PRAISE FOR *FUNDAMENTALS OF ORGANIZATIONAL BEHAVIOUR*

'This book consistently hooked me to the narrative by means of reflective questions and thought-provoking activities, which in turn created a sense of how the content can be quickly and easily applied within the reality of the workplace. Consequently, this is an ideal text to improve one's own performance in the workplace and for educators in organizational behaviour wishing to galvanize their students into action.'
David Deegan, Executive Development Director, Cranfield Executive Development

'A fabulous resource, brimming with insightful observations, up-to-date examples and plenty of resources to reflect, discuss and organize learner-led activities. Ideal for use on apprenticeship programmes focused on professional studies.'
Sam Griffiths, Director, Sagenius

'This new textbook quickly becomes a top choice for my OB teaching due to its contemporary content, approachable format and user-friendly style. Every chapter is rich with helpful elements such as clear learning goals, essential terminology, concise summaries, review questions, exercises for both individuals and groups, real-world cases and insightful points for reflection. I especially enjoyed the mix of individual and group activities. Adding to the book's strengths is its relatively brief size, supplemented with thorough suggestions for further reading, which allow students to actually engage with the activities and deep-dive into the academic literature as needed.'
Minna Paunova, Associate Professor, Copenhagen Business School

Fundamentals of Organizational Behaviour

Principles and applications for improving workplace performance

Chia-Yu Kou-Barrett

KoganPage

First published in Great Britain and the United States in 2024 by Kogan Page Limited

2nd Floor, 45 Gee Street
London
EC1V 3RS
United Kingdom

8 W 38th Street, Suite 902
New York, NY 10018
USA

4737/23 Ansari Road
Daryaganj
New Delhi 110002
India

www.koganpage.com

Kogan Page books are printed on paper from sustainable forests.

© Kogan Page, 2024

ISBNs

Hardback	978 1 3986 1335 5
Paperback	978 1 3986 1333 1
Ebook	978 1 3986 1334 8

British Library Cataloguing-in-Publication Data

A CIP record for this book is available from the British Library.

Library of Congress Cataloging-in-Publication Data
Names: Kou-Barrett, Chia-Yu, author.
Title: Fundamentals of organizational behaviour : principles and
    applications for improving workplace performance / Chia-Yu Kou-Barrett.
Description: London ; New York, NY : Kogan Page, [2024] | Includes
    bibliographical references and index.
Identifiers: LCCN 2023057511 | ISBN 9781398613331 (paperback) | ISBN
    9781398613355 (hardback) | ISBN 9781398613348 (ebook)
Subjects: LCSH: Organizational behavior.
Classification: LCC HD58.7 .K687 2024 | DDC 658.3–dc23/eng/20231213
LC record available at https://lccn.loc.gov/2023057511

Typeset by Integra Software Services, Pondicherry
Print production managed by Jellyfish
Printed and bound by CPI Group (UK) Ltd, Croydon CR0 4YY

CONTENTS

ABOUT THE AUTHOR

Dr Chia-Yu Kou-Barrett 寇家瑜 is a dedicated researcher specializing in unravelling the intricacies of multidisciplinary team dynamics to accomplish complex projects. Born and raised in Taipei, Taiwan, she works and lives in the UK.

Her research has been published in journals such as the *Administrative Science Quarterly*, *Journal of Business Ethics*, *Organization Studies* and *Small Group Research*. She has also contributed to book chapters, with frameworks that serve as practical tools, enabling the application of theory within real-world contexts.

This research has made a substantial impact through her involvement in non-participated consultancy projects, extending her expertise to Fortune 500 and FTSE 100 companies. Her contributions have addressed 'people issues' within organizations. While prioritizing organizational outcomes, her consultancy projects have revolved around optimizing human potential, from inspiring and engaging employees at work to nurturing and preserving their mental well-being. Her efforts in these projects have ensured that the human aspect remains at the forefront, recognizing that motivated and mentally healthy employees are essential for sustainable success.

Dr Kou-Barrett has extensive teaching experience in the field of organizational behaviour. She teaches across various academic levels, ranging from undergraduate studies to full-time and part-time postgraduate programmes, and executive development courses. Her diverse group of students from various fields, such as management, accounting and engineering, stimulated a commitment to bridging the gap between theoretical knowledge and its practical application. As a result, she has crafted an organizational behaviour book that is both practical and applicable for the readers. This book features real-life cases and reflective exercises, enabling readers to draw connections between theoretical constructs and their everyday lives.

Outside of her professional pursuits, Dr Kou-Barrett loves spending time with her furry friends, enjoying the peaceful countryside, making memories with the family and volunteering in the local community.

PREFACE

Organizational behaviour educators use various teaching methods such as case studies, role plays, teamwork, and in-class discussions to apply theory and establish relevance for students in order to bridge the gap between theory and real-world application.

During my doctoral studies at University College London, relevance was a topic of frequent discussion. As a member of a newly created department, and one of the first cohorts of PhD candidates in my field of organizational behaviour, my advisor emphasized the rarity of individuals who pursue a PhD in this discipline straight out of graduate school studies. While some may possess a psychology background and are interested in human behaviours, many only realize the significance of people's issues after years of practical work experience. In essence, organizational behaviour is easier to connect with when individuals have a practical experience to comprehend fully.

The topic of organizational behaviour can be challenging to understand for some students, as they might not see its relevance to their future careers. Though pursuing a management degree, many students tend to focus on technical skills or strategic thinking. However, the study of organizational behaviour, which deals with people issues, is equally important. This issue of relevance has consequently been prevalent throughout my teaching career as well as my graduate study. It is less likely for students who require a higher level of technical skills, such as those with an accounting or engineering background, to see the importance of people issues. Students with an accounting background mainly focus on analysing financial information, whereas engineering students prefer objective solutions to problems. In contrast, organizational behaviour studies are more subjective and less likely to have a one-size-fits-all solution. Instead, they require a best-fitted solution under the given circumstances.

It was this very challenge that led to the birth of this book on organizational behaviour. It aims to bridge the gap between technical skills and people issues, and help students understand the relevance of organizational behaviour to their future careers.

This book emphasizes the importance of people's issues in various aspects of their professional careers. To make it more relevant to the readers, I have incorporated several features. Firstly, each chapter starts with a box story that explains the significance of the given topic in organizational behaviour at work. Secondly, I have included reflective or discussion questions to help readers understand how the theory can be applied to their daily lives. Thirdly, I have included questions that readers may be curious about after an introduction to a theory. Lastly, I have provided international comparisons to give readers a sense of the differences in behaviours and address some of the stereotypes that we may encounter. The aim of these features is to help readers better understand themselves and their stance on a particular people topic. Overall, the book strives to show the relevance of organizational behaviour to our everyday lives and professional careers.

ACKNOWLEDGEMENTS

I must start by thanking my husband, Jason, and my daughter, Nikki, for their support in writing the book and for letting me work evenings and weekends on top of my full-time, already very busy day, job during the book-writing period.

I also must thank the support from my family in Taiwan for understanding I cannot go back to visit them this year due to the workload generated by this project of mine. This decision is particularly difficult since I haven't visited them for five years since the Covid outbreak. My mum decided to travel to the UK in the summer of 2023, which was special.

感謝我的台灣家人理解我的工作, 也特別感謝媽媽飛到英國來看望我和 Nikki。

Special thanks to the Kogan Page team, who contacted me and helped me write this book. I deeply appreciate the publisher's emphasis on practical 'application,' a principle that resonates with my ethos – special thanks to Anne-Marie who has been giving me feedback along the way. Writing a textbook has always been one of the things that I wanted to do in my career. Writing a book takes time and many late nights, but intellectual fulfilment surpasses my initial expectations. With great help from Anne-Marie, I hope that we have created a book that is practical and easy to read for students and practitioners interested in this area.

Lastly, I want to express my gratitude to my students, colleagues, and the universities I have had the privilege of being a part of. This book would not have been possible without the rich experiences and interactions I have had with them in classrooms, offices, and casual conversations across Taiwan, Ireland and the UK.

WALKTHROUGH OF FEATURES

Learning objectives

A bulleted list at the beginning of each chapter summarizes what you can expect to learn, to help you to track your progress.

LEARNING OBJECTIVES

- Define organizational behaviour and its historical evolution.
- Explore the multidisciplinary nature of organizational behaviour and its interdisciplinary foundations.
- Explain the interconnectedness of organizational behaviour with individuals, groups, and organizations.

Chapter outline

This highlights the main issues and topics that will be covered in each chapter.

CHAPTER OUTLINE

- What is organizational behaviour?
- Distinctive features in organizational behaviour
- Organizational behaviour and individuals
  - Enhancing individuals' skill – reflective practice
  - Impact of reflective practice on performance
- Organizational behaviour and team-level factors
- Organizational behaviour and organizational-level factors

Real-world examples

A range of case studies/real-world examples illustrates how key ideas and theories are operating in practice to help you to place the concepts discussed in real-life context.

COMPARING POLITICAL SKILLS: HIGH CONTEXT AND LOW CONTEXT CULTURE

Lvina and a team of researchers (2012) conducted a study involving 1,511 employees from China, Germany, Russia, Turkey and the United States.

Reflection boxes

In each chapter, reflective questions will encourage you to reflect critically on what you have read and reinforce what you have learnt.

REFLECTION

- What is the benefit of understanding different personality traits and types?
- How do individual personalities, experiences and backgrounds influence how people react to the same event or situation?

Exercises

Questions and activities throughout the text encourage you (individually or in groups) to reflect on what you have learnt and to apply your knowledge and skills in practice.

GROUP DISCUSSION

Following the five steps to creating a compensation plan by Kanungo and Mendonca (1988), develop methods to motivate individual team members.

Discussion questions

These can be used in tutorials or small study groups to stimulate debate and critical thinking.

POINTS OF DISCUSSION

- Have I proactively considered how my actions impact my colleagues and the broader organizational environment? Can you think of a recent instance where your actions had a notable effect on your colleagues?
- Reflecting on your team dynamics, how have they influenced your behaviour and contributions? Could you provide a specific example of a situation where team dynamics significantly shaped your actions?

Key terms boxes

These boxes highlight key concepts and terms from each chapter for your learning.

Key terms

- Power
- Legitimate power
- Reward power

Chapter summary and review questions

Draws together the main threads of the chapter and summarizes the key learning points.

CHAPTER REVIEW QUESTIONS

- Define power and explain its significance in an organizational context. Provide examples to support your answer.
- Identify and describe the various forms of power that exist within organizations.

Further reading

Provides some key readings in the area to help you further develop your skills and understanding.

References

Detailed references provide quick and easy access to the research and underpinning sources behind the chapter.

Online resources

This book includes online resources for lecturers and students comprising:

- PowerPoint lecture slides
- Additional exercises
- Further resource and video links

These resources can be accessed through the Kogan Page website: www.koganpage.com/FOB

Introduction to organizational behaviour

LEARNING OBJECTIVES

- Define organizational behaviour and its historical evolution.
- Explore the multidisciplinary nature of organizational behaviour and its interdisciplinary foundations.
- Explain the interconnectedness of organizational behaviour with individuals, groups, and organizations.

CHAPTER OUTLINE

- What is organizational behaviour?
- Distinctive features in organizational behaviour
- Organizational behaviour and individuals
  - Enhancing individuals' skill – reflective practice
  - Impact of reflective practice on performance
- Organizational behaviour and team-level factors
- Organizational behaviour and organizational-level factors

ORGANIZATIONAL BEHAVIOUR AND YOU

Question:

- Reflecting on the aspects of the graduate programme or company that satisfy you, take a moment to jot down the reasons behind this contentment.

- Reflect on what's dissatisfying in the module, programme, or company, and note why.

Look at your answer, and consider what motivates your group members or colleagues.

*NOTE Exercise adapted from Mozahem, N A & Ghanem, C M. 2018, The university is an organization: Teaching organizational behavior by relying on students' university experience, *Management Teaching Review*, 3(4), 271–286.

The purpose of this chapter is to help you become familiar with 'organizational behaviour' by introducing its definition and how organizational behaviour can link to you at the individual level, the people that you work with (at the team level), and the context through which you work (e.g., the organizational level). The chapter includes multiple exercises such as the importance of the 'people factor' at work (as considering only technical knowledge or disciplinary knowledge is insufficient for organizations or individuals).

What is organizational behaviour?

Organizational behaviour (OB) refers to exploring how individuals and groups engage with one another and how these interactions influence the organization's progress in achieving its objectives and working effectively. Studying and observing organizational behaviour is important for the following reasons:

- Knowing what people might do is important in everyday life and organizations. It helps us predict what might happen next.

- Organizational behaviour is about explaining why things happen at work, which is important for managing effectively.

- Managing organizational behaviour means ensuring things get done at work by working with people. It involves understanding, predicting, and taking action based on our knowledge.

Table 1.1   Level of organizational behaviour and corresponding chapters

Individual level	Individual differences (Chapter 2) Motivation (Chapter 3)
Group level	Teams (Chapter 4) Power, status and organizational politics (Chapter 5) Leadership (Chapter 6) Conflict and negotiation (Chapter 7)
Organizational level	Organizational structure (Chapter 8) Organizational culture (Chapter 9) Organizational change (Chapter 10)

Diverse factors influence behaviour within the organizational context and can be broadly categorized into:

- individual/micro-level influences: individual attitudes and behaviours
- group/meso-level influences: looking at how context impacts individuals and groups and emphasizing the interdependence among team members at work
- organizational level (also referred to as macro-level) influences.

This book will explore the most prominent domains within organizational behaviour. Table 1.1 lists which chapters address organizational behaviour at these various disciplinary levels.

Organizational behaviour is a multidisciplinary field (Rousseau, 1997; Staw, 1984; Rousseau & House, 1994), a fusion of knowledge from a range of related disciplines. The individual, micro-level of organizational behaviour studies is rooted in psychology, often covered in publications such as *Journal of Applied Psychology (JAP)* and *Organizational Behavior and Human Decision Process (OBHDP)*. The group meso-level of organizational behaviour studies are rooted in social and organizational psychology, whereas the organizational macro-level of organizational behaviour studies are rooted in sociology, political science and economics. Relevant publications for research may be *Academy of Management Journal (AMJ)*, *Academy of Management Review (AMR)* and *Administrative Science Quarterly (ASQ)*.

EXAMPLE

Organizational behaviour involves the study of how individuals and groups interact within an organization, and how these interactions impact the organization's ability to attain its goals and operate efficiently. Why is it important to consider organizational behaviour or people factors? How does organizational behaviour relate to us? Let's look at the often-cited belief that people who are Asian perform better at university.

Prior to reading on, consider the following question:

- Do Asian people perform better than other ethnic groups in university studies? Give three examples/explanations that support your answer.

In the United States, there is a prevalent belief that Asian students tend to excel at various educational levels. Consequently, much attention from researchers and educators has been directed towards understanding the academic performance of underrepresented and economically disadvantaged ethnic communities. For example, do Asian students perform better than other ethnic groups on standardized admission tests like the SAT, GMAT and GRE?

Lu et al (2022) collected data about East Asians' grades in US law and business schools. In particular, they separated East Asians (e.g., Chinese, Japanese, Koreans) from South Asians (e.g., Indians, Pakistanis) due to their different cultural habits. Using data from six top US universities with over 19,000 students, they found that East Asians' grades were lower than those of South Asians and Caucasians. In particular, they posited that while South Asian culture encourages verbal assertiveness – expressing opinions strongly and confidently – East Asian culture does not, and students are likely to appear less engaged in the discussion in the classroom when the participation is only viewed from the perspective of 'speaking' in the class.

Lu and colleagues explain that the uniqueness of East Asian culture prevents them from being verbally assertive. There is a strong emphasis on traits like humility and harmony instead of being assertive. East Asian students tend to assess their thoughts before speaking, valuing the quality of their contributions over their immediacy. Consequently, their reluctance to assert themselves promptly may lead to a 'ceiling' in their performance, due to missed opportunities for participation. Therefore, the expectation of quick and spontaneous comments and using class participation in a classroom setting can harm the academic performance of East Asians in law and business schools.

Their empirical results can be summarized as follows:

- In both law and business schools, East Asians have lower cumulative overall grades than Caucasians.

- Among the subjects taught in business schools, East Asians do worse in the leadership, marketing and strategy courses where students are required to demonstrate ideas and opinions, i.e., verbal assertiveness when the module is taught in person.

- East Asians' study motivation and English proficiency level are similar to Caucasians.

In their earlier study in 2020, Lu et al similarly showed that East Asians, compared to South Asians and Caucasians, are less likely to achieve leadership positions in the US despite East Asians often being branded as model minorities. Analysing CEOs using historical records, surveying big US companies, observing student leadership selection and conducting controlled experiments revealed that East Asians experienced less bias than South Asians and were equally motivated to seek leadership roles. However, as with the university performance study, exhibiting lower assertiveness levels, which goes against US corporate communication norms for leaders, may have accounted for the leadership attainment gap.

Question:

- How does this example demonstrate organizational behaviour?

- How can a fairer, more inclusive measurement be devised such that individuals with particular characteristics are included?

- In a globalized world, where individuals from diverse cultural backgrounds increasingly collaborate and interact, it becomes imperative to recognize and appreciate the variations in preferences and communication styles among us. The East Asian emphasis on humility and harmony, as highlighted in their approach to communication, serves as a poignant reminder of the importance of thinking differently when working with others.

  o How can you use this information when working with group members from a culture where their level of verbal assertiveness differs from what you do?

  o How can an inclusive environment be established to harness the collective strength of diverse perspectives?

  o In a culturally diverse workplace, how can you assess fairly each individual's contribution to the group work?

Distinctive features in organizational behaviour

Firstly, organizational behaviour views that individuals' behaviours, responses and interactions do not happen in a vacuum. Locating behaviour within organizational settings provides rich insights into the intricate interactions between individuals and their workplaces. Popular areas of study within organizational behaviour studies include motivation, leadership, organizational structuring and organizational change.

The second distinctive feature centres on the outcome factors addressed by organizational behaviour. It encompasses a dual focus, considering not just overall efficiency but also the quality of employees' work experiences (Staw, 1984; Rousseau & House, 1994; Rousseau, 1997; Miner, 2003), for instance:

- job performance
- withdrawal from work (absenteeism)
- employee turnover
- motivation and performance
- job stress
- dissent and whistleblowing
- creativity.

REFLECTION: INDIVIDUALS DO NOT LIVE IN A VACUUM

Take a cue from the chapter titles in Table 1.1 and reflect on how your own actions and responses to a situation are not a standalone item. Reflect on situations in which you found yourself behaving differently in a smaller group as opposed to your behaviour in the larger organization. Explore the potential reasons behind these differences in behaviour when you're alone versus in a group or an organization.

For instance, consider a scenario where you find yourself highly motivated to put in extra effort (Chapter 3: Work motivation) when you're working independently. However, this motivation dwindles when you're working within a group setting. This decline in motivation may stem from consistently shouldering the majority of the workload, frequent emotional conflicts among group members and a prevalence of aggression within the group dynamics.

EXERCISE: ORGANIZATIONAL BEHAVIOUR IS EVERYWHERE

Eskandari and colleagues (2017) interviewed academic and industry professionals to understand better the organizational factors affecting occupational accidents. They identified the following:

- Management's role: management's active support, resource allocation for safety and health programmes and proactive training efforts set the foundation for a safer workplace.

- Communication and psychology safety: the ability of employees to openly discuss and share safety concerns reflects their psychological safety within the organization.

- Organizational culture: a blame culture and the absence of corrective plans for errors contribute to an environment prone to health and safety incidents.
- Continuous improvement: evaluating whether organizational procedures promote continuous improvement in safety measures is crucial.
- Reward systems: the structure of reward systems can influence employee behaviours related to health and safety.
- Employee engagement: employee involvement in reporting health and safety issues is critical to maintaining workplace safety.
- Technical knowledge: individuals' technical knowledge of safety topics plays a significant role in accident prevention.
- Motivation: employee motivation is closely tied to their commitment to following safety protocols.
- Interpersonal relationships: the quality of interpersonal relationships with supervisors can impact communication about safety concerns and the overall safety culture within the organization.

Question:

Utilizing Table 1.1 as a reference point, can you establish connections between the points mentioned earlier and the relevant chapters within this book?

Organizational behaviour and individuals

One recent trend is to link organizational behaviours to not only organizational success but also individuals' professional success. For example, according to the Chartered Management Institute (CMI), the top three skills required in workplaces are (CMI Insights, 2021):

- teamwork
- critical thinking and problem-solving
- communication skills.

The World Economic Forum Future of Jobs report (World Economic Forum, 2023) found that self-efficacy (referred to as dependability at work, motivation, self-awareness and flexibility in the report) and working with others (referred to as empathy, active listening, leadership, influencing and mentoring in the report) is at the top of the priorities for individuals' soft skills. Table 1.2 is a summary of how concepts introduced in this book can be linked to professional skills.

Table 1.2   Description of professional skills and related chapters

Professional skills	Related chapters	Description
Critical thinking and problem-solving	• Reflection and exercises throughout all the chapters	• Reflective exercises in the chapters encourage readers to apply knowledge effectively, fostering problem-solving abilities.
Communication skills, active listening, empathy	• Chapter 1: Individual differences • Chapter 4: Teams	• Chapter 1 on 'Individual differences' fosters empathy by recognizing each person's uniqueness and experiences. It is, therefore, increasing self-awareness, reducing stereotypes, and promoting perspective-taking. Recognizing your natural inclinations and staying attuned to the tendencies of others can help prevent miscommunication. This fosters stronger personal and professional connections, facilitates more efficient communication, and elevates one's emotional intelligence. • Chapter 4 on 'Teams' introduces interaction process analysis to analyse team interactions and communication patterns.
Teamwork	• Chapter 4: Teams	• Understanding the process each team will likely go through (team development) and how individuals can contribute to the team.
Motivation	• Chapter 3: Motivation	• Introducing facets that make individuals feel motivated.
Self-awareness	• Self-reflection (chapter 1) • Reflection exercises throughout the chapters	• Self-reflection practices such as looking at one's strengths, weaknesses, behavioral patterns and context improve self-awareness.

(continued)

Table 1.2   (Continued)

Professional skills	Related chapters	Description
Leadership	• Chapter 1: Individual differences • Chapter 6: Leadership • Chapter 8: Organizational structure • Chapter 9: Organizational culture • Chapter 10: Organizational change • Reflection exercises throughout the chapters	• Chapter 1 on 'Individual Differences' is essential for leadership development as it helps individuals understand the diversity of traits and characteristics people bring to leadership roles. This knowledge enables leaders to tailor their approaches and communication to engage better and motivate their team members. • Chapter 6 on 'Leadership' provides a theoretical framework for leadership development. By learning about different leadership styles and qualities, individuals can use these leadership styles as templates and identify and develop their own leadership strengths. • Chapter 8 on 'Organizational structure' helps leaders understand the elements of structure and the impact of structure on decision-making in the organization. • Chapter 9 on 'Organizational culture' emphasizes facets of organizational culture, allowing leaders to shape the culture in alignment with their vision. • Chapter 10 on 'Organizational change' equips leaders with known steps and factors to consider when navigating organizational change.
Influencing	• Chapter 5: Power, status and organizational politics • Chapter 7: Conflict and negotiation	• 'Power, status and organizational politics' (Chapter 5) and 'Conflict and negotiation' (Chapter 7) improve soft skills for influence by covering power dynamics, politics, conflict resolution and negotiation.

In Susan Cain's books, *Quiet: The power of introverts in a world that can't stop talking* and *Quiet power: The secret strengths of introverted kids,* she sheds light on the importance of understanding individual differences within organizations. Consider an individual with introverted inclinations, as discussed in Chapter 2 (Individual differences – personality and diversity). This introverted individual may be perceived as overly reserved in a society that often highly esteems extroverted and assertive communication styles. When tasked with collaborating in a group primarily composed of extroverted individuals, introverts may find this dynamic overwhelming, leading to potential misjudgements about their capabilities.

However, Susan Cain's research highlights that introverts possess valuable and unique strengths. In leadership roles, introverts excel at identifying potential risks due to their careful and thoughtful nature. They tend to adopt a more cautious approach to decision-making. Additionally, introverts are good at active listening and information processing, ensuring that all perspectives are thoroughly considered before making a decision.

By recognizing and valuing these strengths, organizations can create a more inclusive and effective environment where individuals of all personality types can contribute their best. It underscores the importance of appreciating and accommodating individual differences, as doing so can lead to more balanced, innovative and successful teams and organizations overall.

Enhancing individuals' skills – reflective practice

To enhance employability skills, reflection is a preferred method. Reflection means taking a serious moment to think deeply and carefully about something. For instance, if you decide and later wonder if it was the right choice, you might reflect on it by considering the pros and cons and how it affected you and others. In other words, reflection is an exercise to find your optimal function mode. Your optimal functioning will not happen in the sub-optimal condition. Reflective practices allow you to be more aware of the optimal circumstances for your optimal functioning and allow you to have the opportunity to craft those circumstances to allow you to function at your best (constructing your work environment broadly). Ong et al (2023) suggested that following aspects of reflection at work is particularly helpful, for example:

- self-reflection
- reflecting on one's own work goals
- reflecting on one's working method
- reflecting on work relationships.

For more detailed prompts that you can explore, see Table 1.3.

Table 1.3   Self-reflection prompts to increase leadership effectiveness

Self-reflection	• Assess the impact of your mindset and work approach on collaborative tasks. • Evaluate your effectiveness as a team member. • Reflect on how your mood influences your work. • Consider the energy and enthusiasm you bring to your tasks.
Reflecting on one's own work goals	• Examine your work goals. • Evaluate if you're achieving those goals and consider adjusting them if necessary. • Evaluate work goals considering the evolving circumstances.
Reflecting on one's working method	• Assess your task approach method. • Analyse your decision-making process. • Consider if your contributions propel the project forward. • Explore alternative methods for achieving improved task outcomes. • Reflect on whether you employ the most effective approach for tasks.
Reflecting on work relationships	• Reflect on your ability to work effectively with clients, managers and colleagues. • Evaluate the quality of your work relationships with those directly involved in your tasks and whether your actions contribute to building a strong, productive connection. • Reflect on how the effectiveness of your approach helps to achieve high-quality work relationships within the context of your tasks.

Based on Ong, M, Ashford, S J & Bindl, UK. 2023, The power of reflection for would-be leaders: Investigating individual work reflection and its impact on leadership in teams, *Journal of Organizational Behavior*, 44, 19–41.

Why does reflection help employee skills? Kross et al (2023) articulate the positive impact of reflective practices, including:

- improve performance by drawing insights from past experiences, taking ownership of past performance and boosting confidence in attaining goals
- enhance overall health and well-being by adopting a positive perspective on work, recovering effectively from workplace stress and positively impacting the health and well-being of others
- strengthen relationships and social influence by actively engaging in helpful actions. Reflecting on one's experiences in assisting others bolsters the perception of being a skilled and caring contributor.

Note: Kross et al (2023) also mentioned the negative impact of reflections. When people dwell too much on negative situations like facing mistreatment at work or having an overwhelming workload, they tend to think too deeply about these is-sues, and this can make them anxious. This not only affects their job performance but also has a negative impact on their health, overall well-being and relationships with others.

Impact of reflective practice on performance

Ong et al (2023) studied the relationship between reflective practice and leadership effectiveness. Their research demonstrates that reflecting on various aspects of work, including personal goals, approaches, interpersonal relationships and self-perception, allows individuals to understand their team's needs better. As a result, they are more likely to engage in functional leadership behaviours, ultimately leading to enhanced leadership effectiveness. Dierdorff et al (2019) used a sample of 515 teams (2,658 individuals) to complete a team-based business simulation. Their study revealed that teams comprising of individuals with a heightened sense of self-awareness demon-strated noteworthy improvements in decision quality, enhanced coordination and more effective conflict resolution, ultimately achieving superior team performance outcomes. Conversely, individuals with lower levels of self-awareness tend to encoun-ter greater challenges in decision-making, coordination and conflict management, making them less likely to thrive within a team context.

The Chartered Management Institute (CMI) is an organization that enhances leadership and management excellence. They highlight self-reflection as essential for self-development, personal development and leadership development. For the CMI, self-awareness refers to one's capacity to enhance one's comprehension of one's lead-ership strengths and intentionally learn how to effectively leverage them to empower a team to maximize their own strengths.

- Note down all your weekly achievements. These don't have to be exclusively work- or study-related; they can include relevant readings or conversations with more experienced individuals.

- What are the skills or actions you employed to accomplish these tasks? Did you acquire new skills, overcome challenges or leverage your network?

- Reflect on your personal or organizational goals for the week. How did the completed tasks align with these objectives?

- Could outcomes have been improved, and for whom? This can include things that went well and things that didn't go as planned.

- For the area that identified where improvement was needed, delve into the reasons why things didn't go as well as expected. Examine the steps taken to achieve a goal and pinpoint where things started to go awry.

- After identifying moments that could have been improved, consider how to approach the task or problem differently. It might be as straightforward as ensuring you exchange business cards during networking events.
- Create a list of skills you wish to develop or need to acquire and monitor your progress in honing them.
- Provide actionable steps to summarize your reflections into an actionable list.

Organizational behaviour and team-level factors

In today's business world, people often do their work in teams. We've all enjoyed experiencing moments when a team clicks effortlessly, performs at its best and even forms lasting friendships. Conversely, there are times when team dynamics sour, emotions run high during meetings and performance falters. Why do some teams fail, and why do some teams succeed?

What makes a great team?

It's about how team members work together. In 2012–2014, Google launched its Google Aristotle Project – an internal research initiative to understand what makes teams succeed and fail. They studied 180 teams across different nationalities, looking at team dynamics and individuals' characteristics such as job level, tenure, skills, personality traits and emotional intelligence. The team performance is measured by numbers (e.g., code output, bug fixing and customer satisfaction), performance evaluations from stakeholders (e.g., managers, team leaders, team members and meeting sales targets) and interviews. They found that team members' individual characteristics, backgrounds, skills and personalities matter less than the quality of their interactions and the team's shared norms. They found that teams cultivating a team environment where members feel comfortable taking risks, sharing their ideas, and expressing their concerns without fear of ridicule or retribution – known as psychological safety – tended to perform better and were more innovative.

Google's idea is not new. In the 1970s, Dr. Meredith Belbin, a renowned British researcher and management consultant, formulated the Belbin Team Roles model during the 1970s. His pioneering research took place at Henley Management College in the United Kingdom, where he closely observed teams comprising management students. Surprisingly, he discovered that the biggest factor in success was not whether a team was made up of individuals possessing the highest levels of intelligence or technical expertise, but how well they worked together as a team.

What about the role of manager?

In 2009, Google carried out Project Oxygen to look at the characteristics of outstanding managers within their organization. At the time, some of Google's early leaders and engineers believed that managers represented an undesirable layer of bureaucracy that couldn't be avoided (more on the issue of organizational structure and some interesting cases about how some organizations experiment with structure-less, zero-bureaucracy organizations in Chapter 8: Organizational structure). The research gathered manager performance evaluations and feedback from Google's annual employee surveys. They found that managers played an important role in the team. Teams under effective management were more content and considerably more productive than their counterparts. They found that effective managers are important and influential to the organization, influential performance and the well-being of their team members. Here are the specific things that Google found effective managers did:

1 They fully engaged the team and brought out the best by being a good coach. While challenging team members to perform, good managers also helped them solve their problems.

2 They empowered rather than micromanaged.

3 They were concerned about employees' well-being *before* employees burnt out.

4 They considered that listening to the team is a priority.

5 They showed and created development opportunities for team members' career progression.

GROUP EXERCISE

In Google's research, they found the following factors did not lead to ineffective teams:

- team members collaborating closely within a shared office space
- decision-making relying on consensus within the team
- team members prioritizing diplomacy in their interactions
- the performance of each team member
- workload
- levels of experience and seniority
- the size of the team
- the length of time team members had been with the organization.

However, whether these factors could still impact team dynamics and outcomes in certain contexts or conditions is worth considering. Reflecting on your recent team experiences, ponder the following questions:

1 Did physical proximity to your team members enhance collaboration, or did remote work prove equally effective?

2 Were consensus-based decisions always efficient, or did some situations require a quicker, more authoritative approach?

3 Did prioritizing diplomacy sometimes lead to conflict avoidance, potentially affecting problem-solving?

4 Did individual performance affect team morale or motivation, even if it didn't directly impact outcomes?

5 Did an excessive workload sometimes lead to burnout or decreased quality of work?

6 Were there instances where the team's lack of experience or senior leadership hindered decision-making or innovation, or vice versa?

7 Did long-tenured members bring valuable institutional knowledge, or did they resist change when needed?

As you reflect on these questions, try to recall specific incidents that enable you to paint a detailed picture of the situations. Dive into the setting in which your team functioned, considering how the environmental context could have impacted on the team's effectiveness.

As we saw with individual elements, how team members work together is inherently related to several different themes of research introduced in this book:

Chapter 4: Teams. This chapter delves into the key elements for building successful teams. It defines teams as collaborative groups with shared goals, highlighting the importance of recognizing their unique development stages. Understanding these stages helps you understand the team's challenges at each stage and think about the necessary resources or individuals to best facilitate the team at different stages. Factors to consider include the team composition (not only members' competencies but also their behavioural contribution), communication pattern, conflict resolution and role allocation.

Chapter 5: Power, status and organizational politics. This chapter considers the formal and informal ways of influencing and shaping the outcome of teams and organizations. Starting with power, this chapter covers various forms of power and strategies for individuals to develop power. Status is introduced as an informal influence and the role of organizational politics and how one could develop their political skills by looking at the concept of a political maturity journey.

Chapter 6: Leadership. Leadership theories evolve to reflect changing workplace dynamics and challenges. This chapter introduced leadership theories, key facets to consider what a leader is and different situations when a particular leadership style is exercised, equipping you with the knowledge to adapt your leadership styles to meet the specific needs of your team and organization.

Chapter 7: Conflict and negotiation. In this chapter, we look at the challenges that the team will face – the conflict raised in the team, including task, relationship, process and status conflicts. To resolve conflict, conflict resolution style (the Thomas-Kilmann Conflict Resolution Model) and negotiations were introduced, highlighting the importance of considering context when resolving conflict, as there is no one-size-fits-all solution.

Understanding team dynamics in an organization is crucial to emphasize the significance of grasping organizational behaviour. When a team addresses workplace conflicts, it becomes evident that there is no universal approach to conflict resolution, as discussed in Chapter 6. For instance, within a team, one member may naturally lean towards an empathetic approach, seeking to understand individual perspectives, while another may adopt a more assertive stance, preferring confrontations to address issues directly. These diverse approaches showcase the complexities of individual behaviour within a team setting.

Moreover, the process of resolving conflicts is dynamic, often involving interactions between multiple team members. This means that the ultimate conflict resolution style chosen isn't solely determined by one individual but is influenced by the interactions and interplay between team members. To illustrate, consider a team member who prefers a competitive conflict resolution style. However, they may adapt and evolve as they engage with their colleagues and witness various conflict resolution styles. For example, they might gradually soften their competitive stance when collaborating with a colleague who emphasizes a more collaborative approach, promoting open dialogue and compromise. This adaptation showcases the influence of the team's collective behaviour on an individual's conflict resolution style.

Additionally, how conflicts are handled can also be contingent on the situational dynamics and the preferences of one's colleagues. This underscores the importance of recognizing that organizational behaviour is not a static concept but is influenced by changing circumstances and the behaviours of those with whom we work.

It highlights the intricate interplay between individual preferences, situational factors and the influence of team interactions on shaping how conflicts are managed. This awareness can aid organizations in fostering healthier, more effective team dynamics and ultimately contribute to a more harmonious and productive work environment.

Organizational behaviour and organizational-level factors

Picture two companies and their corresponding organizational structure. One company is characterized by a top-down structure and a profit-driven mission, which may encourage its employees to prioritize efficiency and cost-cutting efforts. Their organizational structure is likely to have the following characteristics:

- job specialization: clear roles and responsibilities, promoting efficiency and expertise
- departmentalization: functional units like finance, marketing and operations for task efficiency
- chain of command: a top-down hierarchy with authority flowing from top management
- span of control: narrow control spans enabling better supervision
- centralization: highly centralized decision-making in upper management for mission alignment and swift action.

These structural characteristics collectively create an organizational environment where employees are encouraged to prioritize efficiency and cost-cutting efforts in alignment with the corporation's profit-driven mission and top-down structure.

On the other hand, the nonprofit organization, guided by a mission centered on community service, may place a higher value on employee engagement and making a positive societal impact rather than solely pursuing financial gains. In this scenario, the behaviour of employees in each organization is significantly moulded by the organization's structure, size and overarching mission, which influence their core values, priorities and actions.

- Job specialization: promotes expertise but often involves diverse responsibilities.
- Departmentalization: encourages cross-departmental collaboration.
- Chain of command: can be decentralized, promoting collaborative decision-making.

- Span of control: wider control encourages employee engagement and mission ownership.
- Centralization: some aspects are centralized for transparency and mission focus. For example, fundraising strategy and financial oversight will likely be centralized to ensure transparency and accountability. This centralization helps maintain the organization's focus on its mission and societal impact.

As can be seen, there are a multitude of factors that influence an organization's performance and behaviour.

Organizational factors and people factors

Robertson and colleagues (2016) summarized two types of human factors that can result in seemingly technical problems: active errors and latent errors. Active errors usually show their effects quickly, but latent errors can hide in the system for a long time without causing problems. They only become a big issue when they combine with other problems and create a potential accident. Active errors are often the fault of people directly operating the system, like control room workers and production operators. On the other hand, latent errors are usually the result of mistakes made by designers, managers and other people who aren't directly in charge of the system's controls.

Consider a major accident or small-scale accidents (such as car accidents) and what factors may contribute to them.

Take the Boeing 737 Max, for example (Gates, 2023):

- The pilot lacked training and was faced with an unfamiliar system. An inexperienced pilot who did not read all the cues that the plane was going too fast rather than too slow.
- Even when the pilot realized the system was the problem, at the time, the pilot and the crew couldn't undertake proper actions due to the stressful, information-overloaded situation.
- Sensor failure. The faulty sensor causes the computer to misunderstand the aeroplane's situation.
- It did not have indicators to tell the pilot what went wrong.
- The system error was not detailed in the flight manual.
- The system pushes the aeroplane nose down and can counter nose-up commands by the pilots.
- Boeing did not signal the danger its system caused and how it could be activated.

The investigation result pointed towards the design of the system, but there were lots of contributing factors involved as well.

GROUP EXERCISE

Analysing the Boeing 737 Max failure and the factors contributing to the incident, it is crucial to emphasize organizational-level elements, including organizational structure and organizational culture, to understand why the failure occurred.

GROUP DISCUSSION

Consider potential instances of active errors and latent errors and analyse how these errors could lead to significant accidents. Start to think about the intricate dynamics between human factors and various facets of the system, including software, hardware and the broader environmental context. Consider how these multifaceted factors interact and contribute to the emergence of significant accidents, moving beyond the surface-level issues like operator fatigue and inadequate training or lack of supervision. Analyse the nuanced interplay between individuals, software procedures, machinery and external factors such as industry competitiveness and stock market pressures.

Similarly, looking at the occupational accidents in Thailand's construction sectors, Hadikusumo et al (2017) concluded that accidents often involve more than technical failures. In particular, they found that 22 organizational factors are important (though only a few are listed here):

- organizational culture
- organizational learning
- leadership and management commitment, resource allocation, training
- reward system, performance evaluation
- coordination of work
- problem identification
- goal prioritization, time urgency
- empowerment
- individual level factors (e.g., knowledge, individual's role and responsibilities).

Therefore, organizational factors are not as removed from people factors as one might assume.

Let's look again at how these relate to the chapter themes of this book:

Chapter 8: Organizational structure. When the organization grows, structures are essential to establish as they can be viewed as how decisions and information flow. This chapter covers the organizational structure and how it evolved according to the development and the choice of certain organizational structures – often linked with the economical challenge at the time and the company's mission.

Chapter 9: Organizational culture. Organizational cultures are often mentioned in the investigation report of a major disaster. But what is organizational culture? This chapter introduces core facets of organizational culture, enabling you to describe it more meaningfully.

Chapter 10: Organizational change. In the examples, typically, after a disaster the investigation report will propose changes to prevent the mistakes from happening again. However, in addition to change passively *after* the accident, organizations can proactively engage change *before* the accident.

EXERCISE: EXPLORING ORGANIZATIONAL BEHAVIOUR CONCEPTS THROUGH FILM OR REAL-LIFE INCIDENTS

Objective: to understand and analyse how key organizational behaviour concepts are manifested in a film, a specific company incident or a real disaster scenario.

Instructions:

- Choose one of the following options:

  o a favourite film

  o a specific incident involving a company (e.g., a product launch, a merger, a crisis or a significant event)

  o a real-life disaster or crisis event (e.g., a natural disaster, a public health crisis or a major accident).

- Identify organizational behaviour concepts: watch the film, research the company incident or study the details of the disaster event. As you do so, look for instances where the following key organizational behaviour concepts are at play. You don't need to choose all the concepts, but here is a list of things you can observe in your chosen case. Once you choose the concept, note down the influence of that concept on outcomes – including numeric performance outcomes as well as quality performance indicators (such as satisfaction, well-being, and how happy they are).

Table 1.4   Organizational behaviour concepts

Related chapter	What to look out for	Outcome
Individual differences (Chapter 2)	• Consider how individual characteristics such as personality preferences and diversity, influence interactions and outcomes.	
Motivation (Chapter 3)	• Examine what motivates individuals or teams in the chosen context and how it impacts their performance.	
Teams (Chapter 4)	• Explore team dynamics, including role allocation. • Analyse communication patterns, considering factors like individual participation levels and actions within the team. • Identify individuals' influence during communication. Note that individual influence may not always correlate with high levels of participation.	
Power, status, and organizational politics (Chapter 5)	• Explore power structures, influence tactics and political behaviours exhibited.	
Leadership (Chapter 6)	• Describe their leadership style in your own words. • Identify the situation background. • Identify other's reactions to the leadership.	
Conflict and negotiation (Chapter 7)	• Identify instances of conflict. • Identify strategies used for resolution or management. • Note down how they negotiated and what words and phrases they used. • Describe the overall feeling of the process – was it full of tension? Or were both parties happy with the result?	
Organizational structure (Chapter 8)	• Describe the organizational structure. • Describe how the organization's structure impacts behaviour, roles and communication.	

(continued)

Table 1.4   (Continued)

Related chapter	What to look out for	Outcome
Organizational culture (Chapter 9)	• What were the observable behaviours and/or objects (e.g., artifacts, buildings) around this organization said about its culture? • What were the norms and beliefs this organization holds? • What were the basic assumptions this organization has?	
Organizational change (Chapter 10):	• What drives the change? • How are change initiatives managed? • How do employees respond to organizational change?	

- Analyse and reflect: write a reflective analysis (500–700 words) that answers the following questions:

  o How are the identified organizational behaviour concepts evident in the chosen film, company incident or disaster scenario?

  o How do these concepts influence the actions and behaviours of individuals and groups within the organization or context?

  o What lessons or insights can be drawn from applying these organizational behaviour concepts in this scenario?

  o Are there any areas where applying these concepts better could have improved the outcome or performance?

- Discussion: discuss your analysis and insights with your peers. Explore different perspectives and interpretations of the organizational behaviour concepts within the chosen context.

Points of discussion

- Have I proactively considered how my actions impact my colleagues and the broader organizational environment? Can you think of a recent instance where your actions had a notable effect on your colleagues?

- Reflecting on your team dynamics, how have they influenced your behaviour and contributions? Could you provide a specific example of a situation where team dynamics significantly shaped your actions?

- In your experience, what specific instances highlight the role of communication and collaboration in moulding group behaviour? Can you share an example of a project or team interaction where effective communication and collaboration positively influenced group behaviour?

- What specific formal policies, procedures, or structural elements do you believe substantially impact behaviour within the organization or institution you are associated with or work for? Can you explain how one of these aspects influenced a recent decision or action?

- Are there particular systemic factors within the organization that you've observed either hindering or enhancing individual and group behaviour?

Chapter summary

This chapter defines organizational behaviour and explores its connection to daily experiences through exercises. Organizational behaviour is portrayed as a multidisciplinary field, emphasizing its applicability and outcome-driven nature. The importance of numerical performance outcomes and individuals' satisfaction and well-being is underscored as essential outcomes in organizational behaviour.

The field of organizational behaviour can be classified into three levels: individuals (micro), groups (meso) and organizations (macro). Examples from Google and historical disasters are utilized to highlight the importance of considering organizational behaviour even in industries traditionally viewed as highly technical engineering incidents.

Furthermore, the author establishes a connection between organizational behaviour and the individual level, particularly regarding skill development. Reflective practices and questions are introduced to aid in personal growth and development, illustrating how organizational behaviour can be applied daily. This chapter serves as a valuable guide for readers to understand and apply the principles of organizational behaviour in their everyday experiences.

Chapter review questions

- What is the definition of organizational behaviour?

- How does the chapter emphasize the multidisciplinary nature of organizational behaviour and its foundations in different disciplines?

- Describe the connection established in the chapter between organizational behaviour and individual skill development.
- What are reflective practices, and how can they aid personal growth and development in the context of organizational behaviour?

Further reading

Gallup (2023) *State of the Global Workplace: Global Insights*. Some interesting reports that talked about the workplace may be a starting point for you to recognize the importance of organizational behaviours.

Miner, J B (2003) The rated importance, scientific validity, and practical usefulness of organizational behavior theories: A quantitative review, *Academy of Management Learning and Education*, 2(3), 250–268. An insightful review article providing a concise summary of the prominent organizational theories currently under study.

References

CMI Insights (2021) *The skills that employers want in the modern workplace*, 28 September 2021.

Dierdorff, E C, Fisher, D M & Rubin, R S (2019) The power of percipience: Consequences of self-awareness in teams on team-level functioning and performance, *Journal of Management*, 2891–2919.

Eskandari, D, Jafari, M J, Mehrabi, Y, Kian, M P, Charkhand, H & Mirghotbi, M (2017) A qualitative study on organizational factors affecting occupational accidents, *Iranian Journal of Public Health*, 46(3), 380, http://www.ncbi.nlm.nih.gov/pmc/articles/pmc5395534/ (archived at https://perma.cc/5BSV-J5F4).

Gallup (2023) *State of the Global Workplace: 2023 Report*.

Gates, D (2023) Final report on Boeing 737 Max crash sparks dispute over pilot error, *The Seattle Times*, 6 January.

Hadikusumo, B H W, Jitwasinkul, B & Memon, A Q (2017) Role of organizational factors affecting worker safety behavior: a Bayesian Belief Network Approach. *Procedia Engineering*, 171, 131–139.

Kross, E, Ong, M & Ayduk, O (2023) Self-reflection at work: Why it matters and how to harness its potential and avoid its pitfalls, *Annual Review of Organizational Psychology and Organizational Behavior*, 10, 441–463.

Lu, J G, Nisbett, R E & Morris, M W (2022) The surprising underperformance of East Asians in US law and business schools: The liability of low assertiveness and the ameliorative potential of online classrooms, *Proceedings of the National Academy of Sciences*, 119(13).

Lu, J G, Nisbett, R E & Morris, M W (2020) Why East Asians but not South Asians are underrepresented in leadership positions in the United States, *Proceedings of the National Academy of Sciences*, 117(9), 4590–4600.

Miner, J B (2003) The rated importance, scientific validity, and practical usefulness of organizational behavior theories: A quantitative review, *Academy of Management Learning and Education*, 2(3), 250–268.

Mozahem, N A & Ghanem, C M (2018) The university is an organization: Teaching organizational behavior by relying on students' university experience, *Management Teaching Review*, 3(4), 271–286.

Ong, M, Ashford, S J & Bindl, U K (2023) The power of reflection for would-be leaders: Investigating individual work reflection and its impact on leadership in teams, *Journal of Organizational Behavior*, 44, 19–41.

Robertson, K, Black, J, Grand-Clement, S & Hall, A (2016) *Human and organisational factors in major accident prevention: A snapshot of the academic landscape*, RAND Corporation

Rousseau, D M (1997) Organizational behavior in the new organizational era. *Annual Review of Psychology*. 48, 515–546.

Rousseau, D M & House, R J (1994) Meso organizational behavior: Avoiding three fundamental biases. In C L Cooper & D M Rousseau (eds.) *Trends in Organizational Behavior*, John Wiley & Sons.

Staw, B M (1984) Organizational behavior: A review and reformulation of the field's outcome variables. *Annual Review of Psychology*. 35, 627–666.

World Economic Forum (2023) *Future of the Jobs Report 2023*.

Individual differences – personality and diversity

02

- Other types of individual differences
  - o Demographic diversity
  - o Neurodiversity

Why is it important for us to consider individual differences, like personality and various forms of diversity? This includes visibly apparent aspects, such as gender, race and age, as well as those that are not immediately visible, like neurodiversity. Understanding your operating tendencies and being aware of other tendencies can avoid misunderstanding. It improves personal and professional relationships, makes communication more effective and enhances overall emotional intelligence. These are essential skills for leaders, team members and individuals.

Consider the situation where you have team member Alex who is good at performing repetitive tasks and has great attention to detail. However, when working with Alex, you noticed that Alex occasionally experiences emotional moments, but no one in the team knows why. These instances of emotional response appear to arise seemingly without explicit triggers. While Alex demonstrates proficiency in handling intricate tasks, interactions can occasionally include a tendency to interpret statements quite literally and communicate with a straightforward and candid approach. Moreover, Alex tends to display some unease in social encounters, notably avoiding customary handshakes. On the surface, team members can view that Alex is good at detail work, but some question whether Alex is good to work with or not given some of their interactions within the work setting.

Now, you have a new piece of information about Alex: Alex is on the autistic spectrum. Autism or autism spectrum disorder (ASD) is a neurological condition, meaning that autistic people's brains are different from a neurotypical person's (neurotypical is a term used to describe individuals whose neurological development and thought patterns are considered typical or within the normal range). Here are some of the challenges that they experience:

- Touch and vision sensitivity – autistic people's touch senses can be skewed and hypersensitive. Some autistic people may find physical contact, like handshakes, uncomfortable or overwhelming, while others may not have a problem with it. They also feel fabrics on their skin differently than neurotypical people do. Certain materials have the potential to trigger a sense of tactile defensiveness, leading to psychological stress or physical pain. They can also be under-sensitive, resulting in clumsiness or blurry peripheral vision.

- Noise – autistic people can be very sensitive to certain sounds. Keyboard typing and eating noise to autistic people might sound like a very loud noise. They can also find it hard to only focus on one sound.

- Light – autistic people may have different reactions to light. Some individuals on the autism spectrum may be hypersensitive to light so that they can be easily overwhelmed. This can lead to discomfort, anxiety and sensory overload.

Ongoing research in the field of autism continually updates our understanding, challenging conventional perspectives. As an example, on the National Health Service UK webpage defining autism, it was mentioned that individuals on the autism spectrum might struggle with interpersonal interactions and communication. However, recent studies have cast doubt on this view of social interactions (Heasman, 2018). Notably, both autistic and non-autistic individuals often demonstrate proficient communication skills when engaging with others who share their neurological characteristics (Morrison et al, 2019). Research has also shown that autistic individuals possess the capability to effectively exchange information while sharing stories in face-to-face contexts, akin to their non-autistic counterparts (Crompton et al, 2020).

Alex processes information differently. Alex sees and feels things differently. Picture yourself in a world where handshaking feels like stinging nettles and office background noise is as loud as aeroplanes taking off – what would you react to? Alex's previous emotionality is now understandable. A work environment taken for granted, such as lighting that can only switch on and off, meeting people and shaking hands, communal area and open office, could be very challenging for some. In recent studies from Ian Iceton (2022), it is not uncommon for autistic employees to be viewed as unhelpful and not team players. Not being viewed as a team player can be particularly challenging, especially the conventional wisdom view that being a team player is as important as operational skills for organizations.

Think about the following questions:

- How would you describe your own personality? What traits do you think are most defining about yourself?

- In what ways might personality differences affect how individuals approach problem-solving and decision-making in the workplace?

- Can you think of any workplace situations where personality differences could be beneficial to achieving organizational or team goals?

- Think of situations when individual differences are detrimental to achieving organizational or team goals.

- How might personality differences influence an individual's communication style or conflict resolution strategies?

- Are there any personality traits that you think are particularly important for success in your desired career field? Why?

Importance of understanding individual differences

At the individual level, understanding one's differences is crucial for personal growth and development. By comprehending one's unique traits, experiences and perspectives, individuals can better understand themselves and connect the dots of their past experiences. Moreover, this knowledge can also aid in seeking relevant training and support to enhance personal and professional capabilities.

Additionally, understanding the differences of others is equally important in building strong relationships and effective leadership. Awareness of others refers to an individual's capacity to perceive, comprehend and acknowledge the thoughts, emotions and behaviours of those around them. Leaders who possess this skill can better understand their team members' needs, perspectives, and motivations, enabling them to delegate tasks and provide support where required. It also reduces misunderstanding (such as the example just described). By recognizing individual strengths and weaknesses, leaders can improve productivity and job satisfaction, leading to positive outcomes for the team and the organization as a whole. Understanding individual differences is critical for promoting positive personal and professional growth, building effective leadership, improving communication and enhancing collective performance.

Individual difference – personality

Definition of personality

Personality is one's tendency to act, think and feel, which is relatively stable over time. It is one's habitual way of thinking and operating. The development of personality is partly innate – inherited genetically – but it continues to develop over the life course (Cloninger, 2009). Key factors that contribute to personality development are:

- Genetics and biology: personality traits are partly inherited through genetic factors. Biological factors such as brain structure and chemistry also influence personality development.

- Early childhood experiences: attachment patterns with caregivers, parental nurturing and exposure to stress and trauma can shape the development of personality traits.

- Environmental factors: cultural norms, social experiences and educational opportunities can shape personality development.

- Socialization refers to how individuals learn and internalize social norms, values and beliefs. Family, peers and other social networks are crucial in socialization and personality development.

- Life experiences: experiences such as work, relationships and education can influence personality development by accumulating knowledge, skills and personal growth.

Trait and type personality theories

Two main approaches to studying personality are trait and type approaches. Trait theory aims to identify and describe the traits that make up an individual's personality and to understand how these traits influence their behaviour. It is a perspective in psychology that suggests that people possess stable and enduring characteristics, called traits, that influence their behaviour, thoughts and emotions. According to trait theory, these traits are relatively consistent across different situations and over time. Type theory, on the other hand, proposes that individuals can be categorized into distinct categories or types based on their personality characteristics. For example, in the Myers-Briggs Type Indicator (MBTI) individuals are classified into one of 16 different personality types based on their scores on four dichotomous dimensions (extraversion vs. introversion, sensing vs. intuition, thinking vs. feeling and judging vs. perceiving).

REFLECTION

- What is the benefit of understanding different personality traits and types?

- How do individual personalities, experiences and backgrounds influence how people react to the same event or situation?

Trait theory

The trait theory of personality emerged in the early 20th century as psychologists began to explore the concept of personality traits, or stable and enduring characteristics (i.e., 'trait') that describe an individual's behaviour. Trait theory aims to identify and describe the traits that make up an individual's personality and to understand how these traits influence their behaviour. It proposes that individuals differ from one another in terms of their levels of different traits. For example, some individuals may be more outgoing and sociable, while others may be more introverted and reserved. Traits can be measured using self-report questionnaires, behavioural observation and peer ratings.

Eysenck's Two-Factor Personality Model   Trait theorists have identified several different traits that are thought to be important in describing personality. Han Eysenck's two-factor personality model and Raymond Cattell's 16-factor model are among the early trait theorists. Eysenck's two-factor theory was based on the idea that human personality can be described along two main dimensions: extraversion/introversion and emotional stability/neuroticism (Eysenck, 1967).

- Extraversion refers to the extent to which a person is outgoing, assertive and sociable.

- Introversion refers to the extent to which a person is reserved, withdrawn and quiet.

- Emotional stability refers to the extent to which a person is calm, stable and in control of their emotions.

- Neuroticism refers to the extent to which a person experiences negative emotions such as anxiety, sadness and anger.

A decade after the two-factor theory was introduced, Eysenck and Eysenck (1976) proposed a third dimension, psychoticism, which relates to qualities such as impulsiveness, aggressiveness and lack of empathy. According to Eysenck, people who score high on psychoticism tend to be cold, hostile and impulsive, whereas those who score low tend to be warm, caring and empathetic. Eysenck's model suggests that personality traits are primarily inherited and biologically determined (in some articles, you might find Eysenck's model is classified as the biological perspective of personality) and that they are relatively stable across the lifespan.

Another early influential work on trait theory is Raymond Cattell's 16-factor model. The 16 factors identified by Cattell (1973) include warmth, reasoning, emotional stability, dominance, liveliness, rule-consciousness, social boldness, sensitivity, vigilance, abstractedness, privateness, apprehension, openness to change, self-reliance, perfectionism and tension.

Five Factor Model (the Big Five)   Given that Eysenck's model was too simple, Cattell's model was too complex for practical use, and other models hosted distinctive individual-differences variables. The Five-Factor model (or the Big Five) was the model that hosted concepts that were central to personality psychologists (McCrae, 2011). McCrae and Costa (1996) identified five broad dimensions or traits that describe the most important aspects of personality. These traits are often referred to by the acronym OCEAN, which stands for Openness to Experience, Conscientiousness, Extraversion, Agreeableness and Neuroticism (or emotional stability). Let's look at each in turn.

- Openness to experience: Openness to experience is a personality trait that describes an individual's receptiveness to new experiences, ideas and perspectives. Individuals who score high on this trait tend to be imaginative, curious and intellectually inquisitive. They are often adventurous and eager to try new things and they tend to approach problems with creativity and an open mind. People with low openness tend to prefer familiar and predictable experiences over new and unconventional ones. They may be less interested in exploring new ideas and perspectives and may be more comfortable with traditional ways of thinking and behaving. As a result, they may be less likely to challenge the status quo or seek out novel experiences.

- Conscientiousness: This trait reflects an individual's level of organization, responsibility and reliability. People who score high on this trait are typically disciplined, dependable and hardworking. They tend to be goal-oriented, strive to achieve their objectives and are conscientious about meeting deadlines and fulfilling their commitments. Conversely, low conscientiousness is a personality characteristic that describes individuals who are more spontaneous, impulsive and flexible. They may be less likely to follow strict routines or adhere to rigid schedules and prefer a more laid-back approach to life.

- Extraversion: This trait reflects an individual's sociability, assertiveness and energy level. People with high extraversion tend to enjoy socializing with others and often seek new experiences and adventures. They tend to be talkative, energetic and confident in social situations, and they often enjoy being the centre of attention. Low extraversion refers to a personality characteristic where an individual is more reserved, introverted and reflective. They tend to be more introspective, thoughtful and cautious in social situations and may prefer to listen rather than speak.

- Agreeableness: This trait reflects an individual's empathy, cooperation and consideration for others. Individuals who score high on this trait are often compassionate, cooperative and friendly. They may be more likely to work well in groups, avoid conflict and be sensitive to the needs and feelings of others. People with low agreeableness may be less concerned with the feelings and opinions of others and may be more inclined to challenge others' ideas or beliefs. They may be less interested in maintaining social harmony and more focused on achieving their goals or objectives, even if it means disagreeing with others or engaging in conflict.

- Neuroticism (or emotional stability): This trait reflects an individual's level of emotional stability, anxiety and moodiness. People with high neuroticism tend to be more sensitive and reactive to environmental stressors and they may experience intense emotional reactions to minor setbacks or challenges. They are also more likely to experience mood swings, feel overwhelmed by stress and struggle with low self-esteem. On the other hand, people with low neuroticism tend to be more emotionally stable, resilient and able to cope with stress and challenges more effectively.

The Big Five is the dominant personality theory. Anglim and O'Connor (2019) noted some of the common misuses of the Big Five. First, the Big Five was developed to measure the stable elements of personality that differentiate among people. In other words, the Big Five suggested that individuals tend to diverge in the five dimensions: extraversion, agreeableness, conscientiousness, neuroticism and openness. Second, because Big Five is not equivalent to one's personality, it cannot explain why people differ.

HOW STABLE IS PERSONALITY?

Openness to experience, conscientiousness, extraversion, agreeableness and neuroticism tended to increase over the lifespan but plateau in mid-life (McCrae & Costa, 1989, 2002). In a close look at extraversion, Roberts, Walton and Viechtbauer (2006) divided it into two facets: traits related to independence and dominance and traits related to activity level and sociability. Using 113 longitudinal samples involving 50,120 participants, which covered the period of adolescence through to old age, they found that individuals' levels of independence and dominance are relatively stable over time. Individuals' activity levels and sociability are relatively stable across life – they may slightly spike during adolescence and slightly decline around the mid-fifties. The workplace can also impact personality (see the Personality and stress section in this chapter on page 39).

HEXACO Personality Inventory   A popular alternative model to the Big Five is the HEXACO Personality Inventory. Kibeom Lee and Dr. Michael Ashton developed the model in the 1990s. HEXACO is a six-factor personality model developed as an extension of the Big Five. While the Big Five has been a widely accepted and influential model, it has been criticized for overlooking certain personality traits that are important for understanding human behaviour. Lee and Ashton identified several traits that were not fully captured by the Big Five, including honesty-humility, which is related to pro-social behaviour and modesty, and emotionality, which is related to anxiety and moodiness (Anglim & O'Connor, 2019). They believed that adding these traits to the Big Five could create a more comprehensive and accurate model of personality. While the Big Five was developed primarily in North America and Europe, the HEXACO model has been shown to have cross-cultural applicability and has been used in research across various cultures and countries. Here are the six factors of the HEXACO model, along with a brief description of each:

- Honesty-humility: refers to an individual's inclination to exhibit modest, sincere and fair behaviour without exploiting others for personal gain. This personality trait has been found to be a significant predictor of various outcomes and behaviours, including ethical conduct, job performance and decision-making. Individuals who score high on this factor tend to be trustworthy, unpretentious and modest, valuing honesty and integrity over personal gain. Conversely, individuals who score low on the honesty-humility factor tend to be more self-centred and less concerned about the welfare of others, leading to unethical or criminal behaviour.

- Emotionality (also known as neuroticism): relates to a person's emotional instability, sensitivity and anxiety.

- Extraversion: relates to a person's sociability, outgoingness and need for stimulation.

- Agreeableness: relates to a person's tendency to be cooperative, compassionate and empathetic.

- Conscientiousness: relates to a person's level of self-discipline, organization and reliability.

- Openness to experience: relates to a person's imagination, creativity and willingness to explore new ideas and experiences.

One of the key differences between the HEXACO model and the Big Five model is the addition of the honesty-humility factor. This factor captures aspects of personality related to ethical and moral behaviour, such as a person's tendency to be honest, sincere and modest. Research has shown that this factor is particularly important in predicting behaviour related to social and moral issues, such as corruption, lying and cheating.

REFLECTION

Personality – personal application

To understand your own personality, you can take the HEXACO Inventory and/or the Big Five personality test for free online. Look at your personality result and think about the following questions:

- How do the personality assessment results align with your personality self-perception? Were there any surprises or unexpected results?

- In what ways might your personality traits influence your interactions with others, both in personal and professional contexts? Think about both positive and negative behavioural examples.

- Are there any aspects of your personality that you feel are particularly well-suited to your current or desired career path? How might you leverage these traits to achieve your professional goals?

- How might your personality traits impact your personal relationships? Can you take any adjustments or approaches in your interactions with others to maximize positive outcomes?

DO PERSONALITY TRAITS DIFFER ACROSS COUNTRIES?

Using a sample of 17,408 participants across 54 countries, Schmitt and colleagues (2007) found the scores across the Big Five were similar. When looking at the ranking of the scores, they discovered some interesting patterns, where South American and European respondents ranked highest in the openness dimension. People from East Asia were significantly different in openness from South America and Europe, where East Asian countries ranked the lowest in the openness ranking (Hong Kong, Japan, South Korea and Taiwan). More recent studies also showed a similar pattern. Using the Big Five personality scale with a sample of 130,602 people across 22 countries, Kajonius and Giolla (2017) found that country of origin can only explain 1.8 per cent of the personality trait variation. In general, their data showed that countries in northern Europe scored comparatively high on openness and low on neuroticism. East Asian countries scored relatively low on all the Big Five personality scales. A study by Murphy, Fisher and Robie (2020) found something similar. They used a sample of over 3 million people across 105 countries (average age 25, standard deviation 1.52). They found that differences between men and women were relatively small. When considering culture, where authors use Hofstede's cultural dimensions, they found that men scored higher on neuroticism/emotional stability than their female counterparts.

Question:

Can you recall some common misconceptions and stereotypes about different personality types across different countries? How can we challenge them?

Type theories

Type theory is a framework which offers that individuals can be classified into particular categories or types based on their personality traits, preferences and tendencies. During the early 1900s, Carl Jung, a Swiss psychiatrist and psychoanalyst, developed his type theory by closely observing his patients and drawing on his own experiences. According to Jung, individuals possess two inherent opposing attitudes (extraversion and introversion) and four functions (thinking, feeling, sensing and intuition). He believed these functions influenced an individual's personality and decision-making processes, shaping their behaviour and interactions with the world. Understanding these preferences can aid in personal growth and development, as individuals can gain insight into their tendencies and learn to navigate relationships and challenges more effectively.

Myers-Briggs Type Indicator   Inspired by Jung's theory, Katharine Briggs and Isabel Myers developed the Myers-Briggs Type Indicator (MBTI). The MBTI assesses personality preferences across four dichotomies: extraversion (E) vs. introversion (I), sensing (S) vs. intuition (N), thinking (T) vs. feeling (F) and judging (J) vs. perceiving (P). It should be noted that MBTI describes preferences – this means that we can all become better at the non-preferred way of working, and it is important to note that people will need both E and I, S and N, T and F, and J and P.

- Extraversion (E) vs. introversion (I): This dichotomy describes how individuals prefer to direct their energy. Extraverts prefer to focus on the external world and other people, while introverts prefer to focus on their inner world and their own thoughts and feelings. Note that extraversion vs. introversion here does not imply one's sociability.

- Sensing (S) vs. intuition (N): This dichotomy describes how individuals prefer to gather information. Sensing types rely on their five senses and direct experience, while intuitive types rely on abstract concepts and patterns.

- Thinking (T) vs. feeling (F): This dichotomy describes how individuals prefer to make decisions. Thinking types prefer to rely on logic and objective criteria, while feeling types prefer to consider personal values and the impact of decisions on others.

- Judging (J) vs. perceiving (P): This dichotomy describes how individuals prefer to organize their lives. Judging types prefer structure and predictability, while perceiving types prefer flexibility and spontaneity.

Each dichotomy describes a fundamental aspect of personality and an individual's preferences for responding and relating to others. Based on an individual's responses to the MBTI questionnaire, they are assigned a four-letter type code that reflects their preferences across these four dichotomies. Each personality type has its strengths and weaknesses, and individuals can use their knowledge of their type to understand themselves and their interactions with others.

What do MBTI preferences mean to managerial behaviours? Gardner and Martinko's (1996) study looked at the MBTI type and managerial behaviours; in comparison to the general population, managers tended to prefer thinking (T) and judging (J) preferences rather than feeling (F) and perceiving (P) preferences. Managers with extroversion preferences (E) are attuned to the surrounding context (outer world) and display confidence and sociability through assertive behaviour. Managers with sensing (S) preferences favour factual information, and they prefer practical, detail-orientation and systematic behaviour. Managers with intuition (N) preference favour abstract information towards idealistic, creative behaviours (e.g., strategic planning activities).

REFLECTION

The Myers-Briggs Type Indicator (MBTI) provides four dichotomies that help us understand how people think and communicate. By using these dichotomies, we can gain insight into why individuals react differently to the same situations and events. It also helps us appreciate these differences and practice self-awareness to recognize our biases or tendencies to take things personally. Using the four dichotomies in MBTI as a framework, think about how people think and communicate, and answer the following questions.

- Consider that you are now about to have a difficult conversation with your friends, team members or colleagues. Considering people have different tendencies in responding to situations, what strategies can you use to ensure you can communicate effectively with people?

- How can we practise empathy and understanding when someone reacts in a way that is different from our own? What might happen in their life or their personality that causes them to react that way?

- How can we develop empathy and understanding for people who react differently than we do? How can we avoid taking these differences personally or becoming defensive?

Personal Construct Theory Kelly's Personal Construct Theory (1955) proposes that individuals develop a set of personal constructs or mental frameworks to understand and interpret the world around them. These constructs are created through an individual's experiences and observations and are unique to each person. According to Kelly, individuals use their personal constructs to anticipate and predict events, to make sense of their own experiences, and to guide their behaviour.

Kelly's theory is based on the idea that individuals inherently desire to understand and make sense of the world around them. He believed that people are naturally inclined to organize their experiences into mental frameworks, or constructs, that help them to predict and understand events in their environment. Kelly proposed that personal constructs are organized into a hierarchical system, with more general constructs at the top and more specific constructs at the bottom. The most general and inclusive constructs are called core constructs, which are fundamental to an individual's sense of identity and understanding of the world. Core constructs may be related to an individual's values, beliefs or self-concept. Kelly also believed that personal constructs are dynamic and subject to change. As individuals encounter new experiences that do not fit into their existing constructs, they may revise or refine their constructs to better account for new information. This process of revision and refinement is known as accommodation.

To understand an individual's mental framework, Kelly developed a repertory. The repertory grid asks the individual to compare and contrast a set of three or more elements, which can be people, objects or concepts. For example, the elements could be family members, emotions or work situations. The individual is then asked to rate the elements on a set of bipolar constructs or dimensions, such as 'warm-cold' or 'friendly-unfriendly' based on how well each element fits that construct. This information can be used to gain insight into the individual's thought processes and decision-making strategies.

Type A and Type B theory Another type theory that particularly looks at the link between personality and stress is Type A and Type B theory, developed by Meyer Friedman and Ray Rosenman. Work stressors can be classified into three categories: (1) individual-level stressors that are related to role stressors and job loss, (2) team-level stressors such as an abusive manager and team conflicts and (3) organizational-level stressors such as organizational change and the environment in which an organization operates. Type A individuals may be prone to stress and may have difficulty relaxing and letting go of their worries.

Type A Personality Characteristics:

- Sense of urgency and impatience: Type A individuals often feel like they are in a hurry and need to accomplish things quickly.

- Competitiveness: Type A individuals are often driven to succeed and may view life as a competition.

- High levels of motivation: Type A individuals are often very motivated to achieve their goals.

- Time urgency: Type A individuals often feel like there is not enough time to get everything done.

- Difficulty relaxing: Type A individuals may have trouble slowing down and relaxing, even in leisure time.

- Aggressiveness: Type A individuals may be more likely to be confrontational and assertive.

- Workaholism: Type A individuals may have a strong drive to work and may struggle to take breaks or vacations.

Type B Personality Characteristics:

- Relaxed and laid-back: Type B individuals tend to have a more relaxed and easy-going approach to life.

- Enjoy leisure time: Type B individuals often enjoy their leisure time and may be good at balancing work and relaxation.

- Less competitive: Type B individuals may be less driven to compete and more focused on personal growth and development.

- Less perfectionistic: Type B individuals may be more accepting of mistakes and flaws.

- Collaborative: Type B individuals may be more likely to work collaboratively with others and may be less interested in dominating or controlling others.

Personality and stress

The way that individuals interpret work stress differs in personality traits. In addition to the Type A and Type B theories mentioned above, existing research also examines how Big Five traits relate to stress. Individuals with high neuroticism may react more negatively to the work stressor than their emotionally stable counterparts (Mroczek & Almeida, 2004), and repeated experience with the work stressor makes individuals hypersensitive, causing one's neuroticism level to continue to increase over time (Smallfield & Kluemper, 2021). Similarly, highly conscientious individuals manage their stress more effectively because they are more likely to respond actively to stress and adverse events (Gilbert, Foulk & Bono, 2018).

It is worth noting that stress is the psychological and *physiological* response to a perceived threat or challenge. Psychologically, stress can impact our thoughts, feelings and behaviours in a number of ways. For example, stress can lead to anxiety, worry or overwhelming feelings, as well as physical symptoms such as muscle tension and fatigue (National Institute of Mental Health). Stress can also affect our ability to concentrate, remember and make decisions (Yaribeygi et al, 2017). The physiological stress response refers to the body's response to a perceived threat or challenge. During the stress response, the body undergoes a range of physiological changes, including increased heart rate and blood pressure, rapid breathing and release of glucose and fatty acids into the bloodstream. These changes prepare the body for fights or flights, allowing it to respond quickly and effectively to perceived threats.

Prolonged exposure can also impact individuals' physiological response to stress, resulting in personality change, particularly neuroticism (Smallfield & Kluemper, 2021). For example, when individuals view stressors as uncontrollable for a prolonged period, it changes individuals' original set-point when they encounter stressors. This is a physiological change that is wired in our brain, including serotonin (the chemical messenger in the brain that regulates our mood, appetite, sleep and other bodily functions, and is often associated with feelings of happiness and well-being), and dopaminergic function where the body releases various hormones when one encounters stress. Under normal circumstances, dopamine can help counteract the effects of stress and promote resilience. However, chronic stress can lead to dysregulation of the dopaminergic system, contributing to a cycle of stress and negative affect.

Chronic stress has been linked to decreased dopaminergic activity, which may contribute to the development of depression and other mood disorders. Another physiological response from the body is the HPA axis, which regulates the body's stress reaction. The HPA axis is a complex set of interactions between the body's hypothalamus, pituitary gland and adrenal glands. The HPA axis is critical in regulating the body's response to stress and various other functions, including metabolism, immune response and mood. Chronic activation of the HPA axis can negatively affect health, including increased risk of depression, anxiety and cardiovascular disease. Dysregulation of the HPA axis has also been linked to a range of conditions, including chronic fatigue syndrome, fibromyalgia and post-traumatic stress disorder (PTSD).

Gilbert, Foulk and Bono (2018) summarized ways for individuals to build personal resources when individuals encounter work stress:

- Journaling can help alleviate stress by allowing individuals to process and express their emotions and experiences in writing.
- Sharing positive events with others can boost mood and foster social connections.
- Taking work breaks throughout the day can help reduce stress and increase productivity.
- Practising positive psychology interventions, such as gratitude exercises where individuals express gratitude towards others or list things they are thankful for, the best possible selves where individuals envision their best self and identifying and utilizing personal strengths in daily life, can promote well-being.
- Mindfulness practices, which focus on present-moment awareness and acceptance, such as meditation, breathing exercises and activities that increase understanding and acceptance of present experiences, can help manage stress and improve overall mental health.
- Spending time in nature can provide a sense of calm and restoration.

Personality at work

Personality and performance

What is our current understanding of personality at work, especially regarding performance? Conscientiousness is the most crucial performance predictor, followed by emotional stability. A study by Barrick, Mount and Judge (2001) examined the relationship between the Big Five personality traits and job performance. The authors found that conscientiousness is the strongest predictor of job performance compared to the other Big Five traits. A high level of conscientiousness is consistently associated with higher levels of job performance across various occupations. Furthermore, individuals scoring high in conscientiousness and low in neuroticism (i.e., high emotional stability) are most likely to perform well in their jobs.

Extraversion, agreeableness and openness can predict context-specific job performance. For example, extraversion becomes a performance predictor when the job requires constant interactions with individuals (e.g., sales, managerial positions). Openness becomes a critical predictor when the job involves change and innovation. Agreeableness becomes a vital performance predictor when teamwork represents the primary means of accomplishing work. When considering the composition of the personality traits within the team, the study found that an individual's levels of emotional stability, agreeableness and conscientiousness are associated with good teamwork. O'Neill and Allen (2011) studied the team-level Big Five in the context of an engineering design team where each team has four members. They found that team-level conscientiousness is the strongest predictor of team performance and team-level openness was negatively related to team performance. Finally, when it comes to training, the study suggests that extraversion and openness are positively associated with training performance. Another way to look at the influence of personality on performance is through work motivation. Neuroticism (emotional stability) and conscientiousness are the most consistent predictors of work motivation. Conscientiousness influences one's willingness to exert effort and neuroticism (emotional stability) affects one's capacity to carry out the task throughout (Barrick & Mount, 2005; Judge & Ilies, 2002).

WHAT ARE THE SOURCES OF STRESS AND WHAT ARE THE EFFECTIVE STRATEGIES TO COPE WITH WORK-RELATED STRESS – LESSON LEARNT FROM HOSPITAL NURSING MANAGER

The nursing manager is responsible for ensuring that patients receive high-quality care. They manage a group of nurses and work closely with other healthcare professionals, such as physicians and administrative staff, to develop and implement care plans that meet the needs of each patient. A nursing manager's duty includes managing and supervising a team of nurses. They are typically in charge of overseeing the daily operations of a healthcare facility's nursing staff, including scheduling, training and evaluating their team. Labrague and colleagues (2018) review nursing managers' sources of stress and how they cope with stress across countries (Belgium, Israel, US, Thailand, Canada, Sweden, China, Japan, United Arab Emirates). They found that the common sources of stressors for nursing managers across countries include heavy workload due to the administrative and managerial duties from their leadership position, resolving complaints and tensions from patients, physicians and nurse teams and lack of resources. Nurse managers who had decision-making authority and control over the tasks that they were performing were less stressed. Social support, such as support from managers, colleagues and administrative staff within the hospital, is also vital to lower work stress.

Think about the following questions:

- Write down a list of what currently makes you feel stressed.

- How do you deal with the stress? Identify your behaviours and evaluate how effective your reactions to stress are.

- Think about a situation when you act out of character – describe the situation and think about your behaviours at the time such that you can identify the triggers of your stress more easily.

- From the incident(s) above, what did you learn from your stress reaction?

- Plan your action when you deal with sudden stress and think about how this planned action will result in a more productive outcome for yourself.

The dark side of the personality

Personality research often talks about the bright side of the personality, such as how individuals differ in their behaviours and motive and, ultimately, its impact on work-related outcomes. However, more research has recently looked into the dark side of personality. The term 'dark side of personality' encompasses a range of negative personality traits that can significantly impact the individual and their social interactions. These traits can be detrimental to personal and professional relationships and have the potential to cause harm to oneself and others. These traits are often characterized by a lack of empathy, impulsivity, manipulation, aggression and dishonesty. Some refer to this set of characters as the dark triad – Machiavellianism, narcissism and psychopathy (Paulhus & Williams, 2002).

- Narcissism: A sense of superiority and entitlement accompanied by a lack of empathy for others. Though charming in the short term, narcissists often find it hard to maintain interpersonal relationships.

- Machiavellianism: A willingness to manipulate and exploit others for personal gain.

- Psychopathy: A lack of remorse or guilt combined with impulsive and thrill-seeking behaviour.

Research by Spain, Harms and Lebreton (2014) highlights the impact of dark personality traits on workplace outcomes. Specifically, the study examines individual performance, creativity and leadership effectiveness in organizations. The authors found a weak relationship between Machiavellianism and psychopathy with poor individual performance and that Machiavellian individuals are more likely to engage in faking during interviews. Furthermore, highly narcissistic individuals are skilled at creating positive first impressions due to their self-promotion skills and enthusiasm. Additionally, the study suggests that narcissists are perceived as creative when they pitch their ideas. However, the research also indicates that narcissistic CEOs tend to be bold and grab attention, but their performance fluctuates more than those of less narcissistic CEOs. Overall, the study sheds light on the impact of dark personality traits on various workplace outcomes, which can be useful for organizations to understand better and manage the behaviours of their employees.

Towards a situational view on personality

While personality is the underlying trait that influences individuals' behaviours across situations, the link between personality and work outcome depends on the situation (Penney, David & Witt, 2011; Judge & Ilies, 2002; Barrick & Mount, 2005), such as job demands (Barrick & Mount, 1991; Tett, Jackson & Rothstein, 1991). Tett and Burnett identified three sources of job demands:

- Task demand arises from the nature of the job itself (e.g., customer service work requiring interaction with customers). The RIASEC model (Holland, 1997) is a helpful framework for thinking about task demands (R – realistic, I – investigative, A – artistic, S – social, E – enterprising and C – conventional).

- Social demand includes factors such as the style of management (e.g., democratic vs. authoritative), the level of teamwork required and informal work occasions (e.g., work parties).

- Organizational demand refers to the implicit demands embedded in the organization's culture, such as its structure, policies and procedures, and reward systems.

According to Tett and Burnett, they further predict the work environments that each of the Big Five personality traits would strive for:

- Conscientiousness: strive for detail precision tasks. Best suited for the production team and management team and the organization that values detail and is outcome-oriented.

- Extraversion: strive for positions that require interpersonal interactions and a teamwork environment. Prefer organizations that are outcome-oriented, team-oriented and show warmth.

- Agreeableness: depend on peers for task completion, thriving in friendly workplace environments, particularly within service teams. Prefer organizations that emphasize teamwork and support.

- Openness: Individuals with high openness prefer tasks that require creativity and learning and belong to a group where individuals are open to others' ideas. Best suited in an innovative organization.

- Emotional stability: best suited when the outcome of the task is beyond one's control. They strive for an organization that is decisive, innovative and values autonomy.

Work environments that will constrain each of the Big Five personality traits:

- Conscientiousness: clearly structured task demands and requirements for close supervision will constrain individuals with high conscientiousness. Groups that favour formal communication, bureaucratic organization and limited promotion opportunities will also constrain highly conscientious individuals.

- Extraversion: tasks that require physical isolation, working with a distributed team or a group of introverted colleagues and a reserved organization constrains extraversion.

- Agreeableness: isolation or the work being highly independent of colleagues and an organization emphasizing efficiency does not serve well for highly agreeable individuals.

- Openness: simple repetitive tasks, inflexible colleagues and a hierarchical organization constrain individuals with high openness.

- Emotional stability: predictability in task demand (e.g., predictable tasks, clear job expectation), social demand (e.g., team collaboration) and organizational demand (e.g., an organization that strives for stability) constraints emotional stability.

REFLECTION

Apply Tett and Burnett's personality trait-based model and think about the following questions:

- How have you experienced task demands in your previous jobs? How did your personality traits influence your response to these demands?

- Think of a social demand you have faced in your workplace. How did you adapt to this demand? Did your response align with your personality traits?

- Reflect on the organizational demands in your current or previous workplace. How did these demands shape your work behaviour and performance?

- Consider a situation where you felt a mismatch between your personality traits and the job demands. How did you manage this situation? What could you have done differently?

An alternative situational view on personality considers whether individuals' expressed behaviour is consistent across situations. Different from Tett and Burnett's personality trait-based mode, where personality may best fit a specific work environment, Dalal and colleagues (2015) consider that individuals act differently in different situations. This view implies that individuals can develop more effective strategies for promoting positive work behaviours and preventing negative ones. The framework proposes that personality strength can be conceptualized as a continuum, ranging from weak to strong. Weak personality traits are those that are easily overridden by situational factors, while strong personality traits are those that are less susceptible to situational influences. Individuals with strong personalities are inclined to make decisions to engage in situations that match their attitudes and behaviours. Moreover, they are more likely to shape situations according to their anticipated behaviours and attitudes. Therefore, personality–situation–behaviours are more interrelated and mutually reinforcing.

Other types of individual differences

Demographic diversity

People can differ in demographics in a number of ways, including age, gender, race/ethnicity, socioeconomic status, sexual orientation, religion, geographic location and disability status. Demographic diversity recognizes that individuals within these categories may have unique experiences and perspectives that can shape their interactions in the workplace. Let's look at these more closely.

- Gender: people's gender identity can impact their experiences of gender discrimination, access to resources and social roles.
- Race and ethnicity: people can differ in their race and ethnicity, which can influence their experiences of discrimination, access to opportunities and cultural practices.
- Socioeconomic status: people can differ in their income, education level and occupation, which can affect their access to resources, social mobility and health outcomes.
- Sexual orientation: people can identify as heterosexual, gay, lesbian, bisexual or queer, which can impact their experiences of discrimination, access to resources and social support.
- Religion: people can identify with different religions or have no religious affiliation, which can affect their values, beliefs and cultural practices.
- Geographic location: people can differ in their geographic location, which can affect their access to resources, cultural norms and social networks.

- Age: people can differ in their age, which can affect their experiences, perspectives and priorities.
- Disability status: people can have different physical or mental disabilities, which can affect their experiences of discrimination, access to resources and social participation. India has around 70 million people of working age with a disability or long-term health condition, with a majority having limited access to education, job skills and employment.

IS AGEISM REAL?

According to United Nations Global Report on Ageism, based on a survey of over 83,000 people from 57 countries, data showed that one in every two people held a moderately or highly ageist attitude. Ageism often comes hand in hand with other types of discrimination (e.g., gender, race).

Ageism incurs significant costs, resulting in compromised health, encompassing physical aspects, like a shorter lifespan and extended illness recovery periods, as well as mental well-being and cognitive capabilities.

Age discrimination can take many different forms. Here are some examples:

- During a job interview, an employer asks an older candidate if they are comfortable using technology, assuming they are not tech-savvy simply because of their age.
- A manager consistently passes over an older employee for promotion and promotes younger colleagues with less experience and skill.
- Younger employees frequently make derogatory comments about their older colleagues, using age-based slurs or jokes.
- A company institutes a mandatory retirement policy for employees over a certain age, even if those employees are still capable and willing to work.
- A job posting specifies a maximum age for applicants, even though this is illegal and discriminatory.
- A company offers older employees different benefits or compensation packages, assuming they are less valuable or productive than younger workers.

What are the factors contributing to ageism?

- Age, gender and education level influence one's likelihood of being highly ageist
- Fear of ageing
- Increasing percentage of older people in the population

- General health – lower life expectancy and poorer health are associated with ageism
- Sectors such as computer, online marketing and start-ups are prone to ageism compared to other occupations
- Media portrayal of older people

What are the factors contributing to reduction of ageism?

- Quality interaction with older people
- Knowledge about aging and death
- Positive portrayal of older people in the media

PROMOTING OPPORTUNITIES FOR THE DISABLED WORKFORCE – TATA

Tata is a multinational conglomerate company headquartered in Mumbai, India. It was founded in 1868 by Jamsetji Tata and has since grown into one of India's largest and most respected companies (Fortune India, 2022), with a workforce of over 935,000 employees across the globe (Tata, 2023). Tata operates in diverse industries, including steel, automotive, telecommunications, information technology and hospitality. In addition to its business activities, Tata is known for its commitment to social responsibility and sustainable development. The company has established numerous philanthropic initiatives to promote education, healthcare and environmental conservation.

Tata has made efforts to promote opportunities for disabled individuals within its workforce. Here are some examples:

- Tata Consultancy Services (TCS) has established an Accessibility Center of Excellence (ACoE) with the aim of promoting the inclusion of disabled individuals in the workforce. The ACoE is dedicated to creating an accessible work environment that accommodates the needs of employees with disabilities and provides accessible products and services for clients.
- Tata Trusts' Enable India Initiative provides a range of services and programmes to support disabled individuals in developing the skills and knowledge needed to secure meaningful employment and lead independent lives. Initiatives include training and skill development, job placement support, accessibility and awareness building.

Neurodiversity

Neurodiversity is a concept that recognizes the natural variation in neurological functioning. It presents how people can process information differently. The term 'neurodiversity' was coined in the late 1990s by an Australian sociologist named Judy Singer. Singer was autistic and used the word 'neurodiverse' to describe the idea that neurological differences are a natural and valuable part of human diversity, similar to differences in race, gender and other characteristics. One key difference between these two concepts is that demographic diversity is typically based on observable factors such as age, gender and race/ethnicity, while neurodiversity is based on differences in neurological functioning that may not be immediately apparent. Neurodiversity, including conditions such as autism, ADHD and dyslexia, represents natural human cognition variations.

- Autism is a developmental disorder that affects social interaction, communication and behaviour. Neuroimaging studies have shown differences in brain structure and connectivity in individuals with autism, particularly in areas related to social contacts, such as the prefrontal cortex and amygdala. There may also be differences in the development and activity of mirror neurons involved in social cognition and empathy.

- Some individuals with autism may have exceptional memory skills, particularly for visual details or specific areas of interest. They may also have a heightened ability to process information in a structured or patterned way, which can be helpful. For instance, Masataka (2017) looked at the aesthetic judgement of music. Compared to neurotypical children (age 4–7, Japanese), she found that children diagnosed with autism are better at the aesthetic judgement of music and demonstrate better musical memory.

- ADHD, or attention deficit hyperactivity disorder, is a condition that affects attention, hyperactivity and impulsivity. People with ADHD often struggle with paying attention, staying focused and completing tasks and may engage in impulsive or hyperactive behaviours. Neuroimaging studies have shown differences in brain structure and connectivity in individuals with ADHD, particularly in areas related to attention and executive function, such as the prefrontal cortex and basal ganglia. There may also be differences in the activity of neurotransmitters, such as dopamine, which are involved in reward and motivation. Some individuals with ADHD may have a hyperfocus ability, which allows them to concentrate intensely on a task that they find interesting or engaging.

- Dyslexia is a learning disorder that affects reading and language processing. People with dyslexia often have difficulty with phonemic awareness, decoding and fluency, making reading and writing challenging. The way dyslexic individuals perceive things varies. For instance, some may incompletely see letters: A as Λ, B as

3, C as ∩, M as ∨. Some may experience the movement of the words despite nothing moving on the printed paper. Rather than spelling the word out, such as 'international', they looked at the overall patterns and shapes of the word and recognized the word that way. Neuroimaging studies have shown differences in brain structure and activity in individuals with dyslexia, particularly in areas related to language processing, such as the brain's left hemisphere. There may also be differences in the development and activity of the magnocellular pathway, which is involved in processing visual information.

The neurodiversity movement advocates for greater acceptance and inclusion of individuals with neurological differences and seeks to challenge the dominant view of these differences as 'disabilities' that need to be cured or fixed. Instead, it promotes the idea that these differences can be seen as strengths and that individuals can make valuable contributions to society. The concept of 'reasonable adjustments' to accommodate individuals with disabilities, including those who are neurodiverse, is gaining recognition in some countries (e.g., the UK, US, EU and Australia).

Examples of reasonable adjustment for neurodiverse individuals, depending on their specific needs, include:

- providing a quiet workspace or designated break area to minimize sensory overload and help the individual stay focused
- allowing flexibility in work hours or schedule to accommodate sensory sensitivities or other needs, such as attending therapy appointments
- providing clear and concise instructions and expectations for tasks and additional training or support as needed
- allowing assistive technology or other accommodations, such as noise-cancelling headphones or visual schedules
- adjusting communication methods or styles to suit better the individual's needs, such as using written instructions instead of verbal ones.

While it is widely acknowledged that having a diverse team can be highly beneficial, it can be challenging for managers actually to achieve this in practice. All too often, managers will unconsciously recruit people who are similar to themselves, perpetuating a lack of diversity within the team. One reason for this is that people tend to gravitate towards others who think, act and even look like them. This can make it more challenging to appreciate the benefits of diversity and work effectively with people with different outlooks or backgrounds.

When you have people who are different in some way, it can mean working with individuals who have contrasting ambitions, views and cultural or custom differences.

They may approach problems differently and have unique ways of thinking about solutions. This can bring fresh perspectives to the team, but it can also mean navigating different perceptions, attitudes and behaviours. As a result, creating a truly diverse team takes a conscious effort and a willingness to embrace different ways of thinking and working.

GROUP EXERCISE

Select a company that piques your interest, ideally opting for a well-recognized corporation since they're more likely to have their Equity, Diversity and Inclusion (EDI) strategy openly available on their official website. For instance, consider EY, a company that showcases a comprehensive EDI strategy and the progress it has achieved. You can explore their EDI strategy and accomplishments by searching for the company's official webpage and reading the documents 'EY US Diversity, Equity and Inclusion report' and 'Global review 2020: Facts and figures'.

Your goal is to gather in-depth insights into the company's approach to EDI. Use other trustworthy sources such as reputable news articles, or annual reports. Consider the following questions:

- How comprehensive and transparent is the company's EDI strategy?
- Are there any unique or innovative approaches to their initiatives?
- How do their actions align with their stated goals?

Chapter summary

The chapter began by defining personality and highlighting its importance in the workplace. Two popular approaches to studying personality, trait and type personality theories provide insight into how personality can influence stress levels and job performance. By understanding the nuances of these theories, individuals can gain insight into their personality traits and how they impact their professional interactions. The chapter explored the dark side of the personality, highlighting the potential adverse effects of personality on workplace dynamics. Recognizing these traits in oneself or others can aid in personal development by providing opportunities for growth and improvement. The chapter also emphasized the importance of situational factors in assessing personality, emphasizing the need to consider both the individual and the context in which they operate. Finally, the chapter identified other types of individual differences, including demographics and neurodiversity and their relevance to personal development in the workplace. By recognizing and valuing individual differences, individuals can enhance their ability to work collaboratively and effectively in diverse teams.

Key terms

Personality

Trait theory

Type theory

Big Five, or Five Factor Model

Type A

Type B

Extroversion

Introversion

Neuroticism

Diversity

Neurodiversity

Chapter review questions

- Define personality and explain its importance in organizational behaviour.
- Compare and contrast trait and type personality theories.
- How does personality influence stress levels in the workplace? Provide examples.
- Describe the relationship between personality and job performance.
- Why is it important to consider situational factors when assessing personality in the workplace?
- How can demographic and neurodiversity impact workplace dynamics? Provide examples.

Further reading

Murphy, S A, Fisher, P A, & Robie, C (2020) International comparison of gender differences in the five-factor model of personality: An investigation across 105 countries.

doi.org/10.1016/j.jrp.2020.104047 (archived at https://perma.cc/X9EE-JXVT). If you are interested to know more about personality and gender differences, this paper will give you a good start.

hubermanlab.com/tools-for-managing-stress-and-anxiety/ (archived at https://perma.cc/WH2C-9NM6). A professor at the Department of Neurobiology at Stanford School of Medicine. He looked at how people react to stress physiologically. By understanding the underlying body and brain reactions to stress, he talked about how to manage stress by breathing.

Gardner, W L & Martinko, M J (1996) Using the Myers-Briggs Type Indicator to study managers: A literature review and research agenda. *Journal of Management*, 22(1), 45–83.

Tett, R P, Burnett, D D (2003) A personality trait-based interactionist model of job performance. *Journal of Applied Psychology*, 88(3), 500–517. doi.org/10.1037/0021-9010.88.3.500 (archived at https://perma.cc/8C6K-Z5L8). The paper presents compelling empirical evidence that supports a model and provides an in-depth discussion of its implications for personnel selection and performance management. The study demonstrates that while personality traits can be valuable predictors of job performance, their effectiveness varies depending on the job requirements and work environment. The paper's framework offers a useful tool for comprehending the intricate interplay between personality traits and job performance, emphasizing the criticality of contextual and situational factors in personnel selection and performance management.

References

Anglim, J & O'Connor, P (2019) Measurement and research using the Big Five, HEXACO, and narrow traits: A primer for researchers and practitioners. *Australian Journal of Psychology*, 71(1), 16–25, doi: 10.1111/ajpy.12202 (archived at https://perma.cc/YBZ3-76X8)

Barrick, M R & Mount, M K (1991) The Big Five personality dimensions and job performance: A meta-analysis, *Personnel Psychology*, 44 (1), 1–26. doi: 10.1111/J.1744-6570.1991.TB00688.X (archived at https://perma.cc/GP87-7FHP)

Barrick, M R & Mount, M K (2005) Yes, personality matters: Moving on to more important matters, *Human Performance*, 18(4), 359–372. doi: 10.1207/s15327043hup1804_3 (archived at https://perma.cc/9ERD-VUTL)

Barrick, M R, Mount, M K & Judge, T A (2001) Personality and performance at the beginning of the new millennium: What do we know and where do we go next?, *International Journal of Selection and Assessment*, 9(1–2), 9–30. doi: 10.1111/1468-2389.00160 (archived at https://perma.cc/AZ7S-H22L)

Bartley, C E, & Roesch, S C (2011) Coping with daily stress: the role of conscientiousness, *Personality and Individual Differences*, 50, 79–83. doi: 10.1016/j.paid.2010.08.027 (archived at https://perma.cc/4HDF-Y3BG)

Cattell, R B (1973) *Personality and mood by questionnaire*, Jossey-Bass.

Cloninger, S (2009) Conceptual issues in personality theory. In P.J. Corr & G. Matthews (eds.), *The Cambridge Handbook of Personality Psychology*. Cambridge University Press, Cambridge. pp. 3–26.

Costa, P T & McCrae, R R (1992) Multiple uses for longitudinal personality data, *European Journal of Personality*, 6, 85–102.

Costa, P T & McCrae, R R (1998) Six approaches to the explication of facet-level traits: Examples from conscientiousness. *European Journal of Personality*, 12, 117–134.

Costa, P T, Jr. & McCrae, R R (2002) Looking backward: Changes in the mean levels of personality traits from 80 to 12. In D. Cervone & W. Mischel (eds.), *Advances in Personality Science* (pp. 219–237). Guilford Press, New York.

Crompton, C J, Ropar, D, Evans-Williams, C V, Flynn, E G, Fletcher-Watson, S (2020) Autistic peer-to-peer information transfer is highly effective, *Autism*, 24, 1704–1712. doi: 10.1177/1362361320919286 (archived at https://perma.cc/S52L-QB2X)

Dalal, R S, Meyer, R D, Patrick Bradshaw, R, Green, J P, Kelly, E D & Zhu, M (2015) Personality strength and situational influences on behavior: A conceptual review and research agenda, *Journal of Management*, 41(1), 261–287. https://journals.sagepub.com/doi/10.1177/0149206314557524 (archived at https://perma.cc/7NX8-KU7K)

Eysenck, H J (1967) *The biological basis of personality*, Springfield. psycnet.apa.org/record/1967-35006-000 (archived at https://perma.cc/FQ7K-CFJX).

Eysenck, H J & Eysenck, S B G (1976). *Psychoticism as a dimension of personality*, Hodder and Stoughton.

Fortune India. *Fortune India 500* (2022) www.fortuneindia.com/fortune-500/company-listing?year=2022 (archived at https://perma.cc/GJH5-9HFE)

Gardner, W L & Martinko, M J (1996) Using the Myers-Briggs Type Indicator to study managers: A literature review and research agenda, *Journal of Management*, 22(1), 45–83.

Gilbert, E, Foulk, T & Bono, J (2018) Building personal resources through interventions: An integrative review. *Journal of Organizational Behavior*, 39(2), 214–228. doi:10.1002/JOB.2198 (archived at https://perma.cc/EE4T-LEWS).

Heasman, B (2018) *Enabling autistic sociality: unrealised potentials in two-sided social interaction*. London School of Economics and Political Science.

Holland, J L (1997) *Making vocational choices: A theory of vocational personalities and work environments, 3rd edition*. Psychological Assessment Resources.

Iceton, I (2022) *What factors influence employers to successfully recruit and then retain autistic employees?* Cranfield University. dspace.lib.cranfield.ac.uk/handle/1826/19088 (archived at https://perma.cc/R2MJ-PJEF).

Judge, T A & Ilies, R (2002) Relationship of personality to performance motivation: A meta-analytic review, *Journal of Applied Psychology*, 87(4), 797–807. doi:10.1037/0021-9010.87.4.797 (archived at https://perma.cc/PM37-RUAV).

Kajonius, P & Giolla, E Mac (2017) Personality traits across countries: Support for similarities rather than differences. *PLOS ONE*. 12 (6), e0179646. doi:10.1371/JOURNAL.PONE.0179646 (archived at https://perma.cc/63LS-8QCD).

Kelly, G A (1955) *The Psychology of Personal Constructs*. Norton, New York.

Labrague, L J, McEnroe-Petitte, D M, Leocadio, M C, Van Bogaert, P & Cummings, G G (2018) Stress and ways of coping among nurse managers: An integrative review. *Journal of Clinical Nursing.* 27(7–8), 1346–1359. doi:10.1111/JOCN.14165 (archived at https://perma.cc/TJ9H-5GGM).

Leszko, M, Iwański, R & Jarzębińska, A (2020) The relationship between personality traits and coping styles among first-time and recurrent prisoners in Poland. *Frontiers in Psychology*, 10, 497931. doi.org/10.3389/fpsyg.2019.02969 (archived at https://perma.cc/SYG9-DUSN).

Masataka, N (2017) Neurodiversity, giftedness, and aesthetic perceptual judgment of music in children with autism, *Frontiers in Psychology*, 8 (SEP), 1595. doi:10.3389/FPSYG.2017.01595/BIBTEX (archived at https://perma.cc/PC7F-UEGP).

McCrae, R R (2011) Personality theories for the 21st century, *Teaching of Psychology*, 38(3), 209–214. doi:10.1177/0098628311411785 (archived at https://perma.cc/47BN-MTCP).

McCrae, R R & Costa, P T (1996) Toward a new generation of personality theories: Theoretical contexts for the five-factor model. In J.S. Wiggins (ed.). *The five-factor model of personality: Theoretical perspectives.* Guilford Press. pp. 51–87. psycnet.apa.org/record/1996-97942-003 (archived at https://perma.cc/W8HK-N3E6).

McCrae, R R, & Costa, P T, Jr. (1989) More reasons to adopt the five-factor model. *American Psychologist*, 44(2), 451–452. https://doi.org/10.1037/0003-066X.44.2.451 (archived at https://perma.cc/W8HK-N3E6).

Morrison, K E, DeBrabander, K M, Jones, D R, Faso, D J, Ackerman, R A & Sasson, N J (2019) Outcomes of real-world social interaction for autistic adults paired with autistic compared to typically developing partners, *Autism*, 24(5), 1067–1080. doi.org/10.1177/1362361319892701 (archived at https://perma.cc/7JQZ-UD7E).

Mroczek, D K & Almeida, D M (2004) The effect of daily stress, personality, and age on daily negative affect, *Journal of Personality*, 72(2), 355–378. doi:10.1111/J.0022-3506.2004.00265.X (archived at https://perma.cc/ND43-9BU4).

Murphy, S A, Fisher, P A & Robie, C (2020) *International comparison of gender differences in the five-factor model of personality: An investigation across 105 countries.* doi:10.1016/j.jrp.2020.104047 (archived at https://perma.cc/N9GJ-LGYA).

O'Neill, T A & Allen, N J (2011) Personality and the prediction of team performance, *European Journal of Personality*, 25(1), 31–42. doi:10.1002/PER.769 (archived at https://perma.cc/JX25-Z3LH).

Paulhus, D L & Williams, K M (2002) The Dark Triad of personality: Narcissism, Machiavellianism, and psychopathy, *Journal of Research in Personality*, 36(6), 556–563. doi:10.1016/S0092-6566(02)00505-6 (archived at https://perma.cc/VDP9-XZVP).

Penney, L M, David, E & Witt, L A (2011) A review of personality and performance: Identifying boundaries, contingencies, and future research directions, *Human Resource Management Review*, 21(4), 297–310. doi:10.1016/J.HRMR.2010.10.005 (archived at https://perma.cc/PL3L-2RGF).

Roberts, B W, Walton, K E, & Viechtbauer, W (2006) Patterns of mean-level change in personality traits across the life course: A meta-analysis of longitudinal studies, *Psychological Bulletin*, 132(1), 1–25. https://doi.org/10.1037/0033-2909.132.1.1 (archived at https://perma.cc/PL3L-2RGF).

Schmitt, D P, Allik, J, Mccrae, R R, Benet-Martínez, V, Alcalay, L, et al (2007) The geographic distribution of Big Five personality trait, *Journal of Cross-cultural Psychology*, 38(2), 173–212. doi:10.1177/0022022106297299 (archived at https://perma.cc/3TT5-UJUL).

Smallfield, J & Kluemper, D H (2021). An explanation of personality change in organizational science: Personality as an outcome of workplace stress, *Journal of Management*, 48(4), 851–877. doi:10.1177/0149206321998429 (archived at https://perma.cc/5DKJ-BV3X).

Spain, S M, Harms, P & Lebreton, J M (2014) The dark side of personality at work, *Journal of Organizational Behavior*, 35(S1), S41–S60. doi:10.1002/JOB.1894 (archived at https://perma.cc/J54C-SPPA).

Tata. *Tata Group Overview*. www.tata.com/business/overview (archived at https://perma.cc/QKG4-UF5P).

Tett, R P & Burnett, D D (2003) A personality trait-based interactionist model of job performance, *Journal of Applied Psychology*, 88(3), 500–517. doi:10.1037/0021-9010.88.3.500 (archived at https://perma.cc/G9UU-95GU).

Tett, R P, Jackson, D N & Rothstein, M (1991) Personality measures as predictors of job performance: A meta-analytic review, *Personnel Psychology*, 44(4), 703–742. doi:10.1111/J.1744-6570.1991.TB00696.X (archived at https://perma.cc/7XZX-L9AW).

U.S. Department of Health and Human Services. *NIH Publication No. 20-MH-8125*. https://www.nimh.nih.gov/health/publications/so-stressed-out-fact-sheet#part_6631 (archived at https://perma.cc/5LYF-JYNU)

Yaribeygi, H, Panahi, Y, Sahraei, H, Johnston, T P & Sahebkar, A (2017) The impact of stress on body function: A review. *EXCLI Journal* 16: 1057–1072. doi.org/10.17179/excli2017-480 (archived at https://perma.cc/3PHU-VMAA).

Work motivation   03

LEARNING OBJECTIVES

- Define motivation and explain its significance in the workplace.
- Analyse and compare need-based theories, including Theory X and Theory Y, Maslow's Hierarchy of Needs theory, Two-Factor theory and Self-Determination theory.
- Analyse process-based theories of motivation, including equity theory, expectancy theory and goal-setting theories, to comprehend the cognitive processes and decision-making involved in motivational behaviour.
- Evaluate the role of motivation in fostering prosocial behaviour within organizational settings and identify strategies to enhance workplace collaboration and cooperation.
- Apply motivation theories to the workplace context, specifically about employee performance.

- Goal-setting theories
- Summary of process theory
- Context-based theory
  - Job design
  - Prosocial behaviour
  - Summary of context-based theory
- Motivation application – work reward and recognition
  - Work-life boundary

WHAT DO PEOPLE WANT AT WORK?

According to McKinsey research (2022), across 16 industries and 18 countries in North America, Europe, Australia, Asia and the Middle East, people share similar expectations and requirements in the workplace.

Workers' reasons for accepting a new job are consistent across different age groups. These common factors include:

- compensation
- career development
- meaningful work
- workplace flexibility.

Reasons behind people leaving their job are also similar across age groups:

- insufficient pay
- limited opportunities for career growth and advancement
- unsupportive leadership.

Regarding why people stay in a company, the top three priorities vary across age:

- age 25–34: workplace flexibility, compensation, career development
- age 35–44: workplace flexibility, compensation, meaningful work
- age 45–54 and 55–64: compensation, meaningful work, workplace flexibility.

Overall, McKinsey's research found that:

- the expectations and needs of people in the workplace are mostly similar

- these findings indicate that numerous organizations continue to face challenges in tackling the primary concerns of their employees: fair and satisfactory compensation, opportunities for career development and supportive leadership.

Why do employees lose motivation?

Clark and Saxberg (2019) found that employees lose their motivation typically due to:

- personal disconnect: employees tend to lose motivation when they find a task uninteresting, lacking intellectual challenges or irrelevant to their self-perception and envisioned roles

- self-efficacy struggle: motivation dwindles when individuals doubt their abilities, feeling inadequate for the task or fearing it requires more energy and effort than they can muster

- emotional impact: a negative emotional state, such as anxiety or depression, can significantly impact on motivation levels, making it challenging to stay engaged and driven

- external attribution: when people cannot pinpoint the cause of their setbacks and attribute them to factors outside their control, their motivation can suffer, leading to a sense of powerlessness and decreased enthusiasm.

What can organizations do to keep people in the company and motivated to do their work? By delving into work motivation theories, organizations can gain valuable insights into creating an engaging and motivating work environment that caters to the diverse needs of their workforce. Employers can use this knowledge to implement effective strategies for talent retention and foster a workplace culture that promotes employee satisfaction and productivity.

Reflective questions:

- Have you ever wondered why some people seem highly motivated and engaged in their work while others appear disinterested? What do you think might be the underlying factors that contribute to these differences?

- How do you feel when working on tasks that align with your interests and passions? Can you recall when you were genuinely motivated to excel in your work? What made that experience so fulfilling and enjoyable?

- Consider a situation when you were demotivated or lacked interest in a particular task or project. What factors do you think contributed to this lack of motivation?

Definition of motivation

Motives and the process of motivation have a significant influence on human behaviour. Motives can be either inherent (drives) or acquired (learnt from society) desirable goals.

Motivation can be summarized as having three key components:

- Direction: motivation guides individuals' behaviour towards specific goals or desired outcomes. It helps individuals focus their attention and efforts on activities aligned with their objectives.

- Intensity: motivation provides the fuel for behaviour. It propels individuals to take action and expend effort towards achieving their goals. This energy manifests as enthusiasm, determination and willingness to make the necessary effort to accomplish tasks or overcome challenges.

- Persistence: motivation influences individuals' persistence or perseverance in facing obstacles, setbacks, or difficulties. It enables individuals to maintain their efforts and commitment to their goals, even when faced with challenges or delays.

Motivation theories: content-, process- and context-based theories

There are three broad approaches to understanding motivation: content-based theories, process-based theories and context-based theories (Kanfer, Frese & Johnson, 2017).

- Content-based theories
  - Content-based theories of motivation focus on understanding what drives and motivates individuals from within themselves rather than from external influences or learning experiences. These theories try to identify the deep-seated preferences and goals that people naturally have. Some content theories look for everyday needs that most people share, while others recognize that individuals may attach different levels of importance to these factors. Overall, these theories help us understand what motivates people at their core.
  - Examples: Maslow's need hierarchy, McGregor's Theory X and Theory Y, Herzberg's two-factors theory, cognitive evaluation theory (intrinsic and extrinsic motivation) and self-determination theory.

- Process-based theories
  - Process-based theories of motivation delve into the cognitive processes and decision-making involved in understanding motivation. Unlike content-based

theories that focus on 'what' types of motivators lead individuals to take action. Process-based theories concern the thought process of how individuals analyse and react to situations. They address why individuals are motivated in a particular way, thus exploring the reason 'why' behind their actions.

- o Examples: equity theory, expectancy theory and Goal-Setting Theory.
- Context-based theories
  - o Context-based theories of motivation examine external factors that affect individuals' motivation. These theories help managers and leaders understand the psychology behind human motivation and create environments that foster productivity and engagement.
  - o Examples: job design and prosocial motivation.

Content-based theories

Maslow's need hierarchy

Abraham Maslow's Hierarchy of Needs Theory suggests that individuals have a set of hierarchical conditions that drive their behaviour and motivation. According to Maslow, these needs are organized in sequential hierarchical order, with the most basic physiological needs at the bottom and higher-level psychological needs at the top. An individual's needs at higher levels in the hierarchy become evident only when the lower needs have been adequately met. In other words, we tend to focus on higher-level needs once our more fundamental needs are satisfied. The hierarchy consists of five levels:

- Physiological needs. The hierarchy's lowest and most fundamental level includes biological needs such as food, water, shelter, sleep and other necessities necessary for survival.
- Safety needs. Once physiological needs are fulfilled, individuals seek safety and security. In the workplace setting, this refers to preferences for a secure, long-term job and insurance such as medical insurance, unemployment insurance, etc.
- Love and belonging needs. These are social and interpersonal needs. Individuals naturally desire love, affection, a sense of belonging and positive relationships with family, friends and colleagues.
- Esteem needs. Esteem needs are about how we view ourselves based on our achievements. It involves wanting external recognition, like respect, status and accomplishments, and feeling self-assured and capable within ourselves. When these needs are not fulfilled, it can lead to feelings of inadequacy and a sense of being powerless.
- Self-actualization needs. This refers to the fulfillment of one's full potential and personal growth.

Maslow's theory suggests that individuals progress through the hierarchy sequentially. Individuals can move up to the next level only when lower-level needs are reasonably satisfied. Though empirical support for Maslow's theory is limited, it has inspired further research into human motivation and needs. Contemporary studies have expanded on his work, creating other theories and frameworks that deepen our understanding of what drives human behaviour. For instance, self-determination theory broadens the notion of basic needs to autonomy, competence and relatedness.

Based on Maslow's theory, Alderfer simplified and reorganized the hierarchy of needs into three broader categories:

- Existence needs: these encompass the basic material necessities required for survival, such as physiological needs (food, water, shelter) and physical safety needs.
- Relatedness needs: this category involves the desire to maintain significant relationships with others, whether with family, peers or superiors. It also includes seeking public recognition and fame. Maslow's social needs and external esteem needs fall into this group.
- Growth needs: this category relates to the aspiration for personal development, self-growth and advancement. It includes Maslow's self-actualization needs and the intrinsic component of esteem needs.

Different from Maslow's theory, Alderfer's model assumes:

- there is no strict hierarchical order
- priorities of any need can change from time to time
- different conditions can be fulfilled at the same time
- progression (Maslow) and regression of the needs (Alderfer's ERG model).

In Maslow's theory, when individuals' lower-level needs are fulfilled, individuals tend to focus more on higher-level needs (i.e., progression to the next level need). On the other hand, in Alderfer's model, when higher-level needs are unmet, individuals may redirect their efforts towards satisfying lower-level needs (i.e., regression to the lower-level needs). For example, individuals may emphasize relatedness or existence needs more if growth needs are not fulfilled. This allows for greater flexibility and complexity in understanding human motivation.

NEEDS ACROSS DIFFERENT COUNTRIES

Using the needs identified in Maslow's Hierarchy of Needs Theory and Alderfer's ERG theories, Mathur, Zhang and Neelankavil (2001) conducted a cross-cultural analysis involving middle managers from China (mainly state-owned companies), India, the Philippines and the United States. Their study encompassed over seven hundred middle managers and they identified fulfilling their full potential and achieving career success as the primary motivators across all managerial groups. In their examination of motivators, which encompass elements like financial rewards, avoidance of failure and rejection, attainment of recognition and respect from others, social interactions, personal growth and self-esteem, researchers seek to determine whether managers from various countries attribute similar levels of importance to each of these motivating factors. However, they observed differences between the countries in terms of motivational factors. Specifically, Chinese managers placed less importance on these motivators than their counterparts in India, the Philippines and the United States.

- Chinese managers place the least importance on financial rewards, whereas Indian, Filipino and American managers consider financial rewards as the most important need. Authors suspect that financial rewards and success are closely linked, i.e., financial reward is seen as successful.

- When considering avoiding failure and rejection, this is rated the least important for Chinese managers, while Indian, Filipino and American managers share similar views without significant differences.

- Social interaction needs are least important for Chinese managers, including gaining admiration, enjoying activities and interacting with others. The other three countries exhibit similar levels of importance, with Indian middle managers assigning minor importance to meeting others' expectations.

- Regarding personal growth and ego needs, Indian managers express the highest need for higher social status, while American managers rank this as the lowest priority.

- Chinese managers consider self-actualization the least important, while American managers think it is the most significant need.

- They found more similarities between India, the Philippines and the United States. The only item that showed a clear difference is safety needs.

Church and colleagues (2012) found that perceived need satisfaction still significantly predicted overall well-being across all cultures studied. They also highlighted the universal importance of need satisfaction in Self-Determination Theory (SDT) to several new cultures, extending support for its relevance and significance across diverse cultural contexts. However, they also observed that some differences between Asians and non-Asians lie in the perceived satisfaction of autonomy, competence and self-actualization needs, as well as in most aspects of eudaimonic well-being.

Questions:

- Reflect on your own motivational beliefs and needs in the workplace. How do they align with the findings of the study?

- This study found that Chinese managers place less importance on financial rewards than managers from India, the Philippines and the United States. What factors might be influencing this difference? (Hint: think about the characteristics of state-owned companies in China vs. private companies.)

McGregor's Theory X and Theory Y

While Maslow's Hierarchy of Needs and Alderfer's model describe an individual's universal motives, McGregor's theory focuses on work motivation and managerial intervention. McGregor believes in the importance of management practice. Individuals are passive and reluctant to accomplish organizational goals without active managerial intervention. Theory X and Theory Y describe different assumptions about human nature and how they influence management practices and employee motivation.

Theory X: Theory X is based on a pessimistic view of human nature and assumes that individuals dislike work and will avoid it whenever possible. Characteristics of Theory X include:

- employees have an inherent dislike for work and will try to avoid it
- employees need to be closely monitored and controlled to ensure productivity
- employees lack ambition and need to be motivated through external rewards and punishments
- employees are inherently self-centred and will prioritize their interests over organizational goals.

Theory Y: Theory Y presents a more optimistic view of human nature. Individuals are motivated, self-controlled and self-directed. Characteristics of Theory Y include:

- employees can view work as satisfying and fulfilling
- employees are capable of self-direction and self-control
- employees possess creativity and problem-solving abilities
- employees can actively seek responsibility and exhibit high levels of motivation.

Applying Theory X and Theory Y in the workplace, you might be able to observe that:

- managers who adopt Theory X may resort to punishments, threats and coercion to drive employees towards achieving organizational goals. They tend to adopt a controlling and directive approach, closely overseeing employees and providing them with limited autonomy

- the responsibility of the management is to create an environment so that people can develop for themselves. Managers who adhere to Theory Y may employ promotions, rewards and recognition as incentives to motivate employees towards organizational objectives. They prioritize building personal and supportive relationships with their staff, allowing them to be self-directed and creative when solving business challenges.

Managers can choose to integrate strategies from both theories into their practices, depending on the specific needs of their organization and employees. For instance, a manager may adopt a more authoritative approach associated with Theory X in situations that require strict control and direction. Simultaneously, they may embrace a more self-directed and creative approach linked to Theory Y in scenarios where employees benefit from increased autonomy and freedom to innovate. The key is to employ a balanced approach that best aligns with the circumstances and individual characteristics of the workforce.

HOW DO MANAGERS' VIEWS ON EMPLOYEES' MOTIVATION INFLUENCE THE PERFORMANCE APPRAISAL?

In essence, Theory X and Theory Y emphasize how a manager's perspective of their employees can significantly impact on how they manage and interact with them. This viewpoint also has a notable influence on how managers conduct employees' performance appraisals. DeVoe and Iyengar (2004) researched how managers' perceptions of whether intrinsic or extrinsic incentives primarily drive their employees affect employee performance evaluation. Using a sample from Argentina, Brazil, Mexico, the Philippines, Taiwan and the United States, they found the following:

- Managers' perceptions of employees' intrinsic motivation strongly influence the outcome of performance appraisals.

- Irrespective of the country, employees perceive themselves as more intrinsically motivated. However, how employees view themselves cannot predict their manager's performance appraisal.

- There are some variations across countries in how managers perceive their employees: North American managers tend to see their employees as more extrinsically motivated, Latin American managers view their employees as more intrinsically motivated and Asian managers perceive their employees as equally motivated by both intrinsic and extrinsic factors.

- Cultural norms can influence employee appraisals in different countries: North American managers may exhibit bias by placing excessive value on uniqueness and qualities that go against the norm. On the other hand, Latin American and Asian managers may favour employees who exemplify their assumptions about ideal employee behaviour.

Discussion questions:

- Have you ever experienced or witnessed a manager's perception of an employee's motivation influence their performance appraisal? How did this impact on the individual's work experience and performance?

- Reflect on the cultural context of your workplace or organization. Are there any noticeable differences in how managers evaluate employee performance based on cultural norms? How do these differences impact on the work environment and employee morale?

- Given the research findings, how can managers ensure they remain objective and fair when conducting performance appraisals? What steps can organizations take to minimize potential biases arising from cultural differences and perceptions of employee motivation?

Herzberg's Two-Factor Theory

Herzberg's Two-Factor Theory, also known as the Motivation-Hygiene Theory, highlights two distinct sets of factors that independently influence job satisfaction and dissatisfaction. A key feature of the Two-Factor Theory is that job satisfaction and dissatisfaction are not merely opposite ends of the same spectrum. Managers and organizations should focus on enhancing motivation factors to promote job satisfaction while minimizing job dissatisfaction by hygiene factors.

Motivational elements constitute the inherent aspects of a job that substantially influence job satisfaction. These encompass the gratifying sense of achievement, wherein employees experience a profound feeling of personal accomplishment and receive due recognition for their contributions to the organization. Moreover, recognition assumes a pivotal role, entailing the receipt of acknowledgement and gratitude for one's devoted efforts and valuable input. Additionally, the notion of responsibility within one's role, encompassing autonomy and decision-making authority, plays a pivotal role in kindling motivation. Opportunities for career advancement, involving growth, promotion and professional development are instrumental in instilling employee motivation. Additionally, personal growth factors in the equation, allowing employees to acquire new skills and knowledge, thereby ensuring their sustained motivation and active involvement.

Hygiene factors encompass a set of external elements crucial for preventing job dissatisfaction. These include fair compensation and benefits, ensuring that employees are rewarded adequately for their contributions. A safe and comfortable working environment is another essential aspect, with job security assuring ongoing employment and stability. Equally vital are well-structured organizational policies that ensure fair and consistent procedures, fostering a sense of equity. Positive interpersonal relationships within the workplace, characterized by harmonious interactions with colleagues and supervisors, complete the roster of factors that help maintain job satisfaction.

Satisfaction is primarily influenced by intrinsic motivators, while dissatisfaction is more closely associated with the absence or dissatisfaction with hygiene factors. In other words, addressing hygiene factors is important to prevent job dissatisfaction, but simply improving these factors will not lead to long-term motivation and satisfaction. To create a motivating environment, Herzberg argued that managers should enhance intrinsic motivators by providing challenging and meaningful work, opportunities for personal growth and recognition.

REFLECTION

Reflect on the factors that contribute to your work satisfaction and dissatisfaction. Do you find that Herzberg's Two-Factors Theory resonates with your experiences in the workplace? How might managers apply this theory to improve satisfaction and motivation in their work or your team?

Cognitive Evaluation Theory – intrinsic and extrinsic motivation

Deci's Cognitive Evaluation Theory (CET) is a motivational theory that focuses on how different types of rewards and feedback influence an individual's intrinsic motivation. According to this theory, there are two main types of motivation: intrinsic and extrinsic.

- Intrinsic motivation: intrinsic motivation refers to the natural, internal drive to engage in an activity because it is inherently enjoyable, interesting or satisfying. In other words, individuals are motivated to do something simply for the pleasure, curiosity or personal sense of achievement it brings. Deci's theory suggests that intrinsic motivation is promoted when individuals experience a sense of autonomy, competence and relatedness while performing the activity.

- Extrinsic motivation: extrinsic motivation involves engaging in an activity to attain an external reward or avoid punishment. These rewards can be tangible, such as money or prizes, or intangible, like praise or recognition.

The effect of intrinsic and extrinsic motivation is mixed and controversial when tested empirically, particularly regarding the detrimental effects of extrinsic motivation on intrinsic motivation. This resulted in a revised theory in the 2000s – self-determination theory.

Self-Determination Theory   A revised version of Cognitive Evaluation Theory is Self-Determination Theory (SDT). The assumption of Self-Determination Theory is based on the idea that humans have a natural tendency to grow, develop and achieve well-being. This psychological growth is closely linked with the notion of intrinsic motivation. In Self-Determination Theory, the main driver for intrinsic motivation is whether the task choice and behaviours are perceived as self-determined (autonomy) vs. not self-determined (controlled). In short, what truly drives employees' highest work motivation is not using rewards and punishments (carrots and sticks) but satisfying their psychological needs. Organizations can foster strong motivation by focusing on fulfilling these needs.

- Autonomy: autonomy refers to individuals' need for a sense of choice, control and volition over their actions. It emphasizes the desire to be self-directed and the freedom to make decisions that align with one's values and interests. SDT suggests that when individuals have autonomy in their actions, they are more motivated, engaged and experience greater satisfaction.
- Competence: competence refers to the need to feel effective, capable and skilled in one's activities. It involves the desire to master challenges, develop skills and achieve a sense of accomplishment. When individuals have opportunities to engage in challenging tasks within their capabilities, it fosters a sense of competence and intrinsic motivation.
- Relatedness refers to the need to feel connected, cared for and understood by others. It involves forming positive relationships, experiencing a sense of belonging and having meaningful social interactions. Self-determination theory proposes that satisfying the need for relatedness contributes to feelings of acceptance, support and social connectedness, which enhances motivation and well-being.

According to Self-Determination Theory, when these three basic psychological needs are fulfilled, individuals experience self-determined motivation. Self-determined motivation is characterized by intrinsic motivation, which arises from internal factors such as personal interest, enjoyment and a sense of personal value, as well as extrinsic motivation integrated with one's values and identity. For anything not driven by their genuine interest and enjoyment in the activity, self-determination theory regards it as extrinsic motivation. Extrinsic motivation has many forms:

- External motivation
  - Individuals feel they need to do so because they can gain rewards or punishment for doing so (or not doing so).
  - Example: employees working on the project solely because they have been promised a financial bonus upon completion.
- Introjected motivation
  - Individuals engage in an activity or behaviour not because they genuinely want to do it but because they feel pressured or compelled by external factors, such as guilt, shame or the desire to gain approval from others.
  - Example: employees may feel pressured to help their colleagues because they fear criticism from their supervisor, who emphasizes the importance of teamwork and collaboration as the group norm. In this situation, their motivation to assist others is influenced by their desire to avoid negative feelings or judgement from their manager and peers.
- Identified motivation
  - Individuals with identified motivation have personally integrated the importance and value of the behaviour into their sense of self. They see the activity as meaningful and aligned with their own values and goals, even though it may still be driven by external factors or rewards.
  - Example: a task-focused manager demonstrates care and sympathy during one-on-one meetings with their direct reports because the manager genuinely believes that being a manager involves showing compassion and affection towards their team members. They see it as an essential aspect of effective management and recognize the importance of building strong relationships and trust with their employees.

Another notable difference between Self-Determination Theory and Cognition Evaluation Theory is the nature of motivation. In Self-Determination Theory, individuals can have multiple motivation forms simultaneously (van den Broeck et al, 2016). For example, when employees put effort into producing quality work, it can be because they enjoy doing it (i.e., intrinsic motivation) and because it is needed for promotion (i.e., extrinsic motivation). This theory is best suited when individuals work under complex tasks. The work environment supports self-determination and enhances other job-related outcomes, such as creativity, job satisfaction, commitment and employee retention.

GROUP DISCUSSION

Imagine a scenario where an employee is passionate about graphic design and genuinely enjoys creating visually appealing content. They have a strong intrinsic motivation for their work, finding fulfilment in expressing their creativity and producing high-quality designs. However, their company introduced a new incentive programme where employees receive monetary bonuses based on the number of design projects they complete within a given period – the company wanted to increase productivity and meet tight project deadlines. Initially, the employee feels encouraged by the potential for earning extra money and maintains their enthusiasm for design projects. However, as time passes, the constant pressure to complete numerous projects solely for extrinsic reward takes a toll. The employee begins to feel rushed and less satisfied with their work as the emphasis on quantity over quality diminishes their genuine interest in the creative process.

In this example, the heavy reliance on extrinsic motivation (monetary bonuses) begins to overshadow the employee's intrinsic motivation (passion for graphic design), leading to a decline in their genuine interest in carrying out their job. Their initial enthusiasm and creativity for their work become compromised, impacting on both their job satisfaction and the quality of their designs.

Based on the example provided, think about a situation in your experience where extrinsic rewards or incentives were introduced to motivate your work. Reflect on the following questions and discuss them in a group.

- Can you recall a specific situation where excessive reliance on extrinsic motivation *diminished* your interest or passion for a job or task?

- Can you recall a specific situation where extrinsic motivation *enhanced* your interest or passion for a job or task?

- What insights did you gain from this experience – what factors motivate and demotivate you the most?

- How might you approach similar situations in the future to maintain a healthy balance between intrinsic and extrinsic motivation to sustain your genuine interest and commitment to your work?

- Imagine you were the manager and actively considering how introducing external rewards or incentives may influence creativity, job satisfaction and overall engagement. What steps can you take to ensure that extrinsic motivation complements and enhances their intrinsic drive rather than overshadowing it, thus fostering a more sustainable and fulfilling work environment for your team?

REFLECTION

As we review the various content-based motivation theories, take a moment to consider which approach resonates with you the most. Reflect on the following questions to delve into your understanding of human motivation and how these theories might align with your experiences and observations.

- Which theory do you find most relatable among Maslow's Hierarchy of Needs, ERG, McGregor's Theory X and Theory Y, Herzberg's Two-Factors Theory, Cognitive Evaluation Theory and Self-Determination Theories? Recall instances in your life that reflect its principles.

- Consider a situation where you felt dissatisfied or unmotivated in your work or studies. Which theory from the list can provide insights into the reasons behind your lack of motivation in that instance?

GROUP DISCUSSION

To better understand and appreciate each team member's unique motivations and how they influence their work, each member should take turns sharing their primary motivations for being part of the project or in the programme.

- Discuss how different motivations can complement and strengthen the team's overall performance and how potential conflicts or misunderstandings can be mitigated.

- Reflect on when the team encountered challenges in accommodating different motivations within your team and brainstorm strategies to address these challenges in the future.

- Explore strategies for supporting and celebrating each other's accomplishments based on their motivations.

Process-Based Theory

Process-based theories of motivation focus on understanding cognitive processes and choice-making. These theories shift the focus from the content of motivation (such as needs) to explore questions of motivation such as where, when and how. These theories provide insights into the cognitive processes that drive motivation and guide behaviour.

Equity Theory

Equity Theory, proposed by J. Stacy Adams in the 1960s, is a process-based theory of motivation that focuses on individuals' perceptions of fairness in social exchanges. Equity Theory suggests that people are motivated to maintain a sense of fairness or equity between the inputs they contribute and the outcomes they receive compared to others. Equity Theory posits that individuals evaluate the fairness of their input-output ratios by comparing them to others and strive to restore equity if it is perceived to be lacking and if they are dissatisfied with the situation.

In the context of Equity Theory, 'fair' refers to the perception of a balanced and equitable distribution of rewards and contributions among individuals within interpersonal relationships or social settings. Fairness is achieved when people believe their inputs (efforts, contributions, or sacrifices) are appropriately matched by the outcomes or rewards they receive. There are three types of fairness that individuals look for:

- Distributive fairness. Distributive fairness, or outcome fairness, refers to the perception of fairness in distributing individual rewards or outcomes. It involves assessing whether the outcomes received are proportional to the inputs or efforts contributed by each person involved.

- Procedural fairness. Procedural fairness pertains to the perceived fairness of the processes, procedures and decision-making mechanisms used to determine outcomes and allocate resources. It focuses on transparency, consistency and participation in decision-making rather than just the outcomes.

- Interactional fairness. Interactional fairness, or interpersonal fairness, relates to the quality of interpersonal treatment and communication between individuals. It involves assessing whether people are treated with respect, dignity and politeness, regardless of the specific outcomes or procedures involved.

In response to perceived inequity, individuals can take several actions to restore equity:

- Change inputs: individuals may modify their effort, dedication, or contributions to align with the perceived equity.

- Change outcomes: individuals may seek to increase or decrease the outcomes or rewards they receive to restore equity.

- Change perceptions: individuals may alter their perception of the inputs or outcomes to perceive equity.

- Change referent others: individuals may choose different comparison points or seek out different referent others to achieve a perception of equity.

- Leave the situation: individuals may choose to leave if they perceive inequity as unresolvable or unbearable.

GROUP DISCUSSION

- Can you recall any specific instances at work where you felt you were treated unfairly? Please describe the situation and the impact it had on your emotions and motivation.

- How do you define fairness at work or in a group and what factors do you consider when evaluating whether a situation is fair or unfair?

- How did you react or respond to address the issue in instances of unfair treatment?

- How can you advocate for fairness and encourage open dialogue?

Expectancy Theory

While Equity Theory addresses the 'when' questions of motivation – when do individuals feel motivated/less motivated at work? – Expectancy Theory addresses the 'how' questions of motivation – how the individual chooses their goal (Kanfer & Chen, 2016a). Empirical research supported Vroom's expectancy and the revised models proposed by Lawler and Suttle (1973).

Expectancy Theory, proposed by Victor H. Vroom in 1964, is a process-based theory of motivation that focuses on individuals' expectations and beliefs about the relationship between their efforts, performance and outcomes. It suggests that individuals are motivated to act in ways they believe will lead to desired outcomes. Expectancy Theory posits that motivation is influenced by three key factors: expectancy, instrumentality and valence. Here's an explanation of each component:

- Expectancy. An individual's belief that their efforts will lead to successful performance. It assesses the perceived relationship between effort and performance. Individuals who believe their endeavours will result in successful performance are more likely to be motivated.

- Instrumentality. The belief that successful performance will result in desired outcomes or rewards. When individuals believe their successful performance will be followed by meaningful rewards, such as recognition, promotion or financial incentives, they are more likely to be motivated.

- Valence. Valence refers to the subjective importance or desirability of the outcomes. Higher-valence outcomes are more likely to motivate individuals, while low-valence outcomes may have limited motivational impact.

Under Expectancy Theory, individuals are motivated when they perceive a high expectancy (effort-performance linkage), a high instrumentality (performance-outcome linkage) and a positive valence (attractiveness of outcomes).

REFLECTION

Think about a recent situation where you were considering whether to pursue a particular goal or task. How did the perceived value or attractiveness of the potential outcomes influence your motivation? Did the anticipated rewards or consequences significantly affect your decision-making process? Reflect on how valence, the positive or negative value attached to the expected outcomes, impacted on your motivation and willingness to put effort into achieving the goal.

GROUP DISCUSSION

Individually, note down the following questions before discussing them in the group:

- As you reflect on your journey, have your motivations remained constant or evolved over time? If they have changed, note what you valued in the past compared to now and the reasons behind these shifts.

In the group discussion, discuss the following questions:

- Share what you wrote and compare it with others. Create a list, as individuals are likely to value different things.

- How did you navigate the differences in what you valued (i.e., valence in Expectancy Theory) in the group and align your efforts to achieve a common group goal?

- Think about a time when you had to compromise or negotiate with someone whose valence for a particular task differed significantly from yours. How did you find common ground to move forward effectively?

Expectancy Theory also highlights that individuals make rational choices based on their expectations, beliefs and preferences. They consider the effort they need to exert, the probability of successful performance and the value of the anticipated outcomes when deciding how motivated they will be to engage in a particular task or behaviour. Expectancy Theory has managerial implications for enhancing employee motivation and performance. It suggests that organizations should:

- provide clear performance expectations and feedback to enhance expectancy

- ensure a strong link between performance and meaningful outcomes to strengthen instrumentality

- understand and consider employees' individual preferences and valence for different outcomes

- provide a variety of attractive rewards that align with employees' valence
- communicate transparently about performance-outcome relationships and reward systems.

Goal-Setting Theory

Goal-Setting Theory was proposed by Edwin Locke and expanded upon by Gary Latham. Unlike Expectancy Theory, which delves into how individuals choose their goals, Goal-Setting Theory centres on exploring the cause-and-effect connection between goals and performance. Several key elements that contribute to its effectiveness in enhancing motivation and performance were identified in goal-setting theory, including:

- Specific. Goals should be specific and clearly defined. Specific goals provide a clear target for individuals to work towards, enabling them to focus their efforts and develop action plans.
- Difficult. Goals should be challenging yet attainable. Setting moderately difficult goals encourages individuals to exert effort, maintain focus and strive for higher performance.
- Goal acceptance and commitment. Individuals must willingly accept and commit to goals to be effective. When individuals are actively involved in setting their own goals or have a say in the goal-setting process, they are more likely to be committed to achieving them.
- Performance feedback. Regular feedback on goal progress is crucial. Feedback provides individuals with information about their performance, allowing them to evaluate their progress, make necessary adjustments and maintain motivation.

A SMART goal is a widely used method that summarizes many beneficial goal-setting activities. SMART stands for Specific, Measurable, Achievable, Relevant and Time-bound. While goal-setting is generally effective, its effectiveness depends on task complexity. The effect on goal and performance is weak when the task is complex. Likewise, rigid goal-setting may not be adaptable or responsive in complex and rapidly changing environments. Goals may become obsolete or irrelevant as circumstances evolve, requiring flexibility and continuous adjustment.

The neuroscience of goals   When we establish a goal, we are programming our brains on a biological level to adapt, develop new behaviours and strive to achieve it. The brain circuit for people to achieve goals involves four key brain areas:

- Amygdala: this part of the brain is closely tied to our emotions. It acts like an emotional calculator, predicting how rewarding or unpleasant the outcomes of various goals and tasks might be.

- Basal ganglia: responsible for controlling whether we take action on something (go for it) or refrain from doing it (don't do it).

- Prefrontal cortex: this region is associated with high-level cognitive skills and abilities. It consciously allocates effort and attention to accomplish tasks, allowing individuals to tackle new challenges.

- Orbitofrontal cortex: this connects our behaviours with their consequences. It keeps track of the relationship between our actions and the results they produce, allowing us to learn from experience ('If I do X, then Y will happen').

These four brain areas are responsible for two kinds of primary functions:

- Determining the worthiness of pursuing a goal: a significant aspect of working towards your goals involves consistently convincing your brain that these long-term objectives are immensely valuable uses of your time and energy. Simultaneously, it's crucial to keep your brain convinced that other distractions may not be as valuable as they appear, preventing them from diverting you from what truly matters.

- Planning the necessary actions for goal achievement: when your brain takes charge of your actions, it assesses and identifies the steps you must take to accomplish your goals and the actions you should steer clear of or resist.

Applying the neuroscience of goals to complex tasks   Therefore, our brain helps us assess the value and decide what to do. In a complex task and having already set up a difficult goal, thinking about the required new behaviours and skills can tighten the likelihood of achieving the goal. Berkman (2018) suggests three questions to consider:

- How does the goal relate to you – beliefs, values and identity? This could create additional subjective value to the goal when the goal is related to one's core values and self. Individuals construe beliefs, values and identities. Individuals may reframe beliefs, values and identities.

- Do you already have the skills required for the new task?

- Is the barrier to accomplishing the new task due to a lack of a way (ability) or a lack of a will?

These questions will aid in identifying the most relevant adaptations needed to achieve the goal, including whether a learning goal (such as acquiring a new skill) is necessary to support you in reaching the objective.

LINKING MANAGERIAL TIPS TO THE NEUROSCIENCE OF GOALS

In business studies, you frequently come across articles that delve into strategies for inspiring managers to encourage individuals to go above and beyond. For instance, Johnson (2006) proposed the following ways to motivate employees to go above and beyond:

- Recognizing necessary new behaviours
- Effectively communicating expectations
- Understanding individual preferences for reinforcement
- Harnessing positive peer influence
- Ensuring proper follow-up on instructions
- Implementing intermittent rewards
- Encouraging employees to relive past successes

Consider Johnson's suggestions to boost employees' motivation. How does each align with the neuroscientific principles discussed by Berkman (2018)?

GROUP DISCUSSION

- How do you personally determine the worthiness of pursuing a goal? Are there any specific strategies you use to convince yourself of the value and importance of long-term objectives?

- Reflect on a time when distractions pulled you away from pursuing a goal. What methods could you employ to convince your brain to better prioritize the goal and resist distractions in the future?

- Have you encountered barriers in accomplishing goals? Reflect on whether these barriers were related to a lack of ability (a 'way' issue) or a lack of motivation (a 'will' issue). How might recognizing these barriers help you overcome future challenges in goal attainment?

- How do you handle situations where you lack specific skills or abilities needed for a new task? What strategies could you implement to acquire the necessary skills and enhance your chances of success?

Context-based motivation theories

Context-based motivation theories look at the impact of environmental factors on individuals' motivation. These theories help managers and leaders to create environments that foster productivity and engagement. Team and leadership are also related to the motivational context and both play significant roles in influencing an individual's drive, enthusiasm and commitment to achieving their goals. For more details on team and leadership, please see Chapter 4, Managing groups and teams (page 91) and Chapter 6, Leadership styles (page 160) for more details.

Job Characteristics Theory Job Characteristics Theory is related to work design. It addresses how job characteristics can affect individuals' motivation and job satisfaction. The model does not delve into the cognitive processes or the choice of goals that drive motivation but rather emphasizes the structural elements of the job itself. The job characteristics model outlines five essential aspects of a job that impact on motivation and work outcomes:

- Skill variety refers to the range of skills required to perform the job. Jobs that involve using diverse abilities can keep employees motivated and prevent boredom.
- Task identity: a clear understanding of the entire task can boost ownership and responsibility, leading to higher motivation and satisfaction.
- Task significance: employees who feel their work is meaningful and contributes to a larger purpose are more motivated and fulfilled.
- Autonomy: autonomy relates to an employee's freedom and decision-making authority in their job. Having control over their work can increase motivation and engagement.
- Feedback: regular and constructive feedback helps employees understand their progress and improvement.

These five dimensions interact and influence three psychological states: experienced meaningfulness of work, experienced responsibility for work outcomes and knowledge of work results. When these states are present, they lead to improved work performance and internal motivation.

- Experienced meaningfulness of the work: this refers to how much the employee perceives their job as intrinsically valuable and meaningful, where they can recognize its significance to others or the external environment.
- Experienced responsibility for work outcomes: this pertains to the extent to which the worker feels accountable and responsible for the results and consequences of their work.
- Knowledge of work results: this is about how well the employee is aware of their performance and the outcomes of their work activities.

The job enrichment model is a job design model closely related to the job characteristics model. While the job characteristics model focuses on the core dimensions of a job that influence motivation and work outcomes, job enrichment puts the principles of the job characteristics model into action by redesigning jobs to be more enriching and satisfying for employees. The goal of job enrichment is to create jobs that are stimulating, provide a sense of accomplishment and foster intrinsic motivation. This involves expanding the depth and scope of responsibilities, providing opportunities for skill development and growth and granting employees more autonomy and decision-making authority.

Five core elements in the job enrichment model include the following:

- Vertical expansion of the job: job enrichment involves redesigning a job by adding more meaningful and challenging tasks and vertically extending the scope of the role. The individual will experience more decision-making autonomy. Note that this is not about adding more tasks from the same level of jobs.

- Increased responsibility: grants individuals greater autonomy and decision-making authority, fostering a sense of accountability and ownership.

- Variety of tasks: variety prevents employee monotony, rigidity and dissatisfaction.

- Self-sufficiency: job enrichment empowers employees with more responsibility and autonomy, necessitating a sense of self-sufficiency. This empowerment enhances their feelings of competence and control over their work.

- Motivation and engagement: job enrichment strives to create positions that cultivate intrinsic motivation and engagement. It draws inspiration from the principles of the job characteristics model, aiming to establish stimulating jobs, provide a sense of accomplishment and foster intrinsic motivation.

EXERCISE

The job characteristics model aims to enhance work motivation through effective job design. This model focuses on specific job context factors impacting on an individual's work motivation, including skill variety, task identity, task significance, autonomy and feedback.

Based on your own experiences, consider how these five factors of job characteristics have influenced your psychological state in the following dimensions:

- Meaningfulness of the work
- Responsibility for work outcomes
- Knowledge of work results

Additionally, consider whether other social context-related factors have influenced your psychological state. Social context factors include relationships with colleagues and supervisors, the organizational culture and the support you receive in your workplace.

Prosocial motivation

Another way to look at the social context impact on the individual environment is by looking at social motivation. Prosocial motivation refers to the desire for an individual to benefit others. Instead of solely focusing on when individuals feel (less) motivated (Equity Theory) or how they choose goals (Expectancy Theory), prosocial motivation takes a different approach. It delves into the social context and interpersonal dynamics that drive people to work harder and collaborate more effectively. Like job design theories, such as the job characteristic and job enrichment models, prosocial motivation is interested in the work context. However, job design theories concentrate on how job characteristics impact motivation. Prosocial motivation focuses on the influence of social factors on people's willingness to contribute and cooperate in their work.

Grant and Shandell (2022) proposed that social motivation is contagious – from colleagues, your team, leaders and even rival competitors. Thinking about Olympic athletes, the presence of a formidable rival pushes the athlete to stay focused on their training and performance. The desire to outperform their rival becomes a driving force, leading them to put in extra effort and dedication to excel in their sport. The energy of a lively audience can elevate an athlete's adrenaline levels, leading to increased focus, alertness and physical performance. Athletes often draw energy from the crowd's excitement, helping them push through physical challenges and deliver exceptional performances.

Grant and Shandell identify ways to design jobs that enable individuals to build strong connections and relationships.

At the individual level:

- Increasing individuals' awareness of the impact of their work
- Direct or indirect contact with beneficiaries. This ranges from speaking to the beneficiaries, knowing who they are, seeing them and reminding individuals about their beneficiaries
- Enhance the impact of beneficiaries by allowing them to share their personal experiences. Instead of managers solely speaking about the project's impact, involve the beneficiaries in sharing how the project affected their lives

At the team level:

- Team's norm to help, for example, providing opportunities to interact through work
- Leaders or managers show appreciation for their work such that individuals feel valued

At the organizational level:

- Celebration events to remind of the long-lasting impact of their work on others
- Nature of the task. Individuals are less likely to help others even with incentives when the task is too challenging
- Role models in the organization
- Inspirational mission and values

REFLECTION

Social motivation can be a double-edged sword: it can be productive and counterproductive for work motivation and performance. Think about the following questions:

- Recall your experience when you have helped others. Why did you do so? Look at Grant and Shandell's list of what triggers social motivation at the individual, team and organizational levels as a cue to think about the context that triggers you to help others.
- Is your prosocial motivation changing during a job, a project or a career?
- What sacrifices do you make when you commit to helping colleagues? What was the benefit and what was the cost to you personally?

Motivation application – work reward and recognition

Motivation application in an organization will be related to the company's compensation system. These three types of work rewards (Kanungo & Mendonca, 1988) include the following:

Performance contingent rewards refer to incentives or benefits directly linked to an individual's performance. These rewards can include financial compensation, opportunities for advancement or promotion, engaging and fulfilling tasks and a sense of fulfilment and achievement.

Intrinsic vs. Extrinsic. The employees self-granted certain rewards, typically offered immediately after task completion. For instance, individuals experience a sense of accomplishment, pride in their achievements and personal growth. In contrast, other rewards were external and bestowed by others, such as profit sharing, promotions, recognition awards and additional benefits.

The rewards can be categorized based on their **recipients.** Some rewards are universal and given to all employees, regardless of performance. These encompass benefits like holidays, breaks, sick leave and financial aid (e.g., education or train ticket). On the other hand, certain rewards are selective and not dependent on performance. These include special allowances and company cars, provided to only a few employees.

Kanungo and Mendonca (1988) further proposed a five-step model to help organizations to design their reward system:

- Step 1: Create a list of all the rewards the organization provides its employees. This list encompasses monetary and non-monetary benefits, including compensatory items such as pay and non-compensatory items like responsibilities, autonomy and challenging assignments.

- Step 2: Identify desired behaviours such that they can be objectively assessed. These desired behaviours may include individuals' knowledge, skills, behaviours needed for specific organizational tasks or desirable work-related behaviours. Note that a reward may be designed to encourage multiple behaviours at once. In such cases, the organization needs to prioritize the specific behaviours they want to promote clearly. In addition, it is important to identify desirable behaviours for the organization and within individual interests.

- Step 3: Survey the employees to understand how they perceive and value each reward the organization offers.

- Step 4: Analyse the survey results and look into cases where employees' perceptions of the behaviour-reward relationship, importance and value differ from the organization's established intentions. These differences suggest that the reward may not achieve management's desired objectives. By investigating these discrepancies, the survey results can offer insights into the reasons behind the misalignment, particularly regarding how employees perceive the reward's importance and relevance.

- Step 5: Review the compensation plan.

EXERCISE

When might promotion not be important or salient to employees?

GROUP DISCUSSION

Following the five steps to creating a compensation plan by Kanungo and Mendonca (1988), develop methods to motivate individual team members.

DISCUSSION

What motivates managers? Are there any cross-cultural differences?

Fey (2005) examined whether there are any cross-cultural differences in how people feel motivated. Using a sample combining 82 Swedish and 86 Russian middle managers, Fey examines whether middle managers across the two cultures would be motivated. He examined how managers would be motivated using need, equity and goal-setting theories. He found that Swedish and Russian managers both find goal setting motivated them to a similar degree.

Russian and Swedish culture

In Russia, a pronounced societal divide between those in positions of power and the broader population underscores the significance of status symbols. When it comes to business interactions, there is a strict adherence to a top-down hierarchy with clear role assignments and task mandates. Russians place a high value on relationship-building, viewing it as vital for gathering information, conducting successful negotiations and making introductions. These connections are expected to be deeply personal, genuine and built on trust, enabling an implicit communication tailored to the recipient's needs. Modesty is special in Russian culture, especially within professional circles such as scientists, researchers and doctors. While dominant behaviour from superiors might be tolerated, it's generally met with disapproval among peers. The Russian approach to communication leans towards the avoidance of ambiguity, leading to a complex bureaucratic system. They prioritize meticulous planning, offering thorough context and background information. Interactions with strangers maintain a formal and respectful tone, emphasizing a degree of distance.

In Sweden, a culture of independence prevails, where hierarchy serves more as a convenience rather than a tool for strict control. Equality and equal rights are highly prized and leaders often take on the role of approachable coaching figures. Power is decentralized, with managers placing trust in their team members' expertise and employees expect to be consulted rather than subjected to a controlling management style. Communication is characterized by its direct and participatory nature. Within this society, there is a strong inclination towards a loosely knit social framework, with individuals prioritizing themselves and their immediate families. The relationship between employers and employees is viewed as a mutual contract founded on merit, with effective management tailored to the needs of individuals. The emphasis in Sweden is on maintaining a harmonious work-life balance and fostering inclusivity. Effective managers actively support their teams and involve them in decision-making. Core values include consensus, equality, solidarity and a commitment to quality. Conflicts are typically resolved through compromise and flexible work arrangements are often favoured. Sweden exhibits a relaxed attitude, valuing practicality over rigid adherence to principles. Deviating from norms is generally well-tolerated and the culture prefers only the necessary rules. Flexibility in work schedules and a measured approach to work efforts are common, with precision and punctuality not being inherent traits in the work culture.

Result

Fey found that managers in Sweden and Russia were motivated for completely different reasons.

- Russian managers
  - The primary motivation for Russian managers stems from salary and bonus incentives.
  - Russian managers' motivation remains consistent regardless of a pleasant work environment.
  - Equity holds less significance for Russian managers; interestingly, their motivation experiences a slight decline in an equitable workplace.
  - The motivation of Russian managers rises in proportion to the level of feedback they receive.
- Swedish managers
  - Swedish managers are motivated by an enjoyable work environment.
  - Increasing the pleasantness of the work environment can boost motivation among Swedish managers.
  - Interestingly, Swedish managers' motivation slightly decreases as their salary increases.

- o Swedish managers can find motivation through perceived equity with their peers.

- o The extent of feedback has a minor adverse impact on the motivation of Swedish managers.

Discussion questions:

- Look at the need theory. Based on the research findings, which hierarchical level does the Russian manager focus on? Which hierarchical level does the Swedish manager focus on? What might be the reasons contributing to this different need focus?

- Russian and Swedish managers have different preferences for an equitable work environment. What might be the reasons contributing to this? (Hint: what does it mean for middle managers when the organization tries to create a low-hierarchical and/or empowered organization when the decision-making style is from an authoritative way to more consensus?)

- Looking at the differences between Russian and Swedish managers in Fey's study, what might be the limitation of equity theory? (When does it become less suitable to apply equity theory?)

- Given the differences between Russian and Swedish managers, how can you motivate them? Consider a few practices you can use to foster a more motivated and engaged workforce – based on the need hierarchy, Equity Theory and Goal-Setting theories and describe why these strategies can work.

WORK–LIFE BALANCE

The notion of work–life balance has gained prominence as individuals seek to manage their work and personal commitments effectively. However, striving for the perfect balance may lead to unrealistic expectations, stress and guilt. The concept of work–life boundaries has recently emerged, acknowledging that perfect balance may not always be feasible. In particular, the emphasis on work–life balance gives an illusion that perfect balance can lead to unrealistic expectations, causing stress and anxiety when it proves unachievable. Additionally, managing this balance might evoke guilt and frustration when one cannot allocate enough time to work and personal life.

Work–life boundaries emphasize the importance of setting clear limits and managing work and personal life integration based on individual preferences. It recognizes that everyone has unique needs and priorities when managing these domains. Establishing designated work hours, technology-free zones and prioritizing self-care and leisure activities can help maintain these boundaries. Controlling the work–life boundaries positively affects individual work outcomes (e.g., reduced turnover, increased engagement) and personal well-being outcomes (e.g., better work–life balance, reduced work–family conflict).

Reviewing over three hundred articles, Kossek, Perrigino and Lautsch (2023) summarize factors that influence work–life boundaries, including:

- society level
  - gender norms – traditional gender roles may place more responsibility on women for caregiving and household duties, leading to challenges in balancing work and family commitments
  - regulation and laws – the presence and effectiveness of laws and regulations related to working hours, parental leave, flexible work arrangements and overtime can significantly impact work-life balance
  - work–life narratives – for instance, if the company culture encourages a constant 'workaholic' mentality, employees may feel pressure to prioritize work over personal life. These narratives of work–life policies were based on beliefs of potential backlash and career disadvantages associated with utilizing such policies. Other narratives centred around 'space' where non-work spaces were considered suitable and adaptable for work-related activities. These narratives supported the implementation of telework and allowed employees to have flexibility in work locations.
- organizational level
  - work–life flexibility policies: such as work location (e.g., virtual work or flexible location), workload (e.g., part-time), work schedule control, likelihood to disconnect work and life (e.g., using a personal device to carry out work) and parental leave.
  - implementation of the work–life flexibility policies: such as managers, organizational culture and other organizational policies. For instance, when employees' performance evaluations are poorly executed and seen as negative or unfair, they can stress employees. This stress can cancel out any positive effects of flexible work policies on work–life balance.
- individual level
  - individuals' preferences to set up clear work and life boundaries.
  - career considerations: perceptions and expectations about future work-related opportunities play a role in determining policy adoption.
  - whether individuals choose to use work–life flexibility policies.

REFLECTION

- What motivates you to use work–life flexibility policies and have you ever chosen not to use them? How do you perceive the impact of using these policies on your productivity and well-being?

- How do you manage work–life boundaries and what factors influence your decisions?

- How do you believe work–life flexibility policies can impact your future career opportunities?

Chapter summary

Understanding motivation theories' content-, process- and context-based views can provide a holistic view of why some employees are more motivated than others by considering multiple dimensions contributing to motivation.

Content theories of motivation seek to understand human behaviour based on innate drives and acquired motives. Such theories, like Maslow's Hierarchy of Needs, ERG theory, Herzberg's Two-Factor Theory, Cognitive Evaluation Theory and Self-Determination theories, address the 'why' questions from an individual perspective – trying to answer what an individual wants and needs. They focus on how to characterize numerous human motives best and what leads to different needs and motives becoming the primary driving force behind our actions. Although not all psychological needs are identified and these Western motivation paradigms are necessarily universal, these content-based theories provide a checklist to understand and solve problems with individuals (Latham, 2012).

Process-based theories, like Equity Theory, Expectancy Theory and Goal-Setting Theory, delve into the cognitive processes that influence employee motivation. These theories consider how employees perceive the fairness of their rewards and outcomes in comparison to others (Equity Theory), their belief that their efforts will lead to performance and desired outcomes (Expectancy Theory) and the relationship between setting goals and performance (Goal-Setting Theory). By understanding these cognitive processes, we can understand why certain employees may be more motivated due to their perceptions and beliefs about work-related rewards and efforts. These theories remain important as it has managerial implications. For instance, when individuals feel unfairly treated, they show affection (e.g., low commitment) and behaviours (e.g., reduced effort); equity theory suggests that the team leader should ensure fairness in recognizing employees' contributions and accomplishments (e.g., a performance recognition programme that acknowledges efforts and results). Based on Expectancy Theory, managerial practice includes strengthening the valence (e.g., clear and specific performance goals, outlining the expected outcomes and the connection between effort and rewards) and improving expectancy (e.g., increasing the belief that effort invested in tasks will lead to successful outcomes through providing training). Based on Goal-Setting Theory, it suggests the team leader collaborates with each team member to set challenging yet achievable performance goals aligned with the organization's objectives, breaking down the larger goals into smaller milestones and providing constructive feedback and acknowledging achievements along the way.

Context-based theories, such as job design and prosocial behaviour, focus on the broader work environment and social context that impact motivation. Job design considers how tasks, roles and responsibilities are structured to provide meaning and autonomy to employees. By understanding the impact of job design and social interactions on motivation, we can recognize why some employees may be more motivated in specific work environments that offer meaningful and socially impactful opportunities.

The chapter has looked at the compensation system and work–life balance for the practical application of motivation theories, highlighting key factors to consider when applying motivation theories at work.

Key terms

ERG

Theory X

Theory Y

Two-Factors Theory

Hygiene factors

Motivational factors

Extrinsic motivation

Intrinsic motivation

Self-Determination Theory

Content-based theory

Process-based theory

Context-based theory

Equity Theory

Distributive fairness

Procedural fairness

Interactional fairness

Expectancy Theory

Expectancy

Instrumentality

Valence

Goal-setting

SMART goal

Job characteristic model

Job enrichment model

Prosocial motivation

Work–life balance

Work–life boundary

Chapter review questions

- How do content-based theories of motivation, such as Maslow's hierarchy of needs and Herzberg's Two-Factor Theory, contribute to understanding why some employees are more motivated than others?

- How do process-based theories like the Equity Theory, Expectancy Theory and Goal Setting Theory help explain differences in employee motivation levels?

- How does the Equity Theory consider employees' perceptions of fairness in rewards and outcomes in relation to others?

- In what ways can the Goal-Setting Theory be applied to enhance motivation and performance in the workplace?

- What are the differences among Equity Theory, Expectancy Theory and Goal-Setting Theories?

- What key elements of job design can contribute to employee motivation and engagement?
- How can social interactions and prosocial behaviour impact employee motivation in the workplace?
- What are the steps to consider when designing a compensation system?

Further reading

Kanfer, R, Frese, M, & Johnson, R. E. (2017) Motivation related to work: A century of progress. *Journal of Applied Psychology*, 102(3), 338–355. A review paper provides a broad overview of the motivation theories.

References

Berkman, E T (2018) The neuroscience of goals and behavior change, *Consulting Psychology Journal*, 70(1), 28–44.

van den Broeck, A, Ferris, D L, Chang, C H & Rosen, C C (2016) A review of self-determination theory's basic psychological needs at work, *Journal of Management*, 42(5), 1195–1229.

Church, A T, Katigbak, M S, Locke, K D, Zhang, H, Shen, J, Vargas-Flores, J & Vargas-Flores, J (2012) Need satisfaction and well-being: Testing self-determination theory in eight cultures, *Journal of Cross-Cultural Psychology*, 44(4), 507–534.

Clark, R E & Saxberg, B (2019) 4 reasons good employees lose their motivation, *Harvard Business Review*, 1–6.

De Smet, A, Dowling, B, Hancock, B & Schaninger, B (2022) Great attrition, great attraction 2.0 global survey. McKinsey & Company.

DeVoe S E & Iyengar S S (2004) Managers' theories of subordinates: A cross-cultural examination of manager perceptions of motivation and appraisal of performance, *Organizational Behavior and Human Decision Processes*, 93(1), 47–61.

Fey, C F (2005) Opening the black box of motivation: A cross-cultural comparison of Sweden and Russia, *International Business Review*, 14, 345–367.

Grant, A M & Shandell, M S (2022) Social motivation at work: The organizational psychology of effort for, against and with others, *Annual Review of Psychology*, 73, 301–326.

Johnson, L K (2006) Motivating employees to go above and beyond, *Harvard Business Review*, 3–4.

Kanfer, R & Chen, G (2016a) Motivation in organizational behavior: History, advances and prospects, *Organizational Behavior and Human Decision Processes*, 136, 6–19.

Kanfer, R, Frese, M & Johnson, R E (2017) Motivation related to work: A century of progress, *Journal of Applied Psychology*, 102(3), 338–355.

Kanungo, R N & Mendonca, M (1988) Evaluating employee compensation, *California Management Review*, 23–39.

Kossek, E E, Perrigino, M B & Lautsch, B A (2023) Work-life flexibility policies from a boundary control and implementation perspective: A review and research framework, *Journal of Management*, 49(6), 2062–2108.

Latham, G P (2012) *Work Motivation, 2nd edition*, Sage.

Lawler, E E & Suttle, J L (1973) Expectancy theory and job behavior, *Organizational Behavior & Human Performance*, 9(3), 482–503. https://doi.org/10.1016/0030-5073(73)90066-4 (archived at https://perma.cc/HL74-DAZV)

Mathur, A, Zhang, Y & Neelankavil, J P (2001) Critical managerial motivational factors: A cross-cultural analysis of four culturally divergent countries, *International Journal of Cross-Cultural Management*, 1(3), 251–267.

Managing groups and teams   04

Working in a team, what was your experience? Some typical positive aspects of working in a team:

- Diverse perspectives and ideas: in a team-based environment, the convergence of diverse backgrounds, experiences and expertise fuels an environment conducive to innovative problem-solving. By embracing a multiplicity of perspectives, teams can more effectively identify potential problems or untapped opportunities that may have eluded individual contributors. The richness of ideas from a collective effort strengthens the overall decision-making process, leading to improved outcomes and long-term success.

- Achieving beyond individual capabilities: the collaborative synergy within a team creates a fertile ground for elevated productivity. Tasks that would be arduous or unattainable for individuals to accomplish alone become feasible and efficient when undertaken collectively. Through the sharing of responsibilities, workload distribution and leveraging complementary skills, teams can achieve goals and deliver results that surpass the capabilities of any individual team member. This heightened productivity not only saves time and resources but also enhances the overall performance of the team.

- Learning and skill development: individuals can expand their skill sets and acquire new capabilities by engaging with teammates with diverse competencies. Communication, the ability to work under pressure and collaborative skills are just a few examples of the proficiencies that can be honed within a team setting. As team members interact and support one another, they naturally acquire and develop essential aptitudes that contribute to their professional growth and resilience in an ever-evolving work landscape.

Working in teams can sometimes present challenges, as follows.

- Coordination and communication difficulties: teams often require coordination and communication between different members, which can be challenging to manage. Miscommunications, delays and breakdowns in coordination can lead to wasted time and effort.

- Groupthink: in some cases, the desire for consensus and harmony within a team can lead to groupthink, where individuals suppress their own opinions to conform to the group. This can lead to poor decision-making and missed opportunities.

- Social loafing: when individuals are working in a team, it can be easy for some members to coast on the efforts of others. This can lead to resentment and decreased motivation among team members.

- Conflicts and disagreements: the benefit of diverse perspectives and backgrounds can also introduce the possibility of conflicts and disagreements. When conflicting viewpoints collide, tension can arise, resulting in communication breakdowns and diminished team performance.

Questions:

- Working in a team, what was your experience? How did those experiences shape your perception of teamwork?
- How do you typically approach working in a team? Are you comfortable taking on leadership roles, or do you prefer to contribute in a more supportive capacity?
- Are there specific tasks or projects better suited for working alone rather than in a team? Why?

Team

Definition of team

A team is a group of individuals working together to achieve a common goal, who are interdependent concerning information, resources, knowledge and skills and who seek to combine their efforts to achieve a common goal. Conversely, a group is a collection of individuals who coordinate their efforts but may sometimes share a different goal. While both teams and groups involve people working together, the critical difference is that teams have a shared goal and a common purpose, while groups may not (noted that sometimes team and group may be used as interchangeable terms because both refer to a collection of individuals).

Additionally, team members are interdependent and rely on each other to achieve their goals, while group members may be more independent and have individual accountability. Kozlowski and Ilgen (2006) outline the fundamental attributes of teams:

- They consist of multiple individuals.
- They engage in social interaction, whether through in-person communication or remote collaboration.
- They share common goals and a unified purpose.
- They embrace diverse roles and responsibilities.
- They operate within a larger context, such as an organization.

A team can also be conceptualized as a system – namely, the input–process–output model (IPO). First introduced by McGrath (1964), it highlights the factors influencing team effectiveness and task completion and helps achieve a satisfying team experience (LePine et al, 2008). Here's a breakdown of each component:

- Input: this phase focuses on the inputs or factors that shape the team. It includes elements such as team composition, member characteristics (skills, expertise, diversity), resources available to the team (technology, funding, materials) and the team's organizational context (goals, structure, culture). For example, in a software team, the input phase involves selecting team members with diverse programming skills, ensuring access to the necessary software and hardware resources and aligning the team's goals with the organization's overall objectives.

- Process: this phase encompasses the actual interactions and activities undertaken by the team. It involves communication, decision-making, problem-solving and coordination among team members. This phase also includes how roles and responsibilities are assigned, how conflicts are managed and how leadership and collaboration are fostered within the team. For example, when a team progresses its task, the process phase includes regular team meetings to discuss project progress, assigning tasks to team members based on their strengths, resolving conflicts during decision-making and maintaining effective communication channels among team members.

- Output: this phase represents the outcomes or results achieved by the team. It includes the tangible deliverables or products of the team's work and the intangible outcomes such as team satisfaction, cohesion and learning. The output phase also considers the impact of the team's work on the broader organization or stakeholders. For example, the output phase consists of the successful execution of tasks, achieving target figures, generating positive client feedback and enhancing the company's brand reputation.

The IPO model emphasizes the interconnectedness of these phases, as the quality of inputs influences the effectiveness of team processes, affecting the outputs or outcomes. Understanding and managing each phase is crucial for building high-performing teams capable of delivering desired results.

Team effectiveness

Team effectiveness refers to the extent to which a team achieves its goals, fulfils its purpose and meets or exceeds performance expectations. It encompasses a team's overall success and performance in achieving desired outcomes. Team effectiveness is not solely determined by individual abilities but is influenced by various factors, including team dynamics, communication, collaboration, leadership and synergy among team members. Cohen and Bailey (1997) developed a model, based on the IPO model, to look at what makes a team effective. In their model, they view team effectiveness as the output of the IPO model and this can be categorized into three major concepts:

- performance, such as goal attainment, efficiency, productivity, response time, quality and quantity and innovation.
- team members' attitude (e.g., job satisfaction, trust)
- behavioural outcome (e.g., turnover).

For Cohen and Bailey, team effectiveness (as an output) will be influenced by the following:

- Input:
  o Task design (e.g., level of autonomy, dependence)
  o Team member composition (e.g., diversity, size of the team, how long they worked together in a team)
  o Context in which team was embedded (e.g., reward)
- Process
  o Team internal process (e.g., conflict and communication within the team)
  o Team external process. This refers to the activities and interactions with people outside the team to share and gather information, coordinate work and maintain effective relationships
  o Team-level psychosocial traits (e.g., norms, cohesion)

Note that the conflict within the team is not necessarily detrimental to the team. For example, when team members disagree over differences of opinion related to the team's tasks (i.e., task conflict), different perspectives, goals, strategies or work processes, when managed constructively, can benefit team performance. It can stimulate creative thinking, encourage critical evaluation of ideas and lead to innovative solutions. However, when task conflicts escalate and become destructive, they can harm team effectiveness by causing tension, impeding collaboration and hindering progress. However, if the team members experience personal clashes, negative emotions or friction among team members that extend beyond task-related issues (i.e., relationship conflict), this tends to have a more negative impact on team effectiveness as it fuels the team misunderstanding and adds stress to the team.

Team and individuals

Group-level perception often influences individuals' behaviour – this is called social influence. It is the power of social interactions and group dynamics to shape individuals' attitudes, beliefs and actions. There are several mechanisms through which social influence operates in group settings, including conformity, obedience and social comparison.

- Conformity occurs when individuals adjust their attitudes or behaviours to align with the perceived norms of the group. For example, individuals may conform to the dress code norms established by the organization to align with the expectations and standards set by the group.

- Obedience involves complying with the directives or instructions of authority figures within the group. For example, in military settings, soldiers are expected to follow orders and directions from their commanding officers without questioning or hesitation.

- Social comparison refers to the tendency to evaluate oneself by comparing one's thoughts, feelings and actions to those of others in the group. For example, employees may engage in social comparison regarding their salaries and compensation packages. They might compare their earnings with their colleagues, leading to satisfaction or dissatisfaction based on perceived fairness or equity.

Team and individual perception

Teams can also influence how individuals perceive and define themselves within the group. This perception strengthens interpersonal bonds and can promote positive social interactions within the group. Two related concepts explain how individuals perceive themselves in the social context: social identity theory and self-categorization theory (Hogg and Terry, 2000). Social identity theory is based on social comparison, where we compare our group with others to feel better about ourselves, i.e., a sense of competition among groups. For example, you strongly identify with your team, feeling a sense of pride and connection. You might compare your work performance favourably with those in other departments, believing your team is the top performer. It is about how being part of a group shapes how we think of ourselves and how we see others in or out of our group.

Self-categorization can be viewed as an extended version of social identity theory. Self-categorization focused on the cognitive process by which individuals identify as members of a particular social group or category. Self-categorization emphasizes the social dimensions of identity and the influence of group membership on an individual's self-concept and behaviour. It involves seeing oneself as part of a collective identity defined by shared characteristics, values and norms. In other words, de-emphasized "self", viewing self as representative characteristics or attributes of the group. Examples include identifying oneself as a student, a professional, a member of a specific cultural or religious group or belonging to a particular team or organization. When individuals strongly identify with a group, the group's norms and values influence their behaviour and attitudes. This identification can lead to a sense of belonging, increased cooperation and a willingness to work towards common goals.

Team and individual effort

In addition to individuals' perception of themselves in relation to the team, individuals may also change their actual input to the collective task. Team can increase an individual's effort (e.g., social facilitation) and decrease an individual's efforts (e.g., social loafing). Social facilitation refers to the tendency for individuals to perform better on simple or well-learnt tasks when they are in the presence of others compared to when they are alone. Social facilitation can lead to an increase in individual effort and performance. Bond and Titus (1983) summarize how arousal can drive individuals to perform better in the team. When individuals are in the presence of others, they experience increased physiological arousal, which can enhance their motivation and alertness. This heightened state of arousal tends to benefit individuals when performing tasks that they are already skilled at or relatively simple tasks. Social facilitation can harm individuals' effort input when working on complex or unfamiliar tasks. In such situations, the heightened arousal caused by the presence of others may increase individuals' anxiety or self-consciousness, leading to a decline in performance. This phenomenon is known as social inhibition or choking under pressure.

A challenge frequently encountered when working in teams, as highlighted in the introductory section of this chapter, involves social loafing. Social loafing refers to the phenomenon where individuals exert less effort or motivation when working in a group than when working individually. It occurs when individuals perceive their contribution to a collective task as less crucial or believe their efforts will be diluted or unnoticed within a group context. Social loafing is closely related to the influence of groups on individual behaviour in several ways (Comer, 1995; Liden et al, 2004; Simms & Nichols, 2014):

- Diffusion of responsibility: in a group, individuals may feel a reduced sense of personal responsibility for the outcome of a task. They may believe that others will compensate for their lack of effort, decreasing individual motivation and performance.
- Lack of individual evaluation: individuals may experience reduced motivation and effort due to concerns about how their performance will be evaluated within the group. They may be less motivated to contribute fully if they believe their efforts will go unnoticed or receive little recognition. This is mainly the case when the size of the team increases.

- Free-riding: social loafing can occur when individuals perceive that their contributions will not be individually evaluated or rewarded. They may exploit the group's collective effort while minimizing their own investment or contribution.

- Perception that others are not doing their work and therefore readjust one's input to the task. Individuals may engage in social comparison within a group, comparing their effort or performance to their peers. If they perceive that others are exerting less effort or performing at a lower level, they may feel justified in reducing their effort, leading to a downward spiral of decreased motivation and performance.

- Unmotivating task. In group settings where individual contributions blend, their motivation wanes and they may be reluctant to exert full energy on the task when the task is non-competitive, mundane and draining (Harkins et al, 1980).

When social loafing continues, team members become more frustrated and resentful towards team members who shirk their responsibilities and find it increasingly challenging to handle the growing workload left undone.

GROUP DISCUSSION

Preventing social loafing

Considering the factors that contribute to social loafing, what proactive measures can you establish as ground rules within the group to prevent social loafing? In other words, what strategies can you implement to discourage and minimize the occurrence of social loafing from the outset?

GROUP ACTIVITIES

Team effectiveness feedback form

Janet Hillier and Linda M. Dunn-Jensen have developed a feedback form designed to help teams discuss team members' responsibilities and expectations and help teams measure the effectiveness of a team. You can access the self-assessed form in the appendix of the article *Groups Meet... Teams Improve: Building Teams That Learn* which can be found online at Sage Journals.

The **team** feedback form is divided into seven sections, each addressing a different aspect of team effectiveness. These sections include:

- team goals and objectives
- communication

- decision-making
- trust and support
- conflict resolution
- performance evaluation
- leadership.

Suggested team activity:

1 Download or obtain a copy of the **team** feedback form.

2 Create a team charter. This is to help your team to identify the skills each team member may bring and expectations of the team are made clear.

3 Review the results as a team and identify areas of strength and areas for improvement from feedback sessions when a team completes a project.

4 Sign the formal team assessment form to carry out self-evaluation periodically. During this time, discuss the findings as a team and develop strategies to address the areas for improvement to be a more effective team.

5 Implement the strategies and monitor progress over time.

Types of teams

The team can be varied in some design features including the following (Reiche, 2023; Stewart, 2006):

- The level of autonomy is the degree of freedom given to the team to make decisions, plan work activities and adapt to the changing demand.
- The level of coordination needed among the team members refers to whether individuals need information and input from others to accomplish a task.

Common types of teams include cross-functional teams, self-managed teams and virtual teams, described as follows.

Cross-functional teams

Cross-functional teams are individuals from different functional areas or departments within an organization collaborating to achieve a specific objective or address a particular problem. These teams bring together diverse expertise and perspectives to tackle complex challenges. Cross-functional teams are well-suited for complex projects that require multidisciplinary expertise, strategic planning and problem-solving that transcends departmental boundaries. Examples include product development, process improvement initiatives and organizational change management.

- Advantages:
  - o Enhanced problem-solving: cross-functional teams leverage members' combined knowledge and skills from various disciplines, enabling comprehensive problem-solving and innovative solutions.
  - o Broader insights: cross-functional teams provide a broader perspective, enabling a more holistic decision-making and strategy development approach.
- Challenges:
  - o Conflicting priorities: members may have differing priorities and objectives due to their respective functional areas, which can cause conflicts and hinder progress.
  - o Communication gaps: different departments may use specific jargon or have different communication styles, leading to misunderstandings and inefficiencies.
  - o Decision-making challenges: reaching consensus within cross-functional teams can be time-consuming and challenging due to diverse opinions and interests.

Self-managing teams

Self-managing teams, also known as autonomous or empowered teams, are individuals with the authority and responsibility to make decisions related to their work processes and goals. They have a high level of autonomy and accountability. Examples of this type of team include temporary teams (e.g., TV and film production).

- Advantages:
  - o Greater motivation and ownership: self-managing teams experience increased motivation and engagement as they have a sense of right and control over their work.
  - o Improved agility: these teams can quickly adapt and respond to changing circumstances, as decision-making is decentralized and team members can make real-time adjustments.
  - o Faster decision-making: with the authority to make decisions, self-managing teams can bypass bureaucratic processes, leading to faster decision-making and increased efficiency.
- Challenges:
  - o Need for strong team dynamics: effective self-managing teams require a high level of trust, collaboration and effective communication among members.
  - o Lack of guidance: team members may face challenges without clear guidance or direction, leading to uncertainty and potential inefficiencies.
  - o Balancing autonomy and alignment: striking a balance between individual freedom and organizational alignment can be challenging, as too much autonomy may lead to conflicting goals or a lack of coordination.

Virtual teams

Virtual teams consist of members who collaborate remotely, using digital communication tools to accomplish their tasks. Geographical or time constraints do not bind these teams; they often operate across different time zones.

- Advantages:
  - Global talent pool: virtual teams allow organizations to tap into a diverse talent pool regardless of geographical location, enabling access to specialized skills and expertise.
  - Cost savings: virtual teams eliminate the need for physical office space and associated expenses, resulting in organization cost savings.
- Challenges:
  - Communication and coordination: virtual teams face communication challenges due to the absence of face-to-face interaction, potentially leading to misunderstandings and reduced collaboration, changing the quality and quantity of informal and formal conversations. This is particularly challenging when the team has just formed but not throughout the entire life of the team (Kou, 2021; Majchrzak et al, 2000).
  - Building trust and rapport: building trust among virtual team members can be more challenging than in-person teams, as building relationships and rapport may take longer.
  - Time zone differences: operating across different time zones can make scheduling meetings and achieving real-time collaboration difficult, potentially impacting productivity.

DISCUSSION

Team type

Utilize a 2x2 matrix (Figure 4.1) to illustrate various types of teams based on the levels of interdependence and autonomy and carry out the following tasks:

- give an example that can describe the kind of team
- describe the level of coordination needed for the team to accomplish the task successfully
- describe what drives individuals to be committed to the team goal.

Figure 4.1   Example matrix

	Level of autonomy	
Level of interdependence	High level of interdependence, low level of autonomy - Example - Level of coordination - Individual source of commitment	High level of interdependence, high level of autonomy - Example - Level of coordination - Individual source of commitment
	Low level of interdependence, low level of autonomy - Example - Level of coordination - Individual source of commitment	Low level of interdependence, high level of autonomy - Example - Level of coordination - Individual source of commitment

Level of autonomy

Adapted from Reiche, B. S. (2023). Between interdependence and autonomy: Toward a typology of work design modes in the new world of work. *Human Resource Management Journal*, 1–17. doi.org/10.1111/1748-8583.12495

BUILDING TRUST IN VIRTUAL TEAMS

Establishing trust relies on consistent and positive interactions. Informal conversations in common areas like the coffee machine and breakrooms can unexpectedly bring colleagues together and foster strong bonds. Similarly, spontaneously informally visiting each other's offices contributes to developing rapport. But how can trust be built when encountering people infrequently?

Dinh and colleagues (2021) suggested ways to build trust among remote colleagues:

- Building trust over delivering tasks:

  o Embracing shared objectives and uncertainties: regularly assess accomplishments and potential risks, fostering a team culture that values collective goals.

  o Establishing boundaries and norms: set clear expectations while respecting individuals' availability. Provide newcomers with learning opportunities through formal training and informal online platforms (e.g., learning teams, virtual chats).

  o Maintaining defined roles: assign roles while considering individual circumstances, clearly define responsibilities and communicate expectations while remaining adaptable.

- o Cultivating mindful engagement: actively acknowledge others' emotions, minimize unnecessary meetings and tasks and evaluate engagement through non-intrusive methods.

- Building affective trust over interpersonal and emotional bonds:
  - o Fostering an inclusive community through psychological safety: celebrate individual and team accomplishments while maintaining informal connections with team members. Encourage the sharing of low-stakes information.
  - o Cultivating commitment: emphasize aligning organizational and individual goals, empower individuals in their work and provide online learning resources.
  - o Nurturing meaningful connections beyond work: demonstrate care for team members and purposefully create opportunities for casual interactions.
  - o Establishing contingencies: encourage backup behaviours, ensure everyone is informed about various tasks within the team and create slack, so that individuals can step in when a team member becomes unavailable.

Likewise, studying in virtual teams across Australia, Brazil, Jamaica, Spain, Suriname and the United States, Gibson and Grushina (2021) also find similar strategies for increasing the effectiveness of virtual teams, including:

- o establishing specific goals and structure to minimize ambiguity, fostering clarity and alignment among team members
- o cultivating a strong sense of identification with the team to enhance commitment and prioritize collective team objectives
- o developing a better understanding of cultural differences within the team to promote inclusivity and effective collaboration
- o purposefully celebrating achievements and encouraging social exchange to foster team cohesion and morale
- o explicitly addressing disagreements and conflicts to ensure open communication and maintain a healthy team dynamic, even in a virtual setting.

Formal and informal teams

In addition to the functional setup of the teams that impact team members' work-place behaviours, we can also view teams in terms of their interactional formality. Formal and informal groups are two distinct types of social structures that exist within organizations. Understanding the differences between these groups is essential for effectively managing and leveraging the dynamics within a workplace. Here's an explanation of formal and informal groups, examples and their respective characteristics.

Formal groups are intentionally created by the organization to fulfil specific objectives and tasks. These groups are formally established and recognized through organizational structure, job design or official assignments. The members of formal groups are brought together based on their job roles, expertise or shared responsibilities (e.g., project teams, functional teams in the organization). Here are some characteristics of formal groups:

- Formal structure and hierarchy
- Clearly defined roles, responsibilities and reporting lines
- Established goals, objectives and tasks
- Official recognition and endorsement by the organization
- Communication and coordination through formal channels
- Accountability to superiors or team leaders

Informal groups, on the other hand, are social structures that emerge naturally within an organization based on shared interests, social interactions or personal relationships (e.g., social circles, reading groups). These groups are not formally designated by the organization but form spontaneously among employees. Here are some characteristics of informal groups:

- Voluntary and self-formed
- Based on social interactions and personal relationships
- Not governed by formal rules or structure
- Communication and coordination through informal channels, such as conversations during breaks or informal gatherings
- Influence and dynamics are driven by social norms, trust and personal connections
- Can have a significant impact on work-related attitudes, morale and productivity

Team development stages

When team leaders understand the various stages of team development, team leaders and members can understand what to expect when forming teams, and understand what to expect at each stage and better support team members. For example, if a team struggles to establish clear goals and roles, the leader can provide guidance and support to help the team move forward. Understanding potential conflicts and challenges that teams face at each stage of development can help leaders anticipate and address problems before they become significant obstacles to team success.

For example, newly formed interdisciplinary teams are tasked to work on a project. In the beginning, team members are all polite and respectful to each other, but as they start brainstorming ideas, disagreements arise and tension rises, with people becoming frustrated with the lack of progress and conflicting opinions. People may begin to talk over each other or become defensive about their ideas. It can feel like chaos and confusion, with no clear direction or consensus. This stage is called the storming stage in team development – a natural part of the team development process. Knowing this in advance can help teams to resolve conflicts in a constructive manner. Team leaders and members can also set realistic performance goals and progress expectations, their approach to tackling the task and allocating resources accordingly.

Gersick's Punctuated Equilibrium Model

The Punctuated Equilibrium Model, created by Gersick in 1988 and 1989, is a way to understand how teams develop. The Punctuated Equilibrium Model is called so because it suggests that teams experience long periods of stability (equilibrium) interrupted by short periods of change (punctuated). Punctuated equilibrium is a concept in evolutionary biology that describes the pattern of long periods of stability followed by rapid bursts of change in the evolution of species. During long periods of stability, species are said to be in a state of equilibrium, where the environment remains relatively constant and there is little selective pressure to evolve. However, during shorter periods, environmental conditions change rapidly and species are subject to increased selective pressures that result in rapid evolutionary change.

Gersick suggested that this pattern of stability and change in evolutionary biology is similar to the pattern observed in team development. In the team setting, this refers to teams going through periods of stability and periods of change. During the first half of their existence, teams establish their goals and work processes and this period is generally stable. However, the second half of a team's existence is marked by change. The team re-evaluates its goals and processes and makes necessary adjustments. This period of change is usually triggered by a significant event, such as a deadline or a change in team membership. After making the necessary changes, the team enters another period of stability and works to achieve its revised goals and processes. This cycle of stability and change continues until the team completes its task or disbands. The punctuated equilibrium model emphasizes that teams must be flexible and adaptable to succeed and be prepared to make changes when necessary.

EXERCISE

Applying the Punctuated Equilibrium Model

Think about a team you have been a part of in the past. Can you identify a period of stability and a period of change in the team's development process? What triggered the change? Based on what you know about the Punctuated Equilibrium Model, what strategies would you suggest to help the team cope with each stage?

Tuckman's Stages of Group Development

Tuckman's Stages of Group Development (or simply Tuckman's model) is a model that explains the process of group development (Tuckman, 1965; Tuckman & Jensen, 1977). The model was developed by psychologist Bruce Tuckman in 1965 and has since become widely used in the study of group dynamics. Tuckman's model suggests that groups may cycle through these stages several times before reaching a state of high performance and productivity. In other words, the frustrating, dysfunctional part of the team development will be overcome. Tuckman's original model in 1965 consists of four stages: 1. forming, 2. storming, 3. norming, and 4. performing. This framework unveils the journey teams undertake – from initial gathering to harmonizing efforts – encompassing interpersonal intricacies, managing challenges and fruitful synergy and accomplishment. It is worth noting that teams may not always spend equal time in each stage – for instance, some teams may be in the storming stage longer than the other stages. Detail of each stage of Tuckman's model is described in Table 4.1.

Later, Tuckman and Jensen (1977) revisited the group process model and proposed the final stage of the model as adjourning. In this final stage, the team disbands or moves on to other projects. Members reflect on their experiences and accomplishments and there may be a sense of loss or sadness – difficulty letting go of the team and lack of closure. The leader's role at this stage is to facilitate a smooth transition and celebrate the team's achievements. An example of this stage is when the team disbands after the project and members move on to other projects. The leader holds a meeting to recognize and celebrate the team's achievements and to provide closure.

Table 4.1 Tuckman's stages of group development

Stage	Forming	Storming	Norming	Performing
Description	• Team members get to know each other interpersonally. • Team members create clear goals.	• Team members start to express their opinions and ideas. • Team comes to agreements and disagreements.	• Team establishes norms and expectations for behaviour. • Show an increase in productivity.	• Team is highly productive and working effectively towards its goals.
Key characteristics	• Team members are polite and friendly, avoiding conflicts. • Individuals are working to understand their roles in the team. • Uncertainty and anxiety.	• Team members try to establish their positions in the team. • Divergent views about tasks and responsibilities are discussed. • Tension arises.	• A sense of 'we' and 'our team.' • Goals are well-understood. • Team works together more effectively, engaging and supportive.	• Fluid roles and responsibilities, seamless collaboration. • Supportive and positive energy in the team.
Potential challenges	• Lack of clarity about goals and objectives. • Difficulty establishing trust among team members.	• Lack of clarity about roles and responsibilities. • Difficulty managing conflicts. • Loss of motivation (e.g., lack of participation).	• Complacency about the sense of we-ness. • Resistance to change. • Risk diminishing the distinctiveness contributed by individuals.	• Few internal problems. • Persistent performance strain may lead to potential burnout.

(continued)

Table 4.1 (Continued)

Stage	Forming	Storming	Norming	Performing
Leaders' role	• Direction the team, set clear goal-related expectations. • Establish or facilitate open communication.	• Conflict resolution. • Promote collaboration among team members.	• Facilitating feedback and solution and collaboration among team members. • Sharing and valuing different perspectives.	• Sustain the team's alignment with goals and objectives while offering facilitation. • Provide group process observation.
Example	A new IT project team is formed to develop a new software application. Members come from different departments and have different backgrounds and skill sets. The leader holds a kick-off meeting to introduce everyone and define the project scope and goals.	IT project team encounters a disagreement about the application's architecture. The leader facilitates a discussion in which all team members can express their views and helps the team decide. Some members argue for a more modular approach, while others prefer a monolithic approach.	After resolving the conflict over the software architecture, the IT project team starts to work collaboratively on specific tasks. The leader holds regular meetings to review progress and provide feedback. Team members begin to develop a sense of trust and mutual respect.	The marketing team in the previous example is now executing the campaign with high efficiency and creativity and achieving success.

Based on Tuckman, B (1965) Developmental sequence in small groups, *Psychological Bulletin*, 384–399.

Tuckman, B W & Jensen, K (1977). Stages of small group development, *Journal of Group & Organisational Studies*, 419–427.

West Chester University. Tuckman's stages of group development. https://www.wcupa.edu/coral/tuckmanStagesGroupDelvelopment.aspx#:~:text=These%20stages%20are%20commonly%20known,more%20collaborative%20or%20shared%20leadership.

EXERCISE

Personality and team development process

In some cases, we may not have the autonomy to select our team members. Team members are often assigned by others. Drawing from the knowledge gained about personality types in the individual difference chapter, what do you expect to be the impact of personality on team process and why so?

DISCUSSION

As many team research studies have been conducted by US scholars or have used US samples, it is important to consider the potential cultural differences and factors that may impact team dynamics. It is also important to recognize that myths or stereotypes about teams from different countries could impact on how they are managed. Using existing empirical evidence, Klett and Arnulf (2020) argued that the view of teams as simply a collection of individuals is overly simplistic and disregards the potential for various cognitive and social processes to differ across cultures and countries. Therefore, it is essential to consider emic (understanding the meaning from inside a particular culture) and etic (understanding the meaning from outside, objective, universal manner) when studying teams to understand their unique characteristics and dynamics better.

In the context of teams, an emic perspective would involve examining how teams operate within a particular culture, taking into account the unique values, beliefs and social systems of that culture. An etic perspective would involve examining teams across different cultures, looking for universal characteristics and behaviour patterns that can be applied across cultures.

Reflective questions:

- Think about the team that you previously belonged to. Which stage of Tuckman's model did your team experience?

- What strategies are effective for managing teams where you come from? Do these strategies align with the strategies suggested in Western team development models?

- Are there any team myths or stereotypes associated with your country? Do any unique values or beliefs influence how teams work in your community?

- Do you think that the emic or etic perspective is more important when studying teams where you come from? Why?
  - An emic perspective would involve examining how teams operate within a particular culture, considering the unique values, beliefs and social systems of that culture.
  - An etic perspective would involve examining teams across different cultures, looking for universal characteristics and behaviour patterns that can be applied across cultures.

Team process

The key to achieving high team performance lies not solely in the individual capabilities of team members but rather in their ability to collaborate effectively: the team process.

Team process refers to the dynamics, interactions and activities within a team as they work together to achieve common goals. It encompasses the way team members communicate, collaborate, make decisions and coordinate their efforts. Team process involves both the formal and informal procedures and behaviours that shape how the team functions and performs. It includes task allocation, goal setting, problem-solving, conflict resolution, decision-making processes and team climate.

Team processes are dynamic, emerging over time and changing their pattern. Marks, Mathieu and Zaccaro (2001) proposed a team process taxonomy, including the following phases:

1 Transition phase: this is the stage when team members evaluate the team's missions, e.g., identifying their key tasks/goals and sub-tasks/goals, developing strategies to accomplish the tasks, resources for the team and teams' broader operational context.

2 Action phase: this is the stage when team members progress to task accomplishment. At this stage, the team often also monitors their progress, monitoring the context in which the team operates, tracking the team's resources, providing feedback and support to the team members and managing interdependent and/or time-sequencing actions.

3 Interpersonal phase: the interpersonal phase exists across the team's lifetime, where team members manage conflicts throughout tasks and regulate members' emotions – including frustration and excitement.

All three phases enhance team performance and team members' satisfaction levels with similar magnitude (Johnson et al, 2018; LePine et al, 2008). Why does team process improve team performance? Through conflict management and collaborative helping (Johnson et al, 2018). Other factors that can either enhance or hinder the effectiveness of team processes, ultimately affecting the overall team performance and outcomes are the following:

- Task interdependence. Task interdependence refers to the degree to which team members depend on one another's efforts, information and resources when completing the task – interdependently or independently (Wageman, 1995, 1999). Team process has a more substantial effect on team effectiveness when team members' task interdependence is high.

- Size of the team. Team process has a more substantial effect on team effectiveness when the team size is larger. Larger teams are more prone to coordination loss due to their complexity and stronger need for effective coordination.

AGILE AND SCRUM METHODOLOGY IN THE IT INDUSTRY

The history of agile methodology can be traced back to the late 20th century when software development practices were often rigid, sequential and heavily dependent on extensive upfront planning. As software projects grew larger and more complex, traditional methods struggled to cope with changing requirements and customer needs. This led to delays, cost overruns and unsatisfactory outcomes. In response to these challenges, a group of 17 software developers gathered in February 2001 at Snowbird, Utah, to discuss and redefine software development approaches (one of the attending companies was called Scrum). This meeting resulted in the creation of the Agile Manifesto, which aimed to promote a more flexible and adaptive approach to software development. The agile manifesto was born and its methodologies focused on iterative development, cross-functional teams, frequent customer feedback and adaptive planning. They aimed to deliver software incrementally and iteratively, responding to changing requirements and incorporating customer input throughout development.

Scrum carries out projects by allocating tasks into small stages called sprints, a subset of the agile methodology. The methodology moves software development projects from a rigid to a more flexible and adaptable approach, enabling teams to navigate complexity, embrace change and deliver value more efficiently, being customer-centric. Scrum focuses on project management and has its specific concepts and practices divided into three categories of roles (a product owner who ensures business goals are reached, a scrum master who carries out task-level tracking and quickly addresses issues that emerge, and a small group of professionals who deliver the project), artifacts (product backlog, sprint backlog and increment) and time boxes (sprint, sprint review, sprint retrospective and daily scrum meeting).

Discussion questions

Research a company case on scrum or agile and answer the following questions:

- Describe the nature of the central business/project the company is carrying out and why scrum or agile were suitable.
- How does the team process in the case study align with the transition, action and interpersonal phases of scrum or agile?
- How did the scrum or agile methodology impact transition, action and interpersonal phases from the team process model?
- What are the challenges related to team dynamics, conflict resolution or decision-making that emerged during the implementation of scrum or agile?
- What insights or lessons can be learnt from the company case and inform your understanding and approach to the team process?

Teamwork behaviours

Teamwork behaviours describe behaviours that improve team performance. According to Rousseau, Aubé and Savoie (2006), teamwork behaviours can be influenced by the nature of subtask arrangements, which set the tone of how team members work together to accomplish their tasks. When the subtasks are highly interdependent, team members do not need to interact extensively to attain the goal. This can be divided into the following five categories:

1 Preparation and planning for the task

   a Purpose and mission of the team, where the team identifies the purpose of the team and ensures everyone in the team understands the team purpose

   b Goal specification

   c Planning action to complete the task

2 Task-related collaborative behaviours, where the team executes the task

   a Coordination

   b Cooperation

   c Exchanging information

3 Work assessment behaviours

   a Monitoring performance

   b Monitoring the team's environment, such as tracking team resources and external environment (e.g., market condition, regulatory change)

4 Team adjustment behaviours

   a Supporting behaviours, such as helping and stepping in when others cannot fulfil

   b Coaching

   c Collaborative problem-solving

   d Team practice innovation

5 Team maintenance behaviours

   a Support

   b Conflict management

Team Roles

An alternative way to look at team behaviours is through team roles. Dr Meredith Belbin defines a team role as one of nine clusters of behavioural attributes, identified by his research at Henley Management College in the UK, as being effective in order to facilitate team progress. (Belbin and Brown, 2023). Each team role has its own unique responsibilities, expectations and contributions to the team's success. Belbin is a British researcher and management consultant who developed the Belbin Team Roles model in the 1970s. Belbin conducted a study at Henley, observing teams of management students in action. He discovered that team success could not be reliably attributed to the intelligence of team members.

He proposed nine team roles:

- Plant: generates creative and unconventional ideas to solve problems and drive innovation
- Monitor evaluator: analyses and evaluates ideas objectively and impartially, weighing the pros and cons of each suggestion
- Resource investigator: acts as the team's external representative, exploring and developing new opportunities through networking
- Coordinator: provides mature leadership by clarifying team goals and delegating tasks effectively
- Implementer: translates plans into action, ensuring deadlines are met efficiently and effectively
- Completer finisher: ensures that all tasks are completed to a high standard, with meticulous attention to detail
- Teamworker: builds strong relationships within the team, resolves conflicts and maintains morale

- Shaper: challenges the team to improve, provides direction and momentum and drives the team forward
- Specialist: brings highly specialized knowledge and skills to the team, providing expert guidance in a specific area

Each role has its own set of characteristics and behaviours that can contribute to the team's success. The theory also suggests that different roles may be more suited to different types of tasks and that teams should be composed of individuals with various roles to ensure that all aspects of the team task are covered. Belbin's Team Roles model encourages team members to be aware of their own strengths and weaknesses, as well as those of their teammates.

By acknowledging and accepting each other's allowable weaknesses, team members can work more effectively together and use their diverse skills and perspectives to achieve common goals. However, non-allowable weaknesses must be addressed and eliminated to maintain a healthy and productive team environment. Allowable weaknesses refer to the less desirable traits or behaviours that are associated with a particular team role. Allowable weaknesses are the flipside of strengths. If someone tried to mitigate these weaknesses, they would be less effective in contributing the corresponding strength. For example, a Plant's tendency to generate many new ideas without considering practicalities can be seen as an allowable weakness because it can lead to creative solutions. Non-allowable weaknesses, on the other hand, are traits or behaviours that are detrimental to the team's success and cannot be tolerated. For example, a Coordinator's tendency to be overly bossy and controlling can be a non-allowable weakness because it can lead to resentment and conflict within the team.

Table 4.2 is a list of the Belbin Team Roles and their corresponding allowable and non-allowable weakness (Belbin & Brown, 2023):

Table 4.2 Belbin Team Role's allowable and non-allowable weakness

Team Role	Allowable weakness	Non-allowable weakness
• Plant	Preoccupied with ideas and neglected things around them (e.g., not paying attention to the meeting, practical consideration around ideas that they generated).	Possessive over their ideas.
• Monitor evaluator	Being critical and evaluating the options with logic.	Excessive skepticism, overly critical.

(continued)

Table 4.2   (Continued)

Team Role	Allowable weakness	Non-allowable weakness
• Resource investigator	Short spur of enthusiasm after the initial excitement.	Not following through with the client due to lack of enthusiasm.
• Coordinator	Delegation to someone else to do the work.	Claiming the contribution without appropriate acknowledgement to the team.
• Implementer	Adhere to existing methods and paths to accomplish tasks.	Does not change and blocking change.
• Completer finisher	Meticulousness and attaining perfectionism.	The pursuit of flawlessness.
• Teamworker	Being hesitant when it comes to critical decisions.	Avoiding confrontational situations.
• Shaper	Shows frustration and irritation.	Inability to maintain the situation, creating a hostile atmosphere in the team.
• Specialist	Pursuing knowledge for his/her own purpose.	Ignorance over other knowledge that's outside of his/her interest.

With kind permission of Belbin Ltd: www.belbin.com

In applying the Team Roles model to organizations, Aritzeta, Swailes and Senior (2007) shed light on the relationship between team roles and organizational dynamics. They emphasized the importance of considering the specific organizational context and its corresponding needs when applying the model. Their findings revealed several noteworthy trends regarding team roles:

- No significant differences in team roles and team performance between managers and non-managers. This suggests that hierarchical organizational positions do not solely determine team role effectiveness.
- Team roles in the organizational environment:
  - Shaper, Plant, Resource investigator and Coordinator roles were better suited for organizations operating in changing and dynamic environments. These roles are more adept at navigating and adapting to evolving circumstances.
  - Conversely, the Implementer and Complete finisher roles were better fitted for organizations striving for stability. These roles ensure tasks are executed efficiently and to completion, which is crucial in environments prioritizing consistency and reliability.

- Senior management positions in different sectors
  - In the public sector, higher percentages of individuals in senior management positions exhibited the Shaper and Implementer roles.
  - The private sector had a higher proportion of individuals with the Plant, Teamworker and Complete finisher roles in senior management positions.

Furthermore, the study highlighted that the Coordinator, Resource investigator and Shaper roles demonstrated a higher level of control over others. These team roles were more likely to assert influence and take charge in decision-making processes. Based on the empirical studies, Aritzeta, Swailes and Senior (2007) summarize team roles and their association with other models:

- Conflict situation
  - Avoid conflict: Complete finisher, Implementer, Teamworker, Specialist
  - Find compromise: Coordinator, Resource investigator
  - Try to dominate: Plant, Shaper, Specialist (otherwise avoided conflict)
- Moral value: roles associated with high moral value include Complete finisher and Implementer
- Emotional intelligence: roles associated with high emotional intelligence include Coordinator, Resource investigator

---

In 2012, Google launched Project Aristotle to investigate why some of its teams performed exceptionally well while others with similar talent struggled. The project involved analysing data from hundreds of Google teams and interviewing team members. The goal was to identify key factors contributing to team success and determine how to improve team performance. The study's results, published in 2016, revealed that the most critical factor in creating a successful team was not individual skills or intelligence but rather the quality of teamwork. The research demonstrated that effective teams exhibited five key characteristics:

1 Psychological safety: team members feel safe to take risks and be vulnerable in front of each other.

2 Dependability: team members can rely on each other to deliver quality work on time.

3 Structure and clarity: team members have clear goals, roles and expectations.

4 Meaning and impact: team members believe their work is meaningful and contributes to the overall mission.

5 Work and personal life balance: team members have a healthy balance between work and their personal lives.

Google also found no one-size-fits-all approach to building effective teams and that different teams had different needs and dynamics. Therefore, it is essential to assess and adjust team dynamics to ensure ongoing success continually.

REFLECTION

Dierdorff et al (2019) found that a higher level of self-awareness among team members impacts team task performance through better coordination, less team conflict and higher team-level cohesion. Teams have a higher level of self-awareness among team members and experience less conflict. In addition, more friction can be exacerbated in teams when team members have lower levels of self-awareness of others. When team members possess accurate self-awareness, they can effectively align their contributions to the team's task. Conversely, when teams lack self-awareness, the coordination among team members tends to suffer. This detrimental effect is particularly noticeable when team members overestimate their abilities.

One way to improve self-awareness among team members is to look at individuals' team roles. Mathieu and colleagues (2014) developed the Team Role Experience and Orientation measure (TREO). They integrated past research and suggested six team roles:

Task-oriented roles:

1 Organizer: an individual who takes the initiative to structure the team's activities and progress. They keep track of achievements, ensuring the team moves forward according to set goals and timelines.

2 Doer: a proactive team member who willingly assumes tasks and efficiently accomplishes them. A Doer can be relied upon to complete work, meet deadlines and take on responsibilities contributing to the team's overall success.

Change-oriented roles:

3 Challenger: someone who actively encourages the team to explore all aspects of a situation and consider alternative assumptions, explanations and solutions. The Challenger often poses thought-provoking questions, engages in debates and offers constructive critiques to stimulate critical thinking.

4 Innovator: a team member who consistently generates fresh and creative ideas, strategies and approaches for handling various situations and challenges. The Innovator frequently contributes original and imaginative suggestions to enhance the team's problem-solving capabilities.

Socio-emotional roles:

5 Team Builder: an individual who helps establish team norms, supports decisions and fosters a positive work environment. The Team Builder offers reassurance and encouragement to team members during stressful times and serves as a motivator when morale is low.

6 Connector: a team member who facilitates connections and bridges the gap between the team and external individuals, groups, or stakeholders. Connectors ensure positive working relationships between the team and those outside, while Team Builders focus on cultivating good relationships within the team.

Access the TREO and calculate your score to determine your team roles based on p. 27 Appendix in Mathieu, J. E., Tannenbaum, S. I., Kukenberger, M. R., Donsbach, J. S., & Alliger, G. M. (2014) Team Role Experience and Orientation: A Measure and Tests of Construct Validity. doi.org/10.1177/1059601114562000

Once you and your team members calculate your TREO result, answer the following questions as a team:

● Look at your TREO result. How does your team role align with your strengths, skills and natural abilities? Provide some behavioural examples to demonstrate how you contribute to the team.

● Reflect on the impact your role has on achieving team goals and maintaining a positive team environment. In what ways does your team role contribute to the overall dynamics and success of the team? Are there any adjustments or improvements you can make to enhance your contribution?

● What learning and growth opportunities does your team role present? How can you actively pursue these opportunities? Reflect on areas where you can further develop your skills, expand your knowledge or seek feedback to continuously improve in your role.

● How does your team role interact with other roles within the team? Reflect on how your role complements and supports the work of others. Are there opportunities for collaboration and synergy with teammates in different roles?

DISCUSSION

Look at the interaction in a group setting

Interaction Process Analysis (IPA) was developed in the mid-20th century by Robert F. Bales, a renowned social psychologist (Bales, 1950). The development of IPA was influenced by Bales' earlier work on small group research and his interest in understanding the patterns and functions of communication behaviours. Bales proposed a coding scheme to analyse group interactions, which involved systematically observing and coding various communication behaviours exhibited by group members. These behaviours were classified into different categories, such as initiating behaviours, reacting behaviours, clarifying behaviours and process behaviours. IPA provides a structured framework for analysing the frequency and distribution of communication behaviours and their impact on group dynamics and outcomes. Through systematically analysing these behaviours, IPA helps identify strengths and weaknesses in the team's communication and collaboration processes.

Group task

Use the following interaction scoring sheet to register the frequency of the behaviours during your team interactions. Ideally, you will want to observe the behaviours over a few meetings.

Table 4.3 Interaction scoring sheet

Behaviours	Team members					
	Name	*Name*	*Name*	*Name*	*Name*	**Total**
Initiating behaviours						
• Content suggestion (e.g., new concept, idea)						
• Process suggestion (the way the group work)						
• Building on suggestions						
Reacting behaviours						
• Agreeing/supporting						
• disagreeing						
• Blocking stating						
• Defending						
Clarifying behaviours						
• Checking understanding						
• Summarizing						
• Seeking information						
• Giving information						
• Disclosure						

(*continued*)

Table 4.3 (Continued)

Behaviours	Team members					
	Name	*Name*	*Name*	*Name*	*Name*	**Total**
Process behaviours						
• Bringing in						
• Shutting out						
TOTAL						

Adapted from Huthwaite International, VBA Communication Overview. www.huthwaiteinternational.com

Answer the following questions as a group:

- What patterns or trends did you observe in the group's communication behaviours during the IPA analysis and how do you think they influenced the overall group interaction? You can use the column totals, which indicate the differences in oral contributions to the discussions by the different members of the group. You can also use the rows showing the group members' different types of oral contributions collectively in this discussion.

- What effect do high or low oral contributions have on the speakers concerned and on the group (e.g., Are high contributors more influential? Are they accepted as group leaders)?

- What effect is predominance or absence of specific contributions (e.g., numerous proposals; little building; little disagreeing) likely to have on the outcomes of a group discussion? How can certain types of contributions be encouraged or discouraged?

- What specific actions prompted changes in the interactions (positive or negative)? Why?

- Were there any surprises or unexpected findings that emerged from the IPA analysis? How did these findings challenge or reinforce your initial assumptions about the group's communication dynamics?

- How can understanding communication behaviours gained through IPA analysis help build more effective and cohesive teams in the future?

Why are professionals deliberately not providing knowledge or knowledge that is not needed when colleagues request it? Knowledge hiding refers to intentionally withholding or concealing information or knowledge from others within an organization or team, resulting in a lack of transparency and collaboration. It occurs when individuals choose not to share relevant knowledge, expertise, or insights with their colleagues, even when it could benefit the team or project.

He and colleagues (2021) concluded that knowledge hiding could be between individuals (e.g., co-workers who purposefully hide knowledge, play dumb and rationalize their own hiding behaviour) and between supervisor-subordinates (e.g., top-down knowledge hiding). They summarize the list of antecedents that contribute positively to knowledge-hiding behaviours:

- Organizational level: such as competition (e.g., organization rewards achievement, focusing on individual performance), politics, injustice, lack of recognition, knowledge sharing cultures
- Team level: leadership (e.g., abusive supervision), management's level of support for knowledge sharing, injustice and distrust, lack of identification and lack of psychological safety. Highly autonomous tasks also lead to a higher level of knowledge hiding.
- Individual level factors such as personality (e.g., the dark side of the personality, high conscientious and low neuroticism/emotional stability), motivation (e.g., goal orientation, extrinsic motivation), individual self-confidence in their knowledge, morally disengaged, stress and pressure increases the knowledge hiding behaviour. When individuals feel they own the knowledge, they are also likely to hide it.

What are the consequences of knowledge-hiding behaviours? There is sometimes a vicious cycle of distrust and retaliation among colleagues, and a negative impact on team effectiveness (team performance and viability), team learning and innovation. At the individual level, knowledge hiding harms individual well-being and job satisfaction and decreases individual creativity. They further suggested ways that can reduce knowledge-hiding behaviour in the teams, including:

- promoting a mastery goal rather than a performance goal
- promotion of group performance rather than individual performance
- establishing reciprocal social exchange
- task design (e.g., interdependent rather than independent)
- team-based reward.

Reflective questions:

- Have there been instances where you witnessed withholding of knowledge or information from others? Are any factors or dynamics contributing to knowledge hiding within the team? Use the findings of He and colleagues (2021) on the team and individual antecedent of knowledge-hiding behaviour as a cue to identify the reasons for knowledge hiding.

- How does knowledge hiding affect trust, communication and collaboration among team members? What impact does it have on overall team effectiveness?
- What strategies or actions can be implemented to create a safe and supportive environment that encourages knowledge sharing and discourages knowledge hiding?

DIVERSE BACKGROUNDS, VIRTUAL TEAMS – HOW DO THEY PERFORM?

Examining competition data from 2019 and 2020 eTournaments that encompassed over 600 students across universities in Hong Kong and Australia, Lau and a team of researchers (2021) undertook an investigation into the performance of cross-country and cross-disciplinary online teams. These teams engaged collaboratively on a digital platform for a four-day duration during each eTournament. The findings of their study suggest that effective communication, adept teamwork skills and proficient leadership are indispensable components for ensuring the success of diverse online teams.

Upon scrutinizing the highest and lowest performing quintiles (46 students), the analysis of chat records unveiled significant discrepancies. The upper echelon teams engaged in notably more extensive dialogues compared to the lower quintile teams, particularly in areas such as problem-solving (6.2 times more frequently in 2020 and 14 times in 2019), collaboration (2.4 times more frequently in 2020 and 2.7 times in 2019), as well as personal learning (3.3 times more frequently in 2020 and 4.6 times in 2019).

Moreover, the superior teams, the top five, exhibited a seamless progression across the phases of discussion, starting from the initial stage of team building (collaboration), advancing to an awareness of Sustainable Development Goals (SDGs), cross-cultural and cross-disciplinary disparities (personal learning) and ultimately culminating in strategic deployment (problem-solving) throughout the course of the eTournament timeline. Essentially, the adept members of these high-performing teams demonstrated a higher propensity for efficiently aligning their efforts towards a shared objective, harnessing the diverse cultural and disciplinary proficiencies.

Chapter summary

This chapter explored teams, their effectiveness and the intricate dynamics between teams and individuals. The chapter began by defining what constitutes a team, emphasizing the collaborative nature and shared goals that distinguish teams from other groups. Understanding the factors that contribute to team effectiveness was a focal point. One crucial aspect explored was the development stages of teams, highlighting the journey teams embark on from their formation to reaching high performance levels. Recognizing the unique challenges and dynamics at each stage enables team members and leaders to navigate the team's progression better and foster a positive and productive environment.

Team process involves a group of individuals combining their skills and knowledge to achieve a common goal through a set of activities, behaviours and interactions. From effective communication and conflict resolution to allocating team roles, these behaviours play a pivotal role in shaping team dynamics and outcomes. Understanding and harnessing the diverse range of team roles and raising awareness of each other's competence allows teams to tap into their members' full potential and talents.

Key terms

Input-Process-Output model (IPO)

Conformity

Obedience

Team effectiveness

Task conflict

Relationship conflict

Social comparison

Self-categorization

Social loafing

Punctuated equilibrium model

Group development stage

Forming

Norming

Storming

Performing

Adjourning

Team process

Transition phase

Action phase

Interpersonal phase

Chapter review questions

- Describe the nature and importance of teamwork in organizations. Why is teamwork crucial for organizational success?

- Explain the stages of team development according to the Punctuated Equilibrium model. What happens during the forming, norming, storming, performing and adjourning stages?

- What is the Input–Process–Output (IPO) model of team effectiveness? How does it explain the relationship between inputs, team processes and outcomes?

- Explain the three phases of the team process: transition phase, action phase and interpersonal phase. What activities and behaviours are typically observed in each phase?

- How can tools like role analysis and interpretative phenomenological analysis (IPA) be used to enhance our understanding of team roles and behaviours? Provide examples of how these tools can improve team dynamics and effectiveness.

Further reading

Cohen, S G & Bailey, D E (1997) What makes teams work: Group effectiveness research from the shop floor to the executive suite, *Journal of Management*, 23(3), 239–290 https://doi.org/10.1177/014920639702300303. (archived at https://perma.cc/74TH-CC6G) Contrary to the newest research, this paper is simplistic and, on p 277, provides a summary of different types of teams. The authors compared different team types (work teams, parallel teams, project teams and top management teams) and their corresponding factors that would impact team effectiveness.

Mathieu, J E, Hollenbeck, J R, van Knippenberg, D & Ilgen, D R (2017) A century of work teams. The authors reviewed the 100 years of work team research – if you want the history of the work team research, primary constructs and their updated findings, this is a great article to start.

Mathieu, J E, Luciano, M M, D'Innocenzo, L, Klock, E A & LePine, J A (2020) The Development and Construct Validity of a Team Processes Survey Measure, *Organizational Research Methods*, 23(3), 399–431 doi: https://journals.sagepub.com/doi/10.1177/1094428119840801 (archived at https://perma.cc/S9ZW-H872). Mathieu and a research team develop a survey measure for the team process where you can measure your team's transition, action and interpersonal phases.

Mathieu, JE, Gallagher, PT, Domingo, MA, Klock, EA (2019) Embracing complexity: Reviewing the past decade of team effectiveness research, *Annual Review of Organizational Psychology and Organizational Behavior*, Behav 6, 17–46. A recent review by Mathieu and colleagues proposed an Input-Mediating-Output to replace the IPO model IMO model provided a greater emphasis on the complexity of team, emphasizing the dynamic, multi-level nature of teamwork.

Delice, F, Rousseau, M, & Feitosa, J (2019) Advancing teams research: What, when and how to measure team dynamics over time, *Frontiers in Psychology*, 10 doi.org/10.3389/fpsyg.2019.01324 (archived at https://perma.cc/DQG7-PWHB). If you are interested to capture the team dynamics in your team, Delice, Rousseau and Feitosa's article gives a summary of what measures you can be using.

Stewart, VR, Snyder, DG & Kou, CY (2023) We hold ourselves accountable: A relational View of team accountability, *Journal of Business Ethics* 183, 691–712 doi.org/10.1007/s10551-021-04969-z (archived at https://perma.cc/3WJK-75ST). Accountability is a fundamental element of group dynamics that significantly contributes to attaining peak performance and accomplishing goals successfully. This paper provides practical methods for self-assessing the level of accountability within the team.

References

Aritzeta, A, Swailes, S & Senior, B (2007) Belbin's Team Role model: Development, validity and applications for team building, *Journal of Management Studies*, 44(1), 96–118, doi.org/10.1111/J.1467-6486.2007.00666.X (archived at https://perma.cc/9YT5-YWHP)

Bales, R F (1950) *Interaction process analysis: A method for the study of small groups* Addison-Wesley, Cambridge, MA.

Belbin, R M & Brown, V (2023) *Team roles at work*, 3rd edition, Routledge.

Bond, C F & Titus, L J (1983) Social facilitation: A meta-analysis of 241 studies, *Psychological Bulletin*, 94(2), 265–292. doi.org/10.1037/0033-2909.94.2.265 (archived at https://perma.cc/V7VM-8LDH).

Casas, Klett T & Arnulf, J K (2020) Are Chinese teams like Western teams? Indigenous management theory to leapfrog essentialist team myths, *Frontiers in Psychology*, 11, 1758, https://www.frontiersin.org/articles/10.3389/fpsyg.2020.01758/full (archived at https://perma.cc/9TVP-ZY7M).

Cohen, S G & Bailey, D E (1997) What makes teams work: Group effectiveness research from the shop floor to the executive suite, *Journal of Management*, 23(3), 239–290. https://doi.org/10.1177/014920639702300303 (archived at https://perma.cc/74TH-CC6G).

Comer, D R (1995) A model of social loafing in real work groups, *Human Relation*, 48(6), 647, https://journals.sagepub.com/doi/10.1177/001872679504800603 (archived at https://perma.cc/F8QB-7EFQ).

Delice, F, Rousseau, M & Feitosa, J (2019) Advancing teams research: What, when and how to measure team dynamics over time, *Frontiers in Psychology*, 10(JUN), 1324 https://doi.org/10.3389/fpsyg.2019.01324 (archived at https://perma.cc/DQG7-PWHB)

Dierdorff E C, Fisher D M & Rubin, R S (2019) The power of percipience: Consequences of self-awareness in teams on team-level functioning and performance, *Journal of Management*, 45(7), 2891–2919. doi.org/10.1177/0149206318774622/ASSET/IMAGES/LARGE/10.1177_0149206318774622-FIG3.JPEG

Dinh, J V, Reyes, D L, Kayga, L, Lindgren, C, Feitosa, J & Salas, E (2021) Developing team trust: Leader insights for virtual settings, *Organizational Dynamics*, 50(1), 100846 doi.org/10.1016/J.ORGDYN.2021.100846 (archived at https://perma.cc/Z3JE-3LJ4).

Gersick, C J G (1989) Marking time: Predictable transitions in task groups, *Academy of Management Journal*, 32(2), 274–309.

Gersick, C J G (1988) Time and transition in work teams: Toward a new model of group development, *Academy of Management Journal*, 31(1), 9–41.

Gibson, C B & Grushina, S V (2021) A tale of two teams: Next generation strategies for increasing the effectiveness of global virtual teams, *Organizational Dynamics*, 50(1) doi.org/10.1016/J.ORGDYN.2020.100823 (archived at https://perma.cc/D3GF-4MZK)

Harkins, S G, Latané, B & Williams, K (1980) Social loafing: Allocating effort or taking it easy, *Journal of Experimental Social Psychology*, 16(5), 457–465. doi.org/10.1016/0022-1031(80)90051-7 (archived at https://perma.cc/KS3U-BNUG).

He, P, Jiang, C, Xu Z & Shen, C (2021) Knowledge hiding: Current research status and future research directions, *Frontiers in Psychology*, 12, 4950 doi.org/10.3389/FPSYG.2021.748237/BIBTEX.

Hillier, J & Dunn-Jensen, L M (2013) Groups meet, teams improve: Building teams that learn, *Journal of Management Education*, 37(5), 704–733. doi.org/10.1177/1052562912459947 (archived at https://perma.cc/L2HJ-V4SF).

Hogg, M A & Terry, D J (2000) Social identity and self-categorization process in organizational context, *Academy of Management Review*, 25(1), 121–140.

Johnson, A, Nguyen, H, Groth, M & White, L (2018) Reaping the rewards of functional diversity in healthcare teams: Why team processes improve performance, *Group and Organization Management*, 43(3), 440–474 doi.org/10.1177/1059601118769192/FORMAT/EPUB.

Klett, C T & Arnulf, J K (2020) Are Chinese teams Like Western teams? Indigenous management theory to leapfrog essentialist team myths, *Frontier Psychology* 11(1758) doi.10.3389/fpsyg.2020.01758 (archived at https://perma.cc/SGL5-QMJZ).

Kou, C-Y (2021) Team boundary spanning in a large engineering project, *Small Group Research*, 52(4), 405–430 doi.org/10.1177/1046496420976836 (archived at https://perma.cc/2JWQ-3PZN).

Kozlowski, S W J & Ilgen, D R (2006) Enhancing the effectiveness of work groups and teams, *Psychological Science in the Public Interest: A Journal of the American Psychological Society*, 7(3), 77–124. doi.org/10.1111/j.1529-1006.2006.00030.x (archived at https://perma.cc/W8H7-GHTK).

Kuipers, B S, Higgs, M J, Tolkacheva, N V & de Witte, M C (2009) The influence of Myers-Briggs Type Indicator Profiles on team development processes, *Small Group Research*, 40(4), 436–464 doi.org/10.1177/1046496409333938 (archived at https://perma.cc/6BWN-NGFQ).

Lau, M, Vuthaluru, R, Mui, L, Kerrigan, S, Kwong, T, Law, L, Wong E Y W & Gibson, D (2021) How online teams with diverse backgrounds worked to excel: Findings from an international eTournament, *Frontiers in Education*, 6, 34 doi.org/10.3389/FEDUC. 2021.624438/BIBTEX.

LePine, J A, Piccolo, R F, Jackson, C L, Mathieu, J E & Saul J R (2008) A meta-analysis of teamwork processes: tests of a multidimensional model and relationships with team effectiveness criteria, *Personnel Psychology*, 61(2), 273–307 doi.org/10.1111/ J.1744-6570.2008.00114.X (archived at https://perma.cc/7LCA-C77V).

Liden, R C, Wayne, S J, Jaworski, R A & Bennett, N (2004) Social loafing: A field investigation, *Journal of Management*, 30(2), 285–304 doi.org/10.1016/j.jm.2003.02.002 (archived at https://perma.cc/P6MA-Y3H9).

Majchrzak, A, Rice, R E, Malhotra, A, King, N & Ba, S (2000) Technology adaptation: The case of a computer-supported inter-organizational virtual team, *MIS Quarterly*, 24(4), 569 doi.org/10.2307/3250948 (archived at https://perma.cc/MD6M-6FE9).

Marks, M A, Mathieu, J E & Zaccaro, S J (2001) A temporally based framework and taxonomy of team processes, 26(3), 356–376 doi.org/10.5465/AMR.2001.4845785 (archived at https://perma.cc/S3C6-3BKL).

Mathieu, J E, Hollenbeck, J R, Knippenberg, D Van & Ilgen, D R (2017) A century of work teams in the journal of applied psychology, *Journal of Applied Psychology*, 102(3), 452–467, doi.org/10.1037/APL0000128 (archived at https://perma.cc/L2RF-L8Y9).

Mathieu, J E, Luciano, M M, D'innocenzo, L, Klock, E A & Lepine, J A (nd) *The Development and Construct Validity of a Team Processes Survey Measure*, doi.org/10.1177/1094428119840801 (archived at https://perma.cc/9XHR-Q7XB).

Mathieu, J E, Tannenbaum, S I, Kukenberger, M R, Donsbach, J S & Alliger, G M (2014) Team role experience and orientation, *Group & Organization Management*, 40(1), 6–34 doi.org/10.1177/1059601114562000 (archived at https://perma.cc/L283-V3YS).

McGrath, J (1964) *Social Psychology: A Brief Introduction*, Holt, Rinehart & Winston, New York.

Peeters, M A G, Rutte, C G, Van Tuijl, H F J M & Reymen, I M M J (2008) Designing in teams: Does personality matter, *Small Group Research*, 39(4), 438–467 doi.org/10.1177/1046496408319810 (archived at https://perma.cc/FZ3W-UM75).

Reiche, B S. (2023) Between interdependence and autonomy: Toward a typology of work design modes in the new world of work, *Human Resource Management Journal*, 1–17 doi.org/10.1111/1748-8583.12495 (archived at https://perma.cc/Z3TW-HB9P).

Rousseau, V, Aubé, C & Savoie, A. (2006) Teamwork behaviors: A review and an integration of frameworks, *Small Group Research*, 37(5), 540–570. doi.org/10.1177/ 1046496406293125 (archived at https://perma.cc/RW9G-6YZC).

Simms A, & Nichols, T (2014) Social loafing: A review of the literature, *Journal of Management Policy and Practice*, 15(1), 58–67.

Stewart, G L (2006)A meta-analytic review of relationships between team design features and team performance, *Journal of Management*, 32(1), 29–54 doi.org/10.1177/0149206305277792 (archived at https://perma.cc/ZPW3-DDNS).

Stewart, V R, Snyder, D G, & Kou, C-Y (2021) We Hold Ourselves Accountable: A Relational View of Team Accountability, *Journal of Business Ethics 2021*, 1, 1–22 doi.org/10.1007/S10551-021-04969-Z (archived at https://perma.cc/3KS8-UGCB).

Tuckman, B W (1965) Developmental sequence in small group *Psychological Bulletin*, 63(6), 384–399 doi.org/10.1037/H0022100 (archived at https://perma.cc/6MYR-NK6Y).

Tuckman, B W & Jensen, M A C (1977) Stages of small-group development revisited, *Group and Organization Management*, 2(4), 419–427. doi.org/10.1177/105960117700200404 (archived at https://perma.cc/DC54-6JVE).

Wageman, R (1995) Interdependence and group effectiveness, *Administrative Science Quarterly*, 40(1), 145–180 doi.org/10.2307/2393703 (archived at https://perma.cc/G7EA-5NWF).

Wageman, R (1999) The meaning of interdependence, In *Groups at work: Advances in theory and research*, Erlbaum, 197–217.

Power, status and organizational politics

05

CHAPTER OUTLINE

- Importance of understanding power, status and organizational politics
- Understanding power
  - Definition of power
  - Forms of power
  - The outcome of power: the impact of power on individual behaviours
  - Developing power
- Understanding status
  - Definition of status
  - Status and power: differences, similarities and what does it mean to organizational life?
  - Factors contributing to the acquisition and maintenance of status
  - Organizational events and status development
- Organizational politics
  - Perception of organizational politics
  - Political behaviour: political will and political skill
  - A journey to political maturity
  - The outcome of political behaviours
  - Gender difference in political skills

Office politics – we've all encountered them, haven't we?

- The meeting monopolizers love the sound of their own voices.
- The power-hungry ones crave control in every aspect.
- The credit thieves conveniently forget about teamwork.
- The chameleons act nice until it's time to impress the higher-ups.

Postma (2021), a seasoned professional with the mentality to get things done, was found blindsided and unprepared, facing an unexpected layoff several years into a promising career. Why was she laid off? Was it due to underperformance? It soon became evident that her termination was not a result of poor performance or failure to meet targets. Instead, it resulted from a crucial oversight – a failure to nurture relationships with influential individuals. There was someone with ulterior motives seeking her removal. The management cleverly masked the situation as budget cuts, but behind the scenes, a powerful individual orchestrated a calculated move to eliminate this unsuspecting employee. It was a disturbing revelation, exposing the darker side of office politics.

Office politics can bring out the worst in people, but we've got to navigate it all.

Questions:

- What word comes to your mind when it comes to politics?
- Based on the account provided above by Postma and her experience with office politics, it's evident that politics is an inescapable aspect of the workplace, even for high-performing individuals. Here are some widely accepted notions of organizational politics. Do you agree or disagree with the following statements?
  - A good person doesn't play politics.
  - We can escape office politics by doing an outstanding job.
  - Job performance and career are merit-based.
  - With the workforce moving online, office politics disappears.
  - Being political at work is an inherent characteristic.
- What is the evil side of office politics?
- What are the good things about office politics? Think about specific examples of how office politics can be beneficial to you.

Take note of your responses now and revisit your answers to the questions after completing this chapter. Are there any alterations to your answers? What insights have you gained?

Importance of understanding power, status and organizational politics

Organizational politics is about how people get things done. How can an individual influence others and get things done? Individuals' capacity to influence is not solely determined by their organizational role. Informal development of status and power through interpersonal interactions also plays a significant role. Two main factors influence a person's ability to have an impact: status and power. Status refers to the level of respect one receives from colleagues, while power is based on controlling valuable resources compared to others. Both status and power enable managers to influence the behaviour of others and achieve leadership goals. To gain influence, one can enhance power or status (ideally, both) by understanding how co-workers and colleagues perceive others' status and power in a sophisticated manner (Magee & Frasier, 2014).

This chapter will start with power and status to gain better insight into how individuals can exert their influence formally and informally at work and it follows with a section on organizational politics to better understand the critical components of organizational politics – political will and political skills.

Understanding power

Definition of power

Power is the capacity of an individual to sway or persuade another person to follow their directives or adhere to their favoured norms. In other words, power is goal-oriented.

The degree to which a person can shape behaviour in alignment with their own intentions determines the extent of their power. Power and dependence are strongly interconnected. When someone relies on someone else, they become susceptible to that person's power. Power is determined by the level of control over information, individuals and resources, as well as the significance of these attributes they possess.

Forms of power

French and Raven (1959) proposed five forms of power. Some powers are gained through position, whereas others are not.

Formal powers gained through position:

- Legitimate power: this comes from the leader's formal position or authority within the organizational hierarchy. It is based on the belief that the leader has the right to make decisions and expect compliance. The effective use of legitimate power requires leaders to use the other forms of power listed next.

- Reward power: this stems from the leader's ability to provide rewards or incentives to followers for their compliance or performance.

- Coercive power: this originates from a leader's capacity to enforce punishment or impose negative consequences when individuals fail to comply with expectations. These consequences may include demotion, redundancy, salary reduction or reassignment to a different position.

Personal power refers to the ability to influence others that stems from a leader's likability and knowledge:

- Expert power: this power is derived from the leader's knowledge or specialized skills that others value. This makes it efficient to carry out the tasks and gain respect from others (e.g., the leader is viewed as a role model by the followers).

- Referent power: referent power is raised from interpersonal relationships, often based on leaders' qualities. It is often divided into affection (likeability) and respect.

Other sources of power included information and relation power. Information power refers to the leaders possessing useful, critical information – noted that some of the information might belong to others but the leader may have privileged access to those information sources. For instance, information power stemmed from the position that leaders held. Examples of information power include information about access to the market, industry trends or knowledge related to an organization's success. Followers listen to leaders with information power because they recognize the information's value and relevance. They trust that the leader's insights and expertise can lead to more informed and effective decision-making.

Additionally, followers may believe that access to such information can provide a competitive advantage or help them achieve their goals. Leaders may also exercise relation power source due to leaders' connections to important figures within or outside the organization. An example of this will be someone who develops a closer relationship with influential leaders in the company. The power source extended from its ability to tap into essential individuals, such that followers wanted to benefit from the relationship or avoid the negative connotations raised from the relationship.

Luke's three faces of power

From political science, Stephen Lukes classified power into visible, covert and institutional power based on how power is exercised. Visible power is the most obvious form of power exercised through decision-making and political action. It primarily concerns observable conflicts that arise in debates. By examining these overt conflicts, each actor's interests and preferences can be uncovered as they participate in decision-making.

The second face of power is covert power. 'Covert' refers to something hidden, concealed or not openly displayed or acknowledged. Covert actions or behaviours are conducted secretly or discreetly, usually to hide them from others or evade detection. Covert power is exercised through non-decision-making, influencing and controlling the topics open for discussion. This allows powerful groups to prevent specific issues from being addressed, thus exerting power through non-decision-making. Problems that are openly debated (i.e., the manager's preferred proposal) demonstrate the manager's power, as they can influence the focus of the discussion and direct attention to their selected option. However, the deliberately excluded problems (i.e., the other alternative ideas) also reveal power dynamics. The manager's influence and authority prevent these alternative ideas from receiving proper consideration, essentially using non-decision-making to control the topics available for discussion. This perspective recognizes not only the overt conflicts where conflicting interests are openly confronted but also the covert conflicts where one group is unable to bring their key concerns to the table for discussion.

The third face of power is institutional power when the powerful transform the people without force. This is the norms – what is normal for people. Power can also be exerted by controlling people's thoughts and making them adopt beliefs not in their best interest. Institutional power is exercised by those who control the institutions that shape society, such as the media, education system and religious institutions. These institutions can shape people's beliefs, values and attitudes and influence their behaviour subtly. For example, an organization may prioritize and promote particular values and beliefs while downplaying others. It is important to note that institutional power can be difficult to identify and challenge due to its covert nature and deep integration within society.

Outcome of power: The impact of power on individuals' behaviours

Power can lead to positive and negative outcomes, depending on how it is exercised. On the positive side, power enables individuals to make significant changes and achieve goals that benefit others. For example, powerful leaders can drive organizational success and make a difference. However, power also has the potential for negative consequences. When wielded irresponsibly or for personal gain, it can lead to abuses and harm to others. According to Magee and Frasier (2014), power can influence individuals' actions in three ways:

- **Power is the facilitator that enables individuals to achieve their objectives.** According to Magee and colleagues (2007), individuals with higher power were more inclined to initiate negotiations and make the initial offer in bargaining situations. This tendency often resulted in better outcomes for those with greater power. Individuals with power also tend to feel empowered to act. A study by Galinsky and colleagues (2003) found that individuals assigned to a high-power condition were more willing to take the initiative than those in a low-power condition. Others found that high-power individuals are more likely to make riskier decisions (Anderson & Berdahl, 2002; Anderson & Galinsky, 2006).

- **Power influences how individuals treat others and their appreciation of others.** Individuals with high power tend to exhibit assertive behaviour in pursuit of their goals, often perceiving others as mere tools or resources to help them accomplish those objectives. In other words, they tend to see others in terms of their value for achieving their own objectives. Additionally, people in positions of power may need to fully understand or appreciate the perspectives and efforts of others working towards common goals. For instance, when individuals are given higher authority to improve workplace efficiency, they might need help remembering important details about their team members and to recognize their unique strengths. This is important because having power can lead to relying on stereotypes and treating subordinates poorly. These behaviours contribute to maintaining the current hierarchy and keeping employees in their assigned roles (Overbeck & Bernadette, 2006).

Individuals who have power also tend to disregard advice from others, even when advice is from experts in their field (Tost, Francesca & Larrick, 2012). High-power decision-makers were more receptive to expert advice when they anticipated a collaborative relationship with them. However, when the experts were presented merely as exceptional performers without a collaborative context, individuals with power felt a sense of competition and were less likely to consider their advice. This demonstrates how the perception of power can influence how people interact with and value the input of others, particularly experts. The implication of the organizational outcome depends on whether a powerful individual pursues individual goals or organizational goals.

To mitigate the negative impact that people with power can have, Ziemianski (2021) created a list of self-diagnostic questions to help individuals to avoid the power trap regarding how high-power individuals perceive others.

- Do managers in the organization acknowledge their limitations in specific areas and actively seek expert advice?

- Do managers prioritize advice from experts over non-experts?

- Does the organization acknowledge and appreciate acts of citizenship behaviour?

- How do employees' actions and behaviour towards others impact on their perception within the organization, especially if they achieve objectives but display negative behaviours?

- Are individuals recognized and appreciated for their unique qualities beyond their job performance?

- Are employee expectations towards new managers managed to ensure effective learning about the organization?

- Are both managers and their subordinates encouraged and recognized for fostering trust-building behaviours?

- **Power influence level of abstraction.** High-level abstraction directs attention towards the essential aspects of an object or event; on the other hand, low-level abstraction entails focusing on specific and concrete details (Trope & Liberman, 2000). High-power individuals tend to be driven by an inquisitive nature, preferring to delve into the motives and reasons behind actions rather than simply focusing on the mechanics of execution. Low-power individuals tend to be more task-oriented, concentrating on the practical aspects of performing a task. Moreover, high-power individuals tend to extract meaning and grasp the entirety of a situation, even when presented with incomplete information. For instance, reading is 'gaining knowledge' rather than 'following lines of print' (Smith & Trope, 2006). A few more examples of how powerful individuals may use higher levels of abstraction: a CEO may view a business challenge as an opportunity for 'strategic transformation' rather than a simple operational issue; a government leader might approach a complex policy decision by considering its implications on 'national security' rather than focusing on specific details. They also create broader categories, including individuals moderately related to a category as part of it. For example, Generation Y representatives may be considered as belonging to a wide group comprising all young people, regardless of their background or specific age, which can then be used to explain various behaviours and attitudes. This tendency may lead to a greater reliance on stereotypes and seeing others through their own perspectives.

Developing power

Magee and Frasier (2014) studied managers in the public sector; they concluded that when it comes to judging someone's power, the main factors considered are their confidence, ability to take assertive action and the appearance of being in control. Here are some ways to demonstrate your power and control:

- Demonstrating that you can do what you want and that the outcomes of your actions are significant
- Taking proactive steps
- Projecting confidence. People who take their time to think through decisions are viewed as less powerful than those who make quick decisions and focus on getting things done (Magee, 2009)
- Taking ownership of the success so that others don't attribute it to luck
- Taking ownership of the failures suggests that they have the power to address the problem going forward

In Pfeffer's work on power, he concluded that individuals fail to gain power typically due to the following three reasons. Firstly, they have self-doubt. Thoughts on avoiding pursuing power and fear of failure and the potential impact on their self-esteem hinder their ability to become more political. Second, following the existing rules favours those already in positions of power. When individuals are excessively polite and modest and prefer to remain in the background, adhering to societal norms and conventional wisdom can hinder their potential to gain power. Third, Pfeffer suggested that the way to view setbacks and failures is not as indicative of personal inadequacy but as learning opportunities. In addition, while inherent talent and aptitude vary among individuals, the most significant differentiating factor in performance is the effort and persistence exerted. Similarly, overcoming self-doubt, embracing resilience and viewing setbacks as valuable lessons are important in pursuing power. By learning from these experiences and maintaining a determined mindset, individuals can increase their chances of achieving success in acquiring power and reaching their goals.

Understanding status

Definition of status

Another primary factor that individuals can use to exert their influence is status – the respect that an individual has in the eyes of others (Magee & Frasier, 2014). Status is defined as the level of respect received from one's peers – the basis of respect in an organization tends to be a judgement about one's competence (Barton & Bunderson, 2014). Individuals rely on 'status cues' to construct their prediction of one's competence and can be derived by job title, position in the organization and past performance. One's ability and competence can also be inferred by stereotypes, such as socioeconomic backgrounds and demographic stereotypes (age, gender, race). These competence cues are signals and may or may not relate to actual competence.

The distinction between status and power is that status is granted willingly by others and is determined by how much an individual is believed to contribute to a group, whereas power is derived from an individual's unequal control over valuable resources (Magee & Galinsky, 2008).

Status and power: Differences, similarities

Magee and Frasier (2014) described that the difference between power and status lies in subjectivity. Status is more subjective than power. Although status and power are subjective, how others perceive and appreciate those qualities and attributes is more important. Regarding power, the worth or importance of resources is based on personal judgement or opinion. However, for power to exist, someone must control how those resources are distributed within a social group or system. In other words, the ability to decide who gets what resources is an essential aspect of power. Given that status is granted through social perception and judgement, while power is derived from resource control, a manager's relationships with employees are crucial in determining their status level within an organization.

Status and power are similar in two aspects. First, both status and power can influence. Second, status and power are context-specific. An individual's level of power or status is determined by the specific social relationships that are important in a given situation. For instance, in a company, employees may hold a high status within their department because of their expertise and contributions. However, this status may not automatically grant them the power to make cross-departmental decisions or have a say in strategic planning meetings at executive level. Likewise, a senior manager may have significant power within his or her department, but this power is context-specific and may vary regarding company-wide decision-making processes involving other departments and higher-level executives. In short, some individuals may have control over resources without earning the respect of others, while others may be respected but lack control over resources.

Individuals' roles can be categorized into four combinations by the level (high and low) of status vs. power (Fragale et al, 2011; Magee & Frasier, 2014). The power and status combination has implications on an individual's behaviour as below:

- Low power, low status (e.g., secretary, bus driver, waiter, clerk): individuals with low power and low status are often seen as submissive and 'warm'. Example: An employee who doesn't have a high-ranking position in the company but is well-liked by everyone due to their friendly and caring nature. Even though they lack power, they are perceived as warm and kind.

- Low power, high status (e.g., emeritus professor, Olympic athlete, member of the advisory board): they seemed neither dominant nor submissive, but they were perceived as warm. For the emeritus professor, they no longer hold a position in the university but still command respect and admiration due to their past accomplishments and contributions. People may perceive them as warm and approachable despite their lack of authority.

- High power, low status (e.g., immigration officer, bouncer): individuals with high power but low status should also be viewed as dominant because of their influential power. An immigration officer at an airport holds considerable power in making decisions about entry into the country. Despite their power, passengers may find them cold or distant.

- High power, high status (e.g., head of state, CEO, dean, vice-president, professor): individuals with power and status are perceived as highly influential, dominant and warm. The president of a country holds both high power and high status. As the head of state and the leader of the nation, they are one of the most prestigious and respected in the country, making them a symbol of leadership and influence. The President's high status in society garners admiration and respect, leading people to perceive them as warm and approachable, especially when they connect with citizens and exhibit empathy and concern for their well-being.

In summary, when people have a lot of power, others tend to see them as less warm or friendly compared to those with less power. However, the effect of power on warmth depends on a person's status. Those with high status, whether they have high or low power, are generally viewed positively as both dominant and warm.

What does it mean for organizational life?

Social evaluations and the resulting behavioural inferences play a crucial role in shaping how people interact with each other. These judgements form the initial and significant stage in determining the dynamics of interpersonal relationships. For instance, although high power and high status are as influential as the low power and high-status combination, the high power and low-status combination was perceived most negatively in Fragale, Overbeck and Neale's study. This has behavioural implications for the organization. When someone expects to deal with a person who is unpleasant and controlling, they may start using strategies to protect themselves from that behaviour, even before they act that way.

Factors contributing to the acquisition and maintenance of status

In general, expectations based on status are crucial in influencing how we perceive others and behave towards them. These expectations also establish boundaries for acceptable behaviour for individuals. When these expectations are violated, the consequences are typically more severe for low-status individuals. The adverse reactions they face serve to maintain the existing hierarchical order.

How to develop status

According to Magee and Frasier (2014), an individual can build status by demonstrating warmth (trustworthiness and agreeableness) and establishing competence.

- Demonstrating warmth
  How others assess warmth typically depends on nonverbal behaviours such as smiling, sitting close, leaning forward during the conversation and mirroring others' behaviours during discussions to signal the warmth; however, this must be genuine. Nonverbal behaviours perceived as insincere will have a negative effect.

- Establishing competence
  Helping and volunteering demonstrate both warmth and competence in accomplishing tasks. Firstly, it provides an opportunity to exert direct influence over the work process. Secondly, thanks to the norm of reciprocity, the recipient of the favour is often inclined to return the gesture of assistance in the future. Individuals can establish a network of support and cooperation by engaging in this mutually beneficial cycle.

EXAMPLE OF DEMONSTRATING WARMTH – INTERVIEW

Imagine a job interview scenario where there are two candidates for a position. Both candidates possess similar qualifications and experience, but their nonverbal behaviours during the interview differ significantly.

Candidate A exhibited warmth by genuinely smiling throughout the conversation, maintaining eye contact, leaning forward and sitting closer to the interviewer to show interest and engagement. A also subtly mirrored the interviewer's positive gestures, such as nodding in agreement and mirroring their open body language.

On the other hand, candidate B tried to appear warm by forcing a smile. B avoided eye contact and maintained a more distant posture during the interview due to nervousness.

In this scenario, candidate A's genuine nonverbal behaviours are perceived positively and as warm and approachable. The interviewer feels comfortable during the conversation, giving a positive impression of candidate A. In contrast, candidate B's nonverbal cues create a negative effect, making it challenging to establish a warm connection. As a result, candidate B's warmth is not perceived as genuine, leading to a less favourable impression during the interview.

Organizational events and status development

Individuals may also develop their status under disruptive events in organizations. According to Wee et al (2023), organizational events disrupt how teams work together and are likely to have behavioural implications. They termed these disruptions 'task-based jolts.' In particular, task-based jolts present opportunities for establishing competencies, particularly useful for lower-status individuals for status development.

For instance, in a case of successful adaptation to organizational change, support from co-workers enhances preparedness, reduces uncertainty about roles and increases commitment to the change process. It often involves helping each other learn new tasks, sharing resources to develop new skills and providing guidance on navigating unfamiliar procedures. In other words, disruptions enable lower-status individuals to contribute more freely even when lower-status individuals view jolts as self-threat. They feel more confident about their abilities to contribute and become more generous towards others. As a result, they gain status in the immediate aftermath of the jolt.

For individuals with higher status, they are likely to see disruptions as threats. This is because the jolt raises the unlikely possibility that they might not have the same level of competence or advantage in the new work environment, putting their goal of maintaining their high standing or reputation at risk. For example, when a task-based jolt occurs, such as introducing new technology that changes how tasks are performed, the high-status individual may feel threatened. They worry that they may not possess the same expertise or advantage in adapting to the new changes as before. This possibility of underperforming and being unable to maintain their status creates a sense of self-threat for them. Wee and colleagues (2023) argue that higher-status individuals are generally more capable of adjusting to task-based changes due to their experience and resources. However, during disruptions, the mere possibility of not being able to live up to their previous performance standards is particularly self-threatening for them.

REFLECTION

To evaluate your self-perceived status, you can consider the following three items suggested by Marr and Thau (2014):

1 How much do your group members hold you in high regard?

2 To what extent do you occupy a high-status position within your work group?

3 How much respect do your group members have for you?

Considering your self-perceived status, reflect on the following questions:

- How does your current perceived status influence your behaviour within your group or work environment?

- Are there any instances where your self-perceived status has influenced your behaviour positively or negatively? Provide examples to illustrate.

- What nonverbal behaviours can you engage in to convey genuine warmth and how can you ensure that your actions are perceived as sincere?

- Have you experienced task-based jolts or disruptive events in your academic or professional journey? How did they impact on your status development?

Organizational politics

Whereas power and status represent an individual's inherent potential to exert influence and command respect, politics pertains to the practical manifestation of influence through actions and behaviours. Power and status signify one's underlying capacity. On the other hand, politics encompasses the active exercise of that influence in organizational contexts.

'Politics' is a general term used to describe the management of social groups and the decision-making processes accompanying it. In the context of organizations, 'organizational politics' specifically refers to the presence of diverse and sometimes conflicting interests within the organization and the strategies employed to handle them. In other words, organizational politics is about how people get things done. Politics, being a form of power, is inherently rooted in relationships and interactions among individuals and can notably impact on the dynamics and outcomes within an organization. How can an individual influence others and get things done? Through power, which is often tied to formal position or through informal influence, such as status.

In the workplace, politics is about different interests and agendas in the organization. Buchanan (2008) surveyed a sample of 250 British managers who perceived organizational politics as necessary. The majority agreed with statements such as 'managers who effectively engage in organizational politics can enhance their careers', 'appropriate game-playing can enhance personal reputations' and 'departments led by skilled organizational politicians attract more resources'.

Perception of organizational politics

When would one engage in political behaviours? It is often associated with an individual's perception of organizational politics. Perception of organizational politics is an individual's judgement of how much their work environment is influenced by co-workers and supervisors who prioritize their interests over others. For instance, if employees perceive that decision-making in the organization is highly centralized and power is concentrated in the hands of a few individuals, they may engage in political tactics to gain influence and control over decision-making processes. According to Ferris and Kacmar (1992) and Hochwarter and colleagues (2020), individuals' perceptions of organizational politics are influenced by the following factors.

Organizational factors: when individuals work in the organization with the following characteristics, individuals associate their work environment as 'political'.

- Centralization. A higher level of centralization means that decision-making is concentrated among a few people. Therefore, there is more significant potential for organizational politics.

- Formalization. Organizations with high levels of formalization, characterized by explicit rules, procedures and guidelines, tend to experience a decrease in the perceived political nature of the organization.
- Hierarchical level. The higher the hierarchical level, the higher the perceived politics.
- The span of control. The span of control refers to the number of subordinates a manager or supervisor oversees. When more subordinates are under one manager, this leads to fewer opportunities for upward communication and feedback, making it harder for employees to have their voices heard and increasing perceptions of a political environment.
- Lack of procedural justice. For example, suppose a company has a clear and unbiased promotion process where employees are evaluated based on objective criteria and everyone has an equal opportunity to compete. In that case, employees are more likely to perceive the organization as fair and less political.

Job/work influences: individuals are less likely to associate their work environment as political when their job and work:

- is autonomous
- requires a variety of skills to complete jobs
- requires cooperation
- receives constant feedback
- has advancement opportunities
- has development opportunities
- has involvement
- has trust.

Personal influences: when individuals possess characteristics such as Machiavellianism (the tendency to manipulate others for personal gain), negative affect and individual political skill, individuals associate their work environment as 'political'. On the other hand, when individuals have a higher level of self-monitoring (awareness and adjustment of behaviour in different situations) and have an external locus of control, they are more likely to view the organization as a political arena. Individuals' interactions and direct relationships with colleagues and managers are also positively related to political perceptions. For instance, in a typical workplace situation, an employee consistently engages in effective communication and collaboration with their co-workers and they maintain a strong working relationship with their immediate supervisor. These positive interactions with colleagues foster trust and cooperation within the team and their rapport with the supervisor allows them to have productive discussions about the organization's policies and decisions. In such an environment, the employee is more inclined to form a favourable perception of the company's internal politics because they feel well-informed and connected, which, in turn, significantly influences their perspective on the political dynamics within the organization.

Demographic factors: demographics such as age, gender, tenure and race also influence perceptions of organizational politics.

GROUP DISCUSSION

Hochwarter et al (2020) summarized the consequences when individuals perceived an organization as political, including:

- psychological impact on an individual, such as stress, anxiety and burnout
- perceptual outcomes: decreased perceptions of fairness, trustworthiness, autonomy, empowerment, support, quality of relationships and increased perceptions of uncertainty
- job-related outcome: lower level of job performance, satisfaction, job involvement, commitment to the organization and link to higher turnover rate
- behavioural consequences: increased absenteeism, reduced organizational citizenship behaviour and a higher likelihood of engaging in counterproductive work behaviours.

This reflection and group discussion aim to help you recognize the importance of managing politics effectively. Take some time to reflect on the following questions regarding the consequences of organizational politics at the individual level. Please write down your thoughts and observations and discuss them in the group.

- Reflect on an experience where you encountered politics (for example, allocation of workload in the project, steering decision-making in the group working for their favours – this can be either from other colleagues or knowledgeable individuals). How did that experience shape your perception of the importance of understanding and acknowledging politics in the workplace?
- Reflect on a personal experience where you have observed or experienced politics. How did it impact you at the individual level? Use Hochwarter et al (2020)'s list above as a cue to think about the impact of perceived organizational politics on you.
- Based on past experiences, what coping strategies have you found effective in dealing with the negative consequences of perceived organizational politics?
- What skills, behaviours or approaches can help individuals mitigate the negative consequences and leverage the potential benefits of organizational politics?

Political behaviour: political will and political skill

Individuals' political behaviour relies on their political will and political skill (Ferris et al, 2007; Treadway et al, 2005; Ferris et al, 2019). Political will refers to the willingness to invest effort in pursuing political objectives – the intrinsic motivation for one to act politically. Political skill is the ability to effectively understand and influence others in the workplace to achieve personal and organizational goals (Ferris et al, 2005; Treadway et al, 2005).

Individual level factors that influence one's political behaviour:

- individuals' needs
- individuals' status
- Machiavellianism
- risk-seeking propensity
- individuals' inclination and capacity to regulate their behaviour and adapt it in a manner that enables them to shape how others perceive them
- individuals' tendency to external loci of control, where individuals believe external forces shape their lives, is associated with engaging in more political behaviours.

In addition to individuals' characters, individuals' life experience also shaped their motivation to act politically. Studying non-managerial individuals' political motivation, Wyatt et al (2022) found that when individuals perceive their environment as threatening and unfair, their motivation to engage in political behaviour stems from self-protection and regaining control. This leads them to navigate secretive and exclusive political cultures, shield themselves from mistreatment by managers and avoid participating in political activities. Conversely, in organizations that explicitly promote a positive political culture, individuals are motivated to engage in political behaviours that benefit others. They perceive political actions as a means to adapt to positive organizational politics, utilize influential gatekeepers to navigate political dynamics and develop personal strategies for engaging in political behaviours.

EXERCISE

Political behaviour and context

Political behaviour is influenced not only by individual antecedents, as discussed earlier, but also by the contextual factors at play. Think of specific examples or scenarios where political behaviours are more likely to emerge.

Politically skilled individuals possess a deep understanding of social dynamics and can adapt their behaviour to meet changing needs and demands. They inspire trust and confidence, enabling effective influence and control over others. Ferris and colleagues (2000) viewed political skill as an interpersonal style that involves being socially perceptive and understanding how to act in different situations. It also means having a likable and trustworthy personality that makes others feel at ease and believe in your authenticity. To characterize political skills, Ferris and colleagues propose four dimensions (Ferris et al, 2007):

- Social astuteness. This refers to the ability of individuals to observe and understand social interactions keenly. Politically skilled individuals are perceptive observers who accurately interpret their own behaviour as well as the behaviour of others. For instance, a politically skilled individual with social astuteness would attentively observe not only the content of the presentations but also the nonverbal cues and dynamics among team members. For instance, if they notice that a team member is feeling hesitant or unsure about their idea, they may offer encouragement or ask follow-up questions to create a supportive and inclusive environment. Their ability to read the social cues and respond appropriately allows them to build rapport and navigate interactions cleverly and effectively. As a result, they are often perceived as imaginative and adept in their interactions with others.

- Interpersonal influence. This involves the skill of adapting and adjusting one's behaviour according to the specific situation to achieve desired outcomes. It entails adapting their approach and tailoring their messages to resonate with each stakeholder. They increase their personal influence to accomplish their objectives. For example, a politically skilled individual with strong interpersonal influence may encounter a situation where they need to gain support for a new project idea from different stakeholders. They understand that each stakeholder has unique priorities, concerns and communication styles. For instance, for a data-driven stakeholder, they may provide detailed analysis and evidence to support their proposal. For a more relationship-oriented stakeholder, they may emphasize the positive impact the project will have on teamwork and collaboration – their chances of achieving their goals by eliciting the desired responses.

- Networking ability. This refers to individuals' ability to form alliances and leverage these connections to create opportunities. Their negotiation and conflict management proficiency enhances their ability to navigate professional relationships and foster successful collaborations. An individual with high networking ability typically demonstrates exceptional skills in building and nurturing professional relationships. They actively participate in industry events, conferences and networking opportunities, approaching conversations with genuine curiosity and a desire to establish meaningful connections. This person excels at maintaining relationships, following up with contacts, offering assistance and sharing valuable resources.

- Apparent sincerity. Politically skilled individuals are perceived by others as having strong integrity and displaying authenticity, sincerity and genuineness. Individuals who behave in a transparent way are perceived by others as being genuine, honest and authentic. These leaders genuinely care about others and are perceived as trustworthy without being seen as manipulative or having hidden agendas. As a result, they earn trust and find themselves in a favourable position to exert influence through various means, such as interpersonal interactions and influence tactics.

Kimura (2015) summarizes three effects of political skill on individuals. First, psychological strain is often associated with the perceived threat of a stressor and an individual's coping mechanisms. However, individuals with high political skills have an advantage in mitigating negative psychological strain through effective coping strategies. They can adapt their behaviours to manage stressors and seek support through their strong networking abilities. Second, political skill is particularly advantageous for career advancement in challenging or unfavourable networking situations compared to favourable ones. Third, political skill is positively related to leadership effectiveness. These indicators include perceived organizational support, work unit performance, leader performance, follower effectiveness, team performance, overall firm performance and entrepreneurial performance (Treadway et al, 2004; Brouer et al, 2013; Douglas & Ammeter, 2004; Ahearn et al, 2004; Tocher et al, 2012).

According to Allen and colleagues (1979) – who studied over 87 supervisors, mid-level managers, senior managers and executive officers – tactics for an individual to engage in organizational politics include:

- criticizing or blaming others
- utilization of information
- impression management
- support building for ideas
- complimenting others, fostering unity
- forming alliances with powerful individuals
- connecting with influential people
- fostering reciprocity.

Surveying 250 managers, Buchanan (2008) summarized a list of political behaviours:

- Most common political behaviours
  - Creating a network of valuable connections
  - Leveraging influential individuals to endorse ideas or initiatives

  o Developing relationships with influential individuals

  o Adapting rules to suit the circumstances

  o Promoting oneself

- Less common political behaviours

  o Shifting responsibility to others for mistakes

  o Taking credit for the work done by others

  o Sacrificing minor matters to achieve significant objectives

  o Gathering opinions through social interactions

  o Assigning others to deliver unfavourable news

  o Intentionally withholding valuable information

  o Emphasizing the errors and weaknesses of others

  o Employing delay strategies to hinder others

  o Violating rules to accomplish goals

  o Making compromises now to gain future benefits

- Rare political behaviours

  o Sending inaccurate information

  o Disseminating false rumours to undermine others

  o Maintaining compromising information to blackmail others

REFLECTION

Look at the lists of political behaviours in the work by Allen and colleagues (1979) and Buchanan (2008) and answer the following questions.

- Reflect on your past experiences: Which political behaviours have you used to influence others? How effective were these behaviours in achieving your desired outcomes?

- Consider the context: In what situations did you employ these political behaviours? Were they appropriate for the specific context?

- Explore alternative strategies: Are there other tactics you could have used to achieve your goals?

- Assess ethical implications: Reflect on the ethicality of the political behaviours you have used. Did they align with your personal values and ethical standards? How could you ensure that your actions remain ethical while still exerting influence?

- Plan for future actions: How will you approach political behaviours more consciously and intentionally? What strategies will you employ to ensure that your actions align with your values and contribute to positive outcomes for yourself and others?

A journey to political maturity

How do individuals become politically savvy? Are they born with it? Or did they learn from the experience? Individuals tend to experience a 'political journey' from a more black-and-white view of organizational politics to a dualist view of organizational politics. Doldor (2017) detailed a leader's political development journey by examining leaders' organizational engagement. She found that leaders may not always start with born political skill and their view of organizational politics changes as individuals move from a naïve stage to a more proficient stage. She classified three stages of an individual's political journey – naïve, coping and proficiency. Each stage shared some characteristics, described below.

Stage 1: Naïve stage

In this stage, people's perceptions of organizational politics can take on a negative hue, perceiving it as a disruptive and harmful force. At the outset, they might hold strong beliefs in the principles of meritocracy, but these convictions can waver when they encounter situations marked by unspoken rules and occurrences that appear to clash with these ideals. In such cases, individuals are prone to attribute the existence of organizational politics to inherent dysfunctions within the system and they often see it as being primarily fuelled by self-interest rather than genuine collective objectives. Consequently, they tend to exhibit hesitancy in actively engaging with organizational politics, describing their experiences as baffling and exasperating. This collective perspective reveals a general skepticism towards the role of politics in the workplace, alongside a clear preference for processes that are more transparent and equitable.

In terms of their political behaviour within the organization, some individuals tend to adopt a rather passive stance, avoiding involvement in political matters whenever possible and only reluctantly engaging when absolutely necessary. These individuals prioritize their focus on the tasks at hand, aiming to excel in their work while keeping a watchful eye on the political landscape. They demonstrate an awareness of the unwritten rules that often govern the organization's dynamics. However, despite their understanding of the significance of relationship-building, these individuals exhibit limited active engagement in this regard. Their behaviour appears to reflect a deliberate choice to strike a balance between maintaining a professional distance and acknowledging the importance of political dynamics within the workplace.

The shift from the initial stage of naïvety to the next stage of the political journey typically occurs in response to a variety of political incidents. These incidents may encompass both work-related challenges, such as encountering roadblocks in getting proposals approved due to a lack of influence, and career-related setbacks, such as struggling to secure a promotion. As individuals progress in their careers, they now have greater managerial responsibilities, which inherently necessitates a more substantial focus on relationship-building. The demand for effective relationship cultivation becomes evident as it becomes increasingly clear that without such connections, critical tasks and objectives may remain unfulfilled. This transition represents a pivotal turning point in individuals' professional journeys, where they recognize the value of political acumen and interpersonal bonds for achieving success in the workplace.

Stage 2: Coping stage

In the coping stage, many may initially recognize certain positive aspects, such as its potential benefits for team dynamics. They maintain the belief that politics largely stems from organizational dysfunction. Individuals acknowledge the omnipresence of politics in daily work tasks, encompassing activities like conflict management, resource allocation and the alignment of diverse motivations and agendas. Despite occasionally finding politics vexing and awkward, they increasingly accept its presence as an integral part of the workplace landscape, demonstrating a growing sense of pragmatism in their approach to this aspect of professional life.

When it comes to their approach to workplace politics, individuals often display a range of behaviours and attitudes that reveal a complex dynamic. Some individuals primarily exhibit reactive behaviour, only becoming politically active in response to specific circumstances. For others, their political actions are more deliberate, reflecting a conscious recognition of the need to engage in political manoeuvring even if they may have some resistance. These individuals tend to demonstrate a certain level of political awareness, enabling them to read between the lines and discern various motives and agendas at play within the organization. Many recognize the importance of practising political skills, particularly as they become increasingly aware of the role relationship-building plays in career progression. Although they often fall short of developing a comprehensive range of strategies for navigating political landscapes, they question whether their political actions align with their authentic selves.

Advancing to the next stage of the political journey is typically spurred by specific political incidents that serve as pivotal turning points in an individual's professional journey. These incidents can range from challenges in the workplace, such as encountering hurdles to implement proposals, to career-related setbacks like the struggle to secure a coveted promotion. Moreover, the accumulation of managerial responsibilities plays a central role in this transition. As individuals climb the corporate ladder, the need to navigate the intricacies of organizational politics becomes increasingly evident. Many find invaluable guidance in mentors or role models who offer insights and strategies for effectively managing political situations, thereby facilitating their progression and ensuring a smoother ascent to this advanced stage.

Stage 3: Proficiency stage

As individuals gain experience in the professional world, their perspective on workplace politics often undergoes a transformation. They come to appreciate that politics is an integral and inherent part of their work environment. With time, they develop the ability to place political behaviour within the context of the workplace, recognizing that it can yield both beneficial and detrimental results, with ethical and unethical dimensions. This nuanced viewpoint underscores the dual nature of politics, where it can serve as a force for good or be a source of disruption. Furthermore, as individuals progress in their careers, they tend to enhance their capacity to manage their emotions, maintaining composure when faced with various political scenarios. This newfound emotional resilience equips them to navigate the political terrain more effectively.

In terms of political actions, individuals evolve to exhibit a depth of political awareness that transcends merely deciphering conflicting agendas. It encompasses a profound understanding of diverse perspectives, requirements and the underlying motivations of those around them. This heightened political awareness fosters a proactive approach, where they anticipate political challenges and make calculated decisions on how to respond. Over time, political actions become an integral and routine aspect of their job, seamlessly integrated into their daily responsibilities. They display notable flexibility and adaptability in navigating the intricate web of political situations that arise within their professional sphere. What sets them apart is their commitment to developing an authentic way of practising politics that aligns harmoniously with their values and identity, ensuring that their actions resonate with their true selves.

REFLECTION

Use the political journey from stage 1 – naïve, stage 2 – coping, and stage 3 – proficient, and the characteristics outline for each stage, thinking about the following questions:

- Reflect on your current stage in your political journey. Where do you perceive yourself to be at this moment?

- Delve into your perception of politics as either positive or negative. Reflect on the factors that have shaped your view and contemplate how altering your mindset might impact on your political journey and effectiveness within your organization.

- Recall a specific political incident from your past, either personal or observed. Reflect on your actions during that event and explore your emotional response at the time. What insights did you gain from the incident? How has it influenced your approach to politics since then?

- Contemplate your progress in navigating organizational politics. Where do you see room for improvement or growth? How can you enhance your ability to navigate political situations effectively while staying true to your values and principles?

COMPARING POLITICAL SKILLS: HIGH CONTEXT AND LOW CONTEXT CULTURE

Lvina and a team of researchers (2012) conducted a study involving 1,511 employees from China, Germany, Russia, Turkey and the United States. Overall, they found that respondents from the United States consistently perceive their political skills as more advanced than individuals from other cultures. Political skill levels, ranked from highest to lowest, were observed as follows: the United States, Turkey, China, Russia and Germany.

They found that when countries have high-context culture, where communication relies heavily on implicit cues, shared experiences and contextual understanding, these countries tend to have higher average scores on political skills. For example, countries like Turkey and China, considered high-context cultures emphasizing the value of relationships and indirect communication, tend to score particularly high on the social astuteness and networking ability aspects of political skill. Conversely, cultures that emphasize uncertainty avoidance, such as Germany, demonstrate a somewhat limited level of endorsement for political skill. When the research team compared the scores between the United States and China, they found that the United States has higher political skill scores than China. Although Chinese and Asian managers are skilled in social situations due to their high-context cultural background, they face challenges in building influence and networks.

Discussion questions:

- According to Ferris, how does your country of origin impact on the development and application of political skills, including social astuteness, interpersonal influence, networking ability and apparent sincerity? What are the practices you use or witness other people using when you/they exercise political skill?

- Compare your observations with individuals from different countries or regions. Do you notice differences in how political skills are demonstrated? Consider the implications for your work outcomes and career progression when collaborating with individuals from different countries/regions or working outside your home country.

REFLECTION

Assessing your political skill

Instruction: Research the 18-item Political Skill Inventory (PSI) developed by Ferris and a team of researchers (2005). Write down your level of agreement with each statement about yourself using the seven-point scale.

Interpreting your political skill score

To calculate your overall political skill rating, add all the individual scores and divide the total by 18. The closer your score is to 7, the higher your general level of political skill.

Under each section, you can also calculate your score for the four dimensions of political skill. An individual dimension score approaching 7 indicates higher self-perceived competence in the area.

Self-reflective questions:

- Reflecting on your beliefs about political behaviour, are you comfortable employing informal tactics to further your interests?

- Among the four dimensions of political skill, in which dimension do you feel the most confident? And in which dimension do you recognize the greatest need for development?

- Are there specific dimensions of political skill in which you feel particularly competent? How do these dimensions align with your career goals?

- How might cultural or contextual factors impact on the effectiveness and application of your political skill in various organizational settings?

The outcome of political behaviours

Ferris and colleagues (2019) summarize the outcome of political behaviour for individuals as:

- increase power
- increase resources
- risk to reputation
- risk to individual relationship.

At the individual level, the outcome of organizational politics includes job performance and other job-related psychological consequences (e.g., job satisfaction, efforts and time spent in the job, stress and burnout) as well as the political outcome for an individual (e.g., one's political perception, reputation, social network and power) (Ferris et al, 2019; Kimura, 2015). At the organizational level, the outcome of organizational politics can impact on the turnover rate and level of absenteeism. The positive consequences of organizational politics are often strategic, including achieving organizational goals, higher productivity, increased communication and flexibility (Landells & Albrecht, 2017; Hochwarter, 2012).

Organizational politics and gender differences

Men and women tended to view organizational politics differently and therefore the extent to which they engaged in political behaviours. While men and women both recognize that organizational politics are necessary in the organization and show an equal willingness to engage in politics, how they act differs. In Buchanan's study of 250 managers, he compared the result of male and female managers and he found that (Buchanan, 2008):

- women tended to be more cautious about potential harm to relationships when engaging in political actions
- women tended to avoid active participation, while men viewed it as necessary and part of their job
- women tended to view political will more negatively than their counterparts
- compared to men, women were more likely to recognize that participating in political activities had helped them progress in their careers.

Doldor et al (2013) also found the gendered situation that female managers find themselves in and political behaviour is a way to navigate it. They found that:

- women perceive the situation as an exclusive 'old boys' club'
- women view political behaviour primarily as a means to pursue self-interest

- due to the gendered nature of the environment, women employ political behaviours to navigate the system, with attitudes ranging from open resistance to reluctant acceptance
- women adopt masculine political practices to increase their personal visibility and establish alliances
- however, women are more mindful of the potential consequences of their actions, considering the impact on others and the implications of their political behaviour within a male-dominated environment
- those who engage in political practices do so by conforming to the widely accepted norms and practices in their gendered situation.

Chapter summary

This chapter has explored the concepts of power, status and organizational politics and their significance within an organizational context. It began by defining power and highlighting its importance in influencing behaviour and shaping outcomes within organizations. Various forms of power were examined, including legitimate power, reward power, coercive power, expert power and referent power. Examples were provided to illustrate how power manifests in different organizational situations. The chapter then delved into strategies and approaches for individuals to develop power within an organization. It explored how individuals can enhance their influence by leveraging their expertise, building relationships and effectively navigating organizational dynamics. Practical tips and techniques were discussed to empower individuals in their pursuit of increased influence and power.

Status was introduced as a form of informal influence. Its definition and relevance within organizations were explained, emphasizing how it impacts on decision-making, access to resources and overall perception within the organizational hierarchy. Factors contributing to the acquisition and maintenance of status, such as status cues, demonstrating warmth and establishing competence, were identified and explored.

Next, the chapter addressed the concept of organizational politics and the importance of political will and political skill. Rather than seeing political ability as an inherent character trait, this chapter introduced the idea of the political maturity journey, describing how individuals move from the naïve stage, to the coping stage and then to the proficient stage. The characteristics and behaviours of each stage were described, allowing individuals to assess their political maturity and understand the progression towards becoming politically astute and effective within organizations.

Gender differences in political skills were then discussed, focusing on the fact that men and women have different perspectives on organizational politics, leading to variations in their engagement in political behaviours. While both genders recognize the importance of organizational politics, their actions and attitudes differ.

Key terms

Power

Legitimate power

Reward power

Coercive power

Expert power

Referent power

Three faces of power

Visible power

Covert power

Institutional power

Level of abstraction

Status

Status cues

Demonstrate warmth

Establishing competence

Organizational politics

Perception of organizational politics

Political will

Political skill

Ferris' political skill inventory

Social astuteness

Interpersonal influence

Networking ability

Apparent sincerity

Political maturity

Chapter review questions

- Define power and explain its significance in an organizational context. Provide examples to support your answer.

- Identify and describe the various forms of power that exist within organizations.

- How can an individual develop power within an organization? Discuss strategies and approaches that individuals can employ to increase their influence.

- Define status and explain its relevance within an organizational setting. Identify and discuss the factors contributing to the acquisition and maintenance of status.

- Describe the three stages of political maturity. Discuss the characteristics and behaviours associated with each stage.

- Consider gender differences in political skills. Discuss the implications of these differences and how organizations can promote gender equality in the context of organizational politics.

Further reading

Postma, N (2021) You can't sit out office politics, *Harvard Business Review*. The author talks about the myth of organizational politics and worksheet that can help you to diagnose your own political skills.

References

Ahearn, K K, Ferris, G R, Hochwarter, W A, Douglas, C & Ammeter, A P (2004) Leader Political Skill and Team Performance, *Journal of Management*, 30(3), 309–327. https://doi.org/10.1016/j.jm.2003.01.004 (archived at https://perma.cc/U83Y-MEL9).

Allen, R W, Madison, D L, Porter, L W, Renwick, P A & Mayes, B T (1979) Organizational politics: Tactics and characteristics of its actors, *California Management Review*, 77–83.

Anderson, C & Berdahl, J L (2002) The experience of power: Examining the effects of power on approach and inhibition tendencies, *Journal of Personality and Social Psychology*, 83, 1362–1377.

Anderson, C & Galinsky, A D (2006) Power, optimism, and risk-taking, *European Journal of Social Psychology*, 36(4), 511–536. https://doi.org/10.1002/ejsp.324 (archived at https://perma.cc/QA7X-JZJE).

Barton, M A & Bunderson, J S (2014) Assessing member expertise in groups: An expertise dependence perspective, *Organizational Psychology Review*, 4(3), 228–257. doi:10.1177/2041386613508975 (archived at https://perma.cc/7NU3-AXBX).

Brouer, R L, Douglas, C, Treadway, D C & Ferris, G R (2013) Leader Political Skill, Relationship Quality, and Leadership Effectiveness: A Two-Study Model Test and

Constructive Replication, *Journal of Leadership & Organizational Studies*, 20(2), 185–198. https://doi.org/10.1177/1548051812460099 (archived at https://perma.cc/UBA5-ZPE2).

Buchanan, D A (2008) You stab my back, I'll stab yours: Management experience and perceptions of organization political behaviour, *British Journal of Management*, 19(1), 49–64. doi:10.1111/J.1467-8551.2007.00533.X (archived at https://perma.cc/AK6K-Q2MV).

Doldor, E (2017) From politically naïve to politically mature: Conceptualizing leaders' political maturation journey, *British Journal of Management*, 28(4), 666–686.

Doldor, E, Anderson, D & Vinnicombe, S (2013) Refining the concept of political will: A gender perspective, *British Journal of Management*, 24(3), 281–462.

Douglas, C & Ammeter, A P (2004) An examination of leader political skill and its effect on ratings of leader effectiveness, *The Leadership Quarterly*, 15(4), 537–550. https://doi.org/10.1016/j.leaqua.2004.05.006 (archived at https://perma.cc/EST4-NFZJ).

Ferris, G R, Ellen, III B P, McAllister, C P & Maher L P (2019) Reorganizing organizational politics research: A review of the literature and identification of future research agenda, *Annual Review of Organizational Psychology and Organizational Behavior*, 6, 299–323.

Ferris, G R & Kacmar, K M (1992) Perceptions of organizational politics, *Journal of Management*, 18(1), 93–116.

Ferris, G R, Perrewe, P L, Anthony, W P & Gilmore, D C (2000) Political skill at work, *Organizational Dynamics*, 28(4), 25–37.

Ferris, G R, Treadway, D C, Kolodinsky, R W, Hochwarter, W A, Kacmar, C J, Douglas, C & Frink D D (2005) Development and validation of the political skill inventory, *Journal of Management*, 31(1), 126–152.

Ferris, G R, Treadway, D C, Perrewe, P L, Brouer, R L, Douglas, C & Lux, S (2007) Political skill in organizations, *Journal of Management*, 33(3), 290–320.

Fragale, A R, Overbeck, J R & Neale, M A (2011) Resources versus respect: Social judgement based on target's power and status position, *Journal of Experimental Social Psychology*, 47, 767–775.

French, J R P, Jr. & Raven, B (1959) The bases of social power. In D. Cartwright (ed.), *Studies in Social Power*, University of Michigan. pp. 150–167.

Galinsky, A D, Gruenfeld, D H & Magee, J C (2003) From Power to Action, *Journal of Personality and Social Psychology*, 85(3), 453–466. https://doi.org/10.1037/0022-3514.85.3.453 (archived at https://perma.cc/AA4D-PDQB).

Hochwarter, W A (2012) The positive side of organizational politics. In: G.R. Ferris & D.C. Treadway (eds.), *Politics in Organizations: Theory and Research Considerations – The Organizational Frontiers Series*, Routledge. pp. 27–66.

Hochwarter, W A, Rosen, C C, Jordan, S L, Ferris, G R, Ejaz, A & Maher, L P (2020) Perceptions of organizational politics research: Past, present and future, *Journal of Management*, 46(6), 879–907.

Kimura, T (2015) A review of political skill: Current research trend and directions for future research, *International Journal of Management Reviews*, 17(3), 279–412.

Landells, E M & Albrecht, S L (2017) The positives and negatives of organizational politics: A qualitative study, *Journal of Business and Psychology*, 32, 41–58.

Lvina, E, Johns, G, Treadway, D C, Blickle, G, Liu, Y, Atay, S, Zettler, I, Solga, J, Noethen, D & Ferris, G R (2012) Measure invariance of the Political Skill Inventory (PSI) across five cultures, *International Journal of Cross Culture Management*, 12(2), 171–191.

Magee, J C & Frasier, C W (2014) Status and power: The principal inputs to influence for public managers, *Public Administration Review*, 74(3), 291–433.

Magee, J C (2009) Seeing power in action: The roles of deliberation, implementation, and action in inferences of power, *Journal of Experimental Social Psychology*, 45(1), 1–14. https://doi.org/10.1016/j.jesp.2008.06.010 (archived at https://perma.cc/A9QR-88HD).

Magee, J C & Galinsky, A D (2008) Social Hierarchy: The Self-Reinforcing Nature of Power and Status, *Academy of Management Annals*, 2(1), 351–398. doi:10.5465/19416520802211628 (archived at https://perma.cc/7ZGD-G469).

Magee J C, Galinsky A D, Gruenfeld D H (2007) Power, propensity to negotiate, and moving first in competitive interactions, *Personality and Social Psychology Bulletin*, 33, 200–212.

Marr, J C & Thau, S (2014) Falling from great (and not-so-great) heights: How initial status position influences performance after status loss, *Academy of Management Journal*, 57(1), 223–248. https://doi.org/10.5465/amj.2011.0909 (archived at https://perma.cc/AHT2-UCPN).

Overbeck, J R & Bernadette, P (2006) Powerful perceivers, powerless objects: Flexibility of powerholders' social attention, *Organizational Behavior and Human Decision Processes*, 99(2), 227–243.

Postma, N (2021) *You can't sit out office politics*, Harvard Business Review.

Smith, P K & Trope, Y (2006) You focus on the forest when you're in charge of the trees: Power priming and abstract information processing, *Journal of Personality and Social Psychology*, 90(4), 578–596. https://doi.org/10.1037/0022-3514.90.4.578 (archived at https://perma.cc/2Y2W-8ERW).

Tocher, N, Oswald, S L, Shook, C L, Adams, G (2012) Entrepreneur political skill and new venture performance: extending the social competence perspective, *Entrepreneurship & Regional Development*, 24:5–6, 283–305. https://doi.org/10.1080/08985626.2010.535856 (archived at https://perma.cc/8VHN-N8QP).

Tost, L P, Francesca, G. & Larrick, R (2012) Power, competitiveness, and advice taking: Why the powerful don't listen, *Organizational Behavior and Human Decision Processes*, 117(1), 53–65.

Treadway, D C, Hochwarter, W A, Kacmar, C J & Ferris, G R (2005) Political will, political skill and political behavior, *Journal of Organizational Behavior*, 26(3), 229–245.

Treadway, D C, Hochwarter, W, Ferris, G R, Kacmar, C J, Douglas, C, Ammeter, A P (2004) Leader political skill and employee reactions, *Leadership Quarterly*, 15, 493–513.

Trope, Y & Liberman, N (2000) Temporal construal and time-dependent changes in preference, *Journal of Personality and Social Psychology*, 79(6), 876–889. doi:10.1037//0022-3514.79.6.876 (archived at https://perma.cc/UP47-RLAY).

Wee, E X M, Derfler-Rozin, R & Carson Marr, J (2023) Jolted: How task-based jolts disrupt status conferral by impacting higher and lower status individuals' generosity, *Journal of Applied Psychology*, 108(5), 750–772.

Wyatt, M, Doldor, E & Tresh, F (2022) To be or not to be political? Racialized cognitive scripts and political motivation, *Human Relations*, 001872672210836. doi: 10.1177/00187267221083660/ASSET/IMAGES/LARGE/10.1177_00187267221083660-FIG2.JPEG (archived at https://perma.cc/25NG-DA9G).

Ziemianski, P (2021) Identifying and mitigating the negative effects of power in organization, *Journal of Applied Social Science*, 16(1), 140–159.

Leadership styles 06

- Evolution of leadership theory
  - o Trait approach
    - − Criticism and application of trait approach
  - o Behavioural approach
    - − Ohio State University Studies
    - − The University of Michigan Studies
    - − Black and Mouton's managerial grid
    - − Criticism and application of the behavioural approach
  - o Contingency approach
    - − Fiedler's contingency model
    - − House and Mitchell's Goal Path Theory
    - − Hersey and Blanchard's Situational Leadership
    - − Leader–Member Exchange Theory
    - − Criticism and application of the contingency approach
- Burns' transformational vs. transactional leadership
- Women in leadership

According to the McKinsey & Company 2021 Global Survey, leadership is considered the most critical area for companies to focus on when it comes to enhancing their skills. Additionally, leadership plays a crucial role in the daily lives of employees. Exceptional managers act as coaches, guiding individuals towards success. They excel in clear communication, offering support and advocacy for their team members and fostering an environment that promotes innovation and collaboration. Likewise, according to Gallup, leaders significantly impact employee engagement within the company. When employees firmly trust their organization's leadership, their engagement levels increase fourfold. Similarly, employees who strongly believe leaders provide clarity on how present changes will shape the organization's future are 7.5 times more likely to feel connected to their company's culture. Furthermore, effective communication between leadership and the rest of the organization reduces the likelihood of employees feeling burnt out by 73 per cent.

But what exactly is leadership? In essence, leadership encompasses guiding and inspiring others towards achieving common goals. As times change, the needs and expectations of leader change. By studying leadership evolution, we gain insights into the shifts in leadership styles, approaches and best practices that have emerged over time.

Group discussion

Choose a leader that inspires you and describe how you perceive this person's leadership. Think about the following questions:

- How did the leader influence others?
- What traits does this leader have?
- What behaviours does this leader exhibit?
- Does this leader lead the same throughout or act depending on the situation? Try to describe the situation the leader faced in as much detail as possible.

What is leadership?

Definition of leadership

The definition of leadership has evolved with time. From the earlier view of leaders, where leaders are viewed as dominating and centralization of power (1900–1929), traits of leaders (1930s), behaviours of leaders (1960s), to a more situational view of leaders (Zhu et al, 2019; Northouse, 2010). In essence, there are four key components of leadership (Northouse, 2010):

- Leadership is a process: it involves ongoing activities where leaders engage in the behaviours and decisions to guide and direct their team or organization, and the leaders are also affected by their team.
- The influence exerted by the leader: the ability of individuals to influence and inspire others towards a set of goals.
- Leadership occurs in a group: leadership is not a solo endeavour but involves a group of individuals and occurs in a group context.
- Pursuing a shared goal: effective leadership involves aligning the efforts of individuals towards a common goal or purpose.

In this view, leadership can be defined as a dynamic process in which individuals exert influence to guide and inspire a collective effort towards attaining a shared objective.

Followership

The concept of followership emerged as a significant aspect within the realm of leadership research, complementing the dynamic nature of leadership itself. Followership refers to the voluntary alignment of individuals or groups with a leader, where they willingly embrace the leader's guidance, direction and influence. The active participation and contribution of followers are vital elements in the intricate dynamics of leadership.

The exploration of followership gained substantial traction during the 1980s and 1990s, marking a notable shift in understanding leadership. Followership is far from passive – followers actively provide essential elements to leaders, such as valuable feedback, unwavering support and assistance. Through these contributions, leaders are empowered to implement effective strategies, make informed decisions and achieve their objectives more efficiently. Followers willingly offer their skills, expertise and efforts to contribute to accomplishing shared goals, thereby enhancing the overall success of the group or organization. Followers also have the potential to introduce new perspectives and constructively challenge the leader's ideas. This interplay of diverse perspectives and constructive dialogue among followers and leaders can lead to novel solutions, greater adaptability and increased creativity.

REFLECTION

What does it mean to lead?

Kotter (1990) distinguishes a leader from an operator/manager. Leadership and management encompass exerting influence, collaborating with individuals and striving towards shared objectives. Leaders lead, whereas the operator focuses on managing and doing. The leader mode refers to a mindset and set of behaviours where individuals embrace a broader perspective and focus on vision, strategy and inspiring others. In this mode, leaders take on the role of guiding and influencing their teams towards achieving collective goals. They have high energy. They prioritize big-picture thinking, decision-making and setting a direction for the organization or group. On the other hand, the operator mode represents a more task-oriented and operational approach. In this mode, individuals primarily focus on executing specific tasks and following established processes. Operators are typically concerned with the day-to-day activities, ensuring things run smoothly and efficiently. Both are complementary and essential to business operations.

- Functions of a leader:
    - Setting big picture and strategies
    - Engaging people through goals, communication and building relationships
    - Inspiring and energizing people
- Functions of an operator/manager:
    - Planning and managing schedules and resources
    - Organizing through providing structure and establishing procedures and rules
    - Monitoring and solving problems

Leadership and management are two distinct yet interconnected aspects of an organization. Leadership and management differ in two aspects. Management primarily emphasizes the execution of tasks and the attainment of formal organizational goals. It involves implementing structured processes and procedures to ensure efficient operations and goal achievement. This formal aspect of management is predominantly carried out within the organizational framework. Managers establish and implement strategies, allocate resources and monitor performance. On the other hand, leadership encompasses a broader scope that goes beyond the formal organizational structure. Leaders operate formally and informally within the organization, utilizing their influence to guide and inspire others. Formal leadership involves setting goals, establishing structures and defining policies. However, leadership also extends to the informal side of the organization. Everyday leadership revolves around building and maintaining relationships, inspiring and motivating employees, celebrating achievements and supporting individuals' professional development. Leaders create a positive work environment that encourages trust, collaboration and personal growth. Leaders act as role models through their actions and behaviours, influencing others to work towards the set organizational goals.

While management emphasizes executing tasks and ensuring goal achievement, leadership emphasizes influencing and inspiring others to contribute to organizational objectives. Leaders use their vision, communication skills and interpersonal abilities to motivate and align employees towards a common purpose.

Reflection questions:

- When do you work in a leader mode and when do you focus more on operational tasks? Try to be as specific as possible and list examples.

- How do you balance the need for strategic thinking and long-term vision with the day-to-day operational demands of your career?

REFLECTION

Leaders often leverage power sources to influence and motivate their followers for different reasons. There are five power sources: legitimate power, reward power, coercive power, expert power and referent power (see Chapter 5, pages 132 and 133). Followers may listen to leaders who possess these power sources due to factors such as the leader's formal authority and position (legitimate power), the expectation of rewards or benefits (reward power), the fear of punishment or negative consequences (coercive power), trust in the leader's knowledge and expertise (expert power), admiration and respect for the leader's personal qualities (referent power), or recognition of the leader's access to valuable information (information power).

Reflective questions:

- Recall a specific incident or situation where you witnessed a leader (or yourself) exerting influence. This could be from your personal or professional life, such as a team project, a community initiative or a workplace scenario.

- Analyse the different power sources that were evident in that situation. Consider legitimate power, reward power, coercive power, expert power, referent power, information power, relation power and any other relevant power sources.

- Reflect on how each power source influenced the leader's (or your) ability to influence and motivate others in that specific incident.

- Consider the impact of these power sources on the dynamics of the group, the followers' engagement and the situation's overall outcomes.

- Reflect on your observations and thoughts regarding the effectiveness of the leader's use of power in that situation.

- Consider any lessons or insights you gained from this reflection and how they may inform your understanding of leadership and power in future situations.

Evolution of leadership theory

Leadership can be understood as a result of the interactions between the leader, the followers and the specific situation such that followers work towards a shared objective. According to the time and the thought leadership at the time, not all three elements of leadership obtained the same weight during the evolution of leadership theory. In the early stage of leadership theory, scholars put more weight on leaders, considering the leader's characteristics, including physical (e.g., height) and psychological (personality traits) attributes. This stream of research has been referred to as the trait theory. In the mid-20th century, scholarly work continued to focus on the leader's role but emphasized leaders' behaviours. Influential studies conducted during this period, such as the Ohio State University and the University of Michigan studies, examined the impact of leader behaviours on follower satisfaction and performance. These studies identified key behavioural dimensions, such as initiating structure (task-oriented behaviour) and consideration (relationship-oriented behaviour) and their effects on organizational outcomes, providing normative advice for leaders.

In the 1960s and 1970s, scholars moved away from the focus on the leader per se to a more comprehensive view of leadership theory while considering the leader, follower and situation-contingency view of leadership. This shift was a response to the recognition that leadership effectiveness is not solely determined by traits or behaviours but also influenced by the specific circumstances or situations in which leaders operate and the character of the followers. Scholars and researchers began to explore how different situational factors interact with leader behaviours to impact outcomes.

Trait approach

The trait approach is one of the earliest leadership theories. In essence, trait theory views that leaders are born. Therefore, this approach is also called the great man theory. Leadership traits can be traced back to ancient times, with philosophers like Plato and Aristotle discussing the characteristics of a good leader. However, the systematic study of leadership traits began in the early 20th century. For instance, in one of the earlier works, Tead (1935) proposed that the following traits are more common among leaders when compared to non-leaders:

- physical appearances
- energy level
- direction
- drive
- friendliness and affection

- integrity

- technical ability

- decisiveness

- intelligence.

Stogdill (1948) classified traits into six categories: physical characteristics (e.g., age, appearance, height, weight), social background (e.g., education, social mobility, social class), intelligence (e.g., IQ, ability, knowledge, determination, speaking fluency, decision making), personality (e.g., aggressiveness, alertness, dominance, independence, creativity, integrity and self-confidence), task-related characteristics (e.g., need for achievement, need for accountability, proactivity, persistence, task-orientation) and social characteristics (e.g., administrative ability, charisma, cooperation, popularity, prestige, sociability, tact and diplomacy).

Kirkpatick and Locke (1991) state that several traits differentiate individuals who assume leadership roles from those who do not. These distinguishing factors encompass various dimensions:

- Drive. The drive is related to high levels of effort in achievement, motivation, ambition, energy, tenacity and initiative.

- Motivation. Motivation refers to a leader who can engage people to complete a common goal.

- Integrity. Integrity refers to whether leaders were truthful and had no double standard in their behaviours.

- Confidence. A leader's belief in solving problems and decision-making processes affects followers' commitments to the common goal.

- Intelligence.

- Technical knowledge and expertise.

Other common leader traits include gender, height and educational background (DeRue et al, 2011). Eagly and Carli and their team of researchers (Eagly & Carli, 2003a; Eagly & Chin, 2010; Eagly et al, 2003; Eagly & Carli, 2003b) conducted an extensive study exploring the relationship between gender and leadership. For example, Eagly et al (2003) found that women demonstrate a propensity to outperform men in leadership aspects that contribute positively to effectiveness, such as building oneself as an exemplar, cultivating trust and the contingent reward behaviours. Conversely, the effect of men's leadership is more noticeable when under management that exists within an imbalance of ownership and responsibility. Their results question the validity of using gender as a reliable indicator of leadership effectiveness. Despite observing differences in how they lead between men and women, the findings suggest that both genders exhibit comparable levels of effectiveness. As for personalities, Judge et al (2002) found that Extraversion in the Big Five model is the most consistent personality trait related to leadership and leadership effectiveness. Conscientiousness is also a strong predictor for leadership but not so much for leadership effectiveness. In more recent trait research, Zaccaro (2007) views trait theory broadly and looks at how leader attributes influence leader performance. In particular, he and his team identified the following attributes and individual competencies that will influence leadership effectiveness.

- Attributes:
  o Cognitive ability. This refers to IQ, critical thinking ability and learnt knowledge through experience
  o Motivation. One's desire to lead and influence others
  o Personalities
- Competencies:
  o Problem-solving skills. Refers to leaders' ability to define problems, gather information, formulate new understandings about the problem and develop solutions
  o Social judgement skills. Refers to the capacity to understand people so leaders can work with and gather support from followers. Social judgement skills refer to one's ability to understand followers' points of view (i.e., perspective taking), understand and adapt how others operate and organize (i.e., social perceptiveness) and communicate leaders' vision to others (i.e., social performance)
  o Technical knowledge

Criticism and application of the trait approach

The trait-based theory has faced criticism for its reliance on a predetermined list of traits to explain leadership and the mixed empirical evidence supporting the relationship between leadership traits and leader effectiveness. These criticisms prompted the emergence of alternative theories, such as behavioural and contingency theories, emphasizing the significance of behaviours and the situational context in assessing leadership effectiveness. These theories shifted the focus from inherent traits to observable actions and the ability to adapt to different situations.

Despite the critiques, trait research still offers valuable insights into leadership. While trait-based theory alone may not fully explain leadership effectiveness, it complements other theoretical views by contributing to a more comprehensive understanding of leadership. It provides a foundation for individuals to aspire to certain traits associated with effective leadership and encourages personal growth and development. It highlights the importance of specific characteristics that can be cultivated and beneficial. This knowledge helps managers enhance their self-awareness by understanding their own traits and how they can influence others. By recognizing their strengths and areas for improvement, managers can work towards developing and honing their leadership skills.

EMOTIONAL INTELLIGENCE

One significant aspect of trait theory – where scholars are concerned with a leader's capacity to inspire and motivate others and build relationships – is its connection with emotional intelligence (EI). EI refers to the ability to recognize, understand and manage one's emotions and the emotions of others. EI concerns the person's capacity to regulate stress and manage relationships effectively.

- Emotional awareness of oneself and emotions in others: leaders with high EI are more attuned to their own emotions as well as the emotions of others. They clearly understand their strengths, weaknesses, values and triggers. Self-awareness allows leaders to accurately recognize their emotional state and how it influences their behaviour and decision-making. They can accurately perceive and understand emotions, which enables them to respond appropriately in various situations. Leaders with strong emotional awareness of others can recognize and understand the emotions of others. They can accurately perceive their followers' emotional cues, body language and verbal expressions. This skill enables leaders to empathize with their followers' experiences, concerns and needs. By recognizing the emotions of others, leaders can respond with appropriate support, guidance and encouragement, fostering a positive and supportive work environment.

- Self-management: leaders must manage their emotions and behaviours effectively to inspire and influence their followers. This aspect of EI aligns with the self-management component, which involves regulating and controlling one's emotions and impulses.

- Relationship building: effective leadership involves building strong relationships with followers, promoting open communication and fostering trust and collaboration. EI plays a crucial role in establishing and maintaining these relationships. Leaders with high EI possess empathy, social awareness and relationship management skills. They can empathize with their followers' perspectives, understand their needs and concerns and effectively communicate and connect with them.

Question: Use trait theory and the EI framework to evaluate why humour is essential for leaders.

Behavioural approach

Leadership can be understood as a function of the leader, the followers and the specific situation such that followers work towards a shared objective. The behavioural approach of leadership continued to focus on the leader's role but emphasized leaders' behaviours – what leaders do. In a broad sense, behavioural scholars classified leader behaviours into two types central for leaders to influence followers to achieve goals: task behaviour and relationship behaviour. Representative studies of the behavioural approaches are Ohio State University, the University of Michigan studies and Blake and Mouton's study.

Ohio State University Studies

The Ohio State Studies on Leadership, also known as the Ohio State Leadership Studies or the Ohio State University Leadership Studies, was a series of research studies conducted at The Ohio State University in the late 1940s and early 1950s. These studies aimed to identify critical dimensions of leadership behaviour and understand how they influence subordinate satisfaction and performance. They focused on two primary dimensions of leadership behaviour, which are commonly known as consideration and initiating structure.

- Consideration: this refers to leaders who show support, empathy and respect for their subordinates' feelings and needs. Leaders create a conducive work environment by being supportive and fostering positive relationships.

- Initiating structure: this pertains to leaders who provide clarity, set goals and organize tasks effectively. They establish clear expectations and guide subordinates to work towards achieving those goals.

Leaders who show consideration by being supportive, empathetic and respectful towards their subordinates' feelings and needs create a positive work environment and foster strong relationships. At the same time, leaders exhibit initiating structure behaviours by providing clarity, setting goals and organizing tasks to enable their subordinates to understand expectations and work towards achieving them. These two dimensions were distinct and independent, allowing leaders to exhibit varying degrees of consideration and initiating structure. i.e., consideration and initiating structure are not the polar extremes on one continuum. By combining consideration and initiating structure, leaders can create a balance that addresses both the interpersonal and task-related aspects of leadership.

Littrell and Valentin (2005) examined the preferred leader behaviours of voluntary manager-level participants from the UK, Germany and Romania. They employed Stogdill's LBDQ XII scale (Stogdill, 1963), which encompasses 12 factors to assess these behaviours. These 12 factors are:

- Representation: evaluates how much the manager acts as the spokesperson for the group
- Demand reconciliation: assesses the manager's skill in resolving conflicting demands and reducing disorder within the system
- Tolerance of uncertainty: measures the manager's capacity to handle uncertainty and postponement calmly
- Persuasiveness: gauges the manager's effectiveness in using persuasion and argumentation
- Initiation of structure: assesses the degree to which the manager clearly defines their role and communicates expectations
- Tolerance of freedom: reflects the manager's willingness to allow followers to take the initiative, make decisions and take action
- Role assumption: measures the manager's active engagement in the leadership role
- Consideration: evaluates the manager's attention to the comfort, well-being, status and contributions of followers
- Production emphasis: measures the extent to which the manager emphasizes achieving productive output
- Predictive accuracy: assesses the manager's ability to foresee and accurately predict outcomes
- Integration: reflects the manager's capability to foster a tightly-knit organization and resolve member conflicts
- Superior orientation: evaluates the manager's effort to maintain harmonious relations with superiors and strive for higher status

According to Hofstede, the cultural value of Romania, German and the UK is as shown in Figure 6.1 (for more information on Hofstede's every dimension, please refer to Chapter 9: Organizational Culture, page 289):

Figure 6.1   Hofstede's culture score: UK, Germany and Romania

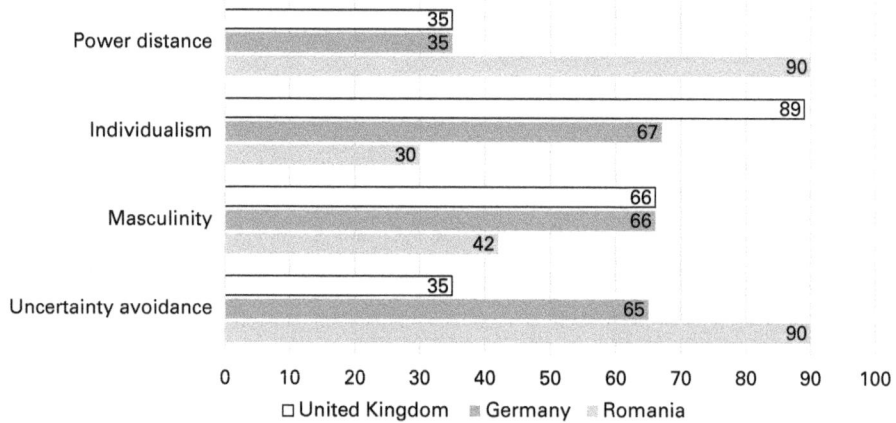

Based on data from: www.hofstede-insights.com

They found that managers from Romania, Germany and the UK shared similar behavioural preferences in consideration, production emphasis and predictive accuracy. However, Romania, Germany and the UK have the following priorities for managers, in particular:

- Demand reconciliation. Romania expected leaders to actively engage in conflicting demands compared to German and UK counterparts.

- Tolerance of uncertainty. Among the three countries, German employees are less tolerant of uncertainty than those in the UK and Romania.

- Initiation of structure. Germans show the highest preference, while Romanians display the lowest. Germans value structure and order, whereas in a collectivist, high power distance society like Romania, such behaviour may not be as necessary or desired.

- Superior orientation. This was a less desirable behaviour among the German group. In Germany, technical competence is typically more valued than company politics. Displaying this behaviour with German employees can lead to respect and trust issues.

Behavioural preferences of managers from the three countries:

- Romanian managers' preferences

    o High preference for demand reconciliation, indicating a solid emphasis on reconciling conflicting demands and reducing disorder in the system. This preference was significantly higher than that of the German and UK samples, aligning with Romania's high uncertainty avoidance score.

- o A low preference for persuasiveness indicates little inclination towards effectively using oral persuasion and argumentation. This score was significantly lower than those of the German and UK samples. This result corresponds to Romania's high power distance score, where subordinates accept and expect significant power differences, making persuasive tactics less necessary.

- German managers' preferences

  - o High preference for demand reconciliation. The German participants rated the leadership factor 'demand reconciliation' as the most desirable among the 12 factors. This finding aligns with the German cultural value of *Ordnung* (order), where effective rules, regulations and procedures play a crucial role in achieving order. Leaders are expected to monitor and enforce laws to establish order.

  - o High preference for representation. This indicated the importance placed on the leader's representation of the group compared to Romania and UK counterparts.

  - o Technical skill is the basis for promotion, not relationships with superiors.

  - o Expecting the leader to display low tolerance for uncertainty and postponement, actively addressing such situations to establish certainty and adhere to schedules (imposing *Ordnung*).

  - o With less preferences on production emphasis, employees are not expected to do long working hours. However, this could present that they are not good enough at their job.

- British managers' preference

  - o High preference for initiation of structure. This is seen as the most important behaviour of a leader in the sample.

  - o High preferences for persuasiveness. Demonstrating strong convictions and effectively utilizing persuasion and argumentation to manage and motivate the followers.

  - o Active involvement and exercise of the leadership role by the leader rather than delegating it to others within the group.

Group discussion:

1 Explore the cultural scores of your country using Hofstede insights (search online) to gain insights into its cultural values and characteristics.

2 Utilize the LBDQ XII factors as a framework to analyse and describe specific managerial behaviours, providing real-life examples to illustrate each behaviour.

3 Engage in a comparative analysis with someone from a different country to identify shared and distinct behavioural preferences among different cultures.

4 Reflect on the potential challenges and opportunities when managing a multicultural team with diverse behavioural preferences.

5 Consider the implications of these findings for management development and identify areas where cultural understanding and adaptation can enhance leadership effectiveness.

The University of Michigan Studies

The University of Michigan and Ohio State Studies focused on leadership and leader behaviours; however, they approach the question differently. While the Ohio State Studies examined specific dimensions of leader behaviour (consideration and initiating structure) and their relationship with leadership effectiveness, the University of Michigan Studies emphasized the importance of employee satisfaction, giving more attention to personal needs.

The University of Michigan Studies focused on identifying two primary leadership styles: employee-oriented (also known as relations-oriented, similar to consideration in Ohio State Studies) and production-oriented (also known as task-oriented, similar to initiating structure in the Ohio State Studies).

- Employee orientation: employee orientation, also known as relations-oriented leadership, refers to a leadership style that emphasizes building positive relationships and supporting the well-being of employees. Leaders with an employee-oriented approach prioritize the needs and satisfaction of their team members. They focus on creating a supportive work environment, fostering open communication and encouraging teamwork and collaboration.

- Production orientation: production orientation, also known as task-oriented leadership, emphasizes achieving task goals, maintaining efficiency and ensuring high productivity. Leaders with a production-oriented approach prioritize task accomplishment and focus on the efficient execution of work. Key characteristics of production-oriented leadership include establishing clear goals and expectations, monitoring task progress, planning and organization and proactively addressing and solving obstacles.

Likert's Four System Approach Combining the insight from the Michigan and Ohio Studies, Rensis Likert developed a Four System Approach, presenting different leadership approaches (Likert, 1979).

- System 1: Exploitative-authoritative. Leadership is autocratic. In this system, decision-making is imposed on employees without their input. There is little emphasis on teamwork or communication; motivation primarily comes from threats and fear.

- System 2: Benevolent-authoritative. A master–servant relationship still exists between managers and employees but with less centralization of decision-making than in System 1. Motivation is driven by rewards.

- System 3: Consultative. Subordinates are consulted over the decision and managers trust subordinates moderately.

- System 4: Participative. The participative system is characterized by trust and confidence in employees. Decision-making was made through participation.

Likert's Four Systems of Management highlight the progression from autocratic and hierarchical approaches to more participative and collaborative leadership styles. Concerning performance, Likert's study found systems 1 and 2 were the least performed. System 4 participative is also linked to better productivity and fostering good quality relationships with followers (Likert & Likert, 1976).

Blake and Mouton's Managerial Grid

Blake and Mouton's Managerial Grid, also known as the Leadership Grid, is a management tool that provides a framework for understanding different leadership styles based on the concern for people and the concern for production. The Managerial Grid is a two-dimensional grid with two axes representing these two dimensions.

The vertical axis represents the concern for people, which refers to the leader's focus on fostering positive relationships, supporting the needs and well-being of team members and promoting employee satisfaction and development. The horizontal axis represents the concern for production, which reflects the leader's emphasis on achieving organizational goals, task accomplishment, efficiency and productivity. Both axes range from low concern (1) to high concern (9).

Combining concern for production and concern for people, the Managerial Grid encompasses a total of 81 leadership styles. From these numerous styles, there are five distinct leadership forms:

- Impoverished style (1, 1): low concern for production and people. Leaders with this style are generally indifferent and detached, showing little interest in either employee satisfaction or task accomplishment. They tend to avoid taking responsibility and focus on maintaining their comfort and avoiding conflicts.

- Country club style (1, 9): low concern for production, high concern for people. Leaders with this style prioritize creating a friendly and supportive work environment and are eager to help, emphasizing employee satisfaction and well-being. However, they may need more effort in driving performance or achieving organizational goals.

- Authority-compliance style (9, 1): high concern for production but a low concern for people. This represents a top-down, autocratic approach to leadership where managers exercise strong control and authority over their subordinates. The purpose of the communication is to give task-related information.

- Middle-of-the-road style (5, 5): reflects a moderate concern for people and production. Leaders adopting this style aim to balance task accomplishment and maintaining positive relationships. They seek to avoid extremes and compromise between employees' needs and the organization's goals.

- Team style (9, 9): high concerns for production and people. Leaders with this style prioritize fostering a collaborative and participative work environment.

Blake and Mouton believe the team management style is the most desirable leadership type. However, there are situations where a more directive and supportive approach might be suitable (Van Wart, 2008).

Criticism and application of the behavioural approach

The criticism of this approach lies in its limited capacity to link the relationship between behaviour and performance. There is a lack of agreement regarding the optimal leadership style. Certain researchers propose that managers prioritizing tasks and people are the most successful (Blake & McCanse, 1991). On the other hand, others contend that there is no definitive correlation between achieving maximum outcomes and overall effectiveness in every situation (Yukl, 1994). A more recent investigation by Cho, Yi and Choi (2018), analyses a longitudinal dataset of Korean education covering the years 2005 to 2007. The objective was to explore the factors that impact academic achievement while considering the influence of family and school principal leadership style. Researchers observed that authority-obedience leadership in the school led to the best academic performance, consistent with earlier studies on Blake and Mouton's managerial grid; however, when family factors were taken into account, the influence of leadership was found to be insignificant.

The behavioural approach provides a framework to assess leadership behaviours. Although different scholars proposed different models, the behavioural approach broadly highlights the importance of the task and relationship dimensions. Northouse (2010) summarized that the strengths of the behavioural approach lie in focusing on a new stream of research beyond leaders' characteristics and looking at what leaders do in different situations. The behavioural approach also provides a framework to study leadership: task and relationship orientations.

GROUP DISCUSSION

- Provide examples from companies of your choice that demonstrate each of the five distinctive leadership styles identified in the managerial grid.
  - Impoverished style (1, 1)
  - Country club style (1, 9)
  - Authority-compliance style (9, 1)
  - Middle-of-the-road style (5, 5)
  - Team style (9, 9).
- Discuss the advantages and disadvantages of each leadership style. Consider the impact on team dynamics, employee motivation and organizational performance.
- Reflect on your leadership style and identify which of the five styles you align with the most. Share examples or anecdotes illustrating how your style has influenced your interactions with team members or colleagues.

Contingency approach

The contingency or situational approach aims to understand leadership holistically, concerned with the interplay among the leader, the followers and the specific situation.

- Leader's behaviour: scholars study the leader's behaviour, such as their task-oriented or relationship-oriented approach and how it aligns with the demands of the situation. Different situations may call for other leadership behaviours to achieve optimal results.

- Situational variables: contingency theorists consider situational variables that impact on leadership effectiveness. These variables can include the level of task structure (the extent to which tasks are well-defined), leader–member relations (the quality of relationships between leaders and followers) and position power (the formal authority possessed by the leader). External environmental factors are also situational factors that contingency theory scholars examined. These include industry-specific challenges, market conditions and external threats.

- Follower characteristics: the characteristics and needs of the followers are also crucial in contingency leadership. Scholars assess followers' readiness, competence, commitment and preferences to determine the appropriate leadership style or behaviours to maximize their performance and satisfaction.

This approach recognizes that there is no universally applicable leadership style and the most effective approach depends on the situation. The goal is to promote leadership flexibility and adaptability, enabling leaders to tailor their approaches to match the specific demands of the situation and the needs of their followers.

Fiedler's Contingency Model

Fiedler proposed that a leader's effectiveness depended on the interaction between their leadership style and the situational context. While he agreed that the leadership approach could be classified into task and relationship orientation, this theory emphasized the need for leaders to adapt their behaviours based on the specific demands of the situation and the quality of leader–follower relationships. The model also describes different types of situational conditions that leaders may face, which are determined by three key factors:

- Leader–member relations (good/poor): the quality of relationships and level of trust between the leader and the team members. Positive relationships enhance the leader's influence and effectiveness.

- Clarity of task structure (high/low): the degree to which tasks are well-defined and structured. High task structure provides clear guidelines and expectations, making it easier for the leader to direct and coordinate the team.

- Position power (strong/weak): the amount of formal authority and power the leader possesses. Greater position power gives the leader more control and influence over their team.

Not all leaders will have high position power. For instance, the CEO of a company wields high position power as they can adjust employee salaries. Conversely, a manager within the same company holds low position power even if the manager is a top performer leading a business deal, as they may lack the ability to exert control over their colleagues through salary adjustments.

The three factors made up eight situations (as seen in Figure 6.2):

Figure 6.2   Fiedler's contingency model

Situation	1	2	3	4	5	6	7	8
Leader–member relations	Poor				Good			
Clarity of task structure	Low		High		Low		High	
Position power	Weak	Strong	Weak	Strong	Weak	Strong	Weak	Strong

Adapted from Fiedler, F E and Chemers, M M (1974) Leadership and effective management. Scott, Foresman, Glenview.

So, what should a leader do in each situation? Fiedler's theory suggests the following:

- The favourable condition for the leader
  - ○ When leader–member relations are positive, the task is well-structured and the leader may have strong or weak positional power.
  - ○ What should a leader do?
  - ○ Task-oriented leaders tend to be more effective. In such circumstances, task-oriented leaders can effectively direct and coordinate their teams to achieve goals and maximize performance. The clarity provided by the well-defined task structure, combined with the leader's focus on goal attainment, contributes to their effectiveness in favourable situations.

- Unfavourable situation for the leader
  - ○ When leader–member relations are strained, the task is ambiguous and lacks clarity or structure and the leader may have strong or weak positional power.
  - ○ What should a leader do?
  - ○ Leaders should primarily adopt a task-oriented approach and minimize their emphasis on relationship orientation. While relationship-building is still essential, the focus is on task accomplishment and overcoming obstacles in unfavourable situations. By prioritizing task-oriented behaviours, leaders can enhance the team's clarity, direction and problem-solving, ultimately striving to improve performance and navigate challenging circumstances more effectively.

The other possible combinations of leader–member relationship, task structure and power position are termed moderate situations for the leader. Under moderate situations, the contingency model suggested that relationship orientation is more important than task orientation.

DISCUSSION

This discussion aims to gain insights into how leaders adapt their behaviours in different situations and the resulting impact on their effectiveness and public perception. It encourages analysing the dynamic nature of leadership and its relationship with situational factors. Reflecting on the follower's perception also allows for an examination of the limitations or weaknesses of the contingency model.

- Identify leaders: ask students to think about leaders they have observed or studied, such as managers, politicians, or historical figures, who have displayed distinct leadership behaviours?

- Identify the situation in each phase: this can range from good times (e.g., when the economy was booming), normal times (e.g., nothing particular happens, functioning as normal) and bad times (e.g., encountering a crisis, pandemic or economic downturn) when the person was in a leadership position.

- Assess the leader's behaviours during each phase: Do they prioritize tasks and goal achievement more in certain periods? Are they more focused on building relationships and fostering collaboration during other periods?

- Explore the effectiveness and outcome of their actions: How did their behaviours impact on the organization, team or society? Did they achieve their objectives or face challenges?

- Analyse the attitudes of followers (if studying a company leader) or the general public (if studying a politician or historical figure) towards the leader across different phases. Was the overall attitude positive, negative, or a mix over time? Why might this be the case?

REFLECTION

Assessing your leadership style

Instruction: Find Fiedler's LPC score online (using Mindtools or a similar website). Consider all the individuals you have collaborated with in various settings, such as work, social clubs, or student projects. Now, focus on the person with whom you encountered the most significant challenges in accomplishing tasks – someone you would prefer not to work with. Describe this individual by selecting the appropriate numbers on each pair of contrasting adjectives. Please respond quickly, as there are no correct or incorrect answers.

Scoring: add all the numbers you circled.

Your total score LPC = _____

What does your score mean?

Fiedler posits that leadership style is ingrained in one's personality and thus challenging to alter. As a result, Fiedler develops his contingency theory, which suggests that the key to successful leadership lies in identifying or creating suitable matches between leadership style and the given situation.

If your score falls at or above 73, you are classified as a 'relationship-oriented' leader. Conversely, if your score is 64 or below, you are classified as a 'task-oriented' leader. Scores ranging from 65 to 72 indicate a combination of both styles and it is left to your discretion to determine which leadership style aligns more closely with your own.

For someone classified as a relationship-oriented leader, they possess the ability to differentiate between a co-worker's personality and their subpar work performance. They believe an individual can perform poorly at work while exhibiting positive personality traits. These individuals:

- prioritize establishing positive interpersonal relations
- show a certain level of consideration towards others
- have lower levels of anxiety
- tend to get along well with their peers
- experience satisfaction from being part of a group
- find fulfilment in successful interpersonal relationships and enjoy group dynamics despite task success
- gain self-esteem through recognition from others.

On the other hand, individuals with a task-oriented leadership style link a co-worker's personality traits to their work performance. They believe that poor work performance is indicative of negative underlying personality traits. These individuals:

- focus more on accomplishing the task
- tend to be more punitive towards co-workers who perform poorly
- display higher efficiency and goal-oriented behaviour
- derive satisfaction from task performance and experience greater enjoyment in group settings when they succeed
- attain self-esteem through successfully executing the assigned task.

Reflection questions:

- What does your LPC score reveal about your leadership style? How does it align with being more task-oriented or relationship-oriented? Reflect on your tendencies and preferences when it comes to leading others.

- Reflect on past experiences where you found yourself in a situation that required adaptation of your leadership approach. How did you respond to the demands of the situation? Did you find it challenging or relatively easy to adjust your style? Based on what contingency theory suggests, explore the potential 'fit' or 'mismatch' between your style and the demands of various work contexts.

- Reflect on the limitations and critiques of contingency theory. In what ways do you agree or disagree with the notion that leadership style is relatively fixed and difficult to change? Consider alternative perspectives or theories that may offer different insights into leadership effectiveness.

House and Mitchell's Goal Path Theory

The Goal Path Theory of leadership, developed by House and Mitchell (House & Mitchell, 1974), incorporates the concepts and principles of motivation into the leadership theory framework. Goal Path Theory focuses on the leader's role in defining goals and clarifying the path to reach the goal. Under Goal Path Theory, leaders remove obstacles and support their followers. In essence, leaders are influential under Goal Path Theory when leaders give what is missing in the follower's environment and support followers to develop. This theory emphasizes the importance of goal-setting and communication in leadership. Although the theory does not emphasize professional development, it provides insights about how one can adapt their leadership style to better suit the situation.

The Goal Path Theory is strongly linked to the Expectancy Theory by Vroom (1964). Expectancy Theory is a motivational theory that suggests individuals are motivated to act in a certain way based on their beliefs about the outcomes of their actions and the likelihood of achieving those outcomes. It posits that three key factors drive people (for more discussion please see Chapter 3: Work motivation, page 56):

- expectancy (individual's belief that their efforts will lead to successful performance)
- instrumentality (a belief that successful performance will be rewarded or result in desired outcomes)
- valence (value or desirability an individual places on the outcomes or rewards associated with performance).

Leaders using Goal Path Theory can align their leadership behaviours with the principles of expectancy theory by:

- clearing obstacles on the goal path and enhancing expectancy: leaders can provide resources, training and support to increase their followers' belief in their ability to achieve the desired goals
- goal and valence alignment: leaders can understand and address their followers' individual needs, preferences and values. By providing rewards and outcomes that are meaningful and desirable to their followers, leaders increase the valence and motivation associated with goal pursuit.

House and Mitchell's Goal Path Theory considers leader behaviours, follower characteristics and task characteristics, as described here:

Four leader behaviours   These leadership styles are believed to influence followers' motivation and goal achievement differently. Here's a description of each leadership style:

- Directive leadership: leaders provide their followers with clear instructions, guidance and specific expectations.

- Supportive leadership: supportive leaders focus on creating a positive and supportive work environment, building on the Ohio State Studies. They are friendly and approachable, treating followers as equals.

- Participative leadership: participative leaders involve their followers in the decision-making process and value their input and suggestions.

- Achievement-oriented leadership: achievement-oriented leaders set high standards and challenging goals for their followers.

Four follower characteristics

- Need for affiliation: the need for affiliation refers to an individual's desire for social interaction, belongingness and interpersonal relationships. Followers with a high need for affiliation seek harmonious and cooperative work environments.

- Need for structure: followers with a high need for structure appreciate clear guidelines, specific instructions and well-established procedures. They respond positively to directive leadership styles that provide clear expectations, guidance and a structured work environment.

- Need for control: this can be internal or external. Followers have an internal locus of control, where they believe that they are in charge of the event themselves. Participative leadership is most suitable for followers with an internal locus of control because they feel in charge of their work. On the other hand, when followers have external locus of control – where external factors determine their life, followers prefer directive leadership.

- Self-perception of ability: self-perception of ability refers to an individual's belief in their competence and capability to accomplish tasks. Directive leadership becomes obsolete and may be perceived as overbearing when followers are confident in their ability to perform tasks.

When considering task structure, Goal Path Theory suggests the following:

- A relationship-oriented leadership style is preferred for structured, repetitive mundane tasks – i.e., a supportive leadership style.

- For ambiguous, unclear rules and structure and complex tasks: task-oriented leadership style – directive leadership is favoured due to its ability to offer guidance and establish a structured framework for followers.

- For ambiguous tasks: participative and achievement-oriented leadership styles are highly valued. Participative leaders contribute to task clarity, facilitate understanding of cause-and-effect relationships and empower followers through autonomy. On the other hand, achievement-oriented leaders inspire and challenge followers by setting high standards for tasks, fostering confidence in their ability to achieve goals.

Hersey and Blanchard's Situational Leadership

Situational Leadership, developed by Hersey and Blanchard (Hersey & Blanchard, 1988), proposes that effective leadership should adapt to the developmental stages of followers. The theory suggests that leaders vary their leadership style based on the followers' level of readiness or maturity to accomplish a specific task or goal. In Situational Leadership Theory, directive behaviour and supportive behaviour are two key components of leadership styles based on the readiness level of followers.

- Directive behaviour:
  o High level: in a high directive behaviour approach, leaders provide specific instructions and clear expectations and closely supervise their followers. The leader takes a more authoritative role, making decisions and guiding the followers' actions. This style is suitable when followers have low readiness or competence levels and require more guidance and structure.

  o Low level: in a low directive behaviour approach, leaders give more autonomy to their followers. They provide less specific instructions and allow followers to take more responsibility for their work. This style is appropriate when followers have a higher readiness level and are more competent and independent.

- Supportive behaviour:
  o High level: in a high supportive behaviour approach, leaders focus on building positive relationships, providing emotional support and facilitating open communication with their followers. They show empathy, listen actively and create a supportive work environment. This style is beneficial when followers have low confidence or low commitment levels and need encouragement and reassurance.

  o Low level: in a low supportive behaviour approach, leaders rely less on emotional support and focus more on task-related aspects. They expect followers to be self-reliant and make decisions independently. This style suits followers with higher confidence and commitment levels and requires less emotional support.

According to the Situational Leadership model, there are therefore four distinct leadership styles:

- Directing style: high directive, low supportive
  o The leader takes charge, gives clear directions and closely monitors the task's progress, providing minimal emotional support or encouragement.
- Coaching style: high directive, high supportive
  o Leaders prioritize attaining goals while also addressing the socioemotional needs of individuals.
- Supporting style: low directive, high supportive
  o Leaders adopting this style focus on building positive relationships and creating a supportive work environment, providing emotional support and listening actively to their followers.

o They encourage collaboration, empower followers and act as a resource for guidance, fostering higher confidence and commitment.

- Delegating style: low directive, low supportive

    o In this style, leaders delegate responsibility and decision-making authority to their followers, allowing them to take ownership of their work and make independent decisions.

    o The leader provides minimal guidance and support, trusting the followers' competence and commitment to accomplish the tasks.

Development level of followers   The second part of situational leadership concerns the development level of followers. Development level refers to the follower's technical capacity and commitment to high competence and confidence in performing tasks. Leader and employees can work independently with minimal support. Employees at the low development level exhibit low competence and confidence in performing tasks and will require direction, guidance and support from the leader to complete tasks effectively.

Leader–Member Exchange Theory

Central to the Leader–Member Exchange Theory (LMX) is the dyadic relationship between leader and followers. The leader and follower interact in the dyadic relationship, including communication, collaboration, influence and support. The LMX model highlights the differentiated and personalized nature of leader–follower relationships. 'In-group' refers to a subgroup of followers who have developed a close and high-quality relationship with their leader. In-group members tend to perceive the problem the same way. In the in-group, leaders tend to provide more communication and support. A more formal and transactional approach characterizes out-group relationships. Leaders have limited interaction and fewer personalized exchanges with followers in the out-group, whereas followers typically focus on fulfilling their job responsibilities and generally disengage from work after completing their tasks. In summary, LMX theory suggests that leaders have different relationships with employees.

Whether someone is seen as part of the 'in-group' or 'out-group' depends on how effectively they collaborate with leaders and fellow team members. If they work well together and provide mutual support, they're likely considered part of the 'in-group.' Additionally, if followers are open to taking on extra responsibilities beyond their assigned roles, it can influence their standing within the group (Northouse, 2010). Harris, Wheeler and Kacmar (2009) found that in-group members view competence as the reason they are the in-group members, whereas out-group counterparts may view it as favouritism and politics.

Graen and Uhl-Bien (1995) proposed a leadership making model to describe the process where the relationship between leader and followers unfolds. Three stages in leader-fellowship development are strangers, acquaintances and maturity.

- Strangers: in the initial stage, leaders and followers are considered strangers. Communication is typically focused on task-related matters and there is minimal personal or social exchange. During this phase, some socio-exchanges were made – either party could offer this and the relationship progressed to the acquaintance stage. For example, leaders and followers may initiate career-related socio-exchange by demonstrating supportive behaviours (e.g., appreciation and help on work).

- Acquaintances: leaders and followers engage in more frequent and meaningful interactions outside the task-related conversation. They share information on a personal and task level. Graen and Uhl-Bien noted that this is a critical stage of leadership development as a genuinely reciprocal relationship awaits development. If this is not moved to the maturity stage, the relationship is likely to revert back to the stranger's stage.

- Maturity: in the maturity stage, the leader and follower have established a high-quality exchange based on mutual trust, respect and shared goals. High levels of commitment, loyalty and support between leaders and followers characterize the relationship. The behaviours also demonstrate emotional support. Reciprocal favours can be observed and the connection is partnership-like (Burns, 1978).

Criticism and application of the contingency approach

The criticism of the contingency approach lies in its no-one-size-fits-all solution for leaders and scholars tended to choose different contingency factors to explain effective leadership style and encompass a broad range of factors. In addition, although contingency theories consider contexts such as the task structure and the level of stableness of the overall environment, these are abstract and do not specifically consider other important organizational structural factors, such as the size of the organization and the structure of the organization (Northouse, 2010). However, different theories in the contingency approach raise awareness of how leaders relate to followers.

See Table 6.1 for a summary table of Fiedler's contingency model, House and Mitchell's Goal Path Theory, Hersey and Blanchard's Situational Leadership and Leader–Member Exchange Theory.

Burns' transformational vs. transactional leadership

One of the most popular approaches to leadership since the 1980s is the transformation leadership proposed by Burns (1978). Transformational leadership focuses on change and developing a united coherent vision and direction for the followers. Transformational leadership consists of four key elements (Bass, 1990):

- Idealized influence. It is demonstrated when a leader effectively communicates a clear sense of purpose and visualizes it accurately.

- Inspiring motivation. This involves a leadership approach that addresses employees' emotional well-being, shows confidence in their abilities and effectively communicates while providing genuine feedback (Rafferty & Griffin, 2004).

- Stimulating intellectual thinking. This refers to a leader's efforts to motivate and encourage employees to be adaptable and embrace new approaches based on the changing circumstances, effectively overcoming obstacles and challenges that arise at different stages (Bednall et al, 2018).

- Providing individualized consideration. This refers to the leader's support for each follower, which may involve training, coaching, assigning tasks based on individual competence and supervising performance (Yuki, 1999).

Transactional leadership, in contrast, primarily focuses on achieving specific goals and objectives through a system of rewards and punishments. They use contingent rewards, such as recognition, bonuses or promotions, to motivate and incentivize their followers. Transactional leaders also employ management-by-exception, intervening only when problems or deviations from the established standards occur (e.g., monitoring mistakes or rule violation). This leadership style is transactional, as it relies on a give-and-take relationship centred around meeting performance expectations and fulfilling predetermined agreements.

The differences between transformational and transactional leadership vary in context, leader power base, how leaders influence followers and the result of leadership on employees.

- Context: transformational leadership is suitable for a dynamic, changing environment, whereas transactional leadership suits a stable environment.

- Power source: transformational leadership influences followers through their referent power whereas transactional leadership tends to be contingent on individual and managing-by-exception.

- Influence: transformational leadership influences followers through inspiration, while transactional leadership influences followers through leaders proactively managing followers, often contingent on rewards.

- Result of the leadership on employees: employees tend to feel intellectually stimulated and inspired and considered individuals under transformational leadership, while employees tend to be more reactive under transactional leadership.

Table 6.1   Leadership theory comparison

	Fiedler's contingency model	House and Mitchell's Goal Path Theory	Hersey and Blanchard's Situational Leadership	Leader–member Exchange Theory
Key focus	• Leader and context • A leader's effectiveness depends on how his style matches the situation	• Leader and context • Vroom's expectancy theory	• Leader and context • Leaders adapt their style to fit the situation	• Leader and follower • Process focus
Assumptions	• The leadership style is fixated and challenging to change • Leadership style needs to match the situation	• Leaders' role in influencing employee motivation	• Leaders are flexible in their approach to treating employees	• A leader does not treat followers the same way
Core dimensions	Situation favourableness is determined by: • Leader–member relations • Task structure • Position power	• Leadership style to remove obstacles to reaching the goal	• Directive behaviour • Supportive behaviour	• In-group • Out-group

Leader behaviours	• Task orientation • Relationship orientation	• Directive • Supportive • Participative • Achievement oriented	• Directing • Coaching • Supporting • Delegating	• Preferential treatment in the level of communication, feedback and support provided
Followers' characteristics	• Leader–member relations (good vs. poor)	• Need for affiliation • Need to structure • Need for control	• Competence • Level of commitment	• Willingness to go beyond their job description. • Level of exchange with leaders. • Self-interests or group interests
Situational factors	Situation favourableness	• Task characteristics • Organization authority system	• Development level of followers	• Work characteristics • Organizational context

Based on: 'The LPC Questionnaire,' in Improving Leadership Effectiveness by Fiedler, F E & Chemers, M M

WHAT DOES TRANSFORMATION LEADERSHIP LOOK LIKE NOW?

Gonzalez and colleagues (2022) examined the attributes of the transformative leaders in Bhutan, Lao People's Democratic Republic and Nepal, where the leaders promoted greater gender equality and social inclusion. Given the deep-rooted social norms and institutional barriers (e.g., policy), this is a difficult challenge for these leaders. They interviewed 19 leaders (nine female leaders and ten male leaders). Their result showed that transformative leaders demonstrate the following qualities:

- Personal values and traits: the data showed compelling evidence of strong social justice, feminist values and strong learning orientations among the leaders.

- Leadership style: focusing on creating buy-in. Leaders adopted a collaborative approach where they were actively involved and gave voice to their followers. They built consensus and convinced others to see the importance of gender equality and social inclusion in their work.

- Actions: leaders' actions were diverse but driven by their personal values and traits, showing integrity. Some activities can be symbolic (e.g., building a breastfeeding room in the government office), while others include awareness building, training initiatives (e.g., mentorship) and proactively incorporating not only women but everyone in the conversation.

- The outcome of their actions: while quantifying the results of this continuous endeavour poses challenges, participants have observed certain advancements, such as diminished negative perceptions associated with female leaders, increased recognition of gender equality and notable shifts in societal norms and national policy formulation.

To empower transformative leaders to enact transformation effectively, this study identified crucial factors such as individual attributes, leadership style and leaders' actions that contribute to their success. These include heightened support in professional and personal domains, knowledge acquisition and continuous learning through education, academic qualifications and mentorships. Personal experiences of facing disadvantages directly or indirectly serve as catalysts, providing direction and motivation for individuals to become transformative leaders.

Women in leadership

Women are underrepresented in leadership and management roles. According to the 2022 Deloitte Women in the Board Report, which analysed data from 51 countries and over 176,340 directorships, women represent 19.7% of board positions. On average, women have a tenure of 5.1 years on boards, shorter than men's average tenure (7.6 years). Here are some of the figures:

- Women on board world average: 19.7%
  - North America: 24.3%
  - Caribbean: 18%
  - Latin and South America: 10.4%
  - Africa: 30%
  - Europe: 30.7%
  - Middle East and North Africa: 10.2%
  - Asia: 11.7%
  - Australasia: 29.9%
- Women in the C-suite world average: 5.0% CEOs, 15.7% CFOs
  - North America: 5.6% CEOs, 13.5% CFOs
  - Caribbean: 4.2% CEOs, 15.2% CFOs
  - Latin and South America: 1.6% CEOs, 7.1% CFOs
  - Africa: 7% CEOs, 22.7% CFOs
  - Europe: 6.7% CEOs, 15.8% CFOs
  - Middle East and North Africa: 1.6% CEOs, 7.7% CFOs
  - Asia: 4.1% CEOs, 19.8% CFOs
  - Australasia: 5.7% CEOs, 15.7% CFOs

Appointing women to boards not only increases gender inclusivity but also increases the participation of ethnic minorities (Vinnicombe & Tessaro, 2023). So what is inclusion? Shore and colleagues (2011) provide a two-by-two framework where inclusive practices are conceptualized by the level of belongingness and uniqueness.

- Inclusion – high uniqueness and high belongingness. When individuals feel included, they are regarded as an insider within the organization, while permitted and encouraged to maintain their unique qualities within the workgroup.
- Exclusion – low uniqueness and low belongingness. Individuals are likely to feel excluded when they are not regarded as an insider with unique value in the workgroup. The exclusion of colleagues and the supervisor harms work attitudes and psychological well-being.
- Assimilation – low uniqueness and high belongingness. When individuals conform to the norms of the organizational or dominant culture and downplay their uniqueness, they are treated as insiders in the workgroup. This typically occurs

when individuals mimic social expectations, e.g., adopting a masculine behaviour to fit the organizational expectation of a particular job role.

- Differentiation – high uniqueness and low belongingness. The individual's unique characteristics are valued and considered essential for the success of the group/organization, even though they are not perceived as an insider within the work-group. In specific organizational environments, employees possessing exceptional and scarce abilities might not be recognized or treated as insiders.

DO WOMEN LEADERS UNDERATE THEMSELVES?

Despite that, empirical work, such as that carried out by Eagly et al (2003), suggests that, compared to male leaders, female leaders tend to possess a set of leadership behaviours that are especially advantageous in today's circumstances. However, traditionally, there are some reasons why women underate themselves because (1) women are perceived more negatively compared to their male counterparts when they brag about their success or competence, (2) women are more sensitive to negative feedback and take it personally, (3) social expectations from leaders still favour male leaders over female leaders, (4) workplace equality.

Taylor et al (2016) tackled the question of whether women leaders are more likely to underestimate themselves by looking at 240 leaders who were assessed by 1700 others (peers, colleagues and bosses). They examined different aspects of leadership, ranging from emotionally intelligent leadership, transformational leadership and leadership competence) from experienced women and men managers. Here is what they found.

- Women perceive their leadership abilities at the same level as men.
- Women receive ratings from their followers and superiors that are not lower than those given to men.

However, although the ratings were similar between women and men leaders, the research team discovered that women generally underestimated *how* others perceived them, including their direct reports, peers and superiors, whereas men did not exhibit the same tendency. They found the reason why women were under-predicting how others viewed them was due to:

- lack of self-confidence and greater self-criticism of women
- lack of feedback
- the social expectation of leaders' role is to be male rather than female.

In the meantime, women leaders were also aware of the implication of under-predicting their performance, such as lack of advancement, decreased level of assertiveness and lower performances due to lack of self-confidence – a self-fulfilling prophecy, as researchers conclude. As the solution to the problem, the authors suggest the importance of fostering a heightened and accurate portrait of self-awareness, such as through training and seeking good feedback.

Questions:

- Reflecting on the research findings, how do you personally relate to the tendency of women to underestimate how others perceive them? Have you experienced or witnessed similar patterns in your own professional journey?

- What role does self-confidence play in accurately assessing one's own leadership abilities?

- How can you develop accurate self-awareness? What models in the organizational behaviour introduced in this book can help you to increase your self-awareness and how would you approach it?

- Thinking about your personal development to become a leader or to be a better leader, what kind of peer feedback could assist you in portraying a more accurate self-awareness rating?

DISCUSSION

Franczak and Margolis (2022) found that employees rated their company as a great place to work and a safe, friendly place when more female employees are in leadership roles. Given that female leaders are underrepresented, they propose several ways to promote gender inclusivity, including:

- rethinking the hiring and recruiting criteria
- re-examining leadership competence
- shifting culture
- establishing diversity goals and making the number visible
- mentorship.

Question: look at the list and critically assess the practicality of approach methods in your context. Do you think this may work? What challenges or barriers might arise when using the above-suggested strategy to promote gender equality?

Chapter summary

The chapter then delves into the evolution of leadership theory, starting with the trait approach. It examines the criticism and application of the trait approach, highlighting its limitations in fully capturing the complexities of leadership. Leaders were proposed to be distinguished from non-leaders based on their individual qualities, including originality, initiative, persistence, knowledge and enthusiasm. Additionally, social traits like tact, patience, prestige and sympathy, as well as physical characteristics such as height, weight and physical attractiveness, were also suggested to play a role in differentiating leaders from non-leaders.

Next is the behavioural approach, where researchers have employed different dimensions of leader behaviour in their studies to identify the specific behaviours that set effective leaders apart from ineffective ones. Ohio State University Studies, the University of Michigan Studies and the Managerial Grid developed by Blake and Mouton were exemplary studies in the behavioural approach to leadership. Broadly speaking, the behavioural approach categorizes leadership behaviours into task-oriented leaders, where the leader focuses on achieving goals, and relationship-oriented, where leaders prioritize building positive relationships with team members. However, this school of thought cannot empirically establish the causality relationships between leader behaviour and follower performance.

A third school of thought is the contingency approach to leadership studies. The contingency approach adopted a more open approach to examine leadership, assuming that employing a specific leadership style in a suitable situation will lead to higher effectiveness than other leadership styles. Exemplary studies under this stream of research include Fiedler's Contingency Model, which emphasizes the interaction between leadership style and situational factors. It further explores House and Mitchell's Goal Path Theory and Hersey and Blanchard's Situational Leadership, shedding light on their significance in understanding leadership in diverse situations. The Leader–Member Exchange Theory is also discussed, emphasizing the importance of leader–follower dyadic relationships.

The chapter concludes by exploring Burns' Transformational vs. Transactional Leadership, focusing on the distinction between these two leadership styles and their impact on organizational outcomes. Finally, the chapter looks at women in leadership and the Shore and colleagues model in promoting an inclusive work environment.

Chapter review questions

- How would you define leadership? Explain the importance of understanding both leadership and followership in the context of organizational dynamics.

- Discuss the various forms of power that leaders can possess and how they influence their followers. Provide examples to illustrate each form of power.
- What are the assumptions, similarities and differences among the traits, behaviour and contingency approaches of leadership?
- What are the two main categories of leader behaviours based on a behavioural approach to leadership?
- Collectively, how did the trait, behavioural and contingency leadership approaches inform about what being an effective leader means?
- Describe inclusiveness, using Shore et al's model.

Key terms

Leadership

Followership

Operator vs. manager

Trait approach

Emotional intelligence

Behavioural approach

Ohio State University leadership study

Consideration

Initiating structure

University of Michigan leadership studies

Relation oriented

Production oriented

Likert's four system approach

Exploitative-authoritative

Benevolent-authoritative

Consultative

Participative

Contingency approach

Blake and Mouton's Managerial Grid

Fiedler's contingency model

House and Mitchell's goal path theory

Directive leadership

Supportive leadership

Participative leadership

Achievement-oriented leadership

Need for affiliation

Need for structure

Need for control

Self-perception of ability

Hersey and Blanchard's situational leadership

Transactional leadership

Transformational leadership

Leader–member exchange theory

Level of belongingness

Level of uniqueness

Inclusion

Exclusion

Assimilation

Differentiation

Further reading

Ethical leadership

Brown-, M E & Treviño, L K (2006) Ethical leadership: A review and future directions, *Leadership Quarterly*, 17, 595–616. doi.org/10.1016/j.leaqua.2006.10.004 (archived at https://perma.cc/6MW4-ASMK).

Lawton, A & Páez, I (2015) Developing a Framework for Ethical Leadership, *Journal of Business Ethics*, 130, 639–649. doi.org/10.1007/s10551-014-2244-2 (archived at https://perma.cc/8GSA-J5M3).

Hassan S, Kaur P, Muchiri M et al (2023) Unethical Leadership: Review, Synthesis and Directions for Future Research, *Journal of Business Ethics*, 183, 511–550. doi.org/10.1007/s10551-022-05081-6 (archived at https://perma.cc/786G-PFMA).

Digital leadership

Cortellazzo L, Bruni, E & Zampieri, R (2019) The Role of Leadership in a Digitalized World: A Review, *Frontiers in Psychology*, 10, 456340. doi.org/10.3389/fpsyg.2019.01938 (archived at https://perma.cc/E4QG-ZKDJ).

This paper examines the intersection between leadership and digitalization, analysing studies across various social science disciplines, such as management and psychology. The paper identifies key themes related to e-leadership, digital tools, ethical considerations and social movements. The findings underscore the vital role of leaders in fostering a digital culture, emphasizing the need for building relationships with diverse stakeholders and facilitating collaborative processes in complex environments. Additionally, ethical concerns are highlighted as crucial for leaders to address.

CEO Genome project (https://ceogenome.com/)

The CEO Genome Project by ghSMART is a research initiative to identify the key factors that set successful CEOs apart. It challenges the notion of the stereotypical 'great man' CEO and highlights the significance of certain traits and behaviours in driving leadership effectiveness. The CEO Genome Project emphasizes that successful CEOs possess a combination of these behaviours rather than conforming to stereotypes or relying solely on educational backgrounds. It highlights the importance of decisiveness, engagement, adaptability and reliability in driving CEO effectiveness. The four key behaviours are:

- Swift decision: Successful CEOs are characterized by their ability to make decisions quickly. They found that being decisive is more important than always making the perfect decision.

- Engaging for impact: Effective CEOs prioritize engaging and influencing stakeholders to gain buy-in and align them towards achieving business goals.

- Adapting proactively: They dedicate a significant portion of their time to long-term thinking, gather information from diverse sources and promptly respond to early indications of change. They perceive setbacks as opportunities for growth and modify their approaches accordingly.

- Delivering reliably: They set realistic expectations, establish strong organizational systems and surround themselves with capable teams.

References

Bass, B M (1990) From transactional to transformational leadership: learning to share the vision, *Organizational Dynamics*, 18(3), 19–31.

Bednall, T C, Rafferty, A E, Shipton, H, Sanders, K & Jackson, J C (2018) Innovative behaviour: How much transformational leadership do you need?, *British Journal of Management*, 29(4), 796–816.

Blake, R R & McCanse, A (1991) *Leadership dilemmas – grid solutions*, Gulf Publishing Company, Houston, TX.

Brown, M E & Treviño, L K (2006) Ethical leadership: A review and future directions *Leadership Quarterly*, 17, 595–616. doi: 101016/jleaqua200610004.

Burns, J M (1978) *Leadership*, Harper & Row, New York, NY.

Cho, K W, Yi, S H & Choi, S O (2018) Does Blake and Mouton's managerial grid work?: The relationship between leadership type and organization performance in South Korea, *International Review of Public Administration*, 23(2), 103–118. doi: 10.1080/12294659. 2018.1471029 (archived at https://perma.cc/JV6K-BHMZ).

DeRue, D S, Nahrgang, J D, Wellman, N & Humphrey, S E (2011) Trait and behavioral theories of leadership: An integration and meta-analytic test of their relative validity, *Personnel Psychology*, 64, 7–52.

Eagly, A, Johannesen-Schmidt, M C & van Engen, M L (2003) Transformational, transactional and laissez-faire leadership styles: A meta-analysis comparing women and men, *Psychological Bulletin*, 129(4), 569–591.

Eagly, A H & Carli, L L (2003a) Finding gender advantage and disadvantage: Systematic research integration is the solution, *The Leadership Quarterly*, 14(6), 851–859 doi: 10.1016/J.LEAQUA.2003.09.003 (archived at https://perma.cc/MY3J-RZKQ).

Eagly, A H & Carli, L L (2003b) The female leadership advantage: An evaluation of the evidence, *Leadership Quarterly*, 14(6), 807–834 doi: 10.1016/J.LEAQUA.2003.09.004 (archived at https://perma.cc/93ZN-KX3H).

Eagly, A H & Chin, J L (2010) Diversity and leadership in a changing world, *American Psychologist*, 65(1), 216–224.

Franczak, J & Margolis, J (2022) Women and great places to work: Gender diversity in leadership and how to get there, *Organizational Dynamics*, 51(4), 100913 doi:10.1016/ J.ORGDYN.2022.100913 (archived at https://perma.cc/79S6-V8JG).

Gallup(nd) *Leadership Effectiveness: How to Be a Better Leader*, www.gallupcom/ cliftonstrengths/en/356072/how-to-be-better-leaderaspx (archived at https://perma.cc/ V62H-R2Z7).

Gonzalez, D, Carrard, N, Chhetri, A, Somphongbouthakanh, P, Choden, T, Halcrow, G, Budhathoki, R, Wangchuk, U & Willetts, J (2022) Qualities of transformative leaders in WASH: A study of gender-transformative leadership during the COVID-19 pandemic, *Frontiers in Water*, 4, 1050103. doi:10.3389/FRWA.2022.1050103/BIBTEX.

Graen, G B & Uhl-Bien, M (1995) Relationship-based approach to leadership: Development of leader-member exchange (LMX) theory of leadership over 25 years: Applying a multi-level multi-domain perspective, *The Leadership Quarterly*, 6(2), 219–247. doi:10.1016/1048-9843(95)90036-5 (archived at https://perma.cc/ENT4-BSP2).

Harris, K J, Wheeler, A R & Kacmar, K M (2009) Leader-member exchange and empowerment: Direct and interactive effects on job satisfaction, turnover intentions and performance, *The Leadership Quarterly*, 20(3), 371–382.

Hassan, S, Kaur, P, Muchiri, M, Ogbonnaya, C & Dhir, A (2022) Unethical leadership: Review, synthesis and directions for future research, *Journal of Business Ethics 2022*, 183(2), 511–550 doi:10.1007/S10551-022-05081-6 (archived at https://perma.cc/E5GQ-PAST).

Hersey, P & Blanchard, K (1988) *Management and Organizational Behavior*, Prentice-Hall, Englewood Cliffs, NJ.

House, R J & Mitchell, T R (1974) Path-goal theory of leadership, *Contemporary Business*, 3, 81–98.

Judge, T A, Bono J E, Ilies, R & Gerhardt, M W (2002) Personality and leadership: A qualitative and quantitative review, *Journal of Applied Psychology*, 87(4), 765–780. doi:10.1037/0021-9010.87.4.765 (archived at https://perma.cc/Y873-QSFK).

Kirkpatick, S A & Locke, E A (1991) Leadership: do traits matter?, *Academy of Management Perspectives*, 5(2), 48–60. doi:10.5465/AME.1991.4274679 (archived at https://perma.cc/HN74-9FJA).

Kotter, J P (1990) *A Force for Change: How Leadership Differs From Management*, Free Press, www.perlegocom/book/779482/force-for-change-how-leadership-differs-from-management-pdf (archived at https://perma.cc/83T3-U74M).

Lawton, A & Páez, I (2015) Developing a framework for ethical leadership, *Journal of Business Ethics*, 130(3), 639–649. https://doi.org/10.1007/s10551-014-2244-2 (archived at https://perma.cc/RM44-K53K).

Likert, R (1979) From production- and employee-centeredness to systems 1–4, *Journal of Management*, 5(2), 147–156.

Likert, R, Likert J G (1976) *New Ways of Managing Conflict*, McGraw-Hill, The University of Michigan.

Littrell, R F & Valentin, L N (2005) Preferred leadership behaviours: Exploratory results from Romania, Germany and the UK, *Journal of Management Development*, 24(5), 421–442. doi:10.1108/02621710510598445/FULL/PDF.

Manuel Batista-Foguet, J, Canboy, B, Cortellazzo, L, Bruni, E & Zampieri, R (2019) The role of leadership in a digitalized world: A review, *Frontiers in Psychology*, https://doi.org/10.3389/fpsyg.2019.01938 (archived at https://perma.cc/KS9B-LPBE)

McKinsey & Company (2021) *McKinsey Global Surveys, 2021: A year in review.*

Northouse, P G (2010) *Leadership: Theory and Practice*, Sage, California.

Rafferty, A E & Griffin, M A (2004) Dimensions of transformational leadership: conceptual and empirical extensions, *Leadership Quarterly*, 15(3), 329–354.

Shore, L M, Fandel, A E, Chung, B G, Dean, M A, Ehrhart, K H & Singh, G (2011) Inclusion and diversity in work groups: A review and model for future research, *Journal of Management*, 37(4), 1262–1289.

Stogdill, R M (1948) Personal factors associated with leadership: A survey of the literature, *Journal of Psychology*, 25(1), 35–71.

Stogdill, R M (1963) *Manual for the Leader behavior description questionnaire-form XII: an experimental revision,* Bureau of Business Research, College of Commerce and Administration, Ohio State University, Columbus.

Taylor, S N, Sturm, R E, Atwater, L E & Braddy, P W (2016) Underestimating one's leadership impact: Are women leaders more susceptible?, *Organizational Dynamics*, 45(2), 132–138. doi:10.1016/J.ORGDYN.2016.02.007 (archived at https://perma.cc/66XM-JYZH).

Tead, O (1935) *The Art of Leadership*, McGraw-Hill, New York.

Van Wart, M (2008) *Leadership in public organizations: An introduction*, M E Sharpe, Armonk, NY.

Vinnicombe, S & Tessaro M(2023)*Female FTSE Board Report 2022, Cranfield University.*

Vroom, V H (1964) *Work and Motivation*, Wiley.

Yuki, G (1999) An evaluation of conceptual weaknesses in transformational and charismatic leadership theories, *Leadership Quarterly*, 10(2), 285–305.

Yukl, G(1994) *Leadership in Organizations*, 3rd edition, Prentice Hall, Upper Saddle River.

Zaccaro, S J (2007) Trait-based perspectives of leadership, *American Psychologist*, 62(1), 6–16. doi:10.1037/0003-066X.62.1.6 (archived at https://perma.cc/YL33-XD6X).

Zhu, J, Song, L J, Zhu, L & Johnson, R E (2019) Visualizing the landscape and evolution of leadership research, *Leadership Quarterly*, 30(2), 215–232.

Conflict and negotiation

07

- Resolving conflicts: conflict management style
- Link between conflict types, conflict management strategies and team performance
- Negotiation
  - Negotiation strategy
  - Cultural difference in negotiation strategies
- Gender and negotiation – when is gender a significant factor to consider in negotiation?

A 2019 research study conducted by Acas and the Centre for Employment Research at the University of Westminster reported that 35 per cent of employees reported experiencing workplace conflict during 2018–2019 (Saundry & Urwin, 2021).

The impact of these conflicts on employees is significant, with 56 per cent reporting stress, anxiety or depression, 40 per cent reporting reduced motivation and commitment and 19 per cent indicating reduced productivity. These conflicts also carry a substantial cost for organizations, including expenses related to recruitment, negative impacts on productivity and the time spent on formal conflict resolution procedures.

Their analysis estimates the total annual cost incurred by employers due to conflicts, encompassing their management and resolution, at a staggering £28.5 billion. This equates to slightly over £1,000 per U.K. employee annually. It becomes evident that early conflict resolution benefits both employees and organizations alike, as it can help mitigate these costs and improve workplace well-being.

Reflective questions:

- Can you think of a recent conflict you encountered in your personal or professional life? What were the key factors or triggers that contributed to the conflict?
- Reflect on your approach to managing the conflict. Did you actively seek resolution or did you initially avoid it? Why did you choose this approach?
- Reflect on the outcome of the conflict. Did you achieve a resolution or compromise? How satisfied are you with the outcome?

Types of conflicts

Conflict emerges when two or more parties find themselves in a situation where their perspectives, objectives or actions are at odds. This divergence can encompass differences in views, goals and behaviours.

Task conflict

Task conflict surfaces when team members have different ideas or perspectives on addressing a specific task, which strategies should be employed or what goals must be pursued. Rather than delving into personal characteristics or relationships, it squarely focuses on work-related content, such as project plans, strategies, methodologies or decisions. An example of task conflict will be when two team members have different opinions on the campaign's theme and messaging. One team member believes a humorous approach will be more effective, while another insists on a more serious tone. Their disagreement centres around designing the campaign, its goals and how to achieve them.

Task conflict can improve decision-making, innovative problem-solving and more favourable outcomes when effectively managed with respect and constructive dialogue. It is typically temporary, linked to particular situations or challenges and in some instances, external mediation or intervention may be necessary if it escalates or becomes counterproductive. In essence, task conflict forms an inherent aspect of group dynamics and organizational functioning, contributing to refining ideas and achieving superior results. In short, when task conflicts are managed effectively, they benefit team performance because they can:

- enhance understanding
- improve decision-making quality
- foster creativity
- increase innovation.

Greer and Dannals (2017) offer a concise overview of what leads to task conflicts. Individual-level elements like distinct perspectives, varying values and personality traits (e.g., extroversion associated with increased task conflicts) come into play. Similarly, at the group level, factors like larger team size, a diverse mix of demographics and a generally negative group atmosphere have contributed to elevated levels of task conflicts.

Relationship conflict

Relationship conflict often harms groups and can be disruptive. Relationship conflict refers to personal disagreements among team members that are unrelated to their work performance or task-related duties. These disputes usually arise due to disparities in individuals' personalities, values and beliefs within the team. An example of relationship conflict is when two team members frequently clash on work-related matters and personal issues during team meetings. They have a history of personal disagreements and find it challenging to work together due to their differing personalities and values. Their disputes are unrelated to the task, creating tension and affecting team dynamics.

The manifestations of relationship conflict commonly include antagonism, rivalry and resentment among team members, signifying the group's strained and contentious interpersonal atmosphere. Relationship conflict also frequently originates from disparities in team members' personalities, values and beliefs. Relationship conflict hinders the performance of the group because relationship conflicts typically:

- generate stress and anxiety
- consume valuable time and energy
- decrease job satisfaction
- diminish the quality of decision-making.

Similar to the antecedent to task conflict, Greer and Dannals (2017) summarized antecedents to relationship conflicts including individual-level factors such as personality, where high level of extroversion and conscientious (Judge et al, 2002; Gilbert, Foulk & Bono, 2018a, 2018b), negative team atmosphere, team level factors such as performance-related feedback (Guenter et al, 2016), diversity and demographics of the team composition can lead to a higher level of relationship conflict.

The impact of relationship conflict on team performance, however, varied. In other words, relationship conflict does not mean hindrance to performance. Research found that avoiding relationship conflict can reduce the negative outcome that relationship conflict may bring to the tasks (Behfar et al, 2008).

WHAT ARE THE SOURCES OF RELATIONAL CONFLICT IN A CONFLICT-LADEN REAL-WORLD CONTEXT?

Vaux and Dority (2020) look at relationship conflict in the construction industry, which is known to have many conflicts due to divergent stakeholder interests, the escalating complexity of construction projects, suboptimal communication practices, distinctive on-site conditions, constrained profit margins and a notable degree of task interdependence. They summarize the studies carried out across North America, Europe and East Asia; the common causes for relationship conflicts include:

- personality clashes
- communication deficit: this encompasses the deliberate withholding of information and a failure to establish mutual understanding from the outset, often resulting in misunderstandings that can intensify as the project progresses
- lack of coordination: given the highly interdependent nature of all parties involved in the construction industry, interpersonal conflict often arises, especially when multiple subcontractors are engaged. For instance, consider a scenario where subcontractors working on various aspects of a building project fail to synchronize their schedules and tasks
- working conditions: stressful, long-hour working conditions heightened the relationship conflict
- different priorities: divergent interests among multiple parties often conflict with overarching project goals, contributing to disputes. For instance, when managing subcontractors, requesting rework to meet quality standards can trigger relationship conflicts, as subcontractors may perceive it as an affront to their competence. This misalignment of interests can overshadow project objectives

Relationship conflicts are frequently recognized as dysfunctional and this observation also extends to the construction industry, as highlighted by Vaux and Dority. Establishing a direct link between overall project outcomes and relationship conflict can be challenging in complex construction projects. Nevertheless, prior research has established a clear connection between relationship conflict and individual health outcomes. For example, individuals involved in such conflicts may endure elevated work-related stress, reduced job satisfaction, sleep disturbances, impaired decision-making abilities and struggles with task concentration.

Group discussion:

- In your personal or professional experience, can you relate to any of the common causes of relationship conflicts mentioned in the construction industry? Share an example of how personality clashes, communication deficits, lack of coordination, stressful working conditions or differing priorities have contributed to conflicts in a team or project.
- The text mentions the impact of relationship conflicts on individual health outcomes. Have you ever personally experienced these effects due to relationship conflicts? How did it emerge and how did you cope with such situations?

- As part of a group activity, please consider sharing any relationship conflicts that have arisen within your previous or current teams. If possible, take notes during multiple group meetings to identify when these conflicts emerged, whether they were successfully resolved and the methods or strategies employed for resolution. Reflect on the consequences of these conflicts, both in terms of team dynamics and project advancement. Additionally, please discuss any specific conflict resolution strategies utilized by the team and evaluate their effectiveness. Are there strategies that have proven more successful than others in addressing relationship conflicts within your teams?

When does conflict become personal?

Task conflict arises when group members hold differing views, opinions or approaches related to the tasks or objectives they are working on. However, as task conflicts intensify and remain unresolved, they can spill over into personal dynamics, fostering frustration, resentment and defensiveness among team members. For instance, in a project team, differences in design preferences mean task conflict as two members debate the best approach for a software application's user interface. Initially, their disagreements were rooted in logic and focused on the project's objectives. However, as time passed, the conflict took on a personal tone. They began to question each other's competence, make disparaging comments about their respective design preferences and limit their collaboration. What commenced as a task conflict regarding design choices ultimately transformed into a relationship conflict, negatively impacting both their teamwork and the project's progress. When this transition occurs, conflicts that were once focused on the task at hand can become deeply personal, impacting the overall team cohesion and hindering collaboration.

When does task conflict become relational conflict?

- Misinterpretations of task conflicts to relationship conflict (e.g., such as viewing the comments as a personal attack).
- Depending on the team members' approach to defuse the task conflict. Task relationships escalate to relationship conflicts when one responds negatively to critique, including perceiving suggestions as personal affronts.
- Identifying task-related arguments as integral to their self-concept (De Dreu & van Knippenberg, 2005).

A Dutch healthcare organization distributed a survey of over 900 employees in the company over six months. Guenter et al (2016) found that task conflicts' impact on relationship conflicts is context-dependent. The findings suggest that when teams are perceived as high-performing, their members tend to prevent these conflicts from escalating into relationship issues. For instance, they show a greater willingness to prioritize the group's interests and make sacrifices for the overall benefit of the team. In contrast, in teams perceived as underperforming, there is a notable connection between task-related conflicts and the subsequent development of relationship conflicts. In such situations, team members' diminished sense of belonging to the team leads them to place less emphasis on team goals and prioritize their objectives. As a result, they vigorously defend their personal positions to safeguard their threatened egos. This defensive behaviour fosters relationship conflicts characterized by tension and animosity, often persisting and hindering the effective resolution of future task-related conflicts.

Process conflict

Process conflict, a type of conflict within teams, occurs when there are disagreements among team members about how the task should be done, such as methods, procedures or approaches used to accomplish tasks or achieve objectives. Among the three types of conflicts, process conflict has the most significant impact on group performance (Greer & Dannals, 2017). It centres on how work should be executed and the strategies employed in the process. When team members with diverse perspectives discuss different approaches to a task, they may discover innovative solutions and identify potential pitfalls that might have been overlooked in a more homogeneous environment.

An example of process conflict occurs when disagreements arise on how tasks should be executed or how the team should operate. Some team members prefer a structured approach to project planning, while others advocate for a more flexible, agile methodology. This process conflict adds complexity to the project's execution as the team grapples with differing views on how to manage the campaign development process.

Similar to the antecedent to task and relationship conflict, Greer and Dannals (2017) summarized antecedents to process conflicts, including negative team atmosphere, diversity and demographics of the team composition, which can lead to a higher level of process conflict. When the team has members with high vs. low power, teams are more likely to experience process conflict.

EXERCISE

Differentiate between task, relationship and process conflict regarding their nature and impact on individuals or groups using your own words.

Why is process conflict considered the most detrimental among task, relationship and process conflicts regarding its impact on team performance?

Status conflict

Status conflict emerges within a group or organization due to disparities in perceived social or hierarchical status among its members (Bendersky & Hays, 2012; Bendersky & Pai, 2018; Bendersky & Shah, 2012). Status conflict centres on issues connected to social standing, authority or perceived power dynamics within the group. It differs from task conflict, which concerns disagreements about work-related tasks and objectives, and relationship conflict, which involves personal disputes unrelated to task performance. (For more on status-related content, please see Chapter 5, Power, status and organizational politics, page 131).

This type of conflict typically arises when individuals within the group discern differences in how they are treated, valued or respected based on their roles or positions in the organization (Sauder, Lynn & Podolny, 2012; Bendersky & Pai, 2018; Bendersky & Hays, 2012; Bendersky & Shah, 2012). Such disparities can trigger emotions like resentment, competition or a desire to assert one's status. In contrast to task conflict, which can lead to productive problem-solving or relationship conflict, often rooted in personal differences, status conflict primarily involves the quest for influence or acknowledgement within the group.

As an example of status conflict, one team member who is a senior member of the department feels that their expertise and experience should give them a higher status within the group. Another team member, a relatively new addition, believes that fresh ideas and a different perspective should be equally valued. Their disagreement revolves around their perceived social standing and influence within the team, affecting their interactions and decision-making processes.

Does status order exist in a flat organization?

While status-seeking behaviours are often associated with formal, hierarchical organizations, Owens (2000) discovered their presence even in flat organizations characterized by highly skilled individuals. Project managers assume a facilitative role in these settings rather than wielding real authority for task allocation and budget control. Individuals can volunteer for tasks that align with their interests and expertise. Owens (2000) studied multidisciplinary design teams and summarized common status-related behaviours in group meetings. These behaviours include the following:

- Dominant behaviours involve actions that provide overarching guidance to groups without directly participating in task execution. High-status group members typically exhibit dominant behaviours. These actions may manifest as interrupting others, arriving late to meetings, frequently summarizing group progress and actively directing the group's focus during discussions, which encompasses steering the meeting topics and emphasizing high-status individuals within the group conversation.

- Engaging in contesting behaviours entails actions aimed at showcasing one's expertise, encompassing knowledge and skills, within the group dynamic. It is called contesting behaviour because it involves a group member highlighting their significance within the group and influencing the progression of the group task. Common behaviours associated with contesting include using specialized terminology to demonstrate technical knowledge, which may inadvertently exclude those unfamiliar with the terminology, attempting to reshape group issues to align with their expertise and proposing task approaches based on their prior experiences.

- Integrating behaviours involve individuals enhancing their standing within the group by bolstering cohesion. They primarily concentrate on the team's social and emotional aspects. These behaviours encompass complimenting others (e.g., acknowledging great ideas), willingly taking on time-consuming tasks in the group and playing devil's advocate when necessary.

Besides behaviour, he also discovered that the frequency of interactions within the group correlated with an individual's status – the more frequently a person spoke, the higher their status within the group. His research found the following:

1 Simply placing members into a titleless group does not ensure their full engagement in the design process. Some structural obstacles and the diverse interests of other group members can make it challenging to achieve equal participation, especially for individuals with low status.

2 The influence dynamics within teams can vary in context. For people with similar disciplinary training and credentials, the extent of influence among group members can significantly depend on the decisions made and implemented.

Discussions:

- How has your group experience shed light on the presence of status-related behaviours, such as dominant, contesting and integrating behaviours?

- Have you observed any specific instances of dominant behaviours within your group and how did these behaviours impact the overall dynamics and decision-making process?

- How can group members ensure that everyone, regardless of status, has an equal opportunity to contribute to the decision-making?

Resolving conflicts: conflict management styles

Effectively resolving conflicts is a crucial skill in personal and professional interactions. One valuable approach to conflict resolution is the Thomas-Kilmann Conflict Resolution Model. This model doesn't advocate for any single conflict-handling mode being universally superior; rather, it emphasizes the importance of adapting conflict resolution strategies to fit the unique demands of each situation.

This model identifies five distinct modes based on two primary dimensions: assertiveness and cooperativeness. These dimensions help individuals understand their approach to conflict resolution by considering their focus on achieving their interests versus those of the other party involved. Here is a breakdown of these two dimensions.

1 The first dimension of conflict management is assertiveness, which relates to how strongly individuals assert their interests, needs or goals during a conflict. This dimension reflects one's level of concern for oneself. Contrary to negative associations with assertiveness, it can be a valuable approach in various scenarios. Firstly, when there is an urgent need for swift results, time is of the essence. Secondly, in cases where ethical or moral considerations are at stake, taking a firm stance becomes important. Thirdly, assertiveness is appropriate when you have confidence in the correctness of your position and are committed to advancing it. Fourthly, assertiveness can offer a decisive course of action when prior attempts to resolve the conflict have proven ineffective. It is particularly relevant when you wield significant power and authority in the given context.

2 The second dimension is cooperativeness. This dimension evaluates how cooperative and accommodating an individual is when addressing the interests, needs or goals of the other party involved in the conflict. It reflects the level of 'concern for others'. In specific situations, prioritizing cooperation over assertiveness can offer distinct advantages. This approach becomes particularly relevant when no clear-cut, superior method for addressing the specific scenario exists. It acknowledges

the possibility that one's own perspective may not always be the definitive or correct solution in every context.

Moreover, when your counterpart is willing to collaborate or exhibits a less confrontational stance, opting for cooperation becomes a strategic decision. Embracing cooperation also plays a role in reducing overall workplace tensions and minimizing the number of adversaries. However, it's important to understand that while cooperation is a versatile approach with advantages in various situations, it may not always represent the ultimate or most suitable course of action.

The identified five modes varied in their degree of assertiveness and cooperativeness, as described below:

Mode 1: Avoiding (low assertiveness, low cooperativeness)

- This style involves withdrawing from the conflict, often by remaining silent or absent.
- Individuals using this style tend to ignore their partner's concerns and avoid direct involvement.
- The outcome is typically lose-lose, as the conflict remains unresolved.

Mode 2: Compromising (medium assertiveness, medium cooperativeness)

- Compromising entails each party giving up something to meet their own and possibly the other party's needs.
- It reflects moderate yet incomplete satisfaction and the approach is characterized by reducing one's demands.
- The outcome is typically a neither win-lose scenario, where both parties give up something.

Mode 3: Integrating (high assertiveness, high cooperativeness)

- Integrating focuses on recognizing mutual interdependence and seeking reconciliation.
- It involves an effort to attain win-win outcomes by addressing the concerns and needs of all parties.
- The outcome is typically a win-win situation, as the conflict is resolved to the satisfaction of all involved.

Mode 4: Accommodating (low assertiveness, high cooperativeness)

- A self-sacrificing approach, where one person yields to the other's needs and goals.
- This style prioritizes maintaining relationships and satisfying the concerns of others over one's own.
- The outcome is typically a lose-win situation, where one party makes concessions to benefit the other.

Mode 5: Dominating (high assertiveness, low cooperativeness)

- Dominating involves a selfish and aggressive approach, where one party seeks to attain its goals at the expense of the other.
- It is characterized by assertive and argumentative behaviour, with little consideration for the concerns of others.
- The outcome is typically a win-lose scenario, with one party achieving its objectives while the other does not.

These conflict resolution styles vary in their concern for self and others and their approach to achieving outcomes. Understanding and selecting the most appropriate style for a situation can be essential for effective conflict resolution.

Look at the five conflict management modes and identify the most suitable scenarios for their application. Please provide examples for each mode to illustrate the ideal usage.

As outlined in the previously provided definition of conflict management modes, maintain a log of your interactions with others over one week. These interactions should encompass diverse communication channels, including email, text messages and face-to-face conversations. Additionally, make note of any pertinent situational factors, such as the specific communication method employed (text, email, phone call or face-to-face) and the level of urgency associated with each interaction (urgent or non-urgent).

Date	Conflict managing style	Describing situation	To whom (e.g., colleague, peer, supervisors)	Other factors

Take note of your conflict management style and the specific situations in which you apply each mode. After a week, review your observations and consider the following questions:

- Which conflict management style did you find yourself using most frequently during the week and why do you think that was the case?

- On the contrary, which conflict management style did you use the least and what factors contributed to its infrequent use in your interactions?

- Considering that the context influences conflict management modes, can you pinpoint specific situational factors that influenced your selection of a particular conflict management style during the week?

- Were there any instances where you noticed a difference in the effectiveness of your chosen conflict management style? If so, what contributed to the variation in outcomes?

- In hindsight, were there any moments where you wished you had employed a different conflict management style? What motivated your choice at that time and what alternative approach might have yielded better results?

Conflict resolution: Three principles

So, what does it take for organizations to manage conflict effectively? Tjosvold et al (2014) suggested three elements to facilitate constructive conflict management:

- mutual benefits
- open discussion
- productive conflicts.

First, mutual benefits are the underlying condition to promote open discussion such that individuals will not use competitive and avoiding strategies when facing conflict. Second, open discussion helps to create productive, not disruptive, conflicts because it reveals deep-rooted differences (e.g., norms, opposing views) and implicit skills and knowledge that one will need for productive conflicts.

Open-minded conversations take place when individuals comprehend each other's viewpoints and stances, objectively assess the rationale behind these stances and strive to incorporate their ideas into solutions that are agreeable to all parties involved. For example, when your colleagues in the team are angry or throw food at you, your immediate reaction might be, 'how dare you?'. However, if we were to look at similar behaviours in a child, we often find evidence against our original belief. For instance, when a child is angry or throws their food on the floor, the parents will not directly think 'what a bad person!', 'why are you mad at me?' or 'how dare you throw the food on the floor?'. Parents are likely to search for various explanations for their child's behaviour. Open-minded discussions start with a generous attitude, proactively looking for different evidence of the actions and behaviours of someone. This can be trying to understand others' ideas, reasoning and ways of doing things. When individuals are open-minded, a more collaborative search for a good solution for all involved is more likely to be applied, resulting in a productive conflict outcome.

Link between conflict type, conflict management strategies and team performance

How does conflict type link to conflict management styles and team outcomes? To investigate this question, Behfar and colleagues (2008) conducted a longitudinal study focused on conflict resolution within high-performing and low-performing teams. Their study involved 57 teams participating in a US MBA programme, characterized by a diverse mix of nationalities, including 34 per cent of students from outside the US and an average of 4.7 years of prior work experience. Notably, these student teams were randomly assigned, marking their first group assignment in the programme. While they are student teams, their composition shares similarities with workplace dynamics, including high workloads, a strong emphasis on achieving top performance to secure future employment opportunities and tuition support, and the likelihood of collaborating with the same individuals in future projects.

Their research revealed distinct patterns in conflict types and resolution strategies across teams with varying performance levels. Interestingly, although the sources of conflict were often similar, such as relationship conflicts stemming from personality clashes, process conflicts and challenges related to time management, the approaches employed by teams to address these conflicts differed significantly.

High team performance, high team satisfaction

They found that high-performing teams where teams perform well and are highly satisfied with the team tended to:

- be mostly free from relationship conflicts

- use open discussions to reach a consensus. Interestingly, although using voting and majority rules is consistently linked to high and steadily increasing task performance, it decreased team satisfaction

- want to work together again.

High team performance, low team satisfaction

When teams performed well but had low team satisfaction, teams were highly task-focused and reported high levels of relationship conflicts. Overall, conflicts are managed. Unlike the high-performing and high team satisfaction groups that use open discussion to reach consensus, these teams use rules to resolve conflicts, using a structural way to avoid the disruptions that conflict may bring to the team. Teams in this category reported the most relationship conflict but these conflicts and tensions persisted throughout the task.

Low team performance, high team satisfaction

Equity-based conflict resolution norms are established to ensure fairness and foster inclusivity for teams with a high level of team satisfaction but did not perform. Team members genuinely care for one another and thoughtfully consider how group decisions might impact individual sentiments. Consequently, these teams tend to shy away from difficult discussions, leading to rare open debates about diverse perspectives. Process conflicts are infrequently encountered within such teams.

Low team performance, low team satisfaction

Several persistent issues emerge for teams with low team performance and low team satisfaction. These include unclear individual roles, ineffective problem identification and resolution and communication marked by tension and strain. These teams struggled to arrive at satisfactory resolutions. While team members are willing to address problems, they frequently find themselves unable to do so effectively, leading to heightened tensions and intense emotions, encompassing relationship and task conflicts. Teams tend to opt for superficial accommodations, such as trial-and-error approaches or conceding out of frustration, to circumvent ongoing conflict. However, these superficial measures often fail to address the underlying issues.

Table 7.1 provides information on the conflicts encountered by high, medium and low-performing teams, including task, relationship and process conflicts, as well as the conflict resolution strategies employed.

Table 7.1 Team performance, conflicts and conflict managing strategies

Team performance	Task conflict	Relationship conflict	Process conflict
High performance and high team satisfaction. 21 teams Preventing conflicts.	71 per cent of the teams addressed. *Conflict managing:* • Compromise to reach solid consensus through deep discussion on conflicting views. • Task-focused and respectful discussions. • Open communication.	Only one team addressed this issue.	33 per cent of the teams addressed. *Example* • Time management. • Impact of dominating personality. • Impact of lack of commitment on group process. *Conflict managing:* • Avoid problem escalation by periodically changing roles. • Address concern for work quality early on. • Adjust individual schedules to prioritize high-quality completion of group tasks.
High/increasing performance but low/decreasing satisfaction. 11 teams Teams structurally manage conflicts.	45 per cent of the teams addressed. *Conflict managing:* • Compromise and consensus were made through voting or majority rules. • Taking turns. • Voting.	55 per cent of the teams addressed. *Example* • Personality clashes. • Direct accusation. • Rude behaviours. *Conflict managing:* • Discuss and debate. • Avoid or ignore the conflict. • Unique solutions (e.g., avoid the trigger point, set rules that don't let emotion interfere with the task).	55 per cent of the teams addressed. *Example* • Time management through rules and procedures. • Workload distribution. *Conflict managing:* • Rotating roles. • Unique solutions.

(continued)

Table 7.1 (Continued)

Team performance	Task conflict	Relationship conflict	Process conflict
Low/decreasing performance, high/increasing satisfaction. 11 teams Strong concern for others. Teams put a strong emphasis on relationship conflict.	64 per cent of the teams addressed. *Conflict managing:* • Open communication but avoid deep debates on perspectives and ideas. • Compromise to reach consensus through accepting all the ideas.	Only two teams addressed. *Example* • Emotional conflicts. *Conflict managing:* • Avoid.	Only two teams addressed. *Example* • Late for the meeting. *Conflict managing:* • Rotating roles. • Different ways of working together.
Low/decreasing performance and satisfaction. 14 teams Teams often fail to pinpoint the root cause, opting for an escape from the painful team dynamics.	64 per cent of the teams addressed. *Conflict managing:* • Discuss and debate. • Consensus was reached through giving in. Problems persisted as teams yielded to avoid the discomfort.	36 per cent of the teams addressed. *Example* • Severe personality crashes. *Conflict managing:* • Open communication, but the problem persisted.	57 per cent of the teams addressed. *Example* • Time management. *Conflict managing:* • Rotating roles. • Avoid the situation. However, the problem persisted.

Based on author's reading of Behfar, K. J., Peterson, R. S., Mannix, E. A. & Trochim, W. M. K. (2008) The critical role of conflict resolution in teams: A close look at the links between conflict type, conflict management strategies and team outcome, *Journal of Applied Psychology*, 93(1), 170–188.

CONFLICT RESOLUTION STYLE AND PERSONALITY

In Chapter 2 (page 30), we discussed personality as the enduring set of characteristics, traits or behaviours. How does one's personality impact one's preference for conflict resolution style? In particular, we talked about the Big Five personality traits:

- openness to experience: a person's willingness to explore new ideas and embrace unconventional thinking
- conscientiousness: a person's level of responsibility and self-discipline
- extroversion: a person's sociability, assertiveness and comfort in social situations
- agreeableness: related to how cooperative, compassionate and empathetic a person is in interactions with others
- neuroticism (or emotional stability): a person's emotional stability or reactivity level.

Tehrani and Yamini (2020) performed a meta-analysis of personality traits and conflict resolution styles with over 5,000 participants. Their results show that:

- Openness to experience: compromising and integrating style.
  Rationale: Individuals who exhibit a high degree of openness tend to consider the viewpoints of others and are more inclined towards divergent thinking and adjusting their objectivity. It is linked to compromising and strongly linked to integrating conflict resolution style.
- Conscientious: compromising style.
  Rational: Conscientious individuals are oriented towards achieving their objectives. Consequently, their motivation may make them more inclined to embrace a compromise approach, which involves a mutually beneficial dynamic.
- Extroversion: strongly linked to compromising, dominating style and integrating style.
  Rationale: Extroversion is an interpersonal component in which people like working with individuals in groups. Therefore, extroversion may lead to greater pro-social orientation, in which individuals have some level of concern for others and desire to work with others, therefore linked to integrating and compromising conflict resolution style. On the other hand, extroversion may express assertiveness, favour being more forceful in communicating their opinions and therefore may be inclined to take a win-lose orientation or a forcing manner to win one's position.
- Agreeableness: strongly linked to compromising and avoiding and negatively linked to dominating style.

Rationale: Out of the five personality traits, agreeableness exhibits the most robust connection with compromising conflict resolution styles, given that agreeableness individuals prefer harmony. While disagreeing with the topic, agreeableness individuals may find it difficult to clarify their ground and prefer avoiding strategy to delay the situation.

- Neuroticism/emotional stability is associated with avoiding style and integrating style.
  Rationale: High emotional stability, characterized by patience and self-confidence, fosters relaxed interactions, promoting win-win conflict resolutions. Conversely, low emotional stability leads to avoidance of conflict due to feelings like anger, anxiety and guilt.

Reflective questions:

When it comes to managing conflicts, how do you typically deal with them when taking your personality trait into consideration? Are there any areas where you excel or struggle? In order to enhance your conflict management skills, here are some questions you can ask yourself to identify your strengths and weaknesses and come up with strategies to improve your approach.

- Think about how you typically approach conflicts. Do you tend to avoid them, confront them assertively or seek compromise as a first instinct?

- Can you recall a recent conflict where your usual conflict resolution style worked well? Conversely, can you remember a situation where it didn't work as effectively?

- Identify aspects of your personality that you believe can be strengths in conflict resolution, such as your ability to understand others, communicate effectively or remain composed under pressure.

- Have you ever encountered a situation where your preferred conflict resolution style clashed with someone else's approach? How did that impact the outcome and what did you learn from it?

- Think about a situation where you needed to deviate from your typical conflict resolution style. Please describe the context, conditions and reasons that prompted you to employ a different approach to resolve the conflict. What were the outcomes or lessons learnt from this adjustment in your conflict resolution strategy?

- What strategies can you develop to enhance your conflict resolution skills, considering both your personality traits and the specific circumstances of future conflicts?

Negotiation

Negotiation plays a pivotal role in resolving conflicts across various situations and is a subject of substantial depth and complexity in advanced academic studies. Fundamentally, it embodies a strategic communication and decision-making process, with the core objective of addressing disputes, securing agreements and discovering common ground among parties holding diverse interests, requirements or goals. Brett and Thompson (2016) put forward a negotiation model emphasizing the pivotal role of negotiators' priorities and interests and negotiation strategies in driving negotiation outcomes. An interesting aspect of Brett's framework is its recognition that biases may influence negotiators' priorities and interests and can evolve during the negotiation process. Factors that can impact include anchoring, overconfidence, and a fixed-pie negotiation mindset see (Table 7.2) wrongly believing the other party's preferences are the opposite of one's own preferences (Jeong, Minson & Gino, 2020).

Table 7.2   Cognitive biases during negotiation

Type of cognitive bias	Implication for negotiation
Anchoring	• Being influenced by the other party's initial offer or proposal. • E.g., When one party starts with an extremely high or low offer, it can anchor the negotiation's direction, potentially leading to suboptimal outcomes.
Overconfidence	• Overestimate one's position or underestimate the concessions needed to reach an agreement. • E.g., A seller overvalues their product's worth, resulting in pricing it too high for potential buyers.
Fixed-pie mindset	• Perceiving negotiations as a zero-sum game, where one party's gain corresponds to the other party's loss. Instead of seeking win-win solutions, individuals with this bias often focus on claiming a larger share of the existing value. • E.g., In a salary negotiation, the employer and employee may view the negotiation as a fixed-pie scenario, making it challenging to find mutually beneficial terms.
False assumption of others	• Assume that other people share the same beliefs, preferences or viewpoints to a greater extent than is accurate. In a negotiation, this can result in misunderstanding the other party's stance, potentially inhibiting effective communication and compromise. • E.g., a seller wrongly assumes that a buyer values certain product features as highly as they do.

(continued)

Table 7.2   (Continued)

Type of cognitive bias	Implication for negotiation
Unconscious biases	• There are unintentional, deeply ingrained stereotyping or attitudes towards others. • E.g., race, gender and appearances (e.g., well-dressed are seen as professional and competent)

Considering gender stereotypes during negotiation, interestingly, when gender stereotypes were implicit, women might have been influenced by the subtle gender-related expectations and behaved in ways that conformed to those expectations, potentially leading to less assertive negotiation behaviour. However, when gender stereotypes were made explicit during negotiations, women tended to negotiate more assertively, with aggressive opening offers and a greater pursuit of value than when stereotypes were implicit. When gender stereotypes are implicit or unrecognized, individuals may inadvertently act following those biases (Kray et al, 2001).

REFLECTION

• Can you recall a negotiation in which you or others perceived it as a zero-sum game, where one party's gain was seen as directly causing the other party's loss? What impact did this mindset have on the negotiation's dynamics and outcome?

• Reflect on seeking win-win solutions versus claiming a larger share of existing value in negotiations. How can negotiators break away from a fixed-pie mindset and encourage more collaborative negotiation approaches, especially when both parties have competing interests?

• Have you ever found yourself making assumptions about the other party's beliefs, preferences or viewpoints in a negotiation? How did these assumptions affect your communication and decision-making during the negotiation?

• Think about instances where you observed or experienced misunderstandings due to false assumptions about the other party's stance. What lessons can be drawn from these situations to improve future negotiations?

OVERCOMING COGNITIVE BIASES

Considering that individuals are susceptible to cognitive biases that can potentially influence negotiation outcomes, exploring strategies for mitigating these biases becomes imperative. Considering your experiences, what strategies or techniques have you found effective in mitigating cognitive biases during negotiations? How did these strategies contribute to achieving more favourable outcomes?

Negotiation strategy

Negotiation strategy can be broadly classified into two categories (Walton & McKersie, 1965):

Distributive strategy (win-lose): this approach primarily involves influencing the other party to make concessions. It employs threats, emotional appeals and single-issue offers to attain one's objectives. The negotiating party that uses distributive strategy may successfully claim a larger portion of the value, but they often miss opportunities that could have generated additional value. There are three different types of distributive strategy:

1 The initial offer was presented as 'take it or leave it.'

2 Justify the fairness of the offer by using objective standards. This is a distributive approach because using objective criteria was a way to persuade the counterpart to accept that the offer is reasonable and that they should make concessions in the negotiation. It is, therefore, not about expanding the overall value of the negotiation but claiming their best gain.

3 Anchoring first offers establishes a reference point for the negotiation, resulting in a favourable outcome for the anchor setter (Galinsky & Mussweiler, 2001).

REFLECTION

- Consider distributive strategies, where the goal is often to secure the best individual gain. Can you recall instances where you or others used tactics like threats, emotional appeals or single-issue offers to influence the negotiation's direction?

- Can you recall a negotiation where you observed or used the 'take-it-or-leave-it' tactic? What was the outcome and how did it feel to be in that position? If you were involved in a take-it-or-leave-it negotiation, how did you assess whether to accept or reject it?

- What are the advantages and disadvantages of employing this strategy from a negotiation perspective and maintaining relationships?

- Can you think of instances where you observed others using objective standards? Did it lead to a more successful negotiation or were opportunities missed for both parties to gain mutual benefits? What could have been done differently?

- When you've been on the receiving end of an anchored first offer, how did you respond? Were you aware of the psychological impact it had on your perception of the negotiation's direction?

Integrative strategy (win-win): in contrast, the integrative strategy focuses on sharing information about interests and priorities, generating higher joint gains. Using an integrative strategy tends to create more overall value in negotiations compared to those heavily relying on a distributive approach (Weingart et al, 1990). Walton and McKersie (1965) identify three ways to create join gains:

1 Dialogues to understand the other negotiator's interests and priorities in the negotiation

2 Finding implicit information about other negotiators' interests and priorities in a distributive negotiation

3 Finding out the potential mutual gain when the negotiation is multi-round negotiations

REFLECTION

Building upon the earlier reflective questions related to situations where you have used or witnessed the use of distributive negotiation strategies, let's delve deeper into how the incorporation of three key mechanisms of integrative strategies can aid in re-evaluating those prior distributive negotiation scenarios.

- Have you ever observed a negotiation involving the 'take-it-or-leave-it' tactic? How did this approach affect the negotiation's outcome and the relationship between the parties? If you were part of such a negotiation, how could integrative strategies have been applied to achieve a mutually beneficial result?

- Think about situations when you used or observed distributive strategies like threats or emotional appeals. How could employing integrative mechanisms, such as open dialogues to understand interests and priorities, have transformed those negotiations into more cooperative and value-creating interactions?

- In negotiations where objective standards were employed, either by you or others, consider how integrative strategies to create value for both parties might have enhanced the negotiation process and led to more favourable outcomes.

Best Alternative to a Negotiation Agreement (BATNA)

In plain English, BATNA means your second-best option. Understanding one's BATNA (Best Alternative to a Negotiated Agreement) is paramount for negotiators because it is a critical reference point during negotiations. Here's a breakdown of its significance:

- Making well-informed decisions. It provides a clear perspective on what can be achieved outside of the ongoing negotiation, facilitating an evaluation of whether the proposed deal surpasses your alternative.

- It informs you about whether to accept the current offer, reject it in favour of pursuing your BATNA, persist in negotiations to secure more favourable terms or not accept unfavourable terms.

- It helps you to concentrate on negotiations that hold the promise of yielding superior results while sidestepping unproductive discussions that might squander your resources.

> Note that not all BATNA is visible – for instance, power can be an important BATNA. Boothby et al (2022) suggested that power can be a way to give an alternative to the current deal. For instance, it can influence the other party to provide a better first offer and strategically anchor the offer. Individuals may likely accept an offer from someone of higher status among the pool of candidates.

Cultural difference in negotiation strategies

According to Gunia et al (2016), culture influences negotiation in three ways:

1 Negotiator's cognitive biases and interests: Individuals exhibit distinct responses to identical contextual influences (such as accountability, team composition, power dynamics and communication methods) based on their biases, objectives and varying levels of trust.

2 Negotiator's strategy: Western cultures lean towards direct information exchange, while East and South Asians often prefer persuasion and making offers. This divergence in strategy can be attributed, in part, to varying levels of trust within these cultural contexts.

3 Importance of the outcome – economic vs. relation: In controlled negotiation scenarios, specific cultures, such as those from the US and Germany, tend to excel in creating greater joint value for parties involved (i.e., making the pie bigger), while others, such as India and China, tend to excel in claiming more value for their own party (gaining the biggest slice of the pie).

Adler and Aycan (2018) identified three dimensions in the context of cross-cultural negotiations:

- Whether one chooses to maintain one's own cultural approach
- Whether one chooses to embrace the cultural approach of others
- Significance of the encounter

Similar to the conflict resolution styles, Adler and Aycan proposed these two dimensions created five ways that can be classified when thinking about how one would interact in a cross-cultural context:

- High own cultural approach, low other cultural approach: dominating, using one's cultural perspective
- Low own cultural approach, high other cultural approach: accommodating, adopting the cultural perspectives of others
- Medium own cultural approach, medium other cultural approach: compromising, crafting a compromised approach
- Low own cultural approach, low other cultural approach: Strategically avoid the issue
- High own cultural approach, high other cultural approach: creating a harmonious solution

The significance of the encounter includes factors such as the depth of the understanding of others' culture, the stakeholders of involved parties (e.g., individual organization or larger society) and the consequences of the encounter. When there are significant and enduring consequences or a need for sustainability, a more strategic approach becomes necessary and it is more important to devise a compromise strategy. When the potential outcomes are less significant, a more tactical approach can be selected and an avoidance strategy may be more suitable in this situation.

Gender and negotiation: when is gender a significant factor to consider in negotiation?

Gender issues in negotiation started with the stereotypes where women are often perceived as expected to exhibit communal behaviour and warmth, while negotiators are commonly associated with expectations of being tough, agentic and assertive (Boothby et al, 2022). Because people internalize these stereotypes, women negotiators face a difficult challenge: they need to act counter-stereotypically (Kulik & Olekalns, 2012). As a result, the important topic is not gender differences in negotiation; rather, it is to understand when gender matters in negotiations.

Bowles et al (2022) proposed a useful model to understand when gender becomes an issue during negotiation. They proposed two dimensions to distinguish the situation where gender issues are likely to emerge. The two dimensions are ambiguity and salience relevance.

Ambiguity refers to the level of clarity over the objective of the negotiation, how to negotiate, whether this can be negotiated and who in the negotiations is clear. Gender biases are more likely to occur during negotiation when negotiation situations are highly ambiguous. Three elements to consider under ambiguity are:

- ambiguity over negotiating what – negotiable elements (e.g., what is negotiable)
- ambiguity over how to negotiate – whether there is information about the negotiation norms. When organizations explicitly outline in their policies that individuals can anticipate negotiating both their work equipment and flexible working arrangements, the explicit rules affirm the organization's norms on negotiation.
- ambiguity over who is involved in the negotiation – the identities of negotiators.

This concept of negotiation ambiguity applies not only to gender but also to minorities in the workplace.

Why does gender (or minority biases) often arise in situations of high ambiguity during negotiations? This can result from individuals not even recognizing the opportunity to negotiate. For example, an exceptionally reliable and dedicated employee may not know they can negotiate aspects of their workload or request additional support to achieve a healthier work–life balance. This might involve redistributing tasks or receiving assistance. Individuals from dominant groups typically have easier access to the information – negotiating what, negotiation method, negotiation parties involved, information and resources. The gendered outcome is likely to be observed with support from their informal social networks compared to underrepresented group members.

Whether gender is relevant to negotiation can be examined from four angles: (a) the larger socio-cultural stereotypes over gender, (b) the various social identities of the negotiators that intersect with gender, (c) the demographics and culture of the organization itself and (d) the specific subject matter being negotiated. For instance, in engineering companies and the field of STEM, gender and power dynamics can be exemplified when men predominantly hold top leadership roles while women are overrepresented in lower-level positions. This creates a notable gender and power imbalance.

There are examples within different industries where there is a noticeable imbalance between gender and power. One example is the engineering industry and the field of STEM, where gender and power dynamics can be exemplified when men predominantly hold top leadership roles while women are overrepresented in lower-level positions. If the subject of gender is relevant to negotiation, it can be examined from four angles:

1 the larger socio-cultural stereotypes over gender

2 the various social identities of the negotiators that intersect with gender

3 the demographics and culture of the organization itself

4 the specific subject matter being negotiated.

Gender becomes a crucial factor in negotiations when there's heightened ambiguity and when gender is prominently relevant in a specific context. However, when the context emphasizes gender but provides clear rules, benchmarks and norms in the negotiation process, the likelihood of gender-related outcomes, while not eliminated, is significantly reduced.

REFLECTION

- Are there clear norms and standards in your workplace that guide negotiation behaviour and assess agreement terms?

- How does gender impact negotiation situations in your organization? Are there specific examples of gendered outcomes observed?

- What are the consequences of gendered outcomes on individual employees in your workplace? How do these outcomes affect their job satisfaction and overall well-being?

- How can we reduce ambiguity in negotiation situations to minimize the potential for gender biases and gendered outcomes? Use Bowles et al's framework as a guide and come up with solutions to reduce ambiguity during negotiation.

Chapter summary

In this comprehensive exploration of conflicts and negotiations, the chapter began by dissecting the various types of conflicts, shedding light on the distinctions between task conflict (on task goals), relationship conflict (rooted in personal differences), process conflict (stemming from methodological disagreements) and status conflict (due to differences in their perceived and actual status in the group). These distinctions form the foundation for effective conflict management strategies. Next, we introduced the Thomas-Kilmann Conflict Resolution Model, emphasizing the importance of two dimensions: assertiveness (the pursuit of one's interests) and cooperativeness (consideration for others). This model unveiled five primary conflict management styles: avoiding, compromising, integrating, accommodating and dominating. This offers a general understanding of common conflict resolution strategies and highlights that the resolution strategy is often context-specific, not the best individual strategy.

We then introduced cognitive biases, such as anchoring, overconfidence, fixed-pie mindset, false assumptions about others and unconscious biases, which were scrutinized for their impact on negotiation outcomes. Recognizing and mitigating these biases became pivotal skills for achieving mutually beneficial agreements. Our exploration then turned towards the influence of cultural differences on negotiation strategies. We uncovered how distinct cultural norms and values can significantly shape the negotiation process and its ultimate outcomes.

The chapter reached its culmination with an examination of the role of gender in negotiation. We identified scenarios where gender emerges as a pivotal factor in negotiation dynamics, influenced by gender stereotypes, societal expectations and established norms. To assess the likelihood of observing gendered outcomes, we adopted the framework proposed by Bowles et al. This framework introduces two critical dimensions, namely ambiguity and salience & relevance in negotiation contexts. The clarity surrounding negotiable aspects, negotiation approaches and the pertinence of gender and other contextual factors aids in identifying the potential for gendered outcomes. Additionally, it provides insights into strategies for creating less gendered negotiation situations and minimizing gender-related disparities. It's important to note that this framework is equally applicable in assessing minority-related outcomes, offering a comprehensive tool for analysing and addressing disparities in negotiation scenarios.

Chapter review questions

- Explain the differences between task conflict, relationship conflict, process conflict and status conflict. Provide examples of each.

- Compare and contrast the five conflict management styles outlined in the Thomas-Kilmann Conflict Resolution Model. Give real-life examples of when each style might be effective.

- How does the type of conflict (task, relationship or process) impact team performance? Provide examples of situations where each type of conflict can either enhance or hinder team performance.

- Describe the differences between distributive and integrative negotiation strategies. Give examples of when each strategy might be appropriate.

- Discuss how cultural norms and values can influence negotiation strategies.

- Explain why gender can be a significant factor in negotiations. How do gender stereotypes and societal expectations impact negotiation dynamics? Provide examples of gender-related negotiation challenges.

- Describe common cognitive biases in negotiation, such as anchoring and overconfidence. How can recognizing and mitigating these biases lead to more favourable negotiation outcomes?
- How do ambiguity and salience of gender and other contextual factors affect negotiation outcomes? How can a nuanced approach minimize gender-related disparities in negotiations?

Key terms

Task conflict

Relationship conflict

Process conflict

Status conflict

Thomas-Kilmann Conflict Resolution Model

Assertiveness

Cooperativeness

Avoiding

Compromising

Integrating

Accommodating

Dominating

Cognitive biases

Anchoring

Overconfidence

Fixed-pie mindset

False assumption of others

Unconscious biases

Distributive strategy

Integrative strategy

Ambiguity in negotiation

Salience and relevance in negotiation

Further reading

More details on gendered negotiations:

Bowles, H R, Thomason, B & Macias-Alonso, I (2022) When gender matters in organizational negotiations, *Annual Review of Organizational Psychology and Organizational Behavior*, 9, 199–223.

Kulik, C T, & Olekalns, M (2012) Negotiating the gender divide: Lessons from the negotiation and organizational behavior literature, *Journal of Management*, 38(4), 1387–1415. doi.org/10.1177/0149206311431307 (archived at https://perma.cc/E2DG-UHCU).

On status dynamics:

Bendersky, C & Pai, J (2018) Status Dynamics, *Annual Review of Organizational Psychology and Organizational Behavior*, 5, 183–199. https://doi.org/10.1146/annurev-orgpsych-032117-104602 (archived at https://perma.cc/GJ53-USVJ).

Emotion and negotiation:

van Kleef, G A & Cote, S (2018) Emotional dynamics in conflict and negotiation: Individual, dyadic, and group processes, *Annual Review of Organizational Psychology and Organizational Behavior*, 5, 437–464.

van Kleef, G A (2009) How emotions regulate social life: The emotions as social information (EASI) model, *Current Directions in Psychological Science*, 18(3), 184–188. doi.org/10.1111/j.1467-8721.2009.01633.x (archived at https://perma.cc/YH42-A23T).

Negotiation in the family:

Livingston, B A (2014) Bargaining behind the scenes: Spousal negotiation, labor, and work–family burnout, *Journal of Management*, 40(4), 949–977. doi.org/10.1177/0149206311428355 (archived at https://perma.cc/BY6M-WCYW).

References

Adler, J J & Aycan, Z (2018) Cross-cultural interaction: What we know and what we need to know, *Annual Review of Organizational Psychology and Organizational Behavior*, 5, 307–333.

Behfar, K J, Peterson, R S, Mannix, E A & Trochim, W M K (2008) The critical role of conflict resolution in teams: A close look at the links between conflict type, conflict management strategies, and team outcome, *Journal of Applied Psychology*, 93(1), 170–188.

Bendersky, C & Hays, N A (2012) Status conflict in groups, *Organization Science*, 23(2), 323–340, doi:10.1287/orsc.1110.0734 (archived at https://perma.cc/8YJM-CLFD).

Bendersky, C & Pai, J (2018) Status dynamics, *Annual Review of Organizational Psychology and Organizational Behavior*, 5 (1), 183–199, doi:10.1146/annurev-orgpsych-032117-104602 (archived at https://perma.cc/5AGJ-CFXJ).

Bendersky, C & Shah, N P (2012) The cost of status enhancement: Performance effects of individuals' status mobility in task groups, *Organization Science*, 23(2), 308–322 doi:10.1287/orsc.1100.0543 (archived at https://perma.cc/U7PH-FMAW).

Boothby, E J, Cooney, G & Schweitzer, M E (2022) Embracing complexity: A review of negotiation research, *Annual Review of Psychology*, 299–332 doi:10.1146/annurev-psych-033020.

Bowles, H R, Thomason, B & Macias-Alonso, I (2022) When gender matters in organizational negotiations, *Annual Review of Organizational Psychology and Organizational Behavior*, 9, 199–223

Brett, J & Thompson, L (2016) Negotiation, *Organizational Behavior and Human Decision Processes*, 136, 68–79. doi:10.1016/J.OBHDP.2016.06.003 (archived at https://perma.cc/L2QZ-MRDA).

De Dreu, C K W, & van Knippenberg, D (2005) The possessive self as a barrier to conflict resolution: Effects of mere ownership, process accountability, and self-concept clarity on competitive cognitions and behavior, *Journal of Personality and Social Psychology*, 89(3), 345–357. doi.org/10.1037/0022-3514.89.3.345 (archived at https://perma.cc/LV9M-LUJT).

Galinsky, A D & Mussweiler, T (2001) First offers as anchors: The role of perspective-taking and negotiator focus, *Journal of Personality and Social Psychology*, 81(4), 657–669.

Gilbert, E, Foulk, T & Bono, J (2018a) Building personal resources through interventions: An integrative review, *Journal of Organizational Behavior*, 39(2), 214–228. doi:10.1002/JOB.2198 (archived at https://perma.cc/BC55-DKLB).

Gilbert, E, Foulk, T & Bono, J (2018b) Building personal resources through interventions: An integrative review, *Journal of Organizational Behavior*, 39(2), 214–228 doi:10.1002/JOB.2198 (archived at https://perma.cc/F9HY-9TST).

Greer, L L & Dannals, J E (2017) Conflict in Teams. In E Salas, R Rico, & J Passmore (eds.) *The Wiley Blackwell Handbook of the Psychology of Team Working and Collaborative Processes*, John Wiley & Sons (pp. 317–343).

Guenter, H, van Emmerik, H, Schreurs, B, Kuypers, T, van Iterson, A & Notelaers, G (2016) When task conflict becomes personal, *Small Group Research*, 47(5), 569–604. doi:10.1177/1046496416667816 (archived at https://perma.cc/MPZ9-YLRY).

Gunia, B C, Brett, J M & Gelfand, M J (2016) The science of culture and negotiation, *Current Opinion in Psychology*, 8, 78–83.

Jeong, M, Minson, J & Gino, F (2020) Psychological shortcomings to optimal negotiation behavior: Intrapersonal and interpersonal challenge. In P. Lange (ed) *Social Psychology*, Guilford Press (pp. 532–544).

Judge, T A, Bono, J E, Ilies, R & Gerhardt, M W (2002) Personality and leadership: A qualitative and quantitative review, *Journal of Applied Psychology*, 87(4), 765–780 doi:10.1037/0021-9010.87.4.765 (archived at https://perma.cc/FJ8B-6YWZ).

Kray, L J, Thompson, L & Galinsky, A (2001) Battle of the sexes: Gender stereotype confirmation and reactance in negotiations, *Journal of Personality and Social Psychology*, 80(6), 942–958. doi:10.1037/0022-3514.80.6.942 (archived at https://perma.cc/N4SJ-7AP7).

Kulik, C T & Olekalns, M (2012) Negotiating the gender divide: Lessons from the negotiation and organizational behavior literatures, *Journal of Management*, 38(4), 1387–1415. doi:10.1177/0149206311431307 (archived at https://perma.cc/G8BB-H7WN).

Owens, D A (2000) Structure and status in design teams: Implications for design management, *Design Management Journal*, 1(1), 55–63. doi:10.1111/J.1948-7177.2000.TB00005.X (archived at https://perma.cc/9NG6-LRCS)

Sauder, M, Lynn, F & Podolny, J M (2012) Status: Insights from organizational sociology, *Annual Review of Sociology*, 38, 267–283.

Saundry, R & Urwin, P (2021) Estimating the cost of workplace conflict, ACAS www.acas.org.uk/estimating-the-costs-of-workplace-conflict-report#endnotes (archived at https://perma.cc/FWH9-J3WD).

Tehrani, H D & Yamini, S (2020) Personality traits and conflict resolution styles: A meta-analysis, *Personality and Individual Differences*, 157, 109794 doi:10.1016/J.PAID.2019.109794 (archived at https://perma.cc/8U85-QU6G).

Tjosvold, D, Wong, A S H & Chen, N Y F (2014) Constructively managing conflicts in organizations, *Annual Review of Organizational Psychology and Organizational Behavior*, 1, 545–568.

Vaux, J S & Dority, B (2020) Relationship conflict in construction: A literature review, *Conflict Resolution Quarterly*, 38(1–2), 47–72. doi:10.1002/CRQ.21286 (archived at https://perma.cc/2DVW-YB8W).

Walton, R E & McKersie, R B (1965) *A behavioral theory of labor relations*, McGraw-Hill.

Weingart, L R, Thompson, L, Bazerman, M H & Carroll, J S (1990) Tactical behavior and negotiation outcomes, *International Journal of Conflict Management*, 1(1), 7–31.

Organizational structure

08

AN EXPERIMENT OF NO STRUCTURE

Treehouse is an internet-based tech school providing a range of courses spanning from novice to advanced levels. These courses encompass web design, web development, mobile development and game development. The primary target audience for these courses is individuals new to the world of coding, seeking to acquire computer coding skills as a foundation for a career in the technology sector. In 2013, the company carried out an interesting experiment – a flat structure, no boss (Rogoway, 2016). Individuals have the authority to manage themselves and evaluate themselves. They do so because engineers typically want to do their 'actual jobs' – designing and implementing the solutions.

This experiment lasted for two years and then the company reverted to the traditional management structure. This no-boss approach was introduced when the company at the time employed 61 people. However, the company grew and the no-boss approach became a hindrance.

Other companies, such as GitHub – a platform and cloud-based service dedicated to software development and version control for developers – also abandoned its flat structure without management or titles (Mittelman, 2016). Founded in 2008, GitHub embarked on its journey with a unique philosophy: a flat corporate structure. This approach aimed to cultivate an environment where software developers could freely innovate and collaborate, fostering a thriving community.

However, this unconventional structure faced challenges – scale effectively and address internal issues – and they needed to transition to a more traditional corporate hierarchy. As GitHub expanded to accommodate approximately 600 employees, introducing managers became essential for better coordination among various departments. This shift allowed the company to achieve notable milestones, including increased engagement in open-source projects and establishing strategic partnerships.

Reflective questions:

- Reflecting on GitHub's unique flat structure experiment, often called a 'bossless company', consider your encounters with organizational structure. Drawing from your professional or academic experiences, share how they align with or diverge from this unconventional approach.

- Describe the organizational structure you've encountered in your personal or professional life. How does it compare to GitHub's initial flat structure?

- Explore the advantages of implementing a structured organizational hierarchy within a company. What positive outcomes or efficiencies can such a structure bring?

- Conversely, examine the potential disadvantages or limitations associated with organizational structure. In your view, what challenges might arise from a structured setup within an organization?

Definition of organizational structure

The organizational structure represents the flow of information, coordination and integration of technology, operational responsibilities and human resources, all working in concert to attain the organization's goals (Duncan, 1979). It encompasses a purposeful arrangement of human resources within an entity, strategically designed to accomplish collective business objectives. It serves as the architectural framework of an organization, delineating its hierarchy and specifying individual roles, functions and reporting relationships. Within this structure, responsibilities for various tasks and processes are allocated among different entities, be it branches, departments, workgroups or individual employees. This allocation ensures the effective and efficient flow of work and information, thereby facilitating the seamless operation of the organization.

The organizational structure serves as a valuable tool for understanding various aspects of an organization:

- Managerial titles: provides insight into the official titles held by managers
- Role accountability: clarifies responsibilities and identifies who is accountable for specific tasks
- Departmental leadership: delineates the managers overseeing each department
- Division and department identification: defines the different divisions and departments within the organization
- Chain of command: offers an overview of the hierarchical order of authority
- Hierarchical positioning: helps determine an individual's position within the organizational hierarchy

Organizational structure, while informative in many aspects, does not provide insights into the following:

- The specific daily tasks and responsibilities of a job
- The actual dynamics and intricacies of communication within the organization
- The extent of managerial authority and control over an individual employee
- The informal influence that individuals may wield within the organization

Designing organizational structures: elements to consider

The organizational structure serves as the structural backbone for both vertical control and horizontal coordination within the organization, enabling it to function cohesively. Shaping an effective organizational structure involves the consideration of six fundamental elements:

Job specialization

Defining specific job roles and tasks within the organization to maximize efficiency and expertise in each area

Example

In IT, job specialization shines in software development teams. Each role has clear responsibilities: architects design software structure, front-end devs create interfaces, back-end devs manage logic, QA testers find issues, DevOps engineers streamline processes, DB admins handle data and network specialists maintain infrastructure. Specialization boosts efficiency, but collaboration is vital for seamless software functionality.

In finance, job specialization thrives within investment banking teams. These teams comprise individuals in various roles. Investment bankers identify opportunities, financial analysts analyse data, risk managers mitigate risks, quants use math for trading, compliance officers ensure regulations, traders execute orders, financial planners advise, credit analysts assess creditworthiness and asset managers optimize portfolios. This specialization enables tailored services, enhancing financial decision quality.

Advantages of job specialization

Job specialization is a pivotal organizational concept for several compelling reasons. Firstly, it fosters skill enhancement through repetition. Employees, by routinely performing the same tasks, cultivate expertise and thereby boost their productivity. Secondly, it may lead to wage stratification, as different skill levels can be matched with complex roles staffed by highly skilled personnel and simpler tasks carried out by less skilled labour. Thirdly, when a significant volume of repetitive work is identified, it opens the door to mechanization possibilities, exemplified by the use of computers for office work. Lastly, job specialization enables the simultaneous execution of a variety of tasks. Using the above example in the IT sector, this means that software development, quality assurance and network maintenance can happen concurrently with different specialists managing each. Likewise, in the finance industry, it ensures that investment banking, financial analysis and risk management can occur simultaneously, with experts in each field contributing their specialized skills.

Disadvantages of job specialization

Despite its advantages, an excessive reliance on job specialization can have detrimental consequences. Extreme specialization may result in employee fatigue, monotony, boredom and job dissatisfaction, potentially leading to issues like absenteeism, high turnover rates and a decline in the quality of work. To mitigate these problems, school administrators have explored alternative approaches that retain the benefits of job specialization while addressing its downsides.

Alternatives to job specialization:

Three prominent alternatives to job specialization include job rotation, job enlargement and job enrichment, as proposed by Herzberg and his colleagues (Paul, Robertson, Herzberg, 1969; Herzberg, 2003). Job rotation involves systematically shifting employees between different roles. For instance, in large school districts, principals may be rotated among schools every five years. Job enlargement broadens the scope of a job by increasing the number and diversity of tasks assigned to an employee. Job enrichment, on the other hand, deepens a job by incorporating 'administrative' activities, such as decision-making, staffing, budgeting and reporting, into an employee's responsibilities. These alternatives provide mechanisms for schools to balance the advantages of job specialization with strategies that prevent its potential negative consequences.

Departmentalization

As the number of specialized roles grows, it becomes challenging for a single manager to oversee them efficiently. To manage this, roles are consolidated into smaller groups and a new role, the group manager, is created, grouping functions and tasks into departments or divisions based on their similarities or common goals. Common bases for departmentalization include functional, product-based, geographic and matrix-based departmentation, detailed in Table 8.1.

DEPARTMENTALIZATION AND CONTINGENCIES

Look at the type of structure in Table 8.1. Delving into the circumstances under which organizations opt for functional, product, geographical or matrix structures, consider the following questions:

- How does the organization's industry and competitive landscape influence its structural decisions?

- Thinking about the company size from small to medium to large, which organizational structure might be most suitable when only the size of the company is taken into consideration?
- Beyond environmental volatility and company size, what other contingent factors might play a significant role in determining the type of departmentalization an organization should adopt?

Table 8.1 Types of departmentalization

Type	Example	Advantages	Disadvantages
Functional: Group jobs based on the essential functions of the organization.	The most common type. The structures may include: • Sales • Marketing • Manufacturing • IT • Finance	• Role clarity. • Efficient coordination • Simplifies decision-making. • The department head is well-versed in a specialized set of skills. • Closer control from the managers.	• Too narrow-sighted and lacks a systematic view. • Prioritize departmental objectives over the broader organizational goals. • Resistance to change.
Product: Based on product or services	• The company's products have key product lines. • Individual divisions act like independent units, responsible for their performance.	• Focus on specific product and market segments. • Extensive knowledge of the division. • Good integration inside the product. • Can handle multiple goals and demands.	• Resource hungry. • Duplication efforts. • Emphasis on division goals can foster competition among divisions. • May lose control over divisions.
Geographical: Based on location.	• Has overarching business policies and guidelines. • Each geographical zone has its own reporting and functional systems.	• Better responding and adapting to the local market. • When operating areas with time zones and physical separations. • Better communication because of using the same language.	• Resource hungry. • Duplication efforts. • Cross-area learning can be limited.

(continued)

Table 8.1   (Continued)

Type	Example	Advantages	Disadvantages
Matrix: A combination of two or more types of organizational structures. Often presented in a grid format.	• Individuals have a dual reporting line – their line manager and a project manager.	• Good integration of the department. • Promotes communication due to the need to liaise among project members. • Handle multiple projects at the same time. • Apply skills in different roles. • Limited investment of resources.	• Require a high level of coordination. • Can cause high stress due to multiple demands. • Might fight for the same expert employees. • Ambiguity in the matrix structure created (e.g., responsibilities and priorities, who makes decisions).

Chain of command

This element is related to who is responsible for what, establishing a clear hierarchy of authority and reporting relationships to ensure accountability and decision-making.

The concept of chain of command, focused on the structured flow of authority and responsibility within an organization, is grounded in two fundamental principles. Firstly, the principle of unity of command dictates that a subordinate should be answerable to a single individual – the source from which they derive their authority and responsibilities. Secondly, the scalar principle outlines that authority and responsibility should follow a direct vertical path, stretching from top management down to the lowest organizational level. It establishes a hierarchical division of labour within the organization.

Advantages of chain of command

One notable advantage of implementing a chain of command is the clear delineation of roles and responsibilities across different organizational levels. This hierarchical structure allows for well-defined reporting relationships and accountability. In financial institutions, there exists a hierarchy within the professional ranks, with each rank representing different levels, each with unique roles and status. In IT firms, this may include positions like software developers, project managers and chief technology officers, while in financial organizations, it can encompass roles such as financial analysts, portfolio managers and senior executives. This clear hierarchy facilitates efficient organizational functioning.

Disadvantages of chain of command

However, there are potential disadvantages to a rigid chain of command. Organizations that adhere strictly to this structure may encounter challenges in adapting to dynamic environments. Rigidity can hinder flexibility and responsiveness to changing circumstances, which is particularly relevant in the fast-paced world of IT and finance. Furthermore, it may limit creativity and innovation, as individuals may be reluctant to deviate from established lines of authority. It can stifle open communication, inhibiting the flow of ideas and information across the organization. Therefore, while the chain of command offers clarity in roles and responsibilities, organizations in IT and finance should strike a balance to avoid potential drawbacks and remain agile in evolving landscapes.

Span of control

This is about how many people a manager can directly oversee. Determining the optimal span of control for a manager involves focusing on the frequency and intensity of actual relationships rather than the sheer number of potential relationships. Not all relationships will come into play and those that do will vary in significance. When we shift our perspective from potential to actual relationships as the basis for determining the ideal span of control, two key factors emerge: the need for required contact and the degree of specialization.

Required contact

For instance, a laboratory team leader may need to engage in frequent discussions and experiments with team members to ensure a research project is completed within the necessary timeframe. Likewise, when tasks have a higher frequency of new problems, more regular contact is needed. Rather than relying solely on written communication, extensive in-depth contact with the team proves beneficial for the organization's research objectives. In general, the greater the job's inherent ambiguity, the more supervision that is needed to prevent conflicts and stress.

Degree of specialization

The more specialized the job, the manager can oversee more subordinates. In cases where work tasks are highly specialized and similar, management can consolidate them into larger departments, as these employees may require less direct supervision.

A critical question here is the maximum width they can attain while maintaining effectiveness. Davison (2003) looked at the ideal ratio of managers to subordinates. In addition to the degree of specialization and required contact, she suggested the need to consider the ability of the manager, such as the manager's time availability, the effectiveness of the managers on leading and delegation and their individual tendencies to manage (level of control). Other environmental issues to consider include the following:

- Change and geographical dispersion of the organization
- Expectations of the staff's work quality: What's the employee training level, performance and tenure? Are there retention and career development measurements?
- Effectiveness of existing coordination mechanisms
- Expected impact on performance.

For a rule of thumb guide, in 1988, Peter Drucker suggested an optimal ratio of one manager to seven subordinates. He emphasized the role of the manager is not replaced by technology. It takes on a significant portion of middle managers' communication responsibilities, enabling organizations to adopt flatter structures by expanding the span of control. As each manager's span broadens, the need for multiple management layers diminishes and employees experience less intensive supervision. Davison (2003) found the median span of the control ratio is one to seven.

GROUP DISCUSSION

In today's fast-paced and technology-driven world, the role of managers has undergone significant changes. The advent of new technologies has not only transformed the way we work but has also raised questions about the traditional role of managers in organizations. Here is a list of possible discussion points:

- Is managerial necessity diminishing in the AI era?
- How can technology enhance the practice of management?
- What are the key skills that modern managers must possess?
- How does technology impact communication and teamwork within organizations?
- What are the ethical considerations surrounding the use of technology in management roles?

Centralization

Clarifying who has the power to make decisions and outlining their associated duties exists on a continuum spanning from centralized to decentralized approaches.

In centralized organizations, top executives or a central governing body hold authority, making significant decisions and outlining departmental roles. This top-down structure creates a clear chain of command, with lower levels following directives from upper management. Conversely, in decentralized setups like agile startups, individuals and teams have more autonomy. They actively participate in decision-making, shaping their roles and responsibilities. This bottom-up approach fosters creativity and agility, enabling diverse inputs in addressing challenges and opportunities.

Centralizing authority within organizations is driven by several factors.

- Manager training programmes can be costly, potentially outweighing the advantages of decentralization.
- Decentralization comes with additional administrative efforts, including the development of accounting and performance systems to inform top management about lower-level decisions.
- There is a cost of functional duplication associated with this. Autonomous units must be self-sufficient, leading to potentially high duplication costs.
- Managers may resist decentralization because decentralization can be interpreted as a loss of control by the managers.

Conversely, individuals and teams have more autonomy in decentralized setups like agile startups. They actively participate in decision-making, shaping their roles and responsibilities. This bottom-up approach fosters creativity and agility, enabling diverse inputs in addressing challenges and opportunities. Benefits of decentralized setups include that it:

- is easier to evaluate performance
- creates a competitive environment
- creates autonomy.

Formalization

This relates to the degree to which an organization relies on established rules, documented procedures and written records to regulate its functioning. Within a highly formalized structure, the organizations define and standardize methods for tasks and undertakings. This promotes consistency and clarity. However, it also brings with it certain drawbacks, such as impeding the speed of decision-making processes, and can foster an atmosphere of rigidity within the organization.

Evolution of structure: linking context to progression

The evolution of the giraffe is a fascinating tale of adaptation. It all began with the ancestors of modern giraffes, which were relatively short-necked creatures. As these early giraffe-like animals roamed the African plains, they encountered challenges in finding food and competing for resources. Over time, natural selection played a significant role in shaping the giraffe's evolution. Some individuals within the population exhibited slightly longer necks, which gave them a competitive advantage. These individuals could reach foliage that was otherwise out of reach for their shorter-necked counterparts, providing them with a more abundant food supply. As generations passed, giraffes with longer necks were more likely to survive and reproduce, passing on their advantageous genetic traits to their offspring. This gradual process of natural selection favoured longer-necked giraffes, leading to the evolution of these iconic creatures we see today.

A more recent and well-documented example of structural evolution is evident in British birds, which have evolved to possess longer beaks. Recent research unveils a notable evolution in British Great Tits, specifically the growth of longer beaks compared to their European counterparts. Analysing genetic and historical data for more than 3,000 birds between UK and Dutch Great Tits, scientists found that the British Great Tit has a longer beak than the Dutch. Scientists have observed this change transpiring over a relatively brief span, sparking speculation about the possible influence of Britain's keen interest in feeding garden birds. Dr. Lewis Spurgin from the School of Biological Sciences at the University of East Anglia noted that the UK's sustained investment in birdseed and birdfeeders, which is significantly higher than that of mainland Europe, has been a long-standing practice contributing to this intriguing adaptation. In 2022, it is estimated that 58 per cent of UK households feed birds regularly. In 2020, the UK was Europe's biggest wild bird food market (PFMA, 2020).

Reflective questions:

- How has the adoption of advanced technologies, such as the ability to mass produce products, shipping products to international markets, using robots in the manufacturing process, the internet and mobile impacted the need for structural adjustments within organizations?

- How does an organization's structural adaptability relate to its long-term survival amid evolving business landscapes?

Organizational structure evolutions

Much like the process of evolution seen in the natural world, the evolution of organizational structure is adaptive, responding to organizational mission, changing environments and challenges. Classic organizational structure models were a witness to the development of the business environment. The evolution of organizational structure is intrinsically tied to its contextual surroundings. Over time, as businesses and institutions respond to changing environments, market dynamics and technological advances, their organizational structures adapt and transform to remain relevant and effective. This relationship between context and structure is evident in the shift from traditional hierarchical models to more flexible and collaborative approaches seen in modern organizations.

We can see the structural evolution through the lens of the operating environment. This is probably most notable from Alfred Chandler's work (1962, 1977), in which he describes the growth of American industry and how it related to organizational structure. Essentially, Chandler's work suggests environment → company strategy → organizational structure.

Before 1850: family-run businesses

The American business landscape primarily comprised tiny enterprises that were personally or family-run, requiring minimal administrative attention. Owners directly participated in functional tasks and there was little requirement for extensive long-term planning. Examples of small businesses at this time are carpenters, tailors, family-based farming and general stores. The need for extensive administrative structures and long-term planning was minimal, reflecting the simplicity and localized nature of these businesses.

Late 19th century: expansion and industrialization

The expansion of industrialization and railroads set the emergence of large-scale industrial enterprises. Companies recognized the need for efficient administrative structures to cope with the challenges of their burgeoning empires. They began implementing formalized management systems, administrative hierarchies and reporting mechanisms to coordinate operations and ensure continued growth.

For instance, consider the historical context of General Motors: William Durant, an entrepreneur, in 1885, started initially selling carts and carriages. Durant focused on high-volume production and vertical integration where GM acquired companies involved in steel production, tire manufacturing and other critical components of car production, leaving other responsibilities through creating a new type of officer to be responsible for marketing, sales, dealership network, finance and administrative duties.

Early 20th century: larger organizations

The organizations grew larger and more complex and there was a need for management control. The management of integrated enterprises faced inefficiencies stemming from the absence of a robust organizational structure, lack of work instructions and lack of accountabilities. This leaned towards centralized control. This approach proved highly inefficient, burdening the headquarters with the complex task of planning and coordinating all units. The multidivisional decentralized structure emerged to address the operational and entrepreneurial complexities of rapidly expanding and diversifying organizations. Businesses focused on adaptation and diversification, further underscoring the need for the multidivisional structure.

During the early 1900s, two major schools of thought drove the development of management principals. At this time, the main concern is productivity and efficiency. Henri Fayol, an advocate of administrative management, put forth a set of principles drawn from his experiences managing a prominent coal mining company in France. He listed 14 management principles:

- specialization
- authorities and responsibilities
- good discipline
- single delegated manager
- one central authority
- shared interests
- reward individuals
- centralization
- scalar chain
- order
- equity
- stability of the workforce
- using initiative to sustain individual motivation
- teamwork.

Max Weber was also concerned with efficiency and an advocate for bureaucracy management. Although bureaucracy is often associated negatively in the 21st century, Weber viewed bureaucracy as the most efficient way to set up an organization. His theory emphasized five key principles: specialization, abstract rules that keep uniformity and coordination of the tasks, clear accountability, clear chain of command and meritocracy-based hiring and promotion.

- Specialization: breaking down tasks into highly specialized roles, enabling individuals to become experts in their specific functions
- Abstract rules for uniformity: these guide individuals to maintain uniformity and coordination. This approach aimed to minimize variances arising from individual differences
- Clear accountability and chain of command: bureaucratic organizations emphasize clear lines of accountability and a well-defined chain of command. Each member was answerable to a designated manager, ensuring efficient decision-making and communication

- Merit-based hiring and promotion: Weber's theory encouraged the recruitment and advancement of employees based on their technical qualifications and merit. This approach guarded against arbitrary personnel decisions and promoted a meritocratic system.

Fayol and Weber's work is representative of the mechanic approach to designing an organization where the organizational performance and efficiencies were due to structural characteristics of the organization – specialization, authority, accountability and functional-based departmentalization.

Another school of thought at the time to improve productivity and efficiencies was the scientific management school. Due to new technologies (recording, the ability to process data), researchers were able to study how to promote efficiency scientifically. They particularly cared about efficiency, improving organizational performance, standardization through dividing tasks into small and specific subtasks to increase performance and managerial control. Popular studies in the early 20th century were influenced by Fayol's time study and Gilbreth's motion studies. Fayol's time study is a method he developed to improve the efficiency of work processes within an organization. It involves meticulously analysing and measuring the time required to complete specific tasks or activities. By breaking down work into its components and timing each step, Fayol aimed to identify opportunities for optimization and efficiency enhancement. Another famous study that analyses workers' activities is Frank Gilbreth's motion analysis. He observed and filmed workers as they performed various tasks. This approach aimed to comprehensively understand and document how tasks were executed within an organization.

Although Fayol's and Gilbreth's studies are old, they are still relevant to today's business world. This reflective exercise aims to help you connect the principles of the scientific management approach to modern operation.

- Can you provide examples of companies or industries that have successfully implemented principles from Fayol's time study or Gilbreth's motion analysis to enhance their operational efficiency?

- In what ways can the concept of standardization, as seen in Fayol's time study, be applied to contemporary businesses to streamline operations and enhance productivity?

- What modern tools and methodologies can be employed to conduct motion analysis, akin to Gilbreth's studies, to improve the understanding of how tasks are performed in an organization?

- How can modern businesses adapt scientific management principles to address current workforce dynamics, including remote work, diversity and the gig economy?

Late 20th century: an unstable environment, focused on adaptability

During the early 20th century, scholars sought to identify the most effective organizational structures for achieving peak performance in specific situational contexts. However, the notion of an ideal, one-size-fits-all structure has become obsolete. Growing complexities and technological advancements, particularly the internet, have made it increasingly clear that a more adaptable approach is necessary. The concept of a universally optimal structure has become challenging to uphold. This era emphasizes team-based organization and acknowledges that companies cannot excel in all areas simultaneously. (See Chapter 4 Managing groups and teams. See the information box on Agile and Scrum methodology on page 111, which is particularly relevant to this current organizational structure.

Project-based structure   The project structure is a popular form. It is designed to efficiently manage and execute specific projects within an organization. Unlike traditional hierarchical structures, where authority and responsibility are delineated by functional departments, a project structure is temporary and task-oriented. The project structure defines each individual's functions and reporting line. It is particularly suitable when the environment is highly dynamic and non-routine tasks.

A particular type of project structure has been developed recently – a multi-team system where expert functional teams come together to work on a meta-goal (Dechurch & Marks, 2006; Marks et al, 2005; Davison et al, 2012; Rentsch & Staniewicz, 2012; Wijnmaalen et al, 2019; DeChurch & Mathieu, 2009; Zaccaro et al, 2020; DeChurch et al, 2011; de Vries et al, 2016; Shuffler & Carter, 2018). The multi-team system is particularly evident in extreme events – such as military services and teams for emergency response to disasters (e.g., in response to earthquakes, space aircraft accidents and firefighting). Multi-team systems can also be seen in less hazardous situations, such as research and development, cybersecurity and other business alliances. Collectively, current research points out the importance of across-team coordination as the key to performance. Campbell et al (2022) found that the multi-team system tended to fail in the following situations:

- Teams frequently dedicate a significant portion of their attention to their internal workings, occasionally overlooking the crucial aspect of interactions with other teams. This tendency becomes more pronounced when teams sense that they are encountering difficulties.

- Teams place a strong emphasis on taking action but sometimes underestimate the importance of closely monitoring their performance and creating comprehensive plans for necessary adjustments.

- When external teams are involved, there is a noticeable inclination to perceive them as distinct entities, leading to limited interaction and a lack of concerted effort in devising strategies for adjustments.

Organizations are also likely to organize their structure in a more modular approach with teams located at different locations. Organizations often outsource the majority of their core functions or operations to independent entities. The virtual network model embraces a free-market ethos where subcontractors can join or exit the system as necessary to adapt to changing requirements. The fundamental idea is for a company to focus on its core competencies while outsourcing ancillary tasks to firms with specialized proficiencies in those specific domains, thereby enabling the organization to achieve more with fewer resources. This approach allows a company to leverage worldwide expertise. However, outsourcing activities may not be the solution for everything and additional coordination costs should be considered. Managing relationships and addressing potential conflicts with contract partners can be time-consuming. There is a risk of organizational disruption if a partner fails to deliver. Moreover, employee loyalty and corporate culture may be weakened because employees may feel replaceable by contract services.

GROUP DISCUSSION

As organizations strive to leverage talent from around the globe, teams, whether they are virtual, project-based or follow agile or scrum methodologies, are becoming increasingly prevalent. It is imperative to investigate their organizational structure, with particular emphasis on how specialization contributes to their success or setbacks. Subsequently, consider the following questions regarding an organization you are familiar with:

- Assess the performance of the selected organization.
- Elaborate on the organizational structure's characteristics and elucidate how they effectively manage geographically dispersed teams.
- Can you identify any challenges or barriers related to team specialization? How does the organization address them?
- Detail the strategies employed to foster inter-team collaboration and cooperation.
- Identify any innovative approaches or practices the organization uses to enhance performance and collaboration.

MECHANISTIC VS. ORGANIC STRUCTURE

In the late 20th century, the contingency view on the organizational structure viewed the importance of 'fit'. Classical management scholars like Fayol and Weber advocated a mechanistic approach to enhance organizational efficiency through formalization, standardization and departmentalization. In stark contrast, the organic approach challenges the potential rigidity of mechanistic structures and underscores the importance of flexibility and human factors within organizations (Likert, 1979).

The rise of the behavioural management movement began with the Hawthorne studies. Hawthorne studies aimed to evaluate how alterations in lighting conditions would impact worker productivity. Surprisingly, the outcomes consistently revealed increased productivity, regardless of improved or reduced lighting. This unforeseen revelation prompted researchers to delve into other elements influencing worker performance. The researcher found that incentives – such as monetary rewards and regular rests – improved productivity regardless of which condition the workers were in. The result suggested that structural elements influence productivity. Mayo pointed out that the importance of job satisfaction is key for employees to be productive. In particular, Mayo found that job satisfaction is likely to be higher when employees have some control over their work (e.g., setting goals for their output), there is a high level of group cohesion and a feeling of being valued at work. Together, these researchers pointed out the importance of people factors such as motivation, emotion and group interactions in improving productivity.

Reflective questions:

- Drawing from your personal experiences, can you identify whether the organizations you've been associated with have predominantly adopted mechanistic or organic approaches to enhance workplace productivity? Was it an effective way to promote efficiency/productivity? List as many factors as possible.

- In your opinion, why might a mechanistic or organic approach be more effective in specific work environments? Consider the stability of the environment and how it influences the choice between these structures.

- Reflecting on your own professional journey, which approach do you believe has the potential to better foster employee productivity: a mechanistic or organic approach? Why do you hold this view?

Formal and informal organizational structure

Another way to look at the organizational structure is from an information process perspective. Common formal structural elements to promote information sharing include:

- formal roles and chain of commands
- rules and procedures

- information repository
- integrator (e.g., project manager to liaise information processing)
- teams.

A formal organizational structure can be intentionally designed to improve information sharing by increasing the predictability, transparency and accountability of each individual's work (Williamson, 1975). For example, thinking about the fundamental elements of organizational structure – specialization, departmentalization and centralization – these have an impact on the clarity of roles and responsibilities, which leads to more effective information sharing, learning and improved decision-making relative to group discussion in the absence of formal structures (Bunderson & Boumgarden, 2010; Stewart & Stasser, 1995; Okhuysen & Bechky, 2009). Formal structures also provide individuals with responsibilities to share information and increase their motivation to share.

Informal structures, such as relationships and networks, also promote information sharing in organizations (Hansen, 1999). Frequent face-to-face interactions, site visits and meetings help organizations overcome cross-location conflicts in coordination by providing opportunities for ongoing informal relationships to develop. Acquaintances or weak ties (i.e., infrequent and distant relationships) provide the effective transfer of information across teams while it is easier to maintain the relationship (Hansen, 1999).

Different forms of structure and company size

Think back to Table 8.1, which covers the different types of departmentalization. How do different forms of departmentalization, such as functional, product, geographic and matrix structures, impact the efficiency, adaptability and overall performance of a company as it varies in size from a small startup to a large multinational corporation?

During the initial phases of a company's development, such as in the early days of a startup or within tightly knit teams, the structure tends to be rather informal. Decision-making processes are often swift and centralized and communication flows freely, fostering an atmosphere of agility and adaptability. This simple structure is low-cost to set up and suitable for small-scale businesses. As the organization becomes bigger and has a range of products, organizations are likely to adopt a functional organizational structure to increase efficiency. Organizational tasks are divided up into functions and employees with similar functions are grouped. Some standardizations of the procedures start to be created at this stage.

As the company strives for further growth and diversification, incorporating different product or service lines becomes imperative. To cater to varying customer needs across products and market segments, the organization may adopt product-based or geographical structures. This approach addresses the demand for more localized information and expertise. Each division takes on profit responsibilities, while the corporate headquarters retains authority over company-wide strategy, training and development and research and development functions. With the increase in size, the establishment of clear hierarchies, departmental divisions and defined reporting lines leads to an increase in the formality of processes and procedures. Although this form gives input insights about the product or local customers, each division is likely to function independently, work as a silo and experience potential resource redundancies. The organization is now big and divisions are now resulting in less responsiveness to strategic changes. To be responsive, the organization adopts a matrix structure. Employees are drawn into specific projects. Employees are likely to come from different teams across geographical areas.

Mintzberg's organizational configurations

Henry Mintzberg identified five fundamental elements that all organizations possess:

- Strategic apex: constitutes the pinnacle of decision-making authority within an organization. Its primary responsibilities revolve around defining the mission and addressing external demands
- Middle managers: serve as the crucial link between the strategic apex and employees. Middle managers ensure the alignment of organizational goals with practical execution
- Operating functions: are responsible for its day-to-day operations
- Technostructure: encompasses multifaceted domains such as product design and development, personnel training and development, financial accounting and research and development – each contributing to the organization's overall functionality and development
- Supporting functions: while not directly involved in profit generation, these are indispensable to an organization's smooth operation. They encompass a wide range of expertise that provides essential support and infrastructure to the core business functions.

Mintzberg further identified six fundamental organizational configurations, each with its unique characteristics and suited to different situations:

- Simple structure
- Machine bureaucracy
- Professional bureaucracy

- Division organization
- Adhocracy
- Missionary

A comparison among these organizational configurations is shown in Table 8.2.

Table 8.2   Comparison among organizational configurations

Forms	Contextual factors	Characteristics
Simple structure E.g., startup • Formalization: low • Complexity: low • Centralization: high • Size: small	• A young startup with a small company size. • Limited or absent establishment of technostructure. • Operating in a stable and predictable environment. • Company executives make decisions.	• Company executives actively drive the company's success. • The company's ownership and management are the same. • The organization maintains a minimal level of departmentalization. • Company executives take charge of coordinating activities across departments. • The company lacks advanced technology and supporting functions.
Machine bureaucracy e.g., public services, military. • Formalization: high • Complexity: high • Centralization: high • Size: large	• Established for a few years, it's now a larger-scale company. • The technostructure has been established. • Operating within a stable and predictable environment.	• Specialization is high, with formalized operating procedures for routine tasks. • Communication has transitioned into a more formalized mode. • Function-based departmentalization is adopted. • The hierarchy and division of labour have become more distinct. • The core of the organization revolves around supporting committees positioned near strategic decision-making.

(continued)

Table 8.2   (Continued)

Forms	Contextual factors	Characteristics
Professional bureaucracy e.g., hospital, law firms, accountancy firms. • Formalization: high • Complexity: high • Centralization: high • Size: medium to large	• The company's age and scale may vary. • Establishing the technostructure proves to be challenging. • It operates within a stable yet complex environment. • Operational functions hold authority.	• The organization heavily relies on specialized functional teams and expertise. • It is not as centralized as in machine bureaucracy. • Employee responsibilities are planned using work design. • The core of the organization revolves around its operational functions.
Division organization e.g., multinational companies. Well-diversified companies. • Formalization: medium • Complexity: high • Centralization: low • Size: medium to large	• Extend to various markets. • The company is established and operates on a larger scale. • It boasts a well-established technostructure, often with further divisions. • The environment can be both stable and complex due to the organization's expansion into different markets.	• Each division manages its own customers, market, or products. • There is low interdependence among divisions. • Each division possesses a high level of autonomy. • Coordination among divisions occurs through goal setting and formal planning. • Middle managers play a pivotal role in the organization.
Adhocracy e.g., project teams. • Formalization: low • Complexity: low • Centralization: high	• The company is often in its early stages. • The technostructure tends to be complex. • The environment is characterized by complexity and instability. • Experts within the company hold significant importance, and they are dispersed throughout the organization.	• Innovation holds a crucial role within the organization. • The organization extensively integrates experts from various fields. • Teams are formed based on the specific tasks at hand. • Experts are responsible for coordination. • It operates as an organic organization, characterized by low formalization. • Supporting functions play a pivotal role within the organization.

(continued)

Table 8.2   (Continued)

Forms	Contextual factors	Characteristics
Missionary e.g., religious groups, and charity organizations. • Formalization: low • Complexity: low • Centralization: low	• The company's age and scale can vary significantly. • It employs a simplified technostructure. • The environment is characterized by its simplicity and stability. • The organization employs missions to guide the actions of its members.	• The mission plays a pivotal role within the organization. • There is a limited degree of specialization. • Individual actions are guided and aligned with the overarching mission.

GROUP EXERCISE

Exploring organizational structures and evolution

Objective: This exercise is designed to enhance your understanding of organizational structures through independent research on a company of your choice, by focusing on the company's organizational history and its evolution. Typically, an organization's life can be classified into four stages:

Exercise:

• Select your company: pick a company that piques your interest. It could be a renowned corporation, a pioneering startup, a nonprofit organization or any entity that captures your curiosity. Ensure that there is ample information available about the company's history and organizational structure.

• Research and background: provide a brief introduction to your chosen company, covering its name, industry, historical context and noteworthy achievements or challenges in a chronological timeline. If you can find out information about the strategic mission of the company at different time points, also note it down in the timeline.

• Describe organizational structure at different time points:

   o Describe the company's original organizational setup at its inception or during its early years.

o Investigate the company's journey regarding organizational structure changes and development. Identify significant transformations or pivotal moments. Analyse whether these changes were driven by growth, shifts in the market, technological advancements or other influential factors.

o Highlight the key catalysts or events that triggered these structural shifts.

● Impact on performance:

o Assess how the evolving organizational structure has affected the company's performance, corporate culture and ability to adapt to industry dynamics.

o Discuss the pros and cons stemming from these structural transformations.

● Finally, answer the following questions to help you gain personal insights from this exercise:

o Share your personal reflections regarding the most intriguing or unexpected aspects of the company's journey in organizational evolution.

o Consider how the company's experiences might offer valuable lessons or insights applicable to other organizations.

INFLUENCE OF STRUCTURE – LINKING ORGANIZATIONAL STRUCTURE TO INSTITUTIONAL DISCRIMINATION

Stamarski and Son Hing (2015) proposed that discrimination at work, or more specifically, gender discrimination, is linked to institutional discrimination in organizational structures, processes and practices. In particular, they pointed out that the HR functions on selection, performance evaluation and training and development can have an impact on how employees feel they are being valued by the organization. They highlight the following factors:

● Gendered organizational structure when women are under- or overrepresented in some departments

● Role assignments and task assignments, such as receiving high strategic-level leadership positions that are important for promotion

● Performance evaluation, such as being evaluated harsher than their male counterparts

● Promotion opportunities and related decision-making processes

The impact of organizational structure on gender discrimination is often tied to a gendered structure where the distribution of women and men is unequal. This can be a gendered department or senior leaders who hold more decision-making power in the structural hierarchy.

Empirical evidence is ample that women experience biased performance evaluation and promotion (Son & Bell, 2022; Mitchell & Martin, 2018; Fan et al, 2019; Kulik & Olekalns, 2012; MacNell et al, 2014; Franczak & Margolis, 2022; Joshi et al, 2015). In a recent empirical study by Ross et al (2022), they used a combination of archival records across 36 major US universities and survey data (sample size = 2660 respondents). Their research findings showed the policies related to task assignment, performance evaluation and promotions varied between women and men across various disciplines from engineering to social sciences. Ross et al noted the following:

- Not taking enough credit. Women tend to downplay their contributions to projects, irrespective of their academic field. This tendency to be less vocal about their achievements is a subtle yet widespread form of gender bias. The authors noted that it is not that women do not want to take credit – rather, it is the structure that prevents them from voicing their credit. In some extreme cases, contribution to the project is completely erased.

- Women contribute significantly more than their male counterparts in the research team. This expanded contribution includes conceptual thinking, data collection, meticulous data analysis, extensive writing and editing, and even administrative duties. Despite these additional efforts, women frequently do not receive the credit they rightfully deserve.

- Damaged career advancement. This lack of recognition takes a toll on women's career advancement prospects, hindering the professional growth of talented women in academia and beyond. These findings underscore the urgency of addressing gender discrimination and promoting a fair and equitable scientific landscape.

In addition, an unbalanced gender structure perpetuates unbalanced career advancement, resulting in fewer women in senior positions. When senior researchers have the authority to make decisions and set up the rules, gender discrimination worsens due to women researchers having less visibility and lack access to people with power (network). As a result, women researchers' careers are impeded and women often feel they need to shout/fight to be heard. Similarly, using Canadian public company data, Ben-Amar et al (2021) found that boards of directors are mainly male-dominated (75 per cent were male). They found that companies' preferences for meritocracy are used to avoid change – and maintain and legitimize their gendered structures and practices.

Reflective questions:

The following questions are aimed at encouraging critical thinking and discussions about the intersection of organizational structure and gender discrimination.

- Can you recall any instances in your own professional or academic journey when you observed or experienced gender discrimination related to organizational structure, role assignments or promotions?

- What does meritocracy mean to you? Is it the objective or subjective measure of contribution and achievement?

- Explore the concept of meritocracy within your organization or industry. Are meritocratic principles used to maintain the status quo and justify gendered structures, or do they genuinely promote fairness and equality?

- Have you witnessed or experienced disparities in performance evaluations between genders in your workplace or academic environment? How do you think such disparities affect individuals' career trajectories?

Organizational design

How can organizations decide their organizational structure? So far, we have pointed out the importance of contextual influences, such as environment and technology, as well as that the growth of the companies may impact the form that the organization chooses. To be able to configure the organizational structural form, theories in organizational design provided a more systematic way to look at the factors that have an impact on the chosen organizational structure. Organizational design is essentially the methodical and intentional process of shaping and structuring an organization to effectively attain its strategic objectives. This entails making informed decisions about crucial aspects of the organization, including its structure, roles and responsibilities, processes, systems and culture. The fundamental objective of organizational design is to establish a framework that harmonizes with the organization's mission and strategic direction, streamlines the allocation of resources, promotes open communication and collaboration and facilitates overall performance and adaptability. Two organizational design theories will be introduced here: Galbraith's STAR model and Burke Litwin's Model of Organizational Design

Galbraith's STAR Model

Galbraith's STAR Model, developed by organizational theorist and consultant Jay R. Galbraith, offers a framework designed to assist organizations in harmonizing their structures, processes, rewards and people practices to support their strategic goals and attain peak performance (Galbraith, 2002, 2008, 2011; Kates & Galbraith, 2010). The Star Model comprises four crucial components, represented by the image of a star:

- Strategy: this component embodies an organization's overarching strategic direction and objectives, encompassing choices such as product or service offerings, target markets, competitive positioning and other strategic decisions. In the STAR Model, strategy serves as the cornerstone upon which the other elements are constructed. It guides the design of the organization's structure and molds its processes, rewards systems and people practices.

- Structure: structure pertains to how an organization is structured and how its various units, functions and roles are organized. Galbraith recognized that different strategies necessitate distinct structures. For example, an organization pursuing innovation and rapid product development may opt for a more decentralized and matrix-based structure, while one emphasizing cost efficiency may favour a more centralized and hierarchical arrangement. Aligning the structure with the chosen strategy is essential for effective implementation.

- Processes: this refers to workflows, routines and protocols governing how work is carried out within the organization. This includes decision-making procedures, information flow, task coordination and resource allocation. Processes should be tailored to support the chosen strategy. For instance, a strategy focused on customer responsiveness might require streamlined and customer-centric processes, whereas a cost-reduction strategy may prioritize efficiency and standardization.

- Rewards and people practices: this element encompasses the organization's systems for recognizing and motivating its workforce. It encompasses areas like compensation, performance evaluation, career development and other human resources practices. Ensuring alignment between rewards and people practices and the selected strategy is vital to motivate employees to pursue strategic objectives. For example, a strategy highlighting innovation may reward creativity and risk-taking, while a cost-focused strategy may incentivize cost control and efficiency.

The STAR Model underscores the interconnected nature of these four elements and underscores the significance of alignment. When an organization aligns its strategy, structure, processes, rewards and people practices, it enhances its capacity to execute its strategy effectively and realize its desired outcomes. This model offers a comprehensive framework for organizations to assess their current state, identify discrepancies or misalignments and make deliberate changes to enhance performance and competitiveness.

Burke Litwin Model of Organizational Design

Burke Litwin's Model is similar to the STAR Model in the sense that the model points out the interrelated factors that matter for organizational design. There are four groups of elements: external environment, transformational factors, transactional factors and performance.

- External environment: this includes elements such as markets, legislation, competitive landscapes and economic conditions. These factors wield considerable influence over organizations, necessitating that change managers maintain continuous vigilence to anticipate issues affecting their teams. In the public sector, legislative adjustments in areas like healthcare and local governance directly impact the scope of work organizations must undertake.

- Transformation factors: these are factors that are embedded in the organizations. Change in these transformational factors will have an impact on the rest of the organizations. Transformation factors include the following:

  o Mission and strategy: an organization's mission statement defines its fundamental purpose for existence. Strategy, then, outlines the broad approach the organization intends to follow in pursuit of its mission.

  o Leadership: this facet pertains to the attitudes and conduct of senior leadership and how their actions are perceived by the entire organization.

  o Organizational culture: beliefs, behaviours, values and norms prevailing in the organization. They are less formal but exist in the organization, guiding individuals' behaviours.

- Transactional factors are related to daily operations in the organizations. They are factors that are influenced by management.

  o Management practices. This refers to managers' activities and behaviours to carry out organizational mission and strategies.

  o Structure refers to the hierarchy, departmentalization and the chain of command in the organization. Shifts in strategy may lead to alterations in the organization's structural framework. These changes can impact relationships, responsibilities and operational processes.

  o Work unit climate refers to the overall team's working environment. Immediate work setting shapes our overall view of the organization and influences job satisfaction.

  o Task requirements and individual skills/abilities

  o Individual needs and values can be monetary (e.g., pay, bonus) and non-monetary (e.g., work-life boundaries) that an individual wants. However, practical constraints may limit the availability to meet these individual's needs.

o Employee motivation. This factor gauges the significance of individual and organizational objectives. Maintaining motivation is crucial for the success of any change initiative. The primary challenge lies in sustaining motivation throughout a change project, especially when such changes are often met with resistance from those affected.

- Performance. Including individual and organizational performance. This serves as the outcome.

Chapter summary

In this chapter, we explore organizational structure, breaking it down into three key stages. Initially, we delve into the fundamental elements of organizational structure, including job specialization, departmentalization, the chain of command and the span of control. Moving forward, we look at the organizational forms, from functional and product structures to matrix configurations. Mintzberg's organizational configurations highlight five pivotal structuring elements within organizations: the strategic apex, middle managers, technostructure, supporting functions and the six fundamental organizational forms, including simple structure, machine bureaucracy, professional bureaucracy, divisional organization, adhocracy and missionary structures. Moreover, we emphasize the significance of organizational structure in conjunction with contextual factors and the size of the organization. Using an evolutionary perspective, the chapter sheds light on how they influence the choice of an optimal structure. As we near the conclusion of the chapter, we provide a comprehensive overview of the organizational design model, presenting an integrated perspective of the multifaceted factors that must be considered when designing an organizational structure.

Key terms

Job specialization

Departmentalization

Functional structure

Product structure

Matrix structure

Chain of commands

Span of control

Centralization

Max Weber's bureaucracy

Mechanic approach

Organic approach

Multi-team system

Project-based structure

Formal organization

Informal organization

Mintzberg's Organizational Configuration

Strategic apex

Middle managers

Operating functions

Technostructure

Supporting functions

Simple structure

Machine bureaucracy

Professional bureaucracy

Division organization

Adhocracy

Missionary

Chapter review questions

- Under what circumstances should an organization consider adopting a functional structure, a product-based structure, a geographical-based structure or a matrix structure? Additionally, what are the advantages and limitations associated with each of these organizational structures?
- Describe how the application of structure depends on the organization's situation.
- Reflect on the potential challenges that a company may encounter when transitioning from: (1) a simple structure to a functional structure, and (2) a functional structure to a matrix structure.

- What are the similarities and differences between the STAR Model and Burke Litwin's model? What are the key takeaways and major limitations of these two models?

Further reading

The research on the span of control peaked around the 70s. A more recent study on span of control considers the implication of span of control on employee satisfaction and equality. Some interesting research articles can help you tap into this area:

Jacobsen, C B, Hansen, A K L, & Pedersen, L D (2023) Not too narrow, not too broad: Linking span of control, leadership behavior, and employee job satisfaction in public organizations, *Public Administrative Review*, 83(4), 775–792.

Lee, M & Kray, L J (2021) A gender gap in managerial span of control: Implication for the gender pay gap, *Organizational Behavior and Human Decision Process*, 167, 1–17.

References

Ben-Amar, W, Bujaki, M, Mcconomy, B & Mcilkenny, P (2021) Gendering merit: How the discourse of merit in diversity disclosures supports the gendered status quo on Canadian corporate boards, *Critical Perspectives on Accounting*, 75. doi:10.1016/j.cpa.2020. 102170 (archived at https://perma.cc/R7CF-6VXW).

Bunderson, J S & Boumgarden, P (2010) Structure and Learning in Self-Managed Teams: Why 'Bureaucratic' Teams Can Be Better Learners, *Organization Science*, 21(3), 609–624. doi:10.1287/orsc.1090.0483 (archived at https://perma.cc/MUM6-Z6E6).

Campbell, L N P, Torres, E M, Zaccaro, S J, Zhou, S, Hedrick, K N, Wallace, D M, Luning, C R & Zakzewski, J E (2022) Examining multiteam systems across context and type: A historiometric analysis of failed MTS performance, *Frontiers in Psychology*, 13(813624).

Cummings, T G & Worley, C G (2005) *Organization Development and Change*, 8th edition, Thomson/South-Western, Mason, OH.

Davison, B (2003) Management span of control: How wide is too wide?, *Journal of Business Strategy*, 24(4), 22–29. doi:10.1108/02756660310494854 (archived at https://perma.cc/ S8JG-GHDN).

Davison, R B, Hollenbeck, J R, Barnes, C M, Sleesman, D J & Ilgen, D R (2012) Coordinated action in multiteam systems, *The Journal of Applied Psychology*, 97(4), 808–824. doi:10.1037/a0026682 (archived at https://perma.cc/MVX4-E7LX).

DeChurch, L A, Burke, C S, Shuffler, M L, Lyons, R, Doty, D & Salas, E (2011) A historio-metric analysis of leadership in mission critical multiteam environments, *The Leadership Quarterly*, 22(1), 152–169. doi:10.1016/J.LEAQUA.2010.12.013 (archived at https:// perma.cc/EPZ8-89YB).

Dechurch, L A & Marks, M A (2006) Leadership in multiteam systems, *Journal of Applied Psychology*, 91(2), 311–329. doi:10.1037/0021-9010.91.2.311 (archived at https://perma.cc/8N62-MDSL).

DeChurch, L A & Mathieu, J E (2009) Thinking in terms of multiteam systems. In E Salas, G F Goodwin & C S Burke (eds.) *Team Effectiveness in Complex Organizations: Cross-disciplinary Perspectives and Approaches*, Taylor & Francis, New York. pp. 267–292.

Duncan, R (1979) What is the right organization structure? Decision tree analysis provides the answer, *Organizational Dynamics*, 7(3), 59–80. https://doi.org/10.1016/0090-2616(79)90027-5 (archived at https://perma.cc/ER7K-LX5J)

Fan, Y, Shepherd, L J, Slavich, E, Waters, D, Stone, M, Abel, R & Johnston, E L (2019) Gender and cultural bias in student evaluations: Why representation matters, *PLOS ONE*, 14(2), e0209749. doi:10.1371/JOURNAL.PONE.0209749 (archived at https://perma.cc/QAQ6-3NPA).

Franczak, J & Margolis, J (2022) Women and great places to work: Gender diversity in leadership and how to get there, *Organizational Dynamics*, 51(4), 100913. doi:10.1016/J.ORGDYN.2022.100913 (archived at https://perma.cc/67YM-JQAQ).

Galbraith, J R (2002) Organizing to deliver solutions, *Organizational Dynamics*, 31(2), 194.

Galbraith, J R (2008) Organization design, *Handbook of Organization Development*, 325–352.

Galbraith, J R (2011) *The star model*, Galbraith Management Consultants, Colorado, USA.

Hansen, M T (1999) The search-transfer problem: The role of weak ties in sharing knowledge across organization subunits, *Administrative Science Quarterly*, 44(1), 82–111. doi:10.2307/2667032 (archived at https://perma.cc/8AGN-KFJT).

Herzberg, F (2003) One more time: How do you motivate employees?, *Harvard Business Review*, 5–16.

Joshi, A, Neely B, Emrich, C, Griffiths D & George, G (2015) From the editors: Gender research in AMJ: An overiew of five decades of empirical research and calls to action, *Academy of Management Journal*, 58(5), 1459–1475.

Kates, A & Galbraith, J R (2010) *Designing your organization: Using the STAR model to solve 5 critical design challenges*, John Wiley & Sons.

Kulik, C T & Olekalns M (2012) Negotiating the gender divide: Lessons from the negotiation and organizational behavior literatures, *Journal of Management*, 38(4), 1387–1415. doi:10.1177/0149206311431307 (archived at https://perma.cc/YV49-5V9K).

Likert, R (1979) From production- and employee-centeredness to systems 1-4, *Journal of Management*, 5(2), 147–156.

MacNell, L, Driscoll, A & Hunt A N (2014) What's in a name: Exposing gender bias in student ratings of teaching, *Innovative Higher Education 2014 40:4*. 40 (4), 291–303. doi:10.1007/S10755-014-9313-4 (archived at https://perma.cc/D2FE-JHBP).

Marks, M A, DeChurch, L A, Mathieu, J E, Panzer, F J & Alonso, H A (2005) Teamwork in multiteam systems, *Journal of Applied Psychology*, 90(5), 964–971. doi:10.1037/0021-9010.90.5.964 (archived at https://perma.cc/MCY9-3ZFQ).

Mitchell, K M W & Martin, J (2018) Gender Bias in Student Evaluations, *PS: Political Science & Politics*, 51(3), 648–652. doi:10.1017/S104909651800001X (archived at https://perma.cc/ZT62-UP8M).

Mittelman, M (2016) Why GitHub finally abandoned its bossless workplace, *Bloomberg News*, 6 September.

Okhuysen, G A & Bechky, B A (2009) Coordination in organizations: An integrative perspective, *The Academy of Management Annals*, 3(1), 463–502. doi:10.1080/194165209 03047533 (archived at https://perma.cc/E4PW-8XSL).

Paul, W, Robertson, K & Herzberg, F (1969) Job enrichment pays off, *Harvard Business Review*, 47, 61–79.

PFMA(2020)*UK Pet Data Report.*

Rentsch, J R & Staniewicz, M J (2012) Cognitive similarity configurations in multiteam systems. In *Multiteam systems: An organization form for dynamic and complex environments*, Routledge/Taylor & Francis Group, New York (pp. 225–252).

Rogoway M (2016) No-boss office brings back the boss: 'We were naive', *Oregonian*, 18 June.

Ross, M B, Glennon, B M, Murciano-Goroff, R, Berkes, E G, Weinberg, B A & Lane, J I (2022) Women are credited less in science than men, *Nature 608*, 135–145. doi:10.1038/ s41586-022-04966-w (archived at https://perma.cc/Q7PS-7GFM).

Shuffler, M L & Carter, D R (2018) Teamwork situated in multiteam systems: Key lessons learned and future opportunities, *American Psychologist*, 73(4), 390–406. doi:10.1037/ amp0000322 (archived at https://perma.cc/M5V4-49RB).

Son, J Y & Bell, M L (2022) Scientific authorship by gender: Trends before and during a global pandemic, *Humanities and Social Sciences Communications*, 9(348).

Stamarski, C S & Son Hing, L S (2015) Gender inequalities in the workplace: the effects of organizational structures, processes, practices, and decision makers' sexism, *Frontiers in Psychology*, 6, 135488. doi:https://www.frontiersin.org/articles/10.3389/fpsyg.2015. 01400/full (archived at https://perma.cc/DJ2A-8DAX).

Stewart, D D & Stasser, G (1995) Expert role assignment and information sampling during collective recall and decision making, *Journal of Personality and Social Psychology*, 69(4), 619–628.

de Vries, T A, Hollenbeck, J R, Davison, R B, Walter, F & van der Vegt, G S (2016) Managing coordination in multiteam systems: Integrating micro and macro perspectives, *Academy of Management Journal*, 59(5), 1823–1844. doi:10.5465/amj.2014.0385 (archived at https://perma.cc/K268-W7UD).

Wijnmaalen, J, Voordijk, H, Rietjens, S & Dewulf, G (2019) Intergroup behavior in military multiteam systems, *Human Relations*, 72(6), 1081–1104. doi:10.1177/0018726718783828 (archived at https://perma.cc/MM7A-GXXG).

Williamson, O E (1975) *Markets and hierarchies: Analysis and antitrust implications*, Free Press, New York.

Zaccaro, S J, Dubrow, S, Torres, E M & Campbell, L N P (2020) Multiteam systems: An integrated review and comparison of different forms, *Annual Review of Organizational Psychology and Organizational Behavior*, 7(1), 479–503. doi:10.1146/annurev-orgpsych-012119-045418 (archived at https://perma.cc/PG7K-Q29L).

Organizational culture

09

- Organizational culture and national culture
  - Hall's context theory
  - Hofstede's national culture
  - The GLOBE study

WHY IS IT IMPORTANT TO STUDY ORGANIZATIONAL CULTURE?

Why did organizational culture gain popularity among managers and scholars?

The initial traction for organizational culture started around late 1970 to early 1980 – due to Japanese economic success: average growth rate for industrial production during the 70s was 13.6 per cent where the average growth rate was 4.9 per cent for 12 European countries and the United States at the same time (Statista, 1991). Cross-country comparisons have gained popularity as a means to identify effective management practices. Additionally, there has been a growing recognition of the significant impact of organizational culture on driving overall performance (e.g., Peter and Waterman's book *In Search of Excellence: Lessons from American's Best Run Companies*, Ochi's book *Theory Z*). Managers and scholars are interested in organizational culture because they want to 'understand how people within organizations interact and how organizations operate to achieve their stated and unstated goals' (Chatman & O'Reilly, 2016, p. 200). Organizational culture can be seen as 'a set of norms and values that are widely shared and strongly held throughout the organization' (O'Reilly & Chatman, 1996, p. 166). Groysberg et al (2018) mentioned the importance of organizational culture for executives to understand because culture is anchored in unspoken behaviours and mindsets.

At the organizational level organizational culture is essential to the company executives because strategic execution goes hand-in-hand with organizational culture – where strategy legitimately orients employees towards the organization's goal and culture expresses the goal through values and beliefs that guide employees' actual behaviours (Groysberg et al, 2018). In addition, this set of norms and values widely shared throughout the organization can impact the employee attrition rate and poor performance. Sull et al (2022) analysed employees' profiles and feedback from the world's 500 leading companies from 40 industries and they found that employees are likely to leave the company when they experience cultures that are:

- noninclusive: the organizations did not provide a fair and inclusive environment regarding gender, race, individual gender identity, sexual orientation, disability and age

- unethical and dishonest: employees used words such as cheating, making false promises and compliance to describe the behaviours that they saw in the organization

- uncollaborative: silo operations escalated to undermining each other or using sabotaging behaviours

- abusive: this behaviour may be from managers, such as bullying, demeaning and condescending.

Sull et al termed these experiences as a toxic culture that is not good for the organization but even worse for the employees themselves.

At the individual level, a toxic organizational culture can result in outcomes from stress, burnout and mental health issues to major diseases such as stroke and heart disease (Goh et al, 2015; Robbins et al, 2012). In a workplace culture where overtime and long working hours are expected (working more than 55 hours a week), it poses a significant personal risk. Using data from 2000–2016 across 194 countries, Pega and colleagues (2021) found that individuals who regularly put in more than 55 hours a week were associated with a 17 per cent higher risk of heart disease and a 35 per cent higher risk of dying from stroke.

Questions

- Have you ever experienced a toxic or healthy organizational culture in a previous job or organization? How would you describe the culture?

- How did it affect you and your work?

What is organizational culture?

Definition of organizational culture

Organizational culture has been much discussed since the 1980s. There is a range of ways to describe culture:

- Physical layout of the workplace, e.g. how organizational members interact with each other (e.g., office layout) or how the organizational members interact with their customers (e.g., parking spaces reserved for the executives vs. parking spaces reserved for the customers)

- Observed behaviours such as the language that people use

- Explicitly articulated principles that the collective tries to achieve, such as high-quality products and services
- Formal celebrations that reflect what is of value to the organization, such as promotion, bonus and project completion
- Implicit standards and values such as fairness
- Shared cognitive frameworks, which guide how organizational members perceive and interpret what they experience
- Emergent shared understanding created by the organizational members
- Unwritten rules which guide the behaviour of individuals, for instance, the company's way of doing things.

This is not to say that each of these is culture but the manifestation of culture. In Edgar Schein's seminal work on organizational culture, he refines the concept of culture from past research. He defined culture as

> 'A pattern of shared basic assumptions that was learned by a group as it solved its problems of external adaptation and internal integration, that has worked well enough to be considered valid and, therefore, to be taught to new members as the correct way to perceive, think and feel in relation to those problems.' (Schein, 2004, p. 17)

Schein further identified the four critical elements of the culture:

- Stability in the collective: culture is not only shared but also stable. It is sustained over time, even when employees leave or join the company
- Deeply embedded such that the culture can become stable among collectives
- Pervasive: culture influences all aspects of how organizations act and respond to their external environment and guides their internal operation
- Patterning or integration. Culture develops as organizational members respond to the environment.

Similarly, Groysberg and colleagues (2018) identified four widely accepted characteristics of culture:

- Shared: collective shared norms and values have to reside beyond the individual level
- Pervasive and applied broadly in the organization
- Enduring and self-reinforcing: the organization chooses the people they think will fit the culture and those who do not leave the company
- Implicit: the individual acts without thinking consciously.

Schein's model of organizational culture

Schein's model (2004) is a widely accepted model for organizational culture (Chatman & O'Reilly, 2016). It describes the culture in three levels. By level, it refers to the extent to which the cultural phenomena can be observed – one can see and feel easily – to be embedded, unconscious assumptions. From the most visible to least visible, Schien's model includes three elements:

Artefacts
Belief and value
Basic assumptions

Artefacts

At the surface level, Schein termed it an artefact. Artefacts are easy to see, hear and feel when someone new joins the organization. Artefacts include physical architecture, buildings, office areas and organizational structures and processes. Here is a list of artefacts that can describe the most visible level of organizational culture:

- physical environment
- language, jokes and slogans
- technology and products produced by the organization
- artistic creation
- emotional display
- stories and past unique achievements talked about in the organization
- norms, for instance, a high-tech company may expect the employees to be innovative, act with integrity, working collaboratively with others and be customer-centric (Chatman et al, 2014).
- published list of values
- observable rituals and celebrations.

Although artefacts are easy to see, this does not mean all outsiders will completely understand their meaning to the organizational members. The observers or the newcomers to the group can describe what they see, but they will not be able to understand the meaning of the artefacts to the groups. For instance, look at the symbol in Figure 9.1; what does this symbol mean to you?

I used this picture in the class where 88 per cent of the students were international students and 12 per cent were UK and EU students. While most of the home students identified this as a roundabout sign (called a traffic circle in the US), the others identified this as a sign of recycling. Indeed, not all artefacts mean the same to everyone – it is linked to their past experience. Individuals' responses to physical artefacts can differ. Therefore, we should be mindful of drawing profound meanings or assumptions solely based on the appearance of artefacts.

Figure 9.1   What does this symbol mean?

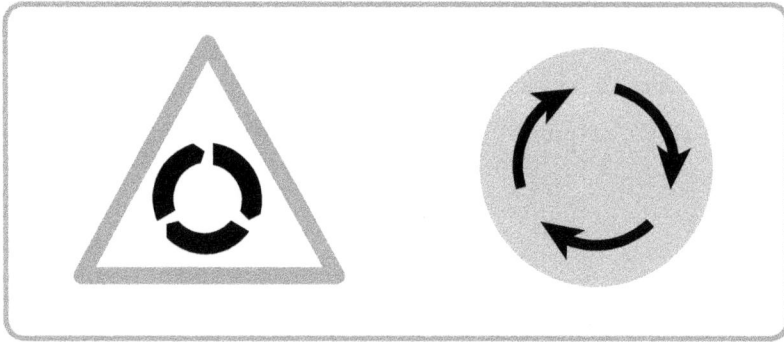

EXERCISE

From artefacts to organizational culture

You are visiting an organization and notice that the senior management has extravagant offices and executive lunchrooms. Looking at the surroundings, how do you describe the organization's culture?

REFLECTION

- What are some visible artefacts of your organization or university's culture, such as the physical space, dress code or company logo? How do these artefacts reflect the values and beliefs of the organization?

- How do the artefacts of the organization's culture affect how customers and clients perceive the organization? Do they convey a positive or negative image?

- What do the artefacts of the organization's culture suggest about the organization's priorities and values? Are these consistent with the stated values and mission of the organization?

- How can the organization's cultural artefacts be leveraged to support positive change and improvement? What changes to the physical space, dress code or company logo could help reinforce the organization's desired values and beliefs?

Espoused values

Espoused values are shared beliefs and norms that guide employees' behaviour. They are publicly declared principles and values that they claim to be working towards and will not be sustained and remain stable until validated by the collective. Many of the values are observable. However, there might be differences between what the organization says its values are and what the organization does. A company might say that they value its people, but the record of its past actions might be against that. Schein, therefore, terms this as espoused values, i.e., the beliefs and values that an organization states as desirable. When the value is believed by organization leaders and groups and employees act on the belief, this value is then gradually transformed into a basic assumption.

Basic assumptions When certain values are successfully implemented many times, they become firmly held within a social unit. They become taken for granted. The major difference between an espoused value and a basic assumption is whether it can be debated and challenged. Value is debatable, whereas basic assumptions are not. For example, a taken-for-granted assumption for engineering will be designing something safe (e.g., can you imagine engineers intentionally creating something unsound or unsafe?). These implicit assumptions guide behaviours that are unquestionable. When the basic assumptions are shared among organizational members, they are mutually reinforced.

Schein (2004) noted that the difference between value and basic assumptions lies in whether they can be challenged. Value can be discussed, whereas assumptions are taken for granted and will not be discussed or questioned. When the basic assumption is challenged, the person who raised the comments is likely to be viewed as an outsider while the rest dismiss those challenges.

REFLECTION

Think about where you were brought up or a place you are familiar with. Think about the taken-for-granted assumptions of your chosen place. How do those commonly held assumptions influence your behaviours and responses? Use the following list (adapted from Schein, 2004, p. 159) as the cue to help you identify those basic assumptions.

- How is time perceived?
- Are humans naturally good, bad or neutral?
- What is the relationship between humans and the environment?
- Regarding the relationships between people – are they competitive or collaborative? Are they individualistic or communal? Are they about conflict avoidance or the embrace of conflict?

Find another person who did not grow up in the same region or country where you come from. Compare your answers to theirs. What are the similarities and differences?

EXERCISE

Application of Schein's model

Imagine that you are working in a professional service firm where the company has a strong focus on innovation. Use Schein's model and describe what the artefacts, beliefs and values of this company are likely to be. Write down behavioural examples when you can.

How does culture form?

An organization's culture and its members are inextricably linked. How do individuals learn organizational culture and then continue to contribute to maintaining or changing the culture? Through socialization (also called assimilation). Socialization refers to 'the process of joining, participating in and leaving organizations' (Kramer & Dailey, 2019), where existing employees influence the newcomers to meet their organizational needs as well as establish satisfying work relationships in the organization. The socialization process is essential for newcomers or individuals who changed their roles to adjust to their new roles in the organization. According to Kramer (2010), there are four stages of the socialization process.

Anticipatory

Anticipatory socialization is when individuals join the organization and expectations are formed before encountering the organization first hand. The anticipation of how the individual should act is formed from their past indirect experience through friends, families, teachers and media, where we form the expectation of how people generally behave in a particular industry. For example, most would expect people to act professionally, respectfully and compassionately in the education industry. We expect doctors and nurses to provide high-quality patient care, communicate clearly and empathetically with patients and their families and maintain confidentiality and respect for patient autonomy. This expectation can also form during pre-organizational experiences (e.g., internship, job hunt process and formal organizational documentation). Individuals' interactions during interviews also inform the individual about their expectations and beliefs about their job, professions and organizations.

Encounter

The second stage of the socialization process is the encounter, typically in the first six months after employment. This is the time when newcomers experience uncertainty. Newcomers start to learn the reality of the organization. Newcomers can learn about the organization passively from the organizational onboarding process, where they learn about the company's operational processes and procedures and learning by observation, modelling their behaviour to match existing employees' actions. Newcomers can also act as a proactive conduit where they read organizational policies and procedures documents, ask direct and indirect questions to existing members and witness or break the rules of the organization. Exposure to this information makes the newcomer more familiar with the organization because they learn about the organizational expectations. Chao and colleagues (1994) identified six types of content information and knowledge exchanged during the socialization process that helps newcomers to learn about the organization's expectation:

- Performance proficiency. This allows individuals to know about the skills required for their role. This includes the skills and experience that the individuals bring when joining the organization and job-role-related knowledge, such as one's job responsibilities and understanding of one's career progression path.

- People. Individuals learn from their co-workers, work groups and their job. Peers and supervisors are the most important source of information for newcomers. Work interactions teach newcomers about good social skills and behaviours in the organization. This also includes whether individuals feel they are part of the 'gang' socially.

- Politics. Information such as how a more knowledgeable or more powerful position than others is helpful for the individuals and how conflicts are resolved in the organization. These include how things 'really work', understanding what needs to be done to achieve a desirable outcome and understanding the motive of other people's behaviours.

- Language. Jargon and slang for the profession or specific for the organization. This trade- or organization-specific language helps individuals understand the organization's explanations and reasoning.

- Goals and values. Organizational goals and values are socialized among the organizational members. Note that this also includes spoken (e.g., espoused value in Schein's model) and unspoken rules and norms in both individuals' immediate work context and the broader organization.

- History. This includes stories and histories of the newcomers' immediate work environment (e.g., the history of the department) as well as broader organization traditions, rituals, ceremonies and celebrations used in the organization. Gaining knowledge about the organization helps individuals learn about what type of behaviours are appropriate and what the organization values.

Metamorphosis

When newcomers no longer feel new to the organization, socialization enters the third stage – metamorphosis – where individuals learn the organizational culture through interpersonal relationships and organizational change (Kramer, 2010;

Kramer & Dailey, 2019). By this time, newcomers have already learnt about the organization and are acting in line with the organization's expectations, adapting their standards to what is expected. Individuals have also learnt about their roles, which results in increasing their self-efficacy and social acceptance (Bauer et al, 2007). When more newcomers join the organization, the people re-experience the first three stages of socialization: anticipatory socialization, encounter and metamorphosis.

Organizational exit

When individuals leave the company, this is the fourth phase of socialization. Not all employees are engaged; at some point, employees may become disengaged and leave the company – organizational exit. Organizational exit can be voluntary or involuntary (Kramer, 2010). A decrease in cultural fit for individuals indicates a likelihood of them leaving voluntarily. Using the six dimensions in the organizational socialization process, Chao et al (1994) found that people were more likely to leave the company when they perceived themselves as misaligning with organizational goals and values and were unfamiliar with its history and traditions. It signals that individuals are ready to leave the company. Individuals who changed jobs within the company showed a decreased cultural alignment in performance proficiency, language, people, politics and history. Likewise, analysis of over ten million internal emails by Srivastava et al (2018) found that newcomers who did not fit in with the organization's culture failed to gain social acceptance and were eventually forced to leave. Those who initially fit in but later become less aligned with the culture tend to disconnect from the organization and leave voluntarily.

REFLECTION

Newcomers often use social media to obtain information about their work, co-workers and organizations. Given the definition of socialization means the process of an individual joining, participating and leaving the organization and learning about the organizational needs, social media equally provides a platform to directly communicate with organizational members and enable newcomers to indirectly seek information – such as observing the interactions from other organizational members.

In a study of how organizational newcomers in their early twenties use social media in China, Huang (2022) found that newcomers connect to the organization's internal and external social media. In addition, highly visible and persistent information provided on social media is constant for newcomers – information seeking is easy for them. Huang also noted the cost of social media. The 24/7, continuous flow of information confuses newcomers. When using work-related external social media, newcomers were unsure of the best way to respond in the social space and questioned the benefit of engagement in social media in completing their daily tasks. Some of the examples from the study demonstrate the paradox that one might experience when individuals use social media or other instant messaging apps:

- Consider the situation when the newcomers wanted to concentrate on working, but the messaging might distract them from doing the work. Newcomers started to want to disengage from the group, but the managers expected them to keep an eye on the message.

- Consider the situation when the manager explicitly asks his employees to be more present in the social media group – because this was the norm in the organization to show one's acknowledgement of the online conversation. However, this norm might contradict the newcomers' role expectations as they do not feel this is directly related to their task.

Question:

How did social media information help you when you first joined the organization? You can think about the first time you entered the company from graduate school – what did you learn about this? Consider the direct message (one-to-one messaging) and indirect information gathered as you read texts, articles, pictures and videos in the public domain. How did the direct and indirect messaging help you learn about the organization and how you are expected to behave now?

The association between organizational culture and performance

A recent survey showed that 78 per cent of Fortune 1000 CEOs and CFOs view culture as one of the top three factors affecting their firm's value (Graham et al, 2016). The empirical evidence supported the link between organizational culture and individual performance. In particular, when individuals' values match with the organizational values (i.e., personal organization fit or value congruence), individuals have higher job satisfaction, higher level of organizational commitment, better individual performance, lower level of work withdrawal and are less likely to leave the company (Kristof-Brown et al, 2005). However, the association between organizational culture and organizational performance is less clear and researchers cannot pinpoint which aspect of the culture is associated with company performance. This may relate to how the culture was measured in the study. For instance, in Chatman and O'Reilly's (2016) seminal work, they identified that culture was rarely directly measured – it often depended on participants' rating of the strength of the culture (e.g., using a Likert scale to assess the organizational culture from a very strong culture to a very weak culture). The link between a company's culture and its performance has some predictive value (i.e. organizational culture can predict organizational performance), but why these connections exist needs to be clarified. It lacks a solid basis of understanding of how it works. Limited conclusive evidence directly connects organizational culture to specific and measurable outcomes at the firm level. Research cannot conclude the impact of the specific substance of organizational culture on organizational performance (Keyton, 2011; Sackmann, 2011; Schneider et al, 2013).

The value of organizational culture to managers: Three different perspectives

What is the instrumental value of organizational culture for managers? Organizational culture could be best viewed through three perspectives, as proposed by Alvesson (2013): culture as a building block, culture as shared understanding and culture as a diagnostic tool for managers. These three perspectives view leaders' ability to shape organizational culture. When managers view culture as building blocks, they see the possibility that it can be engineered and controlled through design. Organizational culture is highly modulable, just like other managerial interventions. When culture is considered as a shared understanding, it implicitly emphasizes managerial actions' influence. It views that leaders influence how employees perceive and develop consensus around the work activities and, therefore, how organizational members understand the culture. A third perspective of culture views culture as non-modulable and managers must adapt to the culture. Here culture is a diagnostic tool where no prescription will be provided. Culture is used to inform managers about what is challenging to achieve given the existing organizational culture in the company (therefore, culture serves as a constraint for managerial actions). Given the limitations in this, how could managers develop practical measures to implement managerial interventions successfully?

REFLECTION

Think about the three perspectives of culture – culture as building blocks, culture as shared understanding and culture as a diagnostic tool for the manager. Describe the limitation of each view when it comes to managerial intervention. Which perspective resonates with you the most? Think of some behavioural examples that informed your cultural perspective.

Common misconceptions of organizational culture

With the popularity of organizational culture, it comes with misguided beliefs about the concept. Alvesson (2013) and Keyton (2011) identified some traps in cultural thinking and being more aware of taking for granted cultural meaning. Here are some of the organizational culture myths.

- Myth: *the organization has a uniform culture. Culture is a shared understanding – a unanimous consensus about what is a company's organizational culture.*

Reality: The notion of collective and shared definition of organizational culture may prompt people to think that an organization has a uniform culture. However, 'shared' does not imply that everyone needs to agree on the organizational culture. Differences are likely to exist among organizational members. For example, the organization can have a dominant culture that may encourage employees to be collegiate, innovative and ambitious in achieving goals. However, people from different teams or departments are likely to have a subculture that differs from the organization's dominant culture. Differentiation is also expected to happen when there is an occupational difference.

EXAMPLE OF NON-UNIFORMED CULTURE: OCCUPATIONAL DIFFERENCES

When software engineers work with hardware engineers, they are likely to find themselves working differently in the following areas:

- Software engineers typically work at a higher level of abstraction, dealing with concepts and algorithms, while hardware engineers work at a lower level of abstraction, coping with the physical components and circuits.

- Software engineering is arguably a more collaborative process, with software engineers working closely with product managers, designers and other stakeholders. On the other hand, hardware engineering usually involves collaboration with other hardware engineers and technical specialists only.

Research has well documented the occupational division between software and hardware engineers and it is particularly challenging when the two occupations need to work together to come up with solutions due to the different professional knowledge that they have and different priorities (Majchrzak et al, 2012; Metiu, 2006; Metiu & Rothbard, 2013; Kou & Harvey, 2021).

Organizations are also likely to have other subcultures when organizational members are located in different geographical locations and use various technologies to complete work across hierarchical levels.

- Myth: *organizational culture does not change and it will last forever.*

Reality: change in organizational culture will take a long time, but organizational culture will not last forever. Positive cultural change is difficult to achieve but can be achieved. For example, Microsoft was known for having a competitive and aggressive culture, with a strong focus on individual performance and a hierarchical management structure. However, as the technology industry evolved, Microsoft recognized the need to adapt its culture to stay relevant and innovative. Satya Nadella became the CEO in 2014 and dedicated himself to transforming Microsoft's culture, shifting it away from a know-it-all, competition/confrontational approach to a more collaborative and growing mindset and finding purpose in their work. Microsoft's cultural transformation embraced startup attributes, such as customer obsession and focusing on usage data rather than sales. They freed up engineering talent, reducing hierarchies and fostering a sense of ownership and innovation. The company organized a large private hackathon, promoting collaboration and solving problems quickly, reflecting a more agile and entrepreneurial approach (Tabrizi, 2023).

Cultural types and their managerial implications

Similar to a personality, where individuals can be described as having different personality types and use those types to describe their preferences and traits, we can also classify organizational culture in types. Popular culture frameworks are Groysberg and colleagues' (2018) culture framework and Cameron and Quinn's (2006) competing value framework. Looking at the different organizational culture types is helpful when one wants to make sense of their culture and identify ways to generate culture change. Similar to the benefit of personality types, where personality types provide a common language for individuals to discuss their strengths and weaknesses, culture types offer a common language to discuss complex desirable organizational fixtures, such as structure, behavioural patterns and leadership for the organization. Considering organizational culture type also makes it possible for the organization to compare to other organizational cultures to analyse the organization and look for aspirations. Groysberg's culture framework and Cameron and Quinn's competing value framework are useful tools for thinking about a company's organizational type and its implications for organizational practices.

Groysberg's Culture Framework

This culture framework was based on Groysberg and his colleagues' study of organizational culture over 200 companies, over 1,000 executives and over 25,000 employees in various industries (e.g., ranging from consumer, financial and professional services, IT to energy and utility) and different organizational types (public, private and nonprofit) across the globe. Their analysis highlights two dimensions that distinguish organizational culture types:

- Attitude towards people interaction: independent vs. interdependent. This refers to an organization's orientation to people interaction. An organization that tends to work independently values autonomy and is highly individualistic. An organization that works interdependently values coordination, integration and focus on group actions.

- Attitude towards change: stability vs. flexibility. This refers to organizations' tendency to emphasize stability or flexibility. An organization that values stability prefers predictability and control and relies on proven processes, whereas an organization that values flexibility prefers adaptability, innovation and openness.

Based on these two dimensions, eight types of cultural styles were identified. Each type of culture has its distinctive way of solving problems and all can be successful. For instance, a culture that focuses on learning and enjoyment will be more tolerant of risk-taking behaviours. A culture emphasizing safety will tend to manage and control the risks when responding to the external environment.

According to Groysberg, every culture type has its strengths and weaknesses. I have described some of these briefly here:

Purpose culture

- Strength: appreciation of social responsibility and sustainability
- Weakness: may overemphasize the long-term focus, resulting in long-term vs. immediate focus conflict

Caring culture

- Strength: focusing on teamwork, engagement, communication, trust and belonging
- Weakness: could overemphasize consensus and therefore could slow down the decision-making process and avoid conflicts, hindering the team's ability to address issues constructively. Task conflict is particularly useful to stimulate healthy debates across different perspectives, improving problem-solving and enhancing performance

Order culture

- Strength: focus on operational efficiency. Respecting rules and being cooperative
- Weakness: emphasizing rules can reduce individualism and creativity

Safety culture

- Strength: focus on risk management and stability
- Weakness: can be too focused on formalization and standardization. Emphasis on risk management and stability could also lead to inflexibility and a hierarchical working environment

Authority culture

- Strength: decisive and responsive to threats and crises
- Weakness: bold decision-making style may lead to conflict and a work environment that does not encourage information exchange (i.e., not a psychologically safe environment)

Result culture

- Strength: focus on execution and achieving goals
- Weakness: emphasizing results could lead to high stress, conflicts and collaboration breakdown in the organization

Enjoyment culture

- Strength: playful and fun-loving, can encourage employee engagement and creativity
- Weakness: overprioritizing fun and employee engagement may compromise overall productivity and performance

Learning culture

- Strength: open and exploring environment that promotes innovation and organizational learning
- Weakness: too much emphasis on exploration could result in the underuse of existing capabilities

Implicitly Groysberg's culture framework emphasizes the CEO and top leaders more because they believe that top leaders have more influence on organizational culture – leaders set strategies and role model the culture. Secondly, they are concerned about culture change – where organizations can assess their culture in relation to the flexibility-stability and interdependent-independent spectrum and setting a culture 'target'. Imagine you are leading in shaping the organizational culture using Groysberg's cultural framework. The eight distinctive types of culture provide some snapshots of the cultural insight and corresponding leadership qualities and capabilities needed to develop a particular culture. Looking at the 'to-be' or aspired culture type versus what type of leaders they currently have, organizations can then identify potential gaps and start thinking about what kind of leaders they need to recruit, what kind of leader behaviours are desirable in shaping the culture (e.g., someone with strong purpose vs. someone is a hands-on operational person).

Cameron and Quinn's Competing Value Framework

Cameron and Quinn's framework started with a focus on critical factors that drive organizational effectiveness. Their framework was developed based on a sample of over 10,000 executives from Fortune 500 companies. Based on their research, they identified six critical dimensions of the organizational culture, including the dominant characteristics of the organization (e.g., the organization is a dynamic place, a result-delivering place, feels like an extended family, a controlled and structured place), leadership style, management of employees, the glue that holds organizational members together, strategic emphasis and criteria for success.

Like Groysberg's culture framework, Cameron and Quinn's competing value framework was set out to explain the organizational phenomenon and diagnose and facilitate organizational culture change. The framework identified two continuums. The X-axis is the spectrum of internal focus and integrating vs. external focus and differentiation. The Y-axis is the spectrum of flexibility and discretion vs. stability and control. The two dimensions then defined four dominant culture types: clan culture, adhocracy culture, hierarchy culture and market culture.

Hierarchy culture

Hierarchical organizing became popular in the early 1900s when companies focused on achieving efficiency-driven goals. Organizations with hierarchical cultures concentrate on having explicit decision-making authority, formal processes and procedures and control mechanisms set up to monitor the progress. It usually has multiple hierarchical layers in the organization. Formal rules and procedures govern what organizational members do and reinforce those rules. In a hierarchy culture, leaders are good organizers, monitors and coordinators, ensuring procedures are followed and maintaining organizational performance. Company examples of hierarchy culture can be found in fast food restaurants (McDonald's, KFC), large multinational conglomerates and the government.

Market culture

Effectiveness is essential to market culture, but the foundation to achieve efficacy differs from hierarchy culture. Whereas hierarchy culture focuses on methods best to organize the company's internal attributes and capabilities, market culture focuses on achieving efficiencies by managing external stakeholders. It emphasizes external control; this trend was popular in the mid-1990s. Under market culture, the external environment is viewed as relatively stable and the organization is result-driven and marching towards its goal. A strong emphasis on winning and market share defines the organization's success. Leaders in the market culture are good at directing and producing results. To be able to do so, they are also good at negotiation and motivating subordinates to exceed expectations. They can seem harsh and demanding. Company examples of hierarchy culture include General Electric and Microsoft.

Clan culture

Clan culture is a family-type organization. This type of organization is not new, but its importance was re-discovered when researchers started studying Japanese companies in the 1960s due to their sweeping economic success. Loyalty and commitment from the employees are central to the clan culture. Clan culture focuses on 'we' – shared values, cohesion and collectiveness. They focus more on teamwork (e.g., reward as a team rather than as an individual, looking at ways to improve individual and organizational performance), employee commitment and participation and companies' commitment to the employee (e.g., providing life-long employment). Where the foundation for hierarchy and market culture lies in efficiencies, clan culture views the best way to achieve performance as working together with internal and external stakeholders. This is particularly evident in turbulent environments. The clan culture leaders are team workers and supporters who facilitate high-performing teamwork. The managers will likely be good at managing interpersonal relationships through creative, constructive feedback and developing subordinates.

Adhocracy culture

An adhocracy culture is flexible and dynamic. It emerged when the global economy entered the information stage in the 21st century. The organizational environment is typically characterized by turbulent and intense competition. Special teams and groups form in response to the need but adjourn when the task is completed. The basic assumption is that companies succeed when they are innovative, and innovation leads to new resources and therefore to succeed financially. Leaders in adhocracy organizations are typically entrepreneurs, visionary and creative – usually very good at communicating their future vision. Adhocracy organizations are high-technology, aerospace, software development, consultancy companies and filmmaking companies.

Strong and weak culture

Another way to measure organizational culture is by its strengths and weaknesses. Chatman and O'Reilly (2016) defined strong culture as widely shared and firmly held among the organizational members. A strong culture is typically maintained and shaped through extensive systems and management practices. On the other hand, a weak culture is one in which employees neither agree on nor are attached to the organization's core values and norms. It is worth noting that a strong culture does not equate to behavioural consistency among organizational members. For instance, when innovation and flexibility are widely shared and firmly held among organizational members, this shared norm is likely to promote behavioural inconsistencies – where individuals can express themselves freely, experiment and take on new opportunities (e.g., Google). On the behavioural side, it lacks behavioural uniformity and seems to suggest the organization does not have a strong culture, despite it actually having a strong culture.

Culture and leadership

Implicitly, the trait-based culture framework underlines the leader's role in influencing culture. A leader's influence on culture can be direct and indirect (Alvesson, 2013; Keyton, 2011; Cameron & Quinn, 2006; Mamatha & Geetanjali, 2020; Kramer & Dailey, 2019; Driskill & Brenton, 2005). Through role modeling, leaders can re-engineer organizational systems, structure and procedures and revise selection, promotion and bonus or reward criteria. In addition, a leader can also make sense of (or reframe) the information for the organization members. For an external threat such as a crisis, a leader can frame it as a time to come together and focus on working on the strong programmes and eliminate the weaker. Leaders can also heighten external threats and shape organizational members' sense of urgency. During the Covid-19 pandemic, many academic institutions had to teach remotely. While a completely online learning offering may have been on the universities' agenda, the Covid-19 pandemic accelerated the adoption of that technology. Many universities saw this as the perfect time to develop online learning programmes.

Likewise, Schein (2004) discussed how leaders could consciously and systematically embed leaders' own beliefs and values in the broader organization. There are six primary ways a leader can influence organizational members' sense-making process:

1 what leaders pay attention to: this includes things that leaders measure and control periodically

2 how leaders respond to critical incidents

3 how they allocate resources

4 by conscious role modeling or through teaching and coaching their organizational members

5 the design of the reward system

6 leaders' criteria for recruitment, selection, promotion and demotion.

Leaders can also influence organizational culture through secondary mechanisms, which include organizational structure, systems, procedures, rituals, design of physical spaces, success storytelling and formal statements of the organizational mission and policies. In particular, Schein argues that leaders need to pay attention to the messages sent out through these actions – consistency of messages is essential. If the leader is unaware of the power of the messages sent out through the primary and secondary mechanisms, any inconsistent messages and behaviours will become a space for organizational members to decipher what the leader 'really' means. Organizational members are likely to create their own narratives of the events. These events include the following:

- Leaders' emotional reactions. An angry response to the situation sends a strong message of what the leader wants.

- An area in which the leader did not react. Organizational members also interpret the situation when the leader does not respond to it. For example, in a project where cost, delivery schedule and product quality are important, which is more important than others? Organizational members would interpret product quality as the most important when the project manager did not get much comment over the delay and spending more money on product development.

- Inconsistency and conflicts that's under the surface. For example, when the organization champions employee involvement, but the top management does all the decision-making, this sends out inconsistent messages to the organizational members, particularly the newcomers, who will find this inconsistency very obvious.

REFLECTION

Choose a leader that you aspire to or are familiar with. Use Schein's primary and secondary mechanisms for leaders to embed their beliefs and values in the organization as a cue to think about how the leader influences organizational culture. How did it influence its organizational members' perception of an event?

- Primary mechanisms:
  o What does a leader pay attention to?
  o How do leaders respond to critical incidents?

- o How did they allocate resources?
- o How does a leader role model or influence through teaching and coaching their organizational members?
- o How do leaders actually give rewards and status?
- o What are a leader's criteria for recruitment, selection and promotion?
- Secondary mechanisms
  - o Organizational structure
  - o Organizational systems
  - o Organizational procedures
  - o Organizational rituals
  - o Design of physical spaces
  - o Organizational success storytelling
  - o Formal statements of the organizational mission and policies

Organizational culture and national culture

How can geographical location influence organizational culture? Geographical location serves as the broader context for the organization and the organization adapts to it. Geographical locations can influence how an organization operates. Hofstede (1983) claimed that management is culturally dependent and leaders will need to adapt managerial practices to local culture, while others addressed the fit between organizational practices and local culture matters (Newman & Nollen, 1996) and the importance of socio-cultural context in defining organization's work culture (Mendonca & Kanungo, 1994). At the more practical level or perhaps the personal level, we are now working with ever more diverse people from different cultural backgrounds. Being more aware of other national cultures gives you insights into how other ways of thinking and behaving might differ from our fundamental ways. Ting-Toomey and Dorjee's (2019) research addressed the mindful communication that occurred in the everyday work setting. Consider the following and how you may respond in the work setting:

- You are due to finish a task, but it was not ready when it was expected. How would you explain this to your manager?

Different languages impose different thinking logically. In English, one is likely to say: 'I cannot give you the report because it is not ready' – you and I are emphasized.

In Chinese, on the contrary, context and contingent conditions (e.g., because, so, then) come up front in the sentence, paving the way for the main point. You and I are de-emphasized in Chinese. Therefore, with Chinese as their native language, one is more likely to say, 'because of so many projects running simultaneously, the report was not finished.' In a cross-cultural communication setting, the latter expression might seem like not taking responsibility to an English speaker, and misunderstanding may occur.

- You are heading to a meeting at 10:30 am. What time do you usually arrive at the meeting?

Different cultures have different understandings and interpretations of time. Some cultures emphasize the past-present times (e.g., African cultures), while others emphasize the future (e.g., Canada and the United States). For instance, if a train arrives more than one minute later than its original schedule in Japan, it is considered late. In Mexico, however, turning 40 minutes late for a scheduled meeting is not uncommon. In Nigeria, a meeting may start anytime between 10:30 and 11:30 am.

REFLECTION

Talk to people you know from other countries and have a conversation about their cultural norms and traditions related to dinner or parties. Specifically, ask them to describe the time their dinner or parties typically begin when guests arrive, the timing of serving dinner and the duration of the dinner party. Compare whether the events begin on time in different countries and how long the dinner parties typically last. Describe your findings on the varying perceptions of time across cultures during these conversations.

Hall's Context Theory

Hall's Context Theory is one of the dominant frameworks in cross-cultural communication. According to Hall, an anthropologist, behaviour and interactions are conditioned by consideration of time and space or the communication context, thus bringing to light non-verbal communication. Hall's work is not without critique (e.g., Cardon, 2008). However, Hall's Context Theory provides a framework for understanding how culture and context shape human behaviour and communication. In Hall's view, 'no communication, no culture'. Communication develops and sustains the organizational culture (Keyton, 2011).

Hall viewed that human interaction can be broadly classified into high and low-context cultures. In low-context cultures, the message is communicated explicitly and directly. The sender of the information (or the speaker) is responsible for clearly communicating so that the receiver understands what is spoken. The sender's intention would be straightforward to the receiver through their content and tone of voice. In low-context cultures, thoughts, opinions and feelings are addressed during a conversation (Ting-Toomey & Dorjee, 2019). People with low-context communication characteristics are likely to call for direct communication and the notions of 'get to the point' or 'I am not a mind reader' reflect it. Countries such as Germany, Switzerland, Denmark and Sweden are at the low end of the continuum.

In high-context cultures, communication is mainly implicit, meaning context and relationships are more important than words. The sender's intent is likely to be camouflaged, sending out information in a more implicit way. The listener is responsible for figuring out the meaning of the information and making sense of the context. Most Asian countries (e.g., Japan, China and Korea) and Arabic countries are towards the high end of the cultural context continuum.

HIGH VS. LOW-CONTEXT COMMUNICATION

Consider the following everyday conversation between two Japanese neighbours to demonstrate the high-context communication style:

> A: *Your daughter is very good at playing piano. We hear the beautiful piano sounds from your house in the evening time.*

> B: *I am very sorry about this.*

Why did B apologize? Although it reads like A is praising B's daughter, what A refers to is the piano noise, but she did not want to point it out directly and used an indirect hint. B understood the indirect hint and therefore apologized for the piano noise. The UK is another example of a high-context communication style and here are some of the British examples:

- *'How are you?'* means 'hi' and the speaker does not want to know how you are in detail. The importance of harmony is usually the reason why they opt for a more implicit way of communication.

- Picture yourself engaged in a discussion, sharing ideas and thoughts. If someone responds with 'This is very interesting,' you might naturally assume they appreciate your idea. In dictionaries, 'interesting' signifies something attention-grabbing due to its uniqueness, excitement, or richness in ideas. However, in the UK, when someone says 'It's interesting!' it often conveys the opposite – they might not actually like it. Sometimes, rather than expressing dislike for something or its taste, people use this phrase as a gentle way of indicating they're not particularly enthusiastic. When conversing with your manager, if they say 'I suggested…' in British English, it often implies a directive rather than a suggestion. It can convey a stronger expectation for action rather than leaving room for flexibility or choice. However, in American or European English, this might be perceived as a simple proposal or recommendation, allowing more freedom to decide whether to act on it or not. Imagine you've just shared a piece of your work with someone. When they respond with 'Not bad,' it might seem lukewarm. However, for British, it is likely to be a positive remark. They're acknowledging your effort and implying that what you've presented is actually quite good or even impressive.

REFLECTION

Cross-culture communication style

Although it is common sense that we should move beyond our preferences, it is not easy to do. What's more, our usual preferences put us in a blind spot, making it harder to identify the potential cultural differences. Sanchez-Burks and colleagues' (2003) experiment examined East-West communication styles. In particular, they looked at how Americans and East Asians (including participants from China, Korea, Thailand, Japan, Singapore and Taiwan) interpreted indirect messages. These indirect messages ranged from avoiding eye contact and looking away, offering indirect verbal praise, to the tone of voice when delivering the message. They found that Americans paid less attention to indirect messages in the work setting compared to the non-work setting. Interestingly, they found that participants from East Asia and America paid similar levels of attention to indirect messages in non-work settings (family and social settings). In other words, Americans can be just as indirect as East Asians in social situations. However, potential misunderstandings could happen in the work situation, such as giving feedback to colleagues and subordinates from different cultures.

In Sanchez-Burks' following study (Brett et al, 2013), the cross-cultural authors further identify different conflict resolution practices. East Asian and Western managers continued to be entirely baffled by colleagues' behaviours – where East Asians can be perceived as passive-aggressive by Western managers and Western managers can be perceived as aggressive by the East Asian manager. Where Western managers tend to confront the situation directly, East Asian managers are more likely to avoid direct confrontation and prefer to be unresponsive.

> **Reflection question:**
>
> Recall a situation when you need to work with someone new to the country or the organization. Have you sent out signals of disagreement to the other person who did not receive the subtle cue? How can you adapt your style to move the conversation forward?

Hofstede's national culture

Hofstede's cultural dimension is among the most used cultural framework. Hofstede's cultural model was developed while working as a researcher at IBM, where he was tasked to study how to manage a global workforce effectively. He sampled 88,000 employees across 72 countries (reduced to 40 countries where he has more than 50 samples). The number of Hofstede's cultural dimensions increases over time. In the early 1980s, there were four dimensions: power distance, uncertainty avoidance, individualism-collectivism, masculinity-femininity and he later added time orientation (long vs. short-term orientation) in the late 1980s. The score for each dimension ranged from 1–100.

- Power distance refers to the degree to which people accepted and expected the power to be distributed unequally. In the high power distance culture, there is a greater acceptance of authority and individuals tend to defer to those in positions of power. People may not question authority or challenge those in power. In low power distance cultures, individuals may challenge authority and those in power and there is a smaller gap between the powerful and the less powerful. Latin American and Asian countries are among the highest power distance countries. Countries such as Austria, Israel, Denmark, New Zealand, Sweden and Switzerland have the lowest power distance scores.

- Individualism vs. collectivism is about how people prioritize individual interests over collective ones. In an individualistic culture, people define themselves primarily by personal characteristics and achievements rather than social identities. On the other hand, collectivism refers to the extent to which people prioritize the interests of the group or community over individual interests. In collectivistic societies, people tend to value interdependence, cooperation and harmony. Research found that performance-based compensation is more prevalent in individualist cultures, whereas group performance-based pay is more prevalent in collectivist cultures (Von Glinow et al, 2002). Highly individualistic countries include the US, Australia, Canada, the UK and the Netherlands. Highly collectivist countries include Venezuela, Colombia, Pakistan, Ecuador, Peru, Guatemala and Panama.

- Masculinity vs. femininity refers to the degree to which a culture values assertiveness, results, success and competitiveness (as a traditionally masculine trait) vs. nurturing and caring, preferring a friendly atmosphere and cooperation (traditional femininity traits). Note that masculinity and femininity are not gender specific. Instead, it is about which traits are valued more in society. In masculine cultures, there is a greater emphasis on performance, ambition and achievement, and success is often measured in material terms, such as wealth and status. In feminine societies, there is a greater emphasis on quality of life, work–life balance and social relationships. Countries with high masculinity scores tend to orient towards career advancement and earnings. Countries with a high score on masculinity are Japan, Hungary, Austria, Venezuela, Italy and Switzerland. Countries with lower scores (i.e., feminine) are Sweden, Norway, the Netherlands, Denmark, Costa Rica and Finland.

- Uncertainty avoidance refers to the degree to which people are comfortable with ambiguity and uncertainty and the extent to which they rely on rules and orders to avoid uncertainty. In low uncertainty avoidance cultures, people tend to be more comfortable with ambiguity and change and may be more willing to take risks and try new things. High uncertainty avoidance culture prefers seniority and a skilled-based reward system, whereas low uncertainty avoidance prefers performance-based pay and employee-shared ownership plans (Von Glinow et al, 2002). Countries with high uncertainty avoidance include Greece, Portugal, Belgium, Japan, France, Spain and Russia. Countries with low uncertainty avoidance include Singapore, Jamaica, Hong Kong, Denmark, Sweden and Norway.

- Long-term vs. short-term orientation is also called Confucian dynamism. People prioritize long-term goals in cultures with a long-term orientation, such as future rewards or a sense of duty and responsibility to society. These cultures often value thrift, perseverance and self-discipline. People tend to respect traditions and social obligations in cultures with a short-term orientation. East Asia countries such as South Korea, Taiwan and Japan scored the highest for the long-term orientation, whereas Anglo countries, Africa and Latin America scored lowest (i.e., short-term orientation).

The GLOBE Study

While Hofstede's study was often criticized for its time-dependent sample, another programme carried out longitudinal research, the Global Leadership and Organizational Behaviour Effectiveness programme (GLOBE). In Hofstede's study, individuals rate their values, such as the significance of personal or family life in their ideal job and the level of independence in their lives. Hofstede focuses on measuring cultural values based on how they influence cultural behaviours. The GLOBE study changed its focus from individuals to society. In the GLOBE study, respondents were asked to describe their ideal leadership style in their culture (Stephan, 2022).

The GLOBE project tested Hofstede's (1980) dimension with some extensions. The GLOBE study retained the terms Power distance and Uncertainty avoidance, but the definitions might have changed. Collectivism was divided into Institutional collectivism and In-Group collectivism, while Masculinity-Femininity was split into Assertiveness and Gender egalitarianism. Long-term orientation was replaced with Future orientation. There were unique dimensions for: performance orientation (emphasis on achievement and performance) and humane orientation (regard for fairness, altruism and caring). The GLOBE research also examined several hypotheses, particularly related to leadership matters. Their culture dimensions include the following:

- Assertiveness: the degree to which people in a culture are assertive, dominant and forceful in their relationship with others

- Future orientation: refers to the degree to which people in a culture are future-oriented and invest in the future. People are not looking for instant gratification

- Gender egalitarianism: refers to the degree to which a culture values gender equality

- Humane orientation: refers to the degree to which a culture values kindness, compassion and support to others

- Institutional collectivism: refers to the degree to which people in a culture encourage collective actions, e.g., company organization, community and society

- In-Group collectivism: refers to the degree to which people are proud of collective achievement and take pride in group members' achievement in the organization or families, e.g., families, friends and inner circle

- Performance orientation: refers to the degree to which people in a culture value achievement, performance and success and are willing to work hard to achieve these goals continuously

- Power distance: refers to the degree to which people in a culture accept power and authority

- Uncertainty avoidance: refers to the degree to which people in a culture rely on rules, procedures, structure and consistencies to reduce the uncertainty of future events. Noted that GLOBE's version is more indicative of the degree to which societies are oriented towards adhering to rules while Hofstede's Uncertainty Avoidance version is known for representing societal stress (Tung & Verbeke, 2010).

Hofstede's model and the GLOBE model are influential. Hofstede's study focused on a single multinational company (IBM) with non-managerial employees, using a management diagnostic approach. GLOBE involved about 170 researchers studying 951 non-multinational organizations. The GLOBE study expanded and improved upon Hofstede's research, incorporating a broader scope, updated methodologies and continued to collect data (their latest data collection effort was in 2020 with data from over 143 countries). How can we understand Hall's, Hofstede's and GLOBE's culture dimension? Friends and Keig (2019) provided some useful examples to apply culture dimensions. In particular, in their view, rather than focusing on the debate and details of each culture dimension, they view these frameworks as theoretical knowledge for cross-cultural application and that they serve as a lens to explore and compare diverse cultural interpretations in business settings, helping in the development of soft skills. They suggested thinking about cultural dimensions before following professional situations:

- before being part of cross-country projects
- prior to partnering with overseas suppliers, customers and colleagues
- before project implementation of cross-country or international campaigns

Given the situation, answering the following questions helps you to use the cultural framework in practice:

- What cultural differences have you observed or might exist?
- Select a specific framework to analyse the situation.
- Offer a rationale for your cultural interpretation of the particular dimension.
- Develop strategies to react to the situation which you identified and explain why you do so.

Practically applying this knowledge should help individuals to: know more about relevant cultural aspects in professional situations, use cultural frameworks to analyse the situations and offer appropriate cultural solutions. It is important to note that cultural dimensions give us language to describe cultural differences; it is crucial to treat each person as an individual, avoiding automatic stereotypes in specific situations.

HOW ARE CULTURES REPRESENTED ON THE INTERNET?

How can culture influence a corporate's website design? In Capece and Di Pillo's (2023) study, they look at whether corporate's online communication is associated with national culture. In collectivist societies, people care about others and look for group consensus and community-based social order. It is, therefore, likely that people in collectivist cultures prefer the design of websites to include forums and chat functions so that they can share their concerns and points of view and look for a consensus in the group. To study this, they choose two countries that exhibit different ends of Hofstede's cultural dimension: India and Australia. They look at 1,000 companies' websites: 500 each from the National Stock Exchange of India and the National Stock Exchange of Australia.

Their research found that the national culture is associated with website design in the following three cultural dimensions:

- Power distance: India (77) has a higher power distance than Australia (36). They found that in India, there are more websites showing corporate headquarters buildings and corporate companies' executives, referring to titles and honours and awards won by the companies. They expect the Indian websites will exhibit more respect for hierarchies.

- Individualism: In comparison to Australia (90), India is a more collectivist country (48). They found this was also reflected in website design, where Indian websites present more group images and individual photos than Australian websites.

- High vs. low context culture: Given that India is high context culture, authors also found that Indian websites use significantly more images and animations accompanied with text, scrollbars and banners. Because of the volume and the variety of content, it also makes the navigation of the Indian website clunky, in their opinion.

EXERCISE

Benefits of cultural misfits

National culture is vital to consider because it is the environment in which the organizations operate. Organizations often adjust to regional, country-specific practices – seeking the 'fit' between an organization and its operating geographical location. However, differences can be beneficial, i.e., cultural misfits. Please think about the potential benefit of cultural differences/misfits.

Chapter summary

Culture is generally a concept that helps explain what the organization is about and how things are done in the organization. There are a number of ways that organizational culture is relevant to organizational members' behaviours. From the angle of organizational members performing and completing tasks, organizational culture helps individuals understand how things are done and the expected response to the problem. At the personal level, organizational culture could impact individuals' physical and psychological health. The organization develops, maintains and is involved over time through socialization across organizational members.

There are different ways to define culture, but Schein's definition of organizational culture is one of the most preferred, where Schein considers organizational culture as contained artefacts, values and patterns of basic assumptions which is developed by a collective as they learn to resolve problems when the organization adapts to the external environment and internal integration. Some view organizational culture as the organization's personality and there are several ways to classify organizational culture. The trait-based classification of organizational culture is a productive way to discuss the differences among organizations. This includes (but is not limited to) the strengths and weaknesses of organizational culture, what kind of leader the organization needs and what type of competencies the leader needs to have to strive in the organization. While organizations do not exist in a vacuum, it is crucial to consider their socio-environmental context – national culture. In particular, understanding the national culture allows us to discuss cross-country differences and their implications.

Chapter review questions

- Explain culture's practical importance from organizational and employee perspectives.
- Describe the critical elements of organizational culture using Schein's three-level organizational culture model.
- Describe how individuals learn an organization's culture.
- Describe different types of cultural frameworks and the implication on leaders' behaviours.
- Contrast different dimensions of Hofstede's' national culture model.

Key terms

Organizational culture

Levels of organizational culture

Manifestation of culture

Organizational socialization process

Culture framework

Competing value framework

Power distance

Individualism vs. collectivism

Masculinity vs. femininity

Uncertainty avoidance

Time orientation

High context culture

Low context culture

Revisiting session exercises

Exercise: From artefacts to organizational culture

Luxurious office space for senior leaders and executive lunchrooms is associated with status. You are likely to expect the company culture to emphasize social order.

Exercise: Application of Schein's model

In Hogan and Coote's (2014) attempt to understand how organizational culture influences companies' innovative behaviours, they used Schein's model to describe the culture of an innovative company from the professional services.

The artefact is the explicit and observable characteristics part of the organizational culture. In a professional service, the artefacts are likely to be:

- Celebration (e.g., award ceremony) of an innovative marketing strategy
- The physical layout of the organization
- Decoration of the building
- Language and metaphor contain messages that value and support innovation.

The organizations are likely to hold the following values:

- Value success where the organization strives for a high standard and challenging goals.
- Openness and flexibility. Appreciation and receptivity to novelty.

- Open internal communication, such as social interactions and cross-fertilization of ideas.
- Professional capabilities. This includes knowledge, expertise and technical skills.
- Cross-functional collaboration and coordination. High level of sharing and effective conflict resolution process.
- A high degree of autonomy and responsibility from individuals. Individuals can take control over their own work and ideas in order to produce innovative outcomes.
- Recognition of employees formally (e.g., reward, formal recognition of innovation) and informally (e.g., feedback, learning opportunities).
- Encouraging risk-taking without the fear of negative consequences or damaging individuals' self-image. Risk-taking behaviours will likely enhance one's professional identity within the company and gain managerial support.

The organizations are likely to hold the following norms:

- Promoting activities that support project execution, such as encouraging teamwork and sharing across teams.

Exercise: Benefits of cultural misfits

According to Caprar et al (2022), a recent review on cross-cultural practices, they identify that cultural differences can generate the following benefits:

- Increase knowledge transfer.
- Increase creativity, such as innovation, exploration and new solutions.
- Cross-pollinated good practices and generating new norms and beliefs (i.e., cultural change)
- Stimulate learning.
- Source of competitive advantage through differentiation.
- Dissimilar cultural practices can complement local business practices, broaden the range of options and create new opportunities.

Further reading

Alvesson, M (2013) *Understanding Organizational Culture*, 2nd edition, Sage.

Keyton, J (2011) *Communication and Organizational Culture: A Key to Understanding Work Experiences*, 2nd edition, Sage.

Chatman, J & O'Reilly, C (2016) Paradigm lost: Reinvigorating the study of organizational culture, *Research in Organizational Behaviour*, 36, 199–224.

Bauer, T N, Bodner, T, Erdogan, B, Truxillo, D M & Tucker, J S (2007) Newcomer adjustment during organizational socialization: A meta-analytic review of antecedents, outcomes, and methods, *Journal of Applied Psychology*, 92(3), 707–721. https://doi.org/10.1037/0021-9010.92.3.707 (archived at https://perma.cc/E8Z2-XGW7)

GLOBE Project: www.globeproject.com/ (archived at https://perma.cc/RW4J-HGE5). The Global Leadership and Organizational Behaviour Effectiveness (GLOBE) project is a large-scale research investigating cultural influences on leadership and organizational behaviour across different countries and regions. The project involves hundreds of researchers from over 60 countries. The GLOBE project aims to advance our understanding of how culture affects leadership and organizational behaviour and to provide insights for global leaders and managers operating in diverse cultural contexts. You will be able to find the following information on their website, including GLOBE cultural dimension, research findings on culture and leadership and individual countries' cultural profile.

If you are interested in exploring the differences, similarities and in-depth discussion about GLOBE and Hofstede's model, the authors themselves have published two papers addressing these topics:

Hofstede, G What did GLOBE really measure? Researchers' minds versus respondents' minds, *Journal of International Business Studies*, 37, 882–896 (2006). doi.org/10.1057/palgrave.jibs.8400233 (archived at https://perma.cc/Z6RN-F8M4)

Javidan, M, House, R, Dorfman, P & de Luque, M S (2006) Conceptualizing and measuring cultures and their consequences: A comparative review of GLOBE's and Hofstede's approaches, *Journal of International Business Studies*, 37, 897–914. doi.org/10.1057/palgrave.jibs.8400234 (archived at https://perma.cc/BV7S-4PFJ).

And this paper critically assesses both cultural dimension: Venaik, S & Brewer, P (2013) Critical issues in the Hofstede and GLOBE national culture models, *International Marketing Review*, 30(5), 469–482. doi.org/10.1108/IMR-03-2013-0058 (archived at https://perma.cc/UTM6-KUTD).

Culture 500: sloanreview.mit.edu/culture500/ (archived at https://perma.cc/ZR5L-X2DM). The Culture 500 website is an initiative of the MIT Sloan Management Review and is part of the broader initiative on Culture 2.0, which aims to promote a more data-driven approach to organizational culture. The Culture 500 database includes information on over 500 companies, allowing users to compare the cultural values of different companies and track changes in cultural values over time. The platform is designed to help companies better understand and measure their own culture, as well as benchmark their culture against industry peers and competitors.

Organizational culture and performance: A longitudinal study. A rare longitudinal study (six years) by using data from 95 car dealerships to investigate the relationship between organizational culture and performance.

Boyce, A, Nieminen, G, Levi, R, Gillespie, M A, Ryan, A M, & Denison, D R (2015) Which comes first organizational culture or performance? A longitudinal study of causal priority with automobile dealerships, *Journal of Organizational Behaviour*, 36(3), 339–359.

Organizational culture and performance: Merger and acquisition. The inconclusive result of organizational culture on performance is also reflected in the research on merger and acquisition, which, instinctively, one would expect the cultural differences and frictions will impact the performance of merger and acquisition. Please see the review articles:

Ye, S, Zhou, J, Jiang, Y & Liu, X (2023) Managers as the bridge: How cultural friction influences the integration of cross-border mergers and acquisitions, *International Business Review*, 32(4), 102138.

Stahl, G K & Voigt, A (2004) Impact of cultural differences on merger and acquisition performance: A critical review and an integrative model, *Advances in Mergers and Acquisitions*, Vol. 4, pp. 51–82. https://doi.org/10.1016/S1479-361X(04)04003-7 (archived at https://perma.cc/7FVX-GWRM)

References

Alvesson, M (2013) *Understanding Organizational Culture*, 2nd edition, Sage.

Bauer, T N, Tucker, J S, Bodner, T, Erdogan, B & Truxillo, D M (2007) Newcomer adjustment during organizational socialization: A meta-analytic review of antecedents, outcomes and methods, *Journal of Applied Psychology*, 92 (3), 707–721.

Brett, J, Behfar, K & Sanchez-Burks, J (2013) How to argue across culture, *Harvard Business Review*.

Cameron, K S & Quinn, R E (2006) *Diagnosing and changing organizational culture: Based on the competing values framework*, Jossey-Bass San Francisco, CA.

Capece, G & Di Pillo, F (2023) Online corporate communication: Should national culture matter?, *Frontier Communication*, 8:1005903. doi: 10.3389/fcomm.2023.1005903 (archived at https://perma.cc/3WMA-3C99).

Caprar, D V, Kim, S, Walker, B W & Caligiuri, P (2022) Beyond "Doing as the Romans Do": A review of research on countercultural business practices, *Journal of International Business Studies*, 53, 1449–1483. doi:10.1057/s41267-021-00479-2 (archived at https://perma.cc/ZC3D-KMX8).

Cardon, P W (2008) A critique of Hall's contexting Model, *Journal of Business and Technical Communication*, 22 (4), 399–428.

Chao, G T, O'Leary-Kelly, A M, Wolf, S, Klein, H J & Gardner, P D (1994) Organizational socialization: Its content and consequences, *Journal of Applied Psychology*, 79 (5), 730–743.

Chatman, J A, Caldwell, D F, O'Reilly, C A, & Doerr, B (2014) Parsing organizational culture: How the norm for adaptability influences the relationship between culture consensus and financial performance in high-technology firms, *Journal of Organizational Behaviour*, 35, 785–808.

Chatman, J A & O'Reilly, C A (2016) Paradigm lost: Reinvigorating the study of organizational culture, *Research in Organizational Behaviour*, 36, 199–224.

Driskill, G W & Brenton, A L (2005) *Organizational Culture in Action: A Cultural Analysis Workbook*, 2nd edition, Sage, Thousand Oaks, CA.

Friends, T & Keig, D L (2019) A scaffolded approach to teaching national culture: From Hall to Hofstede to GLOBE. In Gonzalez-Perez, M. A., Lynden, K, & Taras, V. (eds.), *The Palgrave Handbook of Learning and Teaching International Business and Management*, Palgrave Macmillan.

Graham, J R, Grennan, J, Harvey, C R & Rajgopal, S (2016) Corporate Culture: Evidence from the Field, *Journal of Financial Economics*, Available at SSRN: https://ssrn.com/abstract=2805602 (archived at https://perma.cc/7DPL-YAPN).

Goh, J, Pfeffer, J & Zenios, S A (2015) The relationship between workplace stressors and mortality and health costs in the United States, *Management Science,* 62 (2), 608–628.

Groysberg, B, Lee, J, Price, J & Cheng, J Y (2018) The leader's guide to corporate culture, *Harvard Business Review.*

Hofstede, G (1983) National Cultures Revisited, *Behavior Science Research*, 18(4), 285–305. https://doi.org/10.1177/106939718301800403 (archived at https://perma.cc/K9LU-35XR)

Hofstede, G (1980) *Culture's Consequences: International Differences in Work-Related Values*, Sage, Beverly Hills, CA.

Hogan, S J & Coote, L V (2014) Organizational culture, innovation and performance: A test of Schein's model, *Journal of Business Research*, 67 (8), 1609–1621.

Huang, V (2022) Information experiences of organisational newcomers: Using public social media for organisational socialisation, *Behaviour and Information Technology*, 42(9), 1279–1293. DOI: 10.1080/0144929X.2022.2070545 (archived at https://perma.cc/H59F-E8VK).

Keyton, J (2011) *Communication & Organizational Culture: A Key to Understanding Work Experiences*, Sage.

Kou, C Y & Harvey, S (2021) A dialogic perspective on managing knowledge differences: Problem-solving while building a nuclear power plant safety system, *Organization Studies*, 43(9), 1355–1378.

Kramer, M (2010) *Organizational Socialization: Joining and Leaving Organizations*, Polity Press, Malden, MA.

Kramer, M W & Dailey, S L (2019) Socialization and Organizational Culture. In *Movement in Organizational Communication Research: Current Issues and Future Directions*, Routledge/Taylor & Francis Group, New York, pp. 96–115.

Kristof-Brown, A L, Zimmerman, R D & Johnson, E C (2005) Consequences of individuals' fit at work: A meta-analysis of person-job, person-organization, person-group and person-supervisor FIT, *Personnel Psychology*, 58 (2), 281–342.

Majchrzak, A, More, P H B & Faraj, S (2012) Transcending knowledge differences in cross-functional teams, *Organization Science*, 23 (4), 951–970.

Mamatha, S V & Geetanjali P (2020) Founder Leaders and Organization Culture: A Comparative Study on Indian and American Founder Leaders Based on Schein's Model of Organizational Culture, *IIM Kozhikode Society and Management Review*, 9 (1), 23–33.

Mendonca, M & Kanungo, R N (1994) Managing human resources: The issue of cultural fit, *Journal of Management Inquiry*, 3(2), 189–205.

Metiu, A (2006) Owning the code: Status closure in distributed groups, *Organization Science*, 17 (4), 418–435.

Metiu, A & Rothbard, N P (2013) Task bubbles, artefacts, shared emotion and mutual focus of attention: A comparative study of the microprocesses of group engagement, *Organization Science*, 24 (2), 455–475.

Newman, K L & Nollen, S D (1996) Culture and congruence: The fit between management practices and national culture, *Journal of International Business Studies*, 27 (4), 753–779.

Ochi, W G (1993) *Theory Z: How American Business Can Meet the Japanese Challenge*, Avon Books.

O'Reilly, C A & Chatman, J A (1996) Culture as social control: Corporations, cults and commitment. In B.M. Staw & L.L. Cummings (eds.) *Research in Organizational Behaviour: An Annual Series of Analytical Essays and Critical Reviews*, Elsevier Science/JAI Press, Vol. 18, pp. 157–200.

Pega, F, Náfrádi, B, Momen, N C, Ujita, Y, Streicher, K N Prüss-Üstün, A M, Descatha, A et al (2021) Global, regional and national burdens of ischemic heart disease and stroke attributable to exposure to long working hours for 194 countries, 2000–2016: A systematic analysis from the WHO/ILO joint estimates of the work-related burden of disease and injury, *Environment International*, 154, 106595.

Peters, T J & Waterman, R H (1979) *In Search of Excellence: Lessons from America's Best Run Companies*, Profile Books, New York.

Robbins, J M, Ford, M T & Tetrick, L E (2012) Perceived unfairness and employee health: A meta-analytic integration.: EBSCOhost, *Journal of Applied Psychology*, 97 (2), 235–272.

Sackmann, S A (2011) Culture and performance. In Ashkanasy, N M, Wilderom, C P M, Peterson, M F, (eds.) *The handbook of organizational culture and climate*, 2, Sage, Thousand Oaks, CA, pp. 188–224.

Sanchez-Burks, J, Lee, F, Choi, I, Nisbett, R, Zhao, S & Koo, J (2003) Conversing Across Cultures: East-West Communication Styles in Work and Nonwork Contexts, *Journal of Personality and Social Psychology*, 85 (2), 363–372.

Statista (1991) *Industrial production growth in the US., Japan and Europe per decade 1961–1990*, Statista Research Department.

Schein, E (2004) *Organizational Culture and Leadership*, 3rd edition, Jossey-Bass.

Schneider B, Ehrhart M G, Macey, W H (2013) Organizational climate and culture, *Annual Review of Psychology*, 64, 361–388.

Stephan, U (2022) Cross-cultural innovation and entrepreneurship, *Annual Review of Organizational Psychology and Organizational Behaviour*, 9, 277–308.

Srivastava, S B, Goldberg, A, Manian, V G, & Potts, C (2018) Enculturation trajectories: Language, cultural adaptation and individual outcomes in organizations, *Management Science*, 64(3), 1348–1364.

Sull, D, Sull, C, Cipolli, W & Brighenti, C (2022) Why every leader needs to worry about toxic culture, *MIT Solan Management Review*.

Sull, D, Sull, C & Zweig, B (2022) Toxic culture is driving the great resignation, *MIT Sloan Management Review*.

Tabrizi, B (2023) How Microsoft became innovative again, *Harvard Business Review*. https://hbr.org/2023/02/how-microsoft-became-innovative-again (archived at https://perma.cc/5A8U-5FCS).

Ting-Toomey, S & Dorjee, T (2019) *Communicating Across Cultures*, 2nd edition, Guilford Press, New York.

Tung, R, Verbeke, A (2010) Beyond Hofstede and GLOBE: Improving the quality of cross-cultural research, *Journal of International Business Studies*, 41, 1259–1274. https://doi.org/10.1057/jibs.2010.41 (archived at https://perma.cc/LY2Y-LFX9).

Von Glinow, M A, Drost, E A & Teagarden, M B (2002) Converging on IHRM best practices: Lessons learned from a globally distributed consortium on theory and practice, *Human Resource Management*, 41 (1), 123–140.

Organizational change 10

- Communication and organizational change
  - Type of communication
  - Sensemaking and change
- Culture and change
  - Johnson and Scholes' Culture Web

WHY IS CHANGE IMPORTANT?

At the organizational level, change – or failure to change – is a make-or-break deal for organizations. Here are some examples of when organizations fail to change.

Nokia

Nokia was once the world's largest mobile phone manufacturer. Nokia dominated the market at its peak in 2007, when its market share was around 50 per cent globally (Statista, 2013). But Nokia was slow to adapt to the shift towards touchscreens and app-based operating systems like iOS and Android, which were introduced in 2007. As a result, Nokia's market share declined rapidly. In 2008, its market share dropped to 40 per cent and in 2013 its market share was less than 10 per cent. The company eventually sold its mobile phone business to Microsoft in 2013.

Kodak

For decades, Kodak was one of the leading companies in the photography industry. However, with the advent of digital technology, Kodak's business model became obsolete. Despite early warnings about the shift towards digital photography, Kodak failed to adapt to the changing market. The company continued to focus on its traditional film and print business, while competitors such as Sony and Canon invested heavily in digital technology. As a result, Kodak's sales and profits began to decline rapidly. The company was eventually forced to file for bankruptcy in 2012.

LEGO

Leading toy company LEGO – with a 7.6 per cent market share and branded as the most valuable toy brand – is the largest toy company in the world as of 2023 (Statista, 2023). Lego accounts for the highest annual revenue across the toy brand (Statista, 2023). It is probably hard to imagine that just over two decades ago, LEGO was in trouble. During the early 2000s, LEGO underwent a period of significant expansion within its core product line and expanded a wide range of new products including new markets such as theme parks, retail and video games. Some of the new LEGO sets do not resemble the image of Lego. Open your browser and look up some of the images of the following older LEGO sets online (Znap, Galidor, Scala and Belville). These designs incorporated numerous novel components that lacked compatibility with existing products, leading to an upsurge in their parts inventory and heightened supply expenses. Furthermore, many of these innovative designs did not resonate with the targeted demographic. The only sets that were able to make money were the ones related to Star Wars and Bionicle themes. In 2003, the company lost $300 million. In 2004, the company was $800 million in debt, losing 30 per cent of its market share (Davis, 2017). LEGO turned around this situation by listening to customer feedback and creating new products (e.g., licensed products, such as Star Wars and Harry Potter). LEGO launched the TV series LEGO Ninjago and released its first movie. LEGO expanded their target market – adults. LEGO regained its popularity after a refocus on their strategic direction.

All of the cases highlighted the importance of change and adaptation at the organizational level. In today's fast-paced and rapidly evolving business environment organizations must be able to adapt quickly to changes in technology, consumer preferences, market conditions and the environmental threats (e.g., natural disasters, pandemics) (Kotter & Cohen, 2002; MacCarthaigh, 2014; Mithani, 2020). Change, embracing it and adapting is said to increase organizations' longevity (Bertelli, 2008; Greasley & Hanretty, 2015).

HOW IS CHANGE RELATED TO YOU PERSONALLY?

Individuals are likely to experience significant life changes which can be challenging such as:

- career change or advancement
- starting a family or having another child
- relocating to a new city or country
- significant financial changes, including starting a business, retiring or inheriting
- going back to school or pursuing additional education or training
- health concerns or medical diagnoses
- becoming a caregiver for an ageing parent or family member.

While seeking guidance from loved ones or experts is beneficial for individuals navigating significant life changes, grasping the essence of change models offers valuable insights into behavioural patterns across different stages of transformation. Such comprehension fosters heightened self-awareness regarding coping strategies, granting individuals a sense of empowerment and control over the change process.

At the organizational level, understanding individuals' response to change (see individuals' response to change, or the change curve, on page 307) holds vital importance as it enables organizations to predict reactions, tailor communication, reduce resistance, manage expectations, provide targeted support, minimize disruption and optimize implementation timing.

Questions:

- How do you typically respond to change in the workplace? Are you open to new ideas and ways of doing things or do you resist change? Are you comfortable with uncertainty or do you prefer stability and predictability?

- What skills and competencies do you need to develop to adapt successfully to organizational change?

What is change? Why do we need change?

Change is vital at both the individual and organizational levels. For individuals, we experience changes throughout our life, including changing jobs, learning new skills or adopting new habits. Change can lead to personal and professional growth. Change is also essential for organizations to adjust to meet the demands of the operating environment. Resisting change could lose organizational competitive advantage and fail to meet the changing needs of customers.

Internal and external triggers of change

According to Cummings and Worley (2014) and Dawson (2003), the need for change may be triggered by external and internal disruptions. External disruptions include:

- change in legal requirements: for example, a significant regulatory change in the automotive industry is the implementation of revised emissions standards in many countries. First introduced in 2014, the European Union has implemented the Euro 6 emissions standards, which set stricter limits on the amount of pollutants emitted by vehicles. All new cars and vans in the United Kingdom need zero emissions from 2035. China has also implemented similar emissions standards, known as the China 6 emissions standards. These changes have required automakers to invest heavily in new technologies and make significant changes to their vehicles to meet the new requirements. Governments also introduce tax incentives to promote the development of the electric car

- major technological advancement: for example, in Kodak's case, digital cameras and technological advances made traditional film photography products obsolete. Other industries include music (physical music to digital music streaming), books (printed book to digital e-book and e-reader), shopping (traditional brick-and-mortar stores to online shopping) and online streaming videos (traditional TV network providers and channels to Netflix and Amazon Prime video and on-demand services)

- change in the political landscape: political landscape change such as Brexit and the US–China trade war impacts the company's cost, supply chain and investment decisions in various industries, such as finance, manufacturing, agriculture and technology

- changes in political and/or social attitudes: these can impact consumer behaviour and preferences, which can affect a company's strategies and ongoing projects. For example, the World Bank's Quarterly Pulse Survey of Global Multinational Enterprises (Saurav et al, 2021) demonstrated that companies respond to the market and focus more on sustainable investment.

Internal triggers include:

- change in leadership
- change of ownership, e.g., privately owned company, public listing company, joint venture, merger and acquisition of another company etc.
- change in organizational structure
- change in company strategy
- improvements to operational efficiency and performance
- expansion of the organization
- fluctuations in the business cycle.

McKinsey's 7S model

McKinsey's 7S model was first presented to help organizations align their internal elements and improve performance, but it can also help us outline internal elements that can trigger organizational change. McKinsey's 7S model includes:

- strategy: the organization's plan for achieving its goals and objectives

- structure: the formal and informal systems and processes that govern the organization's operations, including its reporting relationships, roles and responsibilities

- systems: about how the work is done, including tools and processes used to support the organization's operations (e.g. technology, communication channels and performance management systems)

- shared values: the core beliefs, attitudes and values that shape the organization's culture and guide its behaviour

- skills: the competencies and capabilities of the organization as institutions and employees, including their technical expertise, knowledge and experience

- staff: the organization's workforce, including the number, diversity and quality of employees

- style: style embodies the way tasks are approached within the organization, often interchangeable with the term 'culture.' This encompasses the informal side exhibited by the company. Both the leadership approach and the managerial techniques employed to steer the functioning of the company, encompassing choices, interactions and task assignment. Individuals not aligned with this 'style' frequently find themselves relegated to the role of an observer from the outside.

Based on the seven elements, the model suggested three types of internal change stimuli:

- Hard elements: these are the tangible, quantifiable components of an organization, such as its structure, systems and strategy. Changes in these elements can be triggered by external factors such as a shift in market conditions, the introduction of new technologies or changes in regulatory environments. Internal factors such as a desire to improve efficiency or respond to changing customer needs can also trigger changes in these hard elements. For example, a company may restructure its organization to align with changing customer demands or adopt new technologies to improve operational efficiency.

- Soft elements: these are the intangible, less quantifiable components of an organization, such as its culture, leadership style and employee skills and capabilities. Changes in these elements can be triggered by factors such as a desire to improve employee engagement and satisfaction, respond to changing consumer preferences or adapt to new business models. For example, a company may adopt a new leadership style that fosters greater collaboration and innovation or invest in training and development programmes to improve employee skills and capabilities.

- Shared values are the core beliefs and values underpinning an organization's culture and guiding its decision-making. Changes in these values can be triggered by various factors, such as changes in societal norms and expectations, shifts in the competitive landscape or a desire to align better with changing customer needs. For example, a company may shift its values to prioritize sustainability and environmental responsibility in response to growing concerns about climate change and the environment.

Individuals' response to change

Central to change implementation is people – how do organizational members react to organizational change? Generally speaking, the more significant the change, the more negative an individual's response to change becomes (Rafferty & Griffin, 2006) and individuals are likely to experience the process of initial equilibrium–transition–final equilibrium (Elrod & Tippett, 2002). Dr. Walter Menninger conceptualized the 'change curve' to illustrate how individuals react in the face of change. This framework proves invaluable for organizations seeking insights into the predictable psychological reactions exhibited by individuals and groups in the midst of organizational transitions.

Studying volunteers who carry out two-year overseas duties, Menninger's research summarizes a typical psychological process that individuals go through. When individuals first experience change, their morale tends to be high and enthusiastic. Once the volunteers reached the work area, they faced difficulties on-site despite the pre-tour preparation. These difficulties violate their previous taken-for-granted assumption, resulting in a deep dip in morale. As time went by, volunteers accepted the situation, put worries aside, particularly with issues outside their control and focused on what they could change. In the final stage, when the volunteers returned home after two years of service, individuals experienced the same level of response that they experienced at the beginning of their experience. Although the level of morale was the same before and after the trip, volunteers felt that they were different and grew from the volunteering experience. Not everyone goes through these stages at the same pace or in the same order and some people may get stuck in one stage or experience setbacks along the way. However, Menninger's framework provides a helpful guide for understanding the psychological process of change and adapting to new circumstances.

Kubler-Ross' five-stage model originated from studying individuals' emotional responses to death and dying but was further applied to understand the psychological implication of organizational change. The five stages of the Kubler-Ross model are as follows:

- Denial: This stage involves disbelief or shock at the reality of the change. Individuals in this stage may feel numb or disconnected from their emotions.

- Anger: In this stage, individuals may experience frustration, resentment or bitterness about the change, particularly when the change is perceived as unfair.

- Bargaining: In this stage, individuals may negotiate with a higher power to change the situation.

- Depression: This stage is characterized by sadness or despair about the change, particularly when the change involves significant disruption to their work or personal life.

- Acceptance: In this final stage, individuals come to terms with the reality of the loss or change and begin to move forward. They may develop a new perspective or a sense of purpose as they adapt to new circumstances.

Kubler-Ross's change curve can be a helpful tool for organizations seeking to manage change effectively and support their employees through the change process. By recognizing and addressing the emotional responses of individuals to change, organizations can increase the likelihood of successful change implementation and minimize the negative impacts of change on employees.

APPLYING MENNINGER'S CHANGE CURVE AS AN INDIVIDUAL

- Have I experienced the different phases of Menninger's change curve before? How did I respond to each stage and what did I learn from those experiences?

- How can I use the insights from Menninger's Change Curve to understand better and manage my reactions to change? What specific actions can I take during each phase of the change curve?

Applying Menninger's change curve to the team that you work with, answer the following questions:

- How do I typically support individuals and groups during times of change? Are there any areas where I could provide more support or take a different approach?

- How do I communicate about change to others? Consider specific examples of what was spoken to others – e.g., the change's nature, vision, process, benefits and outcome. How can I improve my communication to ensure that individuals and teams are fully informed and engaged?

- How do I celebrate successes and milestones during the change process? Do I take the time to acknowledge progress and achievements or do I move on to the next phase without reflecting on what has been accomplished? How can I create more opportunities for celebration and recognition during change?

To look at the reaction to change in more granular detail, individuals' immediate reactions to change can be positive and negative in three ways (Oreg et al, 2011):

Affective response – how they feel

- Positive affect. This can be change-related satisfaction and increased level of organizational commitment
- Negative affect. When individuals experience change-related stress, anxiety, fatigue and negative emotions

Cognition about the change – what they think of the change

- Individual's views towards change
- Individuals' interpretation of the change

Behavioural reactions – what they intend to do

- Active involvement vs. withdrawal behaviour, such as intention to quit due to change
- Resist vs. support change
- Level of commitment to the change programme

Individuals' approach to change tends to be positive when:

- they view themselves as responsible for what happened to them (internal locus of control), respond positively and have a more positive emotional reaction to change
- the individual has a higher level of self-efficacy, believing they can organize and take necessary actions, readiness to change, engagement and commitment to change problem-focused coping strategy is associated with a higher level of accepting change
- individuals with shorter tenure, higher education, and union membership tend to hold a positive view towards change within the company.

Similarly, people often exhibit a pessimistic attitude towards change under certain circumstances. This can occur when they perceive themselves as having little influence over the events that affect them, also known as an external locus of control. Additionally, individuals who struggle with adapting to new situations are more likely to experience unfavourable emotions and stress brought about by their professional roles.

Individuals' readiness to change

While individuals' core beliefs around change influence individuals' immediate and longer-term positive reactions to change (Oreg et al, 2008; Oreg, 2003; Oreg et al, 2011), how can an organization prepare employees to be mentally ready for the change? One approach to look at this is the readiness to change. Readiness to organizational change refers to how an individual is willing and prepared to adapt to new organizational changes. This includes their attitude, behaviour and emotions towards the initiative (Rafferty et al, 2012). A high individual readiness to change is essential for the success of organizational change initiatives. When individuals are ready and willing to change, they are more likely to be supportive, actively engage in the change process and help to overcome resistance from others. Therefore, it is crucial for leaders to assess and enhance individual readiness to change before implementing any organizational change initiatives.

According to Rafferty et al (2012), the underlying components related to individual readiness for organizational change are:

- the belief that change is needed
- the proposed change is needed
- individuals believe they can implement the change
- principal support: individuals' belief of whether the organization can provide the support to implement the change
- valence: the importance of the benefit of carrying out the change to the individual.

In addition to an individual's self-belief, individual readiness to change is also related to an individual's affective state: an individual's current and future-oriented positive emotional response to the change. For instance, organizational members can experience positivity and optimism when they look forward to a change or future event. One can feel happy and achieve if she/he knows there will be a formal recognition (such as an award ceremony, bonus or promotion).

Group readiness for change

Group level readiness for organizational change is also influenced by the following factors:

- the belief that the change is needed
- believing their capacity to implement change
- benefit the change can bring to the group and organization
- affective responses to change.

The key differences between individual and group-level readiness for change lie in meaning-making. At the group level, the belief of change is fabricated by making sense of the change-related information across organizational members and whether the benefit of the organizational change is in line with the group's interest. For instance, high ambiguity, work overload and group distress lead to lower group belief in the change (Rafferty & Jimmieson, 2009). Individuals are also likely to influence each other's emotional response – emotion is contagious and individuals synchronize their feelings with others in the group (Barsade, 2002).

ASSESS YOUR READINESS FOR CHANGE

Given the importance of readiness to successfully navigate the change initiative, consider the following questions.

1 Assess your past experiences with change: Reflect on how you have responded to change. Consider what went well and what did not go well. Identify what factors contributed to your success or failure in adapting to change.

2 Evaluate your current attitudes and emotions towards change: Consider your current attitude towards the change initiative. Identify any emotions that you are experiencing towards the change. How do you think the change will affect you and your work?

3 Identify potential benefits and costs of the change: Consider the benefits and expenses for yourself and the organization. What opportunities might arise from the change? What challenges might you face? Identify any personal concerns or obstacles that may impact your readiness to change.

4 Assess your characteristics: Consider your characteristics, such as your openness to new experiences, flexibility and adaptability. Identify your strengths and weaknesses and how they may impact your readiness for change.

5 Based on your reflection, identify specific actions that you can take to increase your readiness for change. This might include seeking support from others, learning new skills or knowledge or adopting a more positive attitude towards change.

STRATEGIES TO COPE WITH RESISTANCE

Change can generate resistance in people. According to Cummings and Worley (2014), organizations are likely to experience three types of resistance: cost consideration to implement change, political respect where change can have implications for resource allocation in the organizations, as well as the impact of change on existing 'ways to do things' in the organization. Imagine that you are the senior leader of the organization. What kind of strategy can you employ to mitigate resistance to change?

THE INDIVIDUAL'S TENDENCY TOWARDS CHANGE

Are you willing to change? Do you embrace change? Or do you prefer stability? Oreg (2003) developed the Resistance to Change Scale (RTC scale) which can help you gauge your tendency towards change. To assess your natural tendency to embrace change, please look at Oreg's questions (Oreg et al, 2008, p. 939) and rate each item from 1 (strongly disagree) – 5 (strongly agree).

Resistance to change

Oreg (2003) identified four dimensions of resistance to change, namely routine seeking, where individuals value familiarity and stability at work (items 1–5); the emotional reaction, which refers to the extent individuals experience anxiety or anger in response to change (items 6–9); a short-term focus that describes the extent to which an individual prioritizes immediate concerns over long-term ones (items 10–13); and cognitive rigidity refers to the extent to which an individual has difficulty adapting to new ways of thinking or new information (items 14–17). The total score can range from 19 to 95, with higher scores indicating more significant resistance to change. There is no 'good' or 'bad' score, but this is a starting point to understand your response to change.

A high RTC score generally indicates that an individual is more resistant to change and may struggle to adapt to new situations, processes or procedures. They may prefer stability and routine and feel anxious or uncertain when faced with change. On the other hand, a low RTC score suggests that an individual is more open and adaptable to change and may see change as an opportunity for growth and improvement. They may be more willing to take risks, explore new ideas and feel energized by the challenge of navigating change.

After you calculate the score and look at the total score and individual scores in each sub-dimension of the RTC score, think about the following questions:

- How might my score impact my ability to navigate and adapt to changes at work?
- What support and resources can I draw upon to help me navigate during periods of change?
- How does my score align with my long-term career goals and aspirations?

If you calculate your score more than once, please think about the following question:

- Have there been any changes in my score over time and if so, what might be the reasons for these changes?

Types of organizational change

Considering different types of change is a helpful way to think about what practices and strategies are needed to manage the change. Different types of change have varying complexity, impact and resistance. The kind of organizational change underlines the significant challenges the organization faces and the processes it needs for change is the first step for introducing organizational change.

First, change can be incremental or transformative. Incremental change involves minor improvements to existing systems, processes or products (e.g., implementing a new customer feedback system). It is worth noting that even small changes can be met with resistance as people may feel that the difference that the change brings is unnecessary or threatens their daily work. On the other hand, transformative change involves a fundamental shift in how things are done (e.g., from a physical shop to an online store). Transformative change can be met with significant resistance from employees who may feel threatened by the scale of the change, and the outcome and the impact of the change were not clear when implementing the transformative change. Given the scale of the change, transformative change often requires significant resources and investment.

Change can also be described as proactive or reactive. Proactive change involves anticipating and responding to emerging trends. When change is initiated proactively, individuals may resist due to the change of status quo or feel the change is unnecessary. Reactive change involves responding to the unexpected and the company needs to adjust to accommodate the change. Reactive change can be difficult for organizations as organizations need to adapt to new conditions quickly (e.g., a crisis or economic downturn). Organizations may be unable to respond to the change when they do not have the resources or capacity to do so. For instance, when Covid-19 hit and governments announced lockdowns and social distancing measures to contain the virus, many organizations faced the urgent need to shift operations towards remote work.

This adjustment became crucial as face-to-face interactions dwindled, prompting businesses to adopt digital platforms swiftly. Universities pivoted from traditional in-person classes to online learning models, online curriculum development and virtual events. However, transitions require technology, investment and staffing. On the other hand, imagine a local retail shop that predominantly conducts its business through a traditional brick-and-mortar setup. When the unexpected impact of the Covid-19 pandemic restrictions was introduced, smaller establishments grappled with the need to establish an online presence via e-commerce platforms. Despite this demand, the pace at which smaller shops transition to digital operations takes more time due to resource constraints.

Change can be planned or unplanned. Planned change involves a deliberate, structured process of identifying, designing and implementing change initiatives. Planned change initiatives do not always succeed if key stakeholders, such as senior leaders, employees or customers, do not fully support or understand the rationale for the change. Planned change initiatives can have unintended consequences that are difficult to predict, such as changes in employee morale or unexpected impacts on customer relationships. Unplanned change occurs spontaneously or as a result of unforeseen events. Some of the challenges associated with unplanned change include a lack of control or capacity to respond to external factors and disruptions in the organization's daily operation to adapt quickly to new conditions.

Other classifications of change type include the work of Meyer et al (1990), which classifies change types based on two dimensions: the scale of change (organizational vs. industry) and how the change is taking place (continuous vs. discontinuous change). Mohrman (1989) and Levy (1986) looked at the change in terms of scale and pervasiveness of change (the size of the change in terms of the group of people being affected by the change and in terms of the organizational systems being affected by the change) and depth (behavioural change vs. a paradigm shift). Large-scale change addresses fundamental issues and transforms organizations. Mergers and acquisitions, restructuring and major shifts in business focus are examples of large-scale organizational change, requiring significant resources, time and effort to implement and often affecting the entire organization. On the other hand, small-scale change allows for continuous improvement and adaptation to changing circumstances, improving efficiency and productivity.

Short-term and long-term changes are necessary for an organization's success. Short-term changes can help to address immediate issues and provide momentum for broader transformation efforts. Examples of short-term changes include reorganizing a team, introducing a new product or service or implementing a cost-saving measure. Examples of small-scale change include process improvements, changes to job roles and updates to technology. Long-term changes, however, are critical for building sustainable competitive advantage and adapting to changing market conditions over time. Examples of long-term change include shifting the organization's focus to sustainability, investing in employee development to foster a culture of innovation or implementing a significant technology transformation.

Change process

'How can we best implement planned organization change?' is a question that senior managers and executives like to ask when it comes to planned organizational change. In response to this need, change management scholars developed a sequence of steps for organizations (Stouten et al, 2018). Common organizational change obstacles can be broadly classified into two categories (Hoag et al, 2002):

- perceived external factors: factors that managers believe are outside their control. For example, the organization cannot change because change is too costly. This cost can be money or time invested in the change. Managers believe the change is experienced from the external environment, such as a crisis or governmental regulatory change.

- perceived internal factors: organizational members are perceived to be at fault if the change fails.

Collecting responses from more than 500 human resource managers in the UK, Hoag and colleagues (2002) identified three types of obstacles to organizational change as follows:

- Poor leaders. When leaders have no vision, they do not articulate the need for change effectively to the organizational members. They focus on their personal agenda rather than the organizational agenda and do not recognize the need for change. This can hinder organizational change.

- Weak managers. Hoag identified characteristics of weak managers: dealing with unrelated change challenges rather than focusing on the actual change needed, a hierarchical internal system that makes change untenable and back to the organization's old way, managers seeing themselves as victims of the change and cling to existing status and benefits.

- Culture. Whether existing organizational culture aligns with change, internal politics and fear of change/uncertainty.

Change models

Lewin's Three-Step Change Model

Lewin's Three-Step Change Model was developed as MIT's Group Dynamic Research Centre director. At the time, there were many resistances to change and Lewin's Three-Step Model provides a roadmap for understanding and implementing change within organizations. Despite the model originating in the 1940s and its simplistic three-step process, it remained influential in the field and laid the foundation for the subsequent change management model.

- Unfreeze: The unfreezing stage involves preparing individuals or groups for change by establishing a vision and change plan. Unfreezing is important because employees and organizations must be willing to let go of old behaviours and thinking. An example of this can be setting up a business case that highlights the company's existing equity, diversity and inclusion practices that need to be improved; otherwise, the company will lose business and talent in the company.

- Change: The second stage involves implementing initiatives, such as introducing new policies, procedures or technology, altering organizational structure or making other significant changes to the organization's operations. The company may designate a team to oversee the implementation process, monitor the progress of the change initiatives and address any challenges that arise. During this stage, communication and training are crucial to ensure that stakeholders understand what is expected of them and can adapt to new ways of doing things.

- Refreeze: The third and final stage involves solidifying and integrating the changes into the organization. The change becomes embedded in the organization and organizational infrastructure. Maintaining the change and making new changes to the norm might involve providing ongoing training and support, monitoring progress and making adjustments as necessary and reinforcing the new ways of doing things through recognition.

Kotter's model

Kotter's model was introduced in his 1995 book *Leading Change*. The model was based on his working with large companies and observing how they managed change. Building on Lewin's Three-Step Change Model, Kotter's model provided a more detailed process for implementing change. Central to Kotter's model is the importance of creating a shared sense of urgency around the need for change, communication and stakeholder engagement. Kotter's model has become widely used in change management and has been applied in various settings, including businesses, government agencies and nonprofit organizations. It is valued for its practicality, ease of use and emphasis on communication, collaboration and stakeholder engagement. Here are Kotter's eight steps of the organizational change process:

1 Foster a sense of urgency: leaders should effectively convey the necessity for change in a manner that deeply resonates with stakeholders and propels them to take decisive action. This involves constructing a compelling rationale for the change and generating momentum to propel the change initiative forward.

2 Create a powerful alliance: to steer the transformation, leaders assemble a dedicated group of stakeholders who are committed and possess skills to drive change.

3 Create a vision for change: crafting a distinct and inspiring vision for the organization's future corresponds to the needs of stakeholders and galvanizes them to engage actively.

4 Communicate the vision to ensure that everyone is on board.

5 Enable others to execute the vision: granting the authority to others to act on the vision by eliminating hindrances, furnishing resources and assistance and entrusting them with accountability.

6 Create immediate victories to generate momentum to change.

7 After initial successes, reinforce the advancements and utilize them as a launch pad for further change.

8 Anchor new approaches in the organization's culture: finally, leaders must ensure that the changes become a part of the organization's culture and practices, embedding them in policies, procedures and systems.

Kanter et al (1992) developed ten commandments that viewed change as multi-directional and continuous. They prescribe ten steps to executing change: analyse the organization and the need for change; create a shared vision and direction; separate from the organization's past; create a sense of urgency; a strong leader to support the change; political support; design an implementation plan; enable organizational infrastructure to support change; sustain the change in the organization – such as pilot tests and training; communicate with and involve individuals and embed change in the organization's daily practices.

Lewin et al's change models all aim to guide organizations through the change process; however, their models emphasize different aspects of the change process. In particular, Kanter et al's model strongly emphasizes creating a sense of urgency to motivate and establish momentum towards change. In contrast, Kotter's model emphasizes building a guiding coalition, communicating the vision and empowering others to act on the vision. On the other hand, Lewin's model emphasizes the importance of unfreezing the current state, moving towards the desired state and refreezing the new state.

Other popular change management models include, but are not limited to:

- Beer's six-step change management model focused on an iterative problem-solving approach. Its six steps are: (1) create a sense of urgency and a shared understanding of the need for change among key organizational stakeholders; (2) develop a shared vision and strategy, and involve employees in planning and organizing the change; (3) foster collaboration and commitment to supporting the change effort. This may involve creating cross-functional teams, fostering communication and trust and involving employees in designing and implementing the change effort. (4) Reinforce new approaches; (5) evaluate progress and adjust; (6) embedding the new approaches and behaviours in the organization's culture and system.

- Appreciative enquiry by Cooperrider and Srivastva (1987). This model identifies and amplifies an organization's positive attributes, values and capabilities. It involves a 4D cycle: (1) Discovery: organization identifies its positive attributes, values and capabilities. (2) Dream: stakeholders imagine and articulate a vision of the organization's ideal future based on the discoveries made in the discovery stage. (3) Design: developing a plan or strategy to achieve the desired future. (4) Destiny: change is implemented and evaluated and the organization continues to evolve and improve based on ongoing enquiries.

- Judson's five-step model is based on an analytical approach to address the problem's root cause and evaluate potential solutions. Its five steps are: (1) analysing and planning the change; (2) communicating the change; (3) gaining acceptance for desirable behaviours for the change; (4) transitioning from the status quo to a new state; and (5) consolidating and embedding the change in the organization with ongoing enquiries.

Towards a systematic view of change

Stouten et al (2018) reviewed the empirical evidence of change management models (their review also included other popular change management models). They summarize the ten steps that lead to successful organizational change:

1 Analyse the need for change.

2 Form a guiding coalition.

3 Develop a compelling vision.

4 Communicate the vision.

5 Gain energy for change.

6 Empower others to take action during change.

7 Develop and promote knowledge and capability related to change implementation.

8 Use short-term wins to reinforce change implementation.

9 Monitor and improve the change process continuously.

10 Institutionalize change through company culture, practices and management.

Stouten and colleagues (2018) further pointed out that the success factors in promoting organizational change include the following:

- At the individual level, organizations need to consider individuals' tendency to accept or resist change. When employees have a higher level of commitment to the organization, a higher level of individuals' perceived fairness of change and a higher level of organizational identification will reduce the resistance to organizational change.
- At the team level, organizations should view teams as a way to gain support and small wins. A higher level of quality social relationship among employees, a higher level of agreed shared goals and beliefs, presenting small change initiatives at the team level and gaining team-level support for change are critical to successful change implementation.
- At the organizational level, the fundamental focus of the organization is how to take up new organizational practices. Employees' perception of the leader's competencies, trust in leaders, the nature of change and the organization's readiness for change are linked to the effectiveness of organizational change.

Stouten's review further proposed an effective change intervention and viewed change systematically. Sustainable, effective change requires the collective's capacity to implement change – such as knowledge, skill, resources and commitment – and integrate change into the broader organizational system. Effective interventions include: (1) developing existing leaders: dealing with change themselves and effectively managing the difference from the employees' perspective; (2) developing and communicating a compelling change vision – a goal that can be broadly shared; (3) influence of social networks on employees; (4) supporting change intervention: scope the change scale by goal setting, learning, employee participation in the change and perceived fairness of the change; (5) small-scale experimentation to gain feedback; (6) assess change progress and outcome over time to understand the change's effect; (7) institutionalizing the change to sustain the effectiveness.

Measuring the outcomes of organizational change

According to Armenakis and Bedeian (1999), the success of organizational change outcomes can be measured by the market (such as profitability and market share) or the internal efficiency of the organization (such as operational efficiency), as well as employee-organizational relations (such as individuals' willingness to comply with the organization's rules and procedures), level of organizational identification, with individuals' willingness to associate with the organization socially, level of organizational commitment, level of employees' resistance to change and, ultimately, employee turnover rate. At the individual level, the success of organizational change can be measured by the employees' affective reactions, including the level of employee stress, job satisfaction, complaints and sick leave.

Hartnell et al (2011) suggest there are five types of outcomes to measure organizational performance:

- Employee outcomes: positive employee attitudes (e.g. organizational commitment, job satisfaction, employee satisfaction, perceived organizational support) and positive employee behaviours (e.g., task performance, organizational citizenship behaviour, voice, relationship conflict, turnover rate)

- Innovation outcomes: organization internal innovation (e.g., process and administrative innovation) and technological innovation

- Operational performance: product/service quality (e.g., service quality, defect rate reduction, product reliability improvement) and operational efficiency (e.g., sale/employee ratio, waiting time)

- Customer outcomes: customer loyalty, customer complaints reduction, customer satisfaction, market share, market performance, market effectiveness)

- Financial outcomes: return on assets, return on sales, sales growth, revenue growth

---

LEARNING FROM FAILURE TO CHANGE

Background

Graamans et al's (2020) study took place in a Dutch hospital. The healthcare system faced pressure from cost-cutting as well as to provide good care. The hospital decided to implement a slight change in the way that they source materials. The hospital used this as a test case for future cost-cutting exercises. The hospital launched a tender exercise for surgical suture material. The criteria to decide on the supplier depended on the best value for money, i.e., high quality and low price. When implementing this procedure, the hospital followed Kotter's change management principles – such as building relationships with medical experts, consulting hospital department heads and communicating the change through various channels to the surgeon. The winning supplier was able to produce high-quality sutures and provide additional services, such as online learning, introduction workshops and training workshops to support the surgeon adopting the product, as communicated in emails.

Organizational members' response to change

Intense resistance came from some of the cardiothoracic surgeons. They refused to use the new suture. Cardiothoracic surgeons specialize in operating on the chest organs, such as the heart, lungs and oesophagus. Surgeons were angry, refused to carry out the operation and made managers responsible for the situation of patient death. Some surgeons stocked up their supplies of sutures. Cardiothoracic surgeons wanted to keep the operation environment as controlled as possible and did not want the additional risk. The hospital eventually agreed that cardiac surgeons could use a different supplier.

What can be considered?

- Act on the expressed emotions and feelings promptly. Cardiothoracic surgeons did not feel safe and secure when they were instructed to use new sutures and this feeling is genuine and pressing for the surgeon.
- Occupational knowledge. For cardiothoracic surgeons, open-heart procedures are highly complex and it was an art form where everything and everyone is in implicit attunement in the theatre. When an outsider told surgeons to change the day-to-day working material, it was simply unacceptable.
- While hospital management considered financial pressure, the surgeons were very self-motivated and driven individuals, striving to provide the best possible care for the patient, i.e., money was not a priority.
- Communication on the new suture and subsequent workshop was only via email and busy individuals might easily miss the emails.
- Hospital managers thought they had communicated with the surgeons, but the surgeons did not feel the same way. They felt the change was happening to them, not happening with them.

Questions:

1 What is the role of emotions in this change process?

2 How do negative emotions such as anger impact on the change process and what are the risks of not managing these emotions effectively?

3 What are the causes of anger in the context of organizational change and how can these be addressed?

4 Describe the role that communication and transparency play in managing emotions during organizational change.

Communication and organizational change

'Communication processes are inherently a part of these implementation activities.'
(BORDIA ET AL, 2004, P.96)

Communication and organizational change are inseparably linked processes (Lewis, 1999). Organizations must put their vision to work so communication is vital for organizational change. Organizational members want more information about the change: internal communication is often the reason for organizational change failure, including a lack of communication and involvement from organizational members. Communication is therefore vital to create buy-in. In addition, uncertainty brought with the change requires senior leaders and executives to articulate change-related uncertainty for organizational members (Allen et al, 2007).

According to Russ (2008), communication during organizational change can be viewed in two strands: programmatic and participatory. Programmatic change communication focuses on cascading information around the change from senior leaders and executives to organizational members. Ultimately, senior leaders want employees to commit to the change. It's about telling employees about the change – information such as new strategy, procedures and change process. Key to this process is transferring the right message in the right way so that employees accept (or do not resist) the change. This type of communication mode is often described as command and persuasion. It is often highly centralized and controlled by the top-level managers in the organization. Typical communication activities are one way, mainly using formal communication such as presentations, periodic meetings, newsletters, websites and information communication through the individual network. Successful programmatic communication requires effectively using carefully crafted language for the targeted audience. Programmatic information is quick to reach a broader audience and provide the perception of fair information sharing across employees' roles and hierarchical positions.

Participatory change communication is often considered a more effective way to implement change than the programmatic approach. It assumes that employees should be actively involved in organizational change. Participatory change communication is two-directional communication where employees are involved and the goal is to build consensus and support for the change. The communication involves employees across different levels. Employees are flexible and decisions are made autonomously as employees from all levels work on the best way to implement change. Typical communication activities to facilitate participation include open forums, focus groups, informal conversations, a casual discussion where the supervisor gets feedback from the subordinates, an employee survey and gathering feedback and complaints. The formality of communication varies from very formal to very informal. This continuous exchange of information allows the development of new meanings collectively and mutual understandings, potentially decreasing the resistance to change (Simoes & Esposito, 2014). The participatory approach is particularly good in increasing stakeholder participation, which often reduces change resistance and enables leaders to work with stakeholders and construct change together.

LIMITATIONS OF COMMUNICATION MODES

What are the limitations of programmatic and participatory communication during organizational change?

Lewis et al (2006) provided some communication guidance for during organizational change, which includes the following:

- Communication should focus on increasing employee participation because it is crucial to feel part of the change and take ownership (note that this is not assigning ownership to them).
- Leader needs to communicate and provide a strong justification of why the change is necessary such that the vision of the change is clear to employees.
- It is also essential to set out a communication strategy and this should be participatory-based, not one-directional cascading information.

To achieve the above goals, Lewis and colleagues' review further summarizes communication tactics, as follows:

- Be clear about the vision.
- Ask for help from the employees to solicit more engagement and interaction from them.
- Identify key individuals to include, such as opinion leaders.
- Develop tactics for providing information.
- Be strategic in the content and the style of communication.
- Use motivational communication tactics, such as celebrating small wins and inspiring efforts to motivate organizational members.
- Set up plans for the use of communication channels and the timing of the message.

COMMUNICATION TO WHOM? THINKING ABOUT INTERNAL STAKEHOLDERS

Who should be identified as internal stakeholders? The standard definition of stakeholder is from Freeman (1984, p.46): 'any group or individual who can affect or is affected by the achievement the of organization's objectives.' Stakeholder has some obligation as 'either their legitimate claim to some sort of moral or financial obligation on behalf of an organization or their ability to influence an organization in some meaningful way, regardless of any owed duty or responsibility.' In essence, internal stakeholders and the organization are intertwined and their actions impact on each other, usually referring to employees.

However, when considering the content shared across internal stakeholders, not everyone in the company is likely to receive the same information. For example, employees at different levels (e.g., senior manager, middle manager, first-line manager and employees), different departments and different groups (e.g., management and non-management staff, union vs. non-union) may all receive information at different times.

Sutton et al (2023) studied the top 500 companies in South Africa. Organizations face uncertain and complex internal organizational environments, such as a strong need to bridge stakeholders among different cultures and intense racial tension due to past regimes. They pointed out the importance of thinking about the external environment in which the organization is embedded. In particular, South Africa has undergone significant changes in the past few decades and society faces many political and economic challenges. When organizations face complex external environments, Sutton and colleagues found that the definition of internal stakeholder in their context is broader than just internal employees, including any party that works closely with the organizations, communication consultants and people who represent the organization to external stakeholders.

Discussion questions:

- What are key messages that must be communicated to each internal stakeholder group during the change process?

- How can we ensure that our communication is timely, clear and consistent across all stakeholder groups?

- What potential barriers or challenges do we need to anticipate and plan for when communicating with internal stakeholders during organizational change?

Sensemaking and change

Change creates ambiguity and confusion where individuals need an explanation to understand the event (Maitlis, 2005; Weick & Roberts, 1993). When individuals experience misalignment with their existing way of doing things or encounter ambiguity, they are likely to start their sensemaking process – a process where people create meaning through cycles of interpretation of the actions to understand the environment and act accordingly (Maitlis & Christianson, 2014). All types of change, such as merger and acquisition, organizational restructuring and redefining job roles, new team arrangement, new work practices and change-related interventions (e.g., training sessions to use the new system), require organizational members to make sense of the nature of the change, the organization's new direction and mission and subsequent implications for one's role and one's team (Luscher & Lewis, 2008). Different groups are likely to have their narratives to understand organizational change. Some individuals might see change as advantageous and embrace the benefits of organizational shifts, while others may express resistance through narratives such as showing concerns about the cost-effectiveness and limited advantages of change, being apprehensive about change going too far or even having a sense that the change undertaken isn't comprehensive enough (Loizos & Barrett, 2001; Sonenshein, 2010).

Sensemaking is an ongoing process and changes over time as organizational members experience new events. According to Maitlis and Christianson and Helms Mills et al (2009), senior leaders and managers can shape sensemaking in organizations through:

- appointment of company executive members
- the proactivity of leaders' actions. Leaders have the legitimate power to influence others. This refers to top-down initiatives. The more active are attempts from the leaders to facilitate discussions and promote organizational understanding, the more engaged are the organizational members. Managers also need to be aware of the consistency of their cues, ideas and actions
- the proactivity of middle managers who can synthesize emergent perspectives from various groups. In particular, middle managers' actions, communication and the shared experiences of peers have a direct effect on their subordinates' sensemaking process (Balogun & Johnson, 2004, p. 524). The closeness of middle managers to daily operation means that they can paint a practical acceptable level of certainty for their subordinates during uncertain times of change (Luscher & Lewis, 2008).

In summary, this shows how managers can have an impact on how organizational members construct their meaning, through managers' narratives of change, analogies and metaphors used during change (e.g., use 'learning curve' to describe the low performance during change, use 'dinner table' to describe the interactions and relationships across teams) and the sociocultural context of the organization (e.g., union vs. non-union employees). The ability of managers to influence their team's meaning-making shows that managers can effectively shape the mixed messages that cause confusion and tensions (e.g., emphasize productivity and responsibility but also emphasize well-being).

For instance, studying one of the most successful organizational changes in business history – Lego, Luscher and Lewis (2008) found that managers often craft mixed messages and conflicting demands into complementary demands, guiding their subordinates with a feasible ambiguity by providing temporal directions (e.g., focus on A first and then B, how the current task can eventually lead to the broader goal that team wanted to achieve) or dividing up the task for the team.

REFLECTION

Thinking about a change that has occurred in the organization that you work for or with which you are familiar, answer the following questions:

- What was the reason for the change and what were the triggers of organizational change?

- How did the organization respond to change and what actions did it take? Consider the actions of the senior managers and executives, middle managers and your own action in response to the change.

- Using the answer to the above question, how did these actions influence your understanding of the change?

- How did you engage with others in sensemaking and how did this influence your understanding of the change?

- How did your sensemaking impact your ability to adapt to the changes?

Culture and change

Chapter 9 sheds light on the idea that an organizational culture mirrors its actions, values, beliefs and underlying assumptions. This culture significantly influences how individuals react to organizational change (Ravasi & Schultz, 2006). To ensure the continuity of organizational change, change must be ingrained within the organization, as emphasized by change models. Culture and change initiatives are inextricably intertwined. Understanding the role of organizational culture is critical to the success of organizational change initiatives, especially when an organization experiences significant, radical organizational change. By taking into account the organization's culture, leaders can anticipate and overcome resistance, tailor implementation and communication strategies and build support for change initiatives, increasing the likelihood of success.

Johnson and Scholes' Culture Web

The Culture Web model is a tool used to analyse and understand the elements of organizational culture (Johnson et al, 1992). The model aims to help individuals and organizations identify the critical components of their culture and assess how these components interact with one another to shape organizational behaviour and performance. The Culture Web model can:

- Diagnose problems: by analysing the different elements of organizational culture, the model can help identify potential areas of conflict or dysfunction.

- Identify strengths: the model can also help identify areas where the organization excels and leverage its strengths to achieve its goals.

- Facilitate change: the model can be used to identify areas where change is needed and to develop strategies for implementing change effectively.

At the heart of the Culture Web model is the cultural paradigm, describing the shared beliefs and assumptions of the organization. The Culture Web model uses six elements to describe the cultural paradigm: stories, symbols, power structures, organizational structures, control systems, and rituals and routines.

- Stories: these are the narratives and anecdotes shared within the organization and shape how people think and behave. Stories can be about the organization's history, successes and failures or the experiences of its employees. It should also be noted that the stories are understood by a large proportion of the employees and are passed between them.

- Symbols: these are tangible representations of the organization's values and beliefs, including everything that can be seen, heard or touched in the organization. Symbols can help to reinforce the culture of the organization and create a sense of belonging among employees. Examples of the symbols are language used, office layout, logos etc.

- Power structures: these are the formal and informal hierarchies within the organization that determine who has power and influence. Power structures can be based on position, expertise or personal relationships and can significantly impact how people behave within the organization.

- Control systems: these are the processes and procedures put in place to ensure that the organization operates efficiently and effectively. Control systems can include policies, rules, regulations and systems for monitoring and evaluating performance.

- Organizational structures: these formal frameworks determine how the organization is structured and how work is divided and coordinated. Organizational structures can include departments, teams and reporting lines and can significantly impact how people work and interact with each other.

- Rituals and routines: these are the regular activities and behaviours that are carried out within the organization, such as meetings, celebrations or performance reviews. Rituals and routines can help reinforce the organization's culture and create a sense of continuity and stability.

To apply the Culture Web mode to analyse organizational change, one can use the six elements to identify the cultural elements that are affected by the change initiatives, then, identify potential change tensions that may arise with existing cultural elements. For example, a control system such as initiating a new performance management system may result in resistance from employees who feel like the new system is unfair, does not accurately reflect their contributions or is too burdensome to log their work activities and output. When an organization changes its department structure, there may be resistance from employees who fear losing their jobs or feel like the new structure will make it harder to collaborate with colleagues. New reporting lines can also be confusing. To use the Culture Web model for change, first, spot any culture-related issues. Then, match your plans with these insights to make sure they fit well together.

Organizational culture change does not always need to be grand and large-scale. According to Alvesson (2013), culture change can also be small-scale – local and used in everyday interaction. Few senior managers and a small group of people often drive this type of change. Changes can be more subtle influences and renegotiating meanings with colleagues. Alvesson's concept of everyday reframing highlights the importance of language and communication in shaping our understanding of reality. It also suggests that individuals and organizations have the power to actively construct and reshape their interpretations of the world around them, creating new meanings and new possibilities.

REFLECTION

Consider any organization that you know well. This could be an organization that you have previously worked for or studied. Analyse the organization's culture to identify its strengths and weaknesses in relation to organizational performance.

Chapter summary

Organizational change is a complex and multifaceted process that can significantly impact individuals, teams and organizations. In this chapter, we explored the drivers of organizational change, the various types of change that organizations can undergo, the key strategies and frameworks that can help organizations manage change effectively and towards a more systematic view of managing organizational change. We also looked at individuals' responses to change and readiness to change. The chapter then discussed the importance of clear and effective communication throughout the change process and communication tactics organizations can use to manage change effectively. When considering communication, this chapter also discussed how organizational change can trigger individuals' sensemaking and different organizational cues for individuals to make sense of during organizational change. Finally, we concluded the chapter by discussing the relationship between organizational culture and change. This chapter overviews the drivers, types and strategies for managing organizational change. By understanding the key concepts and frameworks associated with organizational change, individuals and organizations can better navigate this complex process and achieve successful outcomes.

Key terms

Incremental change

Transformational change

Readiness for change

Resistance to change

Sensemaking

Chapter review questions

- What are the different types of changes that an organization may undertake? How do they differ in terms of their objectives and outcomes?
- What are the stages of the change process?
- What are the best practices for ensuring successful organizational change?

- How can sensemaking processes help organizations understand and manage change's impact on employees and stakeholders?

- What is the relationship between organizational culture and change and how can leaders use cultural analysis to identify potential barriers and enablers of change within an organization?

- What are some common challenges that organizations may face when attempting to change their culture and how can they overcome them to facilitate successful change?

Further reading

Baloh, J, Zhu, X & Ward, M (2018) Implementing team huddles in small rural hospitals: How does the Kotter model of change apply?, *Journal of Nursing Management*, 26(5), 571–578. Interesting empirical research that tested Kotter's model in the hospital setting and found mixed support for Kotter's model, highlighting factors such as the scope of the change and the implementation practices are also important to consider when applying the change model.

Burnes, B (2004) 'Kurt Lewin and the planned approach to change: A re-appraisal', *Journal of Management Studies*, 41(6), pp. 977–1002.

Cummings, S, Bridgman, T, & Brown, K G (2016) Unfreezing change as three steps: Rethinking Kurt Lewin's legacy for change management, *Human Relations*, 69(1), 33–60.

Elrod, P D & Tippett, D D (2002) The 'death valley' of change, *Journal of Organizational Change Management*, 15(3), pp. 273–291.

Johansson, C & Heide, M (2008) Speaking of change: Three communication approaches in studies of organizational change, *Corporate Communications*, 13(3), pp. 288–305.

Robinson, P & Shimizu, N (2006) Japanese corporate restructuring: CEO priorities as a window on environmental and organizational change, *Academy of Management Perspective*, pp. 44–75.

Whelan-Berry, K S and Somerville, K S (2010) Linking change drivers and the organizational change process: A Review and Synthesis, *Journal of Change Management*, 10 (2) 175–193.

References

Allen, J, Jimmieson, N L, Bordia, P & Irmer, B E (2007) Uncertainty during organizational change: Managing perceptions through communication, *Journal of Change Management,* 7, pp. 187–210.

Alvesson, M (2013) *Understanding Organizational Culture.*

Armenakis, A A & Bedeian, A G (1999) Organizational change: A review of theory and research in the 1990s, *Journal of Management,* 25(3), pp. 293–315.

Balogun, J, & Johnson, G (2004) Organizational restructuring and middle manager sense-making, *Academy of Management Journal,* 47, 523–549.

Barsade, S G (2002) The ripple effect: Emotional contagion and its influence on group behaviour, *Administrative Science Quarterly,* 47(4), pp. 644–675.

Bertelli, A M (2008) Credible governance? Transparency, political control, the personal vote and British Quangos, *Political Studies,* 56, 807–829.

Bordia, P, Hobman, E, Jones, E, Gallois, C & Callan, V J (2004) Uncertainty during organizational change: Types, consequences and management strategies, *Journal of Business and Psychology,* 18(4), pp. 507–532.

Cooperrider, D & Srivastva, S (1987) Appreciative inquiry in organizational life. In W Pasmore & R Woodman (eds.), *Research in organization change and development* (Vol. 1, pp. 129–169), JAI Press, Greenwich, CT.

Cummings, T G & Worley, C G (2014) *Organization Development and Change,* 9th edition, Cengage Learning.

Dawson, P (2003) *Understanding Organizational Change: The Contemporary Experience of People at Work,* Sage.

Davis, J (2017) How Lego clicked: the super brand that reinvented itself, *The Guardian.* Available at: https://www.theguardian.com/lifeandstyle/2017/jun/04/how-lego-clicked-the-super-brand-that-reinvented-itself (archived at https://perma.cc/9D3Q-LHED)

Elrod, P D & Tippett, D D (2002) The 'death valley' of change, *Journal of Organizational Change Management,* 15(3), pp. 273–291.

Freeman, R E (1984) *The Stakeholder Approach,* Cambridge University Press, Cambridge.

Graamans, E, Aji, K, Vonk, A, ten Have, W (2020) Case study: examining failure in change management, *Journal of Organizational Change Management,* 33(2), pp. 319–330.

Greasley, S, & Hanretty, C (2015) Credibility and agency termination under parliamentarism, *Journal of Public Administration Research and Theory,* 26, 159–173.

Hartnell, C A , Ou, A Y & Kinicki, A (2011) Organizational culture and organizational effectiveness: A meta-analytic investigation of the competing values framework's theoretical suppositions, *Journal of Applied Psychology,* 96(4), pp. 677–694.

Helms Mills, J, Dye, K & Mills, A J (2009) *Understanding Organizational Change,* Routledge, Oxon, UK.

Hoag, B G, Ritschard, H V & Cooper, C L (2002). Obstacles to effective organizational change: the underlying reasons, *Leadership & Organization Development Journal,* 23(1), pp. 6–15.

Johnson, G, Whittington, R, & Scholes, K (1992) *Fundamentals of Strategy,* Pearson.

Kanter, R M, Stein, B & Jick, T D (1992) *The Challenge of Organizational Change: How Companies Experience It and Leaders Guide It*, Free Press, New York.

Kotter, J P, & Cohen, D S (2002) *The heart of change*, Harvard Business School Press, Boston.

Lewis, L K (1999) Disseminating information and soliciting input during planned organizational change, *Management Communication Quarterly*, 13(1), pp. 43–75.

Lewis, L K, Schmisseur, A M, Stephens, K K & Weir, K E (2006) Advice on communicating during organizational change, *International Journal of Business Communication*, 43(2), pp. 113–137.

Levy, A (1986) Second-order planned change: Definition and conceptualization, *Organizational Dynamics*, 15 (1), 5–23.

Loizos, H & Barrett, M (2001) Organizational change as discourse: Communicative actions and deep structures in the context of information technology implementation, *Academy of Management Journal*, 44(4), pp. 755–778.

Luscher, L & Lewis, M W (2008) Organizational change and managerial sensmaking: Working through paradox, *Academy of Management Journal*, 51(2), pp. 221–240.

MacCarthaigh, M (2014) Agency termination in Ireland: Culls and bonfires or life after death?, *Public Administration*, 92, 1017–1037.

Maitlis, S & Christianson, M K (2014) Sensemaking in organizations: Taking stock and moving forward, *Academy of Management Annals*, 8(1), pp. 57–125.

Maitlis, S (2005) The social processes of sensemaking, *Academy of Management Journal*, 48(1), pp. 21–49.

Meyer, A D, Brooks, G R & Goes, J B (1990) Environmental jolts and industry revolutions: Organizational responses to discontinuous change, *Strategic Management Journal*, 11, pp. 93–110.

Mithani, M A (2020) Adaptation in the Face of the New Normal, *Academy of Management Perspectives*, 34(4), 508–530.

Mohrman, A et al (1989) *Large-Scale Organizational Change*, Jossey-Bass.

Oreg, S, Vakola, M & Armenakis, A (2011) Change recipients' reactions to organizational change, *Journal of Applied Behavioural Science*, 47(4), pp. 461–524.

Oreg, S (2003) Resistance to change: Developing an individual differences measure, *Journal of Applied Psychology*, 88(4), pp. 680–693.

Oreg, S, Bayazit, M, Vakola, M, Arciniega, L, Armenakis, A, Barkauskiene, R, Bozionelos, N et al (2008) Dispositional resistance to change: Measurement equivalence and the link to personal values across 17 nations, *Journal of Applied Psychology*, 93(4), 935–944.

Rafferty, A E & Griffin, M A (2006) Perceptions of organizational change: A stress and coping perspective, *Journal of Applied Psychology*, 91(5), pp. 1154–1162.

Rafferty, A E, Jimmieson, N L & Armenakis, A A (2012) Change readiness, *Journal of Management*, 39(1), pp. 110–135.

Rafferty, A E & Jimmieson, N L (2009). Team change climate: A group-level analysis of the relationships among change information and change participation, role stressors and well-being, *European Journal of Work and Organizational Psychology*, 19(5), pp. 551–586.

Ravasi, D, & Schultz, M (2006) Responding to Organizational Identity Threats: Exploring the role of Organizational Culture, *Academy of Management Journal*, 49(3), 433–458. https://doi.org/10.5465/AMJ.2006.21794663 (archived at https://perma.cc/9FW9-VNMG)

Russ, T L (2008) Communicating change: A review and critical analysis of programmatic and participatory implementation approaches, *Journal of Change Management*, 8, pp. 199–211.

Saurav, A, Kusek, P, Kuo, R & Viney, B (2021) *Impact of COVID-19 on Foreign Investors : Evidence from the Quarterly Global MNE Pulse Survey for the Fourth Quarter of 2020*, World Bank, Washington, DC.

Simoes, P M M & Esposito, M (2014) Improving change management: How communication nature influences resistance to change, *Journal of Management Development*, 33(4), pp. 324–341.

Sonenshein, S (2010) We're changing-or are we? Untangling the role of progressive, regressive and stability narratives during strategic change implementation, *Academy of Management Journal*, 53(3), pp. 477–512.

Statista Research Department (2013) Global market share held by Nokia smartphones Q1 2007–Q2 2013, Statista. Available at: https://www.statista.com/statistics/263438/market-share-held-by-nokia-smartphones-since-2007/ (archived at https://perma.cc/8YJK-QJ6U).

Statista Research Department (2023) Worldwide revenue of major toy companies in 2022, Statista. Available at: https://www.statista.com/statistics/241241/revenue-of-major-toy-companies-worldwide/ (archived at https://perma.cc/YE7D-SY7L).

Stouten, J, Rousseau, D & Cremer, D E (2018) Successful organizational change: Integrating the management practice and scholarly literature, *Academy of Management Annals*, 12(2), pp. 752–788.

Sutton, L B, le Roux, & Fourie, L M (2023) Who should be identified as internal stakeholders? An internal communication practitioner and consultant perspective in the South African corporate context, *South African Journal for Communication Theory and Research*, 48 (4), 93–116. https://doi.org/10.1080/02500167.2022.2163268 (archived at https://perma.cc/266V-LJEG).

Weick, K & Roberts, K (1993) Collective mind in organizations: Heedful interrelating on flight decks, *Administrative Science Quarterly*, 38 (3), pp. 357–381.

APPENDIX

Revisiting the chapter exercises

Chapter 1

Organizational behaviour is everywhere

Management's role: Management's support and resource allocation for safety and health programmes align with Organizational Structure (Chapter 8).

Communication and psychology safety: The concept of psychological safety relates to Teams (Chapter 4), as it impacts team dynamics and team members' ability to communicate safety concerns openly.

Organizational culture: The discussion on organizational culture and its impact on safety incidents corresponds to Organizational Culture (Chapter 9), as it explores how an organization's culture shapes its behaviour.

Continuous improvement: Evaluating organizational procedures for continuous improvement links to Organizational Change (Chapter 10), as it addresses the adaptability and evolution of an organization's processes.

Reward systems: Reward systems are connected to Motivation (Chapter 3), as they serve as motivational tools that influence employee behaviour.

Employee engagement: Employee involvement in reporting safety issues is a form of individual engagement, which connects to Individual Differences (Chapter 2), as it considers individual behaviours and characteristics.

Technical knowledge: Individual knowledge on safety topics relates to Individual Differences (Chapter 2) as it involves differences in skill sets and expertise.

Motivation: Motivation is covered in Motivation (Chapter 3) and is essential in driving employees to adhere to safety protocols.

Interpersonal relationships: The quality of interpersonal relationships with supervisors can be associated with Leadership (Chapter 6), as leadership styles and interactions impact these relationships.

Chapter 3

Job characteristic model

The limitation of the job characteristic model lies in it narrowly focused on the job itself but does not consider social context factors. Research has shown that the following social context factors can influence an individual's psychological state (Kanfer & Chen, 2016b):

- social support
- interactions outside the workplace
- interdependent work: this concept encompasses the impact of a job's completion on other jobs in the workflow and how a job's completion relies on the completion of other jobs. In simpler terms, it highlights how your job is influenced by and also influences other people's work
- feedback from others
- opportunities to relate one's job to others, such as helping
- interpersonal relationships at work.

When promotions are not as important

Kanungo and Mendonca (1988) suggested that promotions may not always be important under the following circumstances:

- Inadequate skills: One reason could be that employees lack the required abilities for the higher-level positions. In such cases, providing training to enhance their skills would be a suitable recommendation.
- Contentment with current role: Another reason is that some employees may be satisfied and content with their current job without seeking enhanced self-esteem through promotion. In such instances, counselling might be helpful, followed by training opportunities if needed.
- Perceived inequity: The third reason is that employees may feel that the reward system is unfair, leading them to undervalue the promotion. Addressing issues of perceived inequity is crucial to ensure that the reward is valued by the employees.
- Promotion might be important, but not the financial reward associated with it.
- Promotion is not seen as merit-based. For instance, if a promotion is supposed to be based on superior performance, but employees observe that only those who socialize with supervisors get promoted, they may focus more on socializing than improving their performance. This can lead to a misalignment between the

intended reward system and the actual behaviours employees exhibit, ultimately affecting the effectiveness of the reward programme.

Chapter 4

Applying the Punctuated Equilibrium Model

The Punctuated Equilibrium Model emphasizes the importance of flexibility and adaptability for team success. Teams must be willing to change when necessary to achieve their goals. Leaders can play a crucial role in helping the team navigate these changes by providing guidance and support. Effective communication, active listening and a willingness to compromise are strategies that can promote flexibility and adaptability during periods of change. Overall, remaining flexible, adaptable and open to change is the key to coping with each stage of the Punctuated Equilibrium Model.

Here are suggested strategies (note that these strategies are not fixed and may vary depending on the specific needs and goals of the team):

1 Establishing goals and processes (stability period): During this period, teams should set clear goals, objectives, work processes and procedures. Strategies to cope with this period may include creating a shared understanding of the goals and objectives, clarifying individual roles and responsibilities and developing clear communication channels.

2 Evaluating goals and processes (change period): During this period, the team should re-evaluate their goals and processes and make necessary adjustments. Strategies to cope with this period may include encouraging open and honest communication among team members, identifying and addressing any obstacles that may prevent the team from achieving their goals and creating a safe and supportive environment for feedback and criticism.

3 Achieving revised goals and processes (stability period): The team should work to achieve their revised goals and processes during this period. Strategies to cope with this period may include celebrating achievements and milestones, maintaining open communication, continuing to identify and address any issues or challenges that arise and encouraging a sense of team cohesion and unity.

Personality and team development process

Research finds 'how' teams work together matters more than the composition of personality and diversity. For example, according to Kuipers and colleagues' (2009) work using a sample of 156 teams (1630 individuals in total) in a Swedish manufacturing company, they looked at the relationship between the MBTI profile and team process. They found that the impact of MBTI at the team level is insignificant and the MBTI type does not predict the team process. The presence of personality types such as ENTJ and ENFJ has a significant impact on developing external relations and ESFJ and ISFJ have a significant impact on task management. However, the explanation power was low (17 per cent and 14 per cent variances explained by the personality).

Peeters and colleagues (2008) examined 26 multidisciplinary student teams across three Dutch universities where teams were tasked to design a remote-controlled floating device. They explored the relationship between the composition of personality (Big Five) in the team and the Input-Process-Output team process. They found that:

- the composition of personality matters more during the design phase but not the overall performance of the team
- the team level of agreeableness is positively related to the input-process phase of the team process. Behaving in a friendly and cooperatively way at the team level during the initial step of the team process remains essential
- the team level of conscientiousness is positively related to the process related to decision-making, e.g., including timekeeping and planning time. Interestingly, they found that variation of conscientiousness within a team was also positively associated with team performance (i.e., high conscientious people helped monitor the progress of the task to keep their less conscientious team members to accomplish the job).

Chapter 5

Political behaviour and context

Organizational politics tends to emerge when conflicting views, interests and a lack of agreement on objectives and strategies exist. Here are some specific situations that are likely to encourage political behaviour in an organization:

- Lack of resources: When resources are scarce or limited, individuals may engage in political behaviour to secure a larger share or gain an advantage.

  Example: In a budget allocation meeting, departments compete for a more significant portion of the budget to fund their projects, leading to political manoeuvring and lobbying among department heads.

- Centralized structure: In organizations with a more centralized decision-making structure, political behaviours are intensified as individuals compete for influence and decision-making power.

- Ambiguity around task objectives, roles and decision-making: When there is ambiguity in how tasks should be accomplished, individuals may resort to political tactics to gain clarity, influence decision-making or redefine their roles and responsibilities.

  Example: How teams should work together (e.g., cross-department collaboration), how work is allocated and delegated and how the promotion is carried out (e.g., whether the promotion process and criteria are transparent).

- Organizational change and uncertainty: During periods of change and uncertainty, individuals may engage in political behaviour to protect their own interests, establish their positions or influence the outcome of the change process.

  Example: In a company undergoing a merger or acquisition, employees may engage in political behaviour to secure their positions, form alliances with influential individuals or undermine competitors for better career prospects in the post-merger organization.

Chapter 7

Overcoming cognitive biases

Brett and Thompson (2016) summarized ways to overcome cognitive biases:

- Learning from experiences

  Example: Consider a sales professional who initially struggled with cognitive biases in pricing negotiations. Through years of experience and exposure to various customer interactions, they learnt to recognize biases in both themselves and their customers. This experiential learning allowed them to adapt their negotiation strategies effectively.

- Observation and in-depth discussion

  Example: Observing a real-life negotiation or case and actively participating in discussions allows individuals to draw parallels between the observed situation and their own negotiation experiences. This, in turn, empowers individuals to apply and enhance their negotiation skills effectively.

- Case study with deep discussion

  Example: When individuals witness a negotiation and/or a case on a real negotiation, applying lessons learnt from observing and engaging in discussions helps individuals to capture similarities between the case and their own negotiation situations, enabling them to apply and refine their negotiation skills.

On the other hand, training has limited effectiveness.

Why is process conflict considered the most detrimental among task, relationship and process conflicts in terms of its impact on team performance?

According to Greer and Dannals (2017), process conflict has the most negative impact on team performance out of the three types of conflict because of the following:

- Fairness and equality: Process conflict intertwines with perceptions of fairness and impartiality within a team. When process conflict arises, it can create a sense of unfairness, where individuals may feel that decisions and resource allocations are biased or unjust. For instance, in a project team, if one member consistently receives preferential treatment in task assignments, it could generate feelings of inequity and resentment among other team members.

- Influence on power: Process conflicts often relate to issues of power and authority, as they frequently involve allocating resources and responsibilities within a team. When disputes emerge in these areas, they can disrupt the power balance and trigger internal struggles for control.

- Transparency deficit: Process conflicts tend to thrive in environments where decision-making processes lack transparency or are poorly communicated. When team members are uncertain about how decisions are reached or perceive a lack of transparency, it can foster mistrust and exacerbate conflicts.

Chapter 8

Departmentalization and contingencies

- Cummings and Worley (2005) provided a useful summary of contingencies factors that may impact the choice of departmentalization.

- Company size and the choice of departmentalization: Functional structure is more suitable when the company size is relatively small, whereas geographic, product and matrix structure are more suitable for larger corporations.

- Environmental volatility: A functional structure tends to excel in relatively stable environments, while a geographic or product-based structure becomes more favourable when facing heightened environmental uncertainty. In contrast, a matrix structure often emerges when an organization confronts a multitude of pressures. For instance, consider a software development company operating in a rapidly evolving tech industry. Here, the organization may adopt a matrix structure due to the simultaneous pressures of evolving technology, changing customer demands and the need for cross-functional collaboration to deliver innovative solutions.

- Other factors: technology at the time and the organizational goals.

Chapter 9

From artefacts to organizational culture

Luxurious office space for senior leaders and executive lunchrooms is associated with status. You are likely to expect the company culture to emphasize social order.

Application of Schein's model

In Hogan and Coote's (2014) attempt to understand how organizational culture influences companies' innovative behaviours, they used Schein's model to describe the culture of an innovative company from the professional services.

The artefact is the explicit and observable characteristics part of the organizational culture. In a professional service, the artefacts are likely to be:

- celebration (e.g., award ceremony) of an innovative marketing strategy
- the physical layout of the organization
- decoration of the building
- language and metaphor contain messages that value and support innovation.

The organizations are likely to hold the following values:

- Value success where the organization strives for a high standard and challenging goals
- Openness and flexibility. Appreciation and receptivity to novelty
- Open internal communication, such as social interactions and cross-fertilization of ideas
- Professional capabilities. This includes knowledge, expertise and technical skills
- Cross-functional collaboration and coordination. High level of sharing and effective conflict resolution process
- A high degree of autonomy and responsibility from individuals. Individuals can take control over their own work and ideas in order to produce innovative outcomes

- Recognition of employees formally (e.g., reward, formal recognition of innovation) and informally (e.g., feedback, learning opportunities)

- Encouraging risk-taking without the fear of negative consequences or damaging individuals' self-image. Risk-taking behaviours will likely enhance one's professional identity within the company and gain managerial support

The organizations are likely to hold the following norms:

- Promoting activities that support project execution, such as encouraging teamwork and sharing across teams

Benefit of Culture Misfit

According to Caprar et al (2022), in a recent review on cross-cultural practices, they identify that cultural differences can generate the following benefits:

- Increase knowledge transfer

- Increase creativity, such as innovation, exploration and new solutions

- Cross-pollinated good practices and generating new norms and beliefs (i.e., cultural change)

- Stimulate learning

- Source of competitive advantage through differentiation

- Dissimilar cultural practices can complement local business practices, broaden the range of options and create new opportunities

Chapter 10

Strategies to cope with resistance.

According to Cummings and Worley (2014), there are three strategies to manage resistance to change:

- Be curious and want to learn how individuals experience change. It requires individuals to have lots of empathy and active listening, genuinely interested in how they make sense of the change.

- Communicate what the change is and the potential impact of change on the individuals. Use multiple communication channels to ensure the information is delivered to the individuals. For example, email and messaging can accompany presentations and meetings.

- Involve organizational members in the change process and ensure the voices were heard and acted on. Individuals at the frontline are likely to have the most insight into how the change can impact their daily operations.

Limitations of Communication Mode

According to Russ (2008), here are the limitation of programmatic and participatory approaches.

Limitations of the programmatic approach:

- Employees can interpret the message differently
- There can be too much information for employees to digest
- Top-down communication does not encourage communication and interaction between top-level managers and employees
- One-way communication does not facilitate building a shared vision, distancing employees from the organization.

Limitations of the participatory approach:

- Too much engagement and lost focus
- Can be seen as insincere or mere lip service
- Requires a lot of organizational resources (e.g., employees spend time away from work and managers spend time to listen, document employee voices, make agreed-upon alterations and following up on parties involved)
- Assume employees want to be involved in the change and are motivated to do so fully.

INDEX

Note: Page numbers in *italics* refer to tables or figures.

Looking for another book?

Explore our award-winning
books from global business
experts in Human Resources,
Learning and Development

Scan the code to browse

More books on HR from Kogan Page

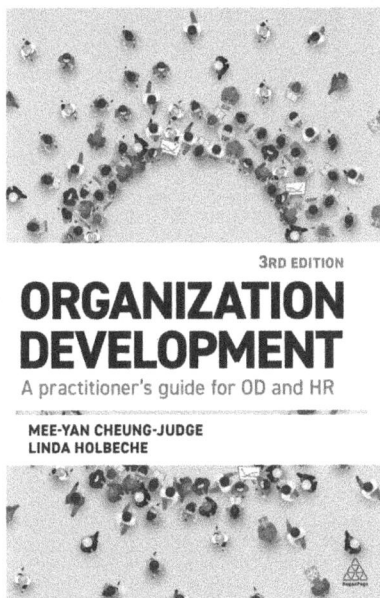

ORGANIZATION DEVELOPMENT
3RD EDITION
A practitioner's guide for OD and HR

MEE-YAN CHEUNG-JUDGE
LINDA HOLBECHE

ISBN: 9781789667912

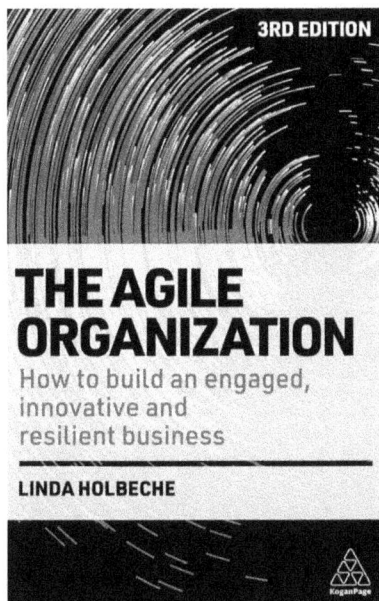

THE AGILE ORGANIZATION
3RD EDITION
How to build an engaged, innovative and resilient business

LINDA HOLBECHE

ISBN: 9781398608665

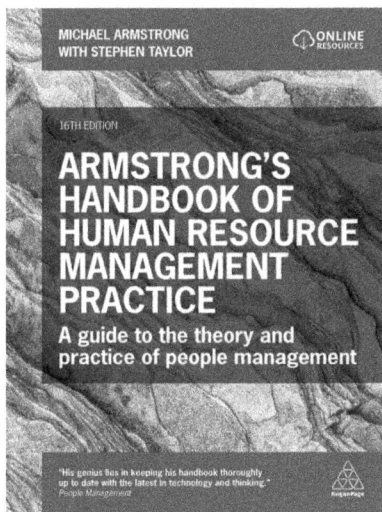

ARMSTRONG'S HANDBOOK OF HUMAN RESOURCE MANAGEMENT PRACTICE
MICHAEL ARMSTRONG
WITH STEPHEN TAYLOR
ONLINE RESOURCES

16TH EDITION

A guide to the theory and practice of people management

"His genius lies in keeping his handbook thoroughly
up to date with the latest in technology and thinking."
People Management

ISBN: 9781398606630

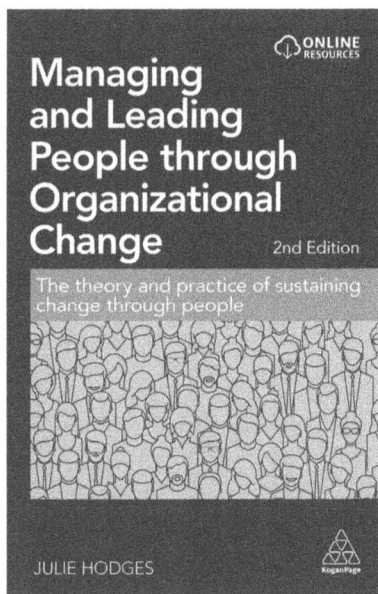

Managing and Leading People through Organizational Change
ONLINE RESOURCES

2nd Edition

The theory and practice of sustaining change through people

JULIE HODGES

ISBN: 9781789667974

www.koganpage.com

KoganPage

From 4 December 2025 the EU Responsible Person (GPSR) is:
eucomply oÜ, Pärnu mnt. 139b – 14, 11317 Tallinn, Estonia
www.eucompliancepartner.com

www.ingramcontent.com/pod-product-compliance
Lightning Source LLC
Chambersburg PA
CBHW052340210326
41597CB00037B/6202